SHETLAND WORDS

SHETLAND WORDS

A dictionary of the Shetland dialect

A & A Christie-Johnston

Contributing Editor: Neil Anderson

The Shetland Times Ltd.
Lerwick
2010

Shetland Words

Hardback ISBN 978-1-904746-57-7
Paperback ISBN 978-1-904746-58-4

British Library Cataloguing-in-Publication Data
A catalogue record for this book is available from the British Library.

The authors welcome comments on Shetland Words for consideration for future editions. Suggested amendments and additions should be sent to Shetland Words at The Shetland Times Ltd., Gremista, Lerwick, Shetland, ZE1 0PX, or by email to shetlandwords@shetland-times.co.uk

Printed and published by
The Shetland Times Ltd.,
Gremista, Lerwick,
Shetland, Scotland. ZE1 0PX

CONTENTS

FOREWORD

HERODOTUS wrote of "the whole Greek community, being of one blood and one tongue". For at the beginning of the fifth century BC, tongue *was* blood. Societies were small; those who spoke like you usually were related to you. Now, some two and a half millennia later, most of us inhabit multicultural megacities within multilingual nations. We've also belatedly come to the realisation that we are equal voyagers on this small and lonely planet hurling through the ineffable vastness of space. All the same, we still cannot deny sensing that similar speech embraces. We do feel best around those who speak as we do. Tongue is still Home.

This is only right. If it's true that "to learn a second language is to acquire a second soul," as Goethe penned, then surely its corollary must obtain, too. That is, to learn more about one's own tongue, to expand our skill with it, to preserve it for future generations – all of these endeavours must only enrich that first soul of ours, that mother tongue we were born with, our true umbilical cord planted in our native earth.

For language is geography, too. As we are rooted to our soil, so are we rooted to our soil's speech. We appreciate that this speech must change with time, as must our gardens, hedgerows, fields, beaches: language alters in just the same way as Nature alters; it is the biological imperative. Our personal language, our idiolect, changes too as we age, though its rate of change increasingly slows, like the growth of a mature oak. Hence, the 'living dictionaries' that our eldest neighbours embody.

But "the tongue can no man tame," as the Book of James will tell us. Language will always be a wild thing, one that the younger generation will wield like a weapon. There is perhaps some consolation in language's historical irony here: our grandchildren will be horrified by the speech of their own grandchildren.

All the more reason, then, to preserve what we can, while we can, of what we know and what we still cherish so profoundly. It is an homage to those who came before, a duty to those we share our land with, and a bequest to those who will come. Above all, it safeguards the social cement, ensuring that a folk's very identity – their blood, their tongue – will thrive long past the individual's three-score-and-ten.

My congratulations to Alastair and Adaline Christie-Johnston, with concomitant admiration for their assiduous, selfless dedication in just this regard. Shetland must only flourish after this linguistic transfusion. Herodotus himself would be pleased.

Dr Steven Roger Fischer
linguist, historian, author
Waiheke Island, New Zealand
30th November, 2009

ACKNOWLEDGEMENTS

IN setting out to compile a dictionary of the Shetland dialect I must first give credit to those who have gone this way before. Jakob Jakobsen, *The Etymological Dictionary of the Norn Language in Shetland*, 1932 (reprinted in 1985 by the Shetland Folk Society) and John Graham, *The Shetland Dictionary*, Shetland Times, 1979 (current revised reprint 2009) have been my main resources and I am indebted to these men for their research – a work undertaken long before the labour-saving convenience of computers.

Many online dictionaries have proved invaluable for cross-referencing. Of these the most notable resource (not least because it gives due recognition to the Shetland dialect) has been *the Dictionary of the Scots Language* (DSL) which combines a 12 volume *Dictionary of the Old Scottish Language* (DOST) covering the period from 12th to 17th century and the 10 volume *Scottish National Dictionary* (SND) which spans the era from 17th century to 1970.

Neil Anderson of Tingwall, Shetland (himself an enthusiastic proponent of the dialect) has generously assisted my research giving freely of his time (hundreds of hours) to correct mistakes, submit additional entries and offer advice. I am especially grateful and indebted to him.

To attempt a work of this sort without first-hand knowledge of the dialect would be extremely difficult if not nigh on impossible. I am therefore immensely grateful to my wife Adaline Jamieson of Cullivoe, Shetland, for her patience and per-severance in directing me back to the right paths when I became lost in the fog of mispronunciation and misunderstanding. Researching origin of words is a tedious and at times convoluted business. Having to live in the same house as someone so engaged definitely warrants special acknowledge-ment and thanks. Adaline's extensive knowledge and use of the dialect, together with Neil Anderson's invaluable contributions, has led to the inclusion of an additional 700 words in confirmed usage (known by at least two persons and understood by a third in conversation) that are not listed in John Graham's *Shetland Dictionary*.

A full bibliography is included on page 122, however I make special mention here of D. Malcolm's *Shetland's Wild Flowers* (The Shetland Times, 2003) and Margaret Stout's *Cookery for Northern Wives* (T. & J. Manson, 1925) for flower and food words I have included which were not listed in previous dictionaries. I also wish to acknowledge the support and encouragement given by Robert and June Wishart without which I might never have persevered and am indebted to Dr Steven Roger Fischer for his generously worded 'Preface'. Others who have helped me include James Ericson (for extensive research of haaf fishermen's tabu words – see addenda), Derek Herning and Bill Moore (for preliminary editing of the 'A' & 'B' list), Prof. Raphael Rish, Dr Ian Tait, Lawrence Tulloch, Winnie Tulloch, Charles Umphray and many others too numerous to mention. To all of them, a very sincere "thank-you".

Alastair Christie-Johnston
Aywick, Yell, July 2010

INTRODUCTION

THE demise of the Norn (Norrøna) language in Shetland probably began in the latter half of the 16th century when judicial matters were controlled by governing Scots. Scottish influence in Shetland was reinforced after the marriage of King James III of Scotland to Princess Margaret of Denmark (1469) and the assumption of Scottish rule that followed. In 1611 all remaining Norse laws were proscribed and Scots law was imposed in Shetland. By the mid-18th century historians and visiting linguists were noting and recording the decline of Norn. One hundred and fifty years on, at the end of the 19th century, Jakob Jakobsen collected and recorded 10,000 Norn words still known at the time (if not necessarily in everyday use) to produce his *Etymological Dictionary of the Norn Language in Shetland*. By 1970, less than 80 years later, John Graham was unable to muster more than 15 per cent of these to compile his *Shetland Dictionary*. This new work seeks to stem the tide by recording not only what is left of supposed authentic Norn but such other dialect words as we have been able to uncover during our research over the past three years – words known and used in modern-day Shetland speech and words describing objects and actions that, while no longer a part of daily life, are still remembered from recent history.

Usage is obviously the key to preservation of a language, however we believe knowledge of the source of words is an important part of the lock mechanism, especially when seeking to encourage a younger generation to explore language they may not be wholly familiar with; therefore the main purpose of this work has been our attempt to provide some qualified etymology to existing word lists. We claim no scholarship in this regard and stress that all [bracketed] material alongside each word is provided in order that readers may compare and confer on a wider scale according to their individual interest.

The value of such probing can be demonstrated by reference to Jakobsen's dictionary where he gives an example of a word becoming confused in meaning through misunderstanding of its origin. Thus **bonnhoga**, which joins two Old Norse words *barn* (child) and *hagi* (pasture) to give us *the place of one's childhood* – i.e. *barn-hagi* = child-pasture; spiritual home. Ironically this word came to mean *a good trip*, or *a piece of good work*, presumably from French *bon* (good) and Old Norse *haga* (to manage). The island of Yell took the confusion even further with expressions like *dey got a bonhagi de day*, meaning *they got nothing out of their trip or errand*. Such a departure from the original etymology is difficult to understand.

While the word **bonhoga** was listed in Graham's dictionary with its correct meaning, it has subsequently fallen out of general usage and many would argue for deleting it altogether (notwithstanding its being adopted as the name for an art gallery in Weisdale). To do so might begin an avalanche which would certainly do nothing for the survival of the dialect. In choosing to list the word we are more tempted to revert to the original spelling of *barn-hagi*, if only to preserve the correct meaning. After all, we come a lot closer to Old Norse when we call a child a *bairn*. However, dictionaries are not about individual preference; they must reflect the language of the people.

The use of the diacritical to indicate pronunciation can be misleading at times as it may give a false impression of Germanic or Norn origin. Words like **böt** (boot); and **pör** (poor); are good examples of this. The Shetlandic pronunciation of **böt** may come from the Scots form of *buit* and not from the Norn which is rendered as *bot* or *bootsen*; **pör** has its origin in the Old French *poure* or *povre* (Scots *puir*). Various representations of the word **göd** raise further difficulties owing to subtle differences in pronunciation. Thus **göd** can mean 1) *God*; 2) *good* (O.Sc. *gude*); 3) *went* (pt of *go*, O.Sc. *gaed*). In the case of **gödless** with the given example in Graham's dictionary *He wis most gödless coorse*, it is uncertain whether this should be interpreted as *God-less* or *good-less* (arguably the same thing). A similar word **gödably**, is rendered in O.Sc. as *guidably* – another misleading example. Notwithstanding these observations we have adhered to Graham's spelling of such words for the good reason he gives in his dictionary – namely that over time the Norn tongue has influenced pronunciation of words borrowed from Scots and English and vice versa.

An important part of the evolution of Shetland language is the change that has taken place in the spelling of words over the last century. To help trace this (and to some degree assist in establishing nuances in pronunciation) we have shown Jakobsen's and other renderings of some words in brackets alongside the accepted modern-day version wherever it has been possible to determine this. As is the case in all languages, some new words have appeared in the intervening years.

In analysing the present-day list some interesting facts emerge. Many of the words Jakobsen collected refer to implements, utensils or activities that have ceased to be a part of Shetland life so it will come as no surprise to discover this side of the dictionary is severely depleted. Of the remainder we have identified 152 words connected to the sea, fishing and boats, while a further 94 relate to the weather (an ever-present topic of conversation). On the subject of crofting, over 90 words have to do with sheep and cattle while no fewer than 30 are used to describe the multiplicity of things one might do with rope. Owing to the absence of trees in the islands, rocks and stones are still put to many uses and their particular shapes or purposes run to 24 words. And perhaps in acknowledgement of a past where the daily grind was significantly harder than it is today, there are no fewer than 12 dialect words for **exhausted**: daddit, debaetless, depooperit, disjasket, forfochen, hurless, maegered, mankit, moyenless, ootmaagit, pooskered, pyaagit.

Most birds, fish, animals and wildflowers continue to be known by the old dialect words – chiefly Norn – and the enquiry into history of origin adds some interesting insights. It may be conjectured that these are the things learned in early childhood prior to going to school and therefore taught by parents and grandparents who continue to use the old words when speaking of familiar everyday things. **Blaand**, **stap**, **krappen** and **sooins** are virtually unheard of these days (along with many other dubious culinary wonders), however it seems a shame to deprive the present generation of at least an insight – if not a taste.

With the loss of many obsolete words we tend to find an increasing proportion of what is left falls into the category of what Jakobsen called words *of an insignificant character and apparently of a lower class, half comic, sometimes bantering, sometimes derisive, mere dialect-words*. This is not to say they are irrelevant; however their survival in a more sophisticated modern society appears to be diminished. And yet, as has so often been found to be the case with dialect, the more quaintly descriptive the word, the better its chances of remaining as a part of the life and character of a society.

Word-play is like any other play. We love to invent new words or twist old ones into clever new meanings and so *We ax for what we want* appears on the Guizer Jarl's Seal of the Up-Helly-A' Proclamation and any superficial wounding is presumably done with the pen only; or we trumpet *Shetland ForWirds* and hope to advance support for the dialect. From time to time odd discrepancies appear. The installation of **showers** in Shetland bathrooms began in the mid-20th century and so the word gets its English pronunciation while the rain continues to fall in **shooers**. Similarly one might say *De* **power** *is geen aff* when referring to an electricity failure yet speak of a man's strength as ***pooer*** *in his airm*.

Outsiders sometimes lightly mock Shetlanders' mispronunciations of some English words but it could be the locals who have the last laugh. A word like *mattress* (English: ***matt-ress***, Shetland: ***matt-rass***) has its origins in Arabic and came to us via the French *materas* – from which a Shetlander may well be entitled to say *I rest my case*.

To a degree the word **knap** (*k-nap*) is still used to reveal a sense of frustration at the imposition of English over the mother tongue. The word comes from *snap* and in Old Scots referred to an affected or pretentious manner of speaking 'proper' English. John Graham's example of usage – *Hear du him knappin awa laek a föl* – makes it plain that the word has overtones of disdain for the one who knaps. King James of Scotland was said to consider *knapping suddrone* (suddrone being English) as bordering on traitorous behaviour; surely a chilling remark from a king's lips.

Our dog can spell w-a-l-k, by which we mean she is able to recognise the individual sounds of the letters when spelt out in the correct order and immediately responds by barking ecstatically and rushing to and fro. If we change the pronunciation however, making the 'w' into a 'v' in the Germanic manner; 'a' into 'au'; 'l' into 'ull' and shorten 'k' to 'kh', she will merely cock one ear, tilt her head and give a quizzical look as if to say *have you taken leave of your senses?*

When approaching the fascinating challenge of preparing this dictionary we quickly came to realise the importance of pronunciation (and not simply because it matters to our dog). As pronunciation is by no means universal throughout the islands the subject has posed something of a problem. An amusing exchange took place in the House of Lords in 1736 during an examination of the Magistrates of Edinburgh regarding some shooting incidence. The Duke of Newcastle asked the Provost with what kind of shot the town-guards loaded their muskets and was told *Ou juist as ane shutes deuks and sic lik fules wi*. The reply caused uproar and the Provost was at risk of being held in contempt of the House until the Duke of Argyle (who must have been highly amused) translated the remark into English as *shot used for ducks and waterfowl*. [*Reminiscences of Scottish Life and Character* by Dean Ramsay: T. N. Foulis, London & Edinburgh (1912)] Getting it right is obviously important.

Historically most Shetland words have arisen out of an oral tradition rather than a literary one. To this day even the most fluent speakers of the dialect tend to be reticent when it comes to writing it and by and large prefer to use English. When eventually the words came to be written it was done in a phonetic manner and therefore presumed to be self-explanatory. For example, *pin* is written as **preen** in Shetland. The pronunciation is obvious. A word like **aabody** (everybody) is more problematic. Not all Shetlanders would agree on this one; some rendering the *aa* as the 'a' in *all* while others would have it 'a' as in *art*. The way in which the Westside district of Walls got its name has frequently been documented over the years; nevertheless it is worth repeating it here as a means of highlighting the difficulties which can arise between the spoken and the written word. Hearing the name being pronounced as 'vaas' a cartographer misunderstood this to be the Lowland Scots word 'waas' (walls) and proceeded accordingly. (Any visitor to the district, on seeing the large number of dry-stone enclosures in the surrounding hills might readily agree with the nomenclature). In fact the village gets its name from the way the sea encroaches in a series bays, the Norn word for which is 'va' – (pl) 'vaas'.

There can be little doubt that many of the entries in this dictionary, having evolved in spoken dialect over centuries, have become subtly changed phonetically to the point that they are no longer accurate representations of their origins. A good example of this is **taegirse** (wild thyme). In Scots, **tae** = toe and **girse** = grass. Clearly this is wrong – unless we try to suggest the herbal properties of

thyme, which were used to treat athlete's foot, gave rise to the name. Or we might conjecture what is intended here is **teg-girse** – grass growing in a strip of field, i.e. along road verges – from O.N. **teigr** (*measured strip of land*). A good try but still highly unlikely as in most cases plants derive their names from their appearance. Following some brilliant sleuthing on the part of Neil Anderson, we were led to O.N. **tág** (*root fibre*) (N. **taag**) which is rendered in the plural as **tæger** to mean, in a general sense, *tough, fibrous substance*. Could **taegirse** in fact be **tæger**? We think so, especially as the variety found in Shetland is *Thymus praecox* or creeping thyme.

Not wishing to complicate the matter unduly we have kept to a few simple rules bearing in mind at all times that it is non-Shetlanders who are looking for help in the main. To this end we have included a phonetic version of any words which are likely to cause difficulty. Where the normal spelling of the word is itself phonetic we have let this suffice. Newcomers to the dialect might care to start with the well known exchange said to have taken place between two women at a parish show. They are discussing a piece of knitted hand-spun.

Oo?
Aye oo.
Aa oo?
Aye aa oo.
Aa ee oo?
Aye aa ee oo (**Yes, all one wool**)
    i.e. made from the one fleece.

While the exchange is not originally Shetlandic it comfortably fits within the parameters of the dialect and equates with that other Scottish tongue-twister *it's a braw bricht moonlicht nicht* – the Germanic/Scots pronunciation of which raises a point. When comparing Graham's preferred spelling of words to modern-day usage it is apparent that some changes have continued to take place in recent years and we have attempted to accommodate these where it is thought appropriate to do so. One example is the word *night* which appears in many of Graham's phrases with the standard Scots spelling *nicht*. Many 21st century Shetlanders favour the spelling and pronunciation of *nite* – *In aboot da nite*, while John M. Tait (*Shetlandic in a Context of Linguistic and Cultural Identity*) – an internet on-line dissertation – suggests *nycht* as a better rendering of the word.

In regard to diminutives (much favoured in the Scots language), it is difficult to apply any hard and fast rule. Graham employs all three forms 'i' 'ie' and 'y' and as his dictionary has been in common usage in Shetland for almost thirty years, we have maintained his rendering (with a few exceptions) in the interest of standardisation.

Discovering the origin of words greatly enriches their meaning. It also helps explain the pronunciation variables. To this end we are indebted to Jakob Jakobsen, who first travelled to Shetland in 1893 visiting extensively throughout the islands meeting many people in order to complete his two-volume work. In comparing usage of Norn words from place to place, he observed that the outlying parishes and islands preserved the greatest diversity. Commenting on Unst's popularity as a tourist destination, coupled with its lively trade and fishing industry of the day, he states: *Yell is in reality more isolated than Unst and this larger island, with its still very rich Norn vocabulary, will certainly be the part of Shetland where the old dialect with its intermixture of Norn will maintain itself longest.* Arguably, this has proved to be the case, especially as in the intervening years Unst became even more cosmopolitan with the establishment of an RAF Base there after the Second World War. (If we appear to have relied too heavily upon Jakobsen's scholarship when researching the history of Norn words – especially when some modern-day scholars would favour treading more cautiously; we reiterate our own limited scholarship in this regard and point out that Jakobsen has stood as a primary source in this particular field for the greater part of the last century.) Readers wishing to explore the recorded history of Norn in greater detail will find Michael Barnes, *The Norn Language of Orkney and Shetland* (The Shetland Times Ltd, 1998) a very informative resource.

Strictly speaking, this ought to be a dictionary of words that are exclusive to Shetland, or at least have meanings that are peculiarly Shetlandic, else we would be required to include all the words that a Shetlander might be expected to use in everyday language. Clearly that would be tiresome and of little value. However there are some grey areas

John Graham obviously experienced the same problems we have encountered in this regard, for example he included the word *affront* giving its usage as *I wis black affrontit ta see his onkerry.* As *affront* is a Standard English word we chose rather to go with *affrontit.*

On the other hand we were *not* persuaded to exclude all words or meanings which have died out of usage simply because they refer to things or actions that have ceased to be part of Shetland life. If we keep leaving out the old words where will modern day writers of historical novels go for their resources? Not to mention all those poets who love the word play of intriguing onomatopoeia. By the same token we were not convinced to include some of the extraordinary modern-day attempts to twist spelling for the mere sake of doing so. Words like *faece* for *face* do nothing for the integrity of the dialect, particularly when they do not appear to significantly alter pronunciation and sentences such as *Dey washed der faeces*, are downright ridiculous.

In compiling a Shetland dictionary which aims to give due emphasis to the Norse origins of many of the words, it is worth noting that the Old Norse alphabet did not include the letter **c**, thus a number of commonly spelt **c** words such as **crö**, **crex**, **creeksit**, should perhaps be spelt with a **k**. (Jakobsen's Norn dictionary went from **b** to **d** and had only *calf*, *corn* and *craw* described as 'anglicised' words which he listed under **k**.) Similarly the letter **q** is absent from Old Norse, the sound being substituted with **kv**, pronounced in Shetland as **kw** (**kwar** (*where* – Westside)). Nevertheless we have maintained most of Graham's usage – again in the interest of continuity. Pedants and poets will make their own **k** adjustments and very probably want to argue the inconsistencies of **c** versus **k** in this dictionary. It is all grist to the mill of debate and no doubt will contribute to keeping the language alive and well.

A cursory glance at the few existing published dictionaries and glossaries of Shetland words will very quickly determine that no satisfactory system of representing the spelling and pronunciation of the dialect has yet been devised. Individual writers, when providing glossaries to assist their readers, give differing representation of the words they use – in some cases clearly implying different pronunciations. Not surprisingly, Shetlanders corresponding with one another tend to become reticent when penning the dialect however fluently they may speak it. In something as basic as the definitive article *the*, Graham favoured **da** while Jakobsen preferred the more Norn **de** (as English *the* and French *le*) and many writers are happy to go with **d** – *He göd ta d foy.* Observing the tendency of newcomers to the dialect to lengthen **da** to **daa** – *daa street*, we have consequently favoured **de** in most examples of usage (**da** is *grandfather* in Shetland).

If this also leads to discouraging the modern-day practice of rendering the second personal pronoun **dee** (*you*) as **de**, so much the better. Having said this, a more scholarly argument for using **de** rather than **da** can best be explained as follows:

In English, pairs of characters used to write one phoneme or unit of sound are referred to as **digraphs**. The digraph **th** in Old English was represented either by the letter **dæt** (**ð**) which in modern English is called an **eth** or **edh**, or alternately by the letter **þ** which is called a **thorn** or **þorn**. These two letters are also represented in Old Norse. The **ð** represents the 'soft' **th** sound referred to as a **voiced dental spirant** while the **þ** represents the 'hard' **th** sound referred to as a **voiceless dental spirant**, both pronounced with the tongue between the teeth. In Shetland dialect the two **th** sounds are represented either by a **d** (voiced **th**) or **t** (voiceless **th**). When comparing the following English words with their Shetland counterparts it can be seen that apart from changing the **th** to either **d** or **t** (the modern equivilant of **ð** and **þ**) the words by and large remain the same.

Voiced Dental Spirant **th** (**d**)	Voiceless Dental Spirant **th** (**t**)
the = de	think = tink
this = dis	thin = tin
they = dey	thistle = tistle
there = dere	thunder = tunder
them = dem	thanks = tanks
that = dat	thick = tick
thee = dee	three = tree
than = dan	thief = tief
variant:	variants:
their = dir	thirst = trist
	thorny = toarny
	thought = towt
	thrash = tresh
	throat = trot
	thread = treed
	thumb = toom

The rule also applies when **th** appears elsewhere in a word:

mother = midder	month = munt
father = faider	fifth = fift
brother = bridder	
heather = hedder	
gather = gadder	
bother = budder	
tether = tedder	

There are many more but the point is in all cases the rule holds true and thus becomes a compelling argument for using **de** in preference to **da** for the definite article *the*, while at the same time

acknowledging speech patterns sometimes dictate otherwise.

Dialect, unlike English, tends to be written as a phonetic representation of the spoken word, e.g. *For siccan a onkerry whin shö drappit de mylk jug an he göd in shalmillens* (There was such a carry on when she dropped the milk jug and it went in smithereens).

It can be said the sentence has a number of essentially English words – *when she dropped* and *milk jug* – yet only *jug* is correctly spelt according to English usage while the others are changed to facilitate pronunciation of the dialect. The difficulty lies in that not all Shetlanders would agree on the precise spelling of these words owing to subtle variations in pronunciation and so some might prefer to change *shö* to *shuh* and *mylk* to *mjlk*, while *siccan* could happily become *sic*.

All this has led to hesitancy on our part when attempting to lay down guidelines despite the obvious need for some. In particular it is commonplace to introduce a vowel-change to facilitate pronunciation in words such as **beat** and **meat** where the **ea** switches to **ae** to become **baet** and **maet**. Likewise **ai** changes to **e** in words like **paint** (**pent**) and **faith** (**feth**) for a similar reason and **au** becomes **o** in **daughter** (**dochter**, **dowter**), **aught** (**ocht**, **owt**) and others. It is also the case that in some English words beginning with **ch**, this is changed (*shenged*) to **sh** – again to facilitate pronunciation, and some words ending in -**ed** are changed to -**it**, particularly -**ked** endings, e.g. **liked** becomes **laekit** and in this instance (as in several others) there is a slight break in pronunciation, thus *laek-it*. Notwithstanding all of the above, unless there is a significant change in the way English words are pronounced in the dialect, it is generally better to adhere to the English spelling, and here we are reminded of John Graham's comment – *Outlandish forms, used perhaps in a misdirected zeal to emphasise the non-English character of the dialect, should be avoided as far as possible*. (*The Shetland Dictionary*, The Shetland Times Ltd., 2009). For further guidance, students of the dialect may like to visit John Tait's online article titled *Shetlandic in a Context of Linguistic and Cultural Identity* and click on the *Shetland and Scots Language* pages where they will find a very good in-depth guide to pronunciation.

In the main we have favoured giving alternative spellings in the word list wherever it appears useful to do so. As a rule of thumb the headword should be considered the most popular although in the case of **c** versus **k** and **y** versus **j** (as mentioned earlier) the jury may still be out. Bracketed words following the headword provide alternative spellings (and to some extent pronunciations), e.g. **aald** (**ald**, **auld**, **ould**, **owld**) while first or second syllable emphasis is given in italics, e.g. **salist** sa-*list*.

As indicated previously, for simplification we have adhered to Graham's practice of using the diacritic **ö** in words like **blöd** (blood) and **shön** (shoes) although many have a preference for **bluid** and **shoon**. However we were tempted to change other spellings like **grind** (gate) to **grinnd** in order to differentiate from English **grind** (crush) – **grinnd** having the vowel quality of *hit*, while **grind** has a diphthong as in *bite*. We got round it with the italics *grin-d*. Incidentally, the ö symbol indicates a sound similar to the *oe* in German *Goethe* (the sound can be approximated by rounded the lips as for the 'a' in *ate* and pronouncing an 'e'), while the **ch** in *acht*, *dicht*, *licht*, *fecht*, *soch*, *tocht*, etc. sounds the same as the German *achtung* or Scots *loch* and not as English *church* and definitely not as *lock*.

As a further aid to exploring the source of words, we have used the colour blue to render all words that appear to have a strong connection to Scandinavian languages – Norn if you like. This does not necessarily mean the words came into the Shetland language directly from this source although in most cases that would appear to be Jakobsen's view. We are aware that informed scholarship frequently disputes some of the assertions made by Jakobsen and others and in all probability will disagree with many of our findings. With the passage of time the imposition of other tongues has overlaid the original phonetics and influenced oral tradition to some extent making it difficult to accurately determine sources. We can only repeat that all [bracketed] material in this dictionary is offered as tentative etymology only and we encourage interested readers to dig deeper. If wiser heads than ours believe we have got it wrong, we welcome their critical comment and will be pleased to amend subsequent editions.

While the majority of Shetland words not of Norn origin are directly linked to Old Scots, English or some provincial dialect of Britain in general, some interesting anomolies have crept in and held on down through the centuries. In the same way in which the 'Auld Alliance' saw many French words introduced into the Scots tongue – e.g. *ashet*, *aumry* – so Dutch fishermen, who regularly visited Shetland in the 18th and 19th centuries, left their mark on the dialect with words like **cabbi-labbi** (M.Du. *kibbelen*: to wrangle); **maed** (M.Du. & Ger. *made*: maggot) and many more.

According to the experts, the rule of thumb for including a word in a dictionary is that it must have been in general use for five years. It is less certain at what point words should be considered to be obsolete. About 80 years ago Jessie Saxby wrote a book [*Shetland Traditional Lore*, Jessie M. E. Saxby: Grant & Murray Ltd, Edinburgh (1932)] in which she used many interesting words. Most of the words in her glossary were still in use when John Graham set out to compile his dictionary although twenty were excluded from that work. It is worth noting that of those twenty words, my wife still uses six. For what it is worth, we list here some of Jessie Saxby's words which are *not* included in John Graham's dictionary:

fiels	– hill grazing
grulik	– guizer
heogue	– hillock
knockit	– ground in a hand mill
murge (mirge)	– multitude
riggie	– back

As all but one of these words are believed to be of Norn derivation and still known in the North Yell district (if not necessarily extensively used), we have included them in the dictionary. In fact (as mentioned in the *Acknowledgements*) the criteria for including words in this dictionary is that they be known by at least two persons and understood by a third in conversation.

Old English pronunciation of words like **knee** [*k-nee*] and **gnash** [*g-nash*] were once commonplace throughout Britain. Today the speech anomoly survives in only a few provincial pockets with Shetland arguably having the most words still in everyday use – **knap** [k-nap], **knep** [k-nep], **knoilt** [k-noilt], **knowe** [k-nowe], and others, while the Westside renders most **wh**- words as **kw**-, **white** thus becoming **kwite**, with the prefix being slightly drawn out in the **kn** manner. Incidently, in Mrs Saxby's book she had a delightful instruction on the pronunciation of the word **knockit** – *when saying the word you must give full effect to the 'K' sending it through the nose with emphasis!* So much for phonetics.

When it comes to grammar, it is not our intention to enter that particular minefield and so we refer readers to *Grammar and Usage of the Shetland Dialect*; [T.A. Robertson & John J. Graham: The Shetland Times Ltd. (1991)] with one brief comment on the usage of **wiz/wis**, and **wir**. **wiz/wis** (either spelling) can mean both **us**, **was** and **were** depending on usage while **wir** can mean **our**, **were** or **we are** –

> *He **wis** at de hill cuttin **wir** paets*. He **was** at the hill cutting **our** peats
> ***Wir** dy bairns playin wi **wir** dug?* **Were** your children playing with **our** dog?
> ***Wir** aye blyde to hae dee stayin wi **wiz**.* **We are** always glad to have you stay with **us**.
> *Dey **wir** in Lerook wi **wiz** aa day, **wis** du no?* They **were** in Lerwick with **us** all day, **were** you not?

Now you know why we have left the rest to Messrs Robertson and Graham.

And finally, spare a thought for the ever-increasing number of 'sooth-moothers' now living in Shetland who must learn to speak the dialect just in case the locals ever take it into their heads to emulate the Old Testament Gileadites

> *The Gileadites captured the fords of Jordan leading to Ephraim, and whenever a survivor of Ephraim said, "Let me cross over", the men of Gilead asked him, "Are you an Ephraimite?" If he replied "No" they said, "All right, say, Shibboleth." If he said, "Sibboleth" because he could not pronounce the word correctly, they seized him and killed him…"*
>
> [Judges 12: verses 5-6]

Not being particularly adept at pronouncing words like **crö** I'd be the first to lose my head!

A. Christie-Johnston

ABBREVIATIONS

adj.	adjective		M.Du.	Middle Dutch
adv.	adverb		M.E.	Middle English
aux.	auxiliary		M.Ger.	Middle German
C.E.	Common English		M.L.Ger.	Middle Lower German
cf.	compare		Mod.Fr.	Modern French
colloq.	colloquial		n.	noun
conj.	conjunction		N.	Norwegian
D.	Danish		N.Amer.	North American
der. exclam.	derived exclamation		N.Fr.	Northern French
deriv.	derivative		O.E.	Old English
dial.	dialect		O.F.	Old French
dimin.	diminutive		O.N.	Old Norse
DOST	Dict. of Scots Tongue		obs.	obscure
DSL	Dict. of Scottish Language		opp.	opposite
Du.	Dutch		orig.	origin
E.	English		Ork.	Orkney
Edm.	Thomas Edmondston		O.Sc.	Old Scots
esp.	especially		O.Sh.	Old Shetland
exp.	expression		p.	proverb
Fær.	Faroese		pl.	plural
fig.	figurative		poss.	possibly
Finn.	Finnish		pp.	past participle
Fr.	French		ppl.	past participle applies
Gael	Gaelic		pt.	past tense
Ger.	German		prep.	preposition
Gr.	Greek		pron.	pronoun
Icel.	Icelandic		prop.	properly
id.	idem (same as)		S.Amer.	South American
interj.	interjection		Sc.	Scottish
Jak.	Jakobsen		Sh.	Shetland
L.	Latin		SIC	Shetland Islands Council
L.Ger.	Lower German		st.	street
Lapp.	Lapland		Sw.	Swedish
lit.	literally		v.	verb
L.Sc.	Lowland Scots			

A

a (aux v) have. *Du could a come as weel*; (prep) of. *A cup a tae*; (also see **o**).

aa (adj) all; every one. *Aa da sheep wis moorit*; (n) everything. *I'm telt dee aa I keen* (I've told you all I know). [L.Sc. *aa*: all]; (v) to owe. *Foo muckle did he aa dee?* [E. owe]

aaber (aber, awber) (adj) eager; enthusiastic; keen. [Sw.dial. *apra*, D.dial. *abre*: set to work energetically]

aaberknot (n) magic knot, such as may be used to tie a **wrestin treed** to effect a cure. [O.N. *apr*: sharp; hard; bad]

aaber-up (v) liven up. *Aaber up de fire* (Poke up the fire). [Sw.dial. *apra*, D.dial. *abre*: set to work energetically]

aabody (pron) everybody; all the people. [L.Sc. *aabody*]

aafil (aaful) (adv) (colloq) very; thoroughly. *Shö's aafil lik her midder*; (also see **terrible**); (n) a large quantity. *Yun's a aafil o tatties du's peelin*. [L.Sc. *awful*, in similar meanings]

aald (ald, auld, ould, owld) (adj) old; aged; belonging to the past (note differing spellings as being indicative of variations in pronunciation throughout Shetland). [Sc. *auld*: old]

aald daa (n) great-grandfather; (sometimes) grandfather; (see **daa**).

Aald Rock (De) (n) sentimental, affectionate or poetic name for Shetland. [Sc. *auld*: old – rock]

aalie lamb (alilam, ali-lamb) (n) pet lamb (also **allie-caddie**). [O.N. *alidýr*: tame animal; domesticated animal]

aamos (amos, amus) (n) alms; a gift made in the expectation that a wish will be granted to the donor. The donor is said to *lay on a aamos* and if the wish is granted, this person is said to *have won an aamos*; (adj) poor; wretched; deserving of alms (also see **pör aamos**). [O.N. *almusa*, E. *alms*: money given in charity; O.E. *ælmesse*: alms]

aamos bairn (n) a child (usually born on a Sunday) capable of winning alms. [see above]

aamos body (-ting) (n) an indigent person deserving of alms. [see **aamos**]

aamos kirk (n) a church considered to have the power of winning alms. In early days such buildings continued to be visited even after falling into disuse and people left tokens of money in the expectation of receiving alms. [see **aamos**]

aandoo (andu) using oars to hold a boat in position against tide drift or wind; row slowly against the tide; also used metaphorically to describe a person walking slowly, dawdling. [O.N. *andæfa*]

aari (adj) bitter. [Sc. *oorie*: dismal; gloomy; cheerless; cf. *eerie*]

aarisay (arrisie) (n) dislike; loathing. [N. *arrig*: cross; ill-tempered]

aathing (pron) everything.

aboot (prep) about; during. *In aboot da nycht* – an evening visit. [E. *about* but with extension of meaning *near in time or place*]

aboot de banks along the shoreline; beachcombing – *ta geng aboot de banks* being a favourite pastime of old fishermen and crofters esp. in hope of finding some timber washed up by the sea (see **banks**).

abön (abune) (prep) above; overhead. [Sc. *abune, aboon*]

ach (interj) expression of dismissal, exasperation or impatience. *Ach! A'm hed enough a dis*. [same as Sc. *och*]

acht (n) a treasured possession; (v pt) owned. [O.Sc. *aucht*: to possess or own]

acquant (adj) acquainted. *Wir neebor wiz acquant wi de wey o him*. [O.F. *acointer*; L. *adcognitum*]

admire (v) to surprise; astonish. *Hit admired me tae see her* – hence admiration. Obs. usage elsewhere in Sc. and E. [L. *ad*: at + *mīrāri*: to wonder]

aer (n) 1) an oar. [O.N. *ar*: an oar]; 2) a minute quantity. [Icel. *ar*: a mote; a speck of dust]

aert (n) earth. [L.Sc. *eart, ert*]

aertbark (n) tormentil (*Potentilla erecta*) – used medicinally and in tanning leather.

aert-bile (n) a bog; specifically a small area where trapped water makes a patch of ground swell up and is like a jelly when stood on; a quagmire.

aert-fast (adj) firmly grounded. [L.Sc. *eart, ert*]

aert-kent (adj) universally known. *He's as aert kent as de moorit yowe o Hascosay*. [L.Sc. *eart, ert*: earth + *kent*: known]

aeshins (esins) (n) top of house gable, inside roof. [O.N. *áss*: ridge; beam]

aest (n) east. (**nort**; **sooth**; **wast** – north; south; west)

aester (v) to shift eastwards, as wind.

aestard (n) an easterly direction. *Bring her boo up a point tae de aestard*.

aet (et) (n) state of agitation; eagerness. *He wis in a aafil aet owre yun*. [O.N. *at*: agitation; *etja*: to incite]

aet (v) eat; (pt) **öt**; (pp) **aetin (ötten)**. [M.E. *eat(e)*, *ete*; O.N. *eta*]

aetmell (n) oatmeal.

aets (n) oats. [O.Sc. *ait(t)s*]

aff (adv) off; usage in phrases: **geng aff** go fishing in a boat; **had aff** wait; keep away. *Had aff a me a min*; **lay aff** speak volubly. *Wid du lay aff wi dee argie-bargie*; **tak aff** abate (as sea or wind). *Da Bressa ferry'll no geng till dis wadder taks aff*; poke fun at, copy. *He can fairly tak her aff*; (v) **taen aff** taken aback. [O.N. *af*]

affbidden (affsettin) (adj) off-putting. [N. *bjoda mot*, Icel. *bjoda vid*: arouse dislike; repugnance]

affcuttins (n) hocks of cattle.

afflay (n) voluminous talk; garrulousness.

affroad (affröd) aff-*rod* (v) to dissuade; discourage. *Du'll meybe try an affröd him fae gaan;* to chatter; speak volubly. *Dir a affröd wi her.* [N.dial. *avröd*: dissuaded; Fær. *avráða*: to dissuade]

affrontit (v) to cause to feel ashamed, humiliated. *I wis black-affrontit at de wye o him.* [O.F. *affronter*: to strike on the forehead; to insult]

affrug (afrog, aafrugg) *aff*-rug (n) the back-surge of waves after having broken on the shore (also see **rugg**). [O.N. *reka*: drift, cf. Fær. *rák*: set of current]

afftak (aaftak) *aff*-tak (n) 1) mocking remark; taunt; 2) last ring of stitches at the lower end of a sock before making the heel. [L.Sc. *afftak*: a 'taking off' or send-up]

afkled (v) to undress. [O.N. *afklæðask*]

afore (adv, prep) before. *He göd afore de idders.* [L.Sc. *afore*]

aft (adv) frequently. [Sc.]

aftest (adv) most frequently.

ag (agg, aug) (n) the dash of waves on the shore as caused by rising wind. *He's surely comin a gale fur der an agg apo de sea.* [cf. N. *ag* (n): swell]

agg (ug) (v) to feel sick; to gag in act of vomiting. [N. *aga*: to feel sick]

aggle (agl, agel) (n) a mess; (v) to make a mess; to dirty; to soil. *Dunna aggle in yun bruck.* [N. *alka*: to dirty; defile]

agment (n) unrest; anxiety. [cf. N. *agg*: drift, in sense of unrest; movement; *aggast*: to be anxious]

ahint (ahent) (prep) behind. [O.E. *hindan*]

aidge o a time (adv) infrequently. *Wir eens geng ta da kirk at de aidge o a time.*

ain (adj) own. *I wiz on me ain.* [O.N. *eiginn*; D. *egen*; L.Sc. *ain*]

ajee (ajie) a-*jee* (adj) ajar. [E. *ajar*]

akkadör (v) to endure; forbear; persevere. [orig. obs. poss. 'act to endure']

akker (aker) (n) (in) remnants; fragments; ruin. [orig. O.N. *akr*: field; seed; crop; connected to L.Sc. *aiker*: ear (of corn) but also *aker*: a crushed mass]

alamootie (alamuti) (n) storm petrel (*Hydrobates pelagicus*) (also see **scooty-alan**). [Jakobsen suggests the word may be derived from D. & Sw.dial. *adel*: urine, liquid manure; on account of the stormy petrel's habit of squirting out a yellowish oil through its nostrils as a form of defence (and attack); *mootie* = small; O.N. *motti*: a moth; mite; tiny insect]

alan (aalin) (n) arctic skua (*Stercorarius parasiticus*) (also **scooty-alan**). [orig. uncertain, cf. Sc. *allan-hawk*; Sw.dial. *auk*; O.N. *alka*]

alane a-*lane* (adj) alone. [Sc.]

aless a-*less* (conj) unless; (prep) except; (interj) alas, in exp. *less aless* – sympathetic remark at hearing bad news; (also **less**). [Sc. *less, aless*]

aliplukkins (n) wool plucked from the belly of a sheep. [O.N. *alidýr*: tame animal, domesticated animal + E. *pluck*: to pull out (wool, feathers, etc.)]

almark (n) a rogue sheep that breaks through fences or jumps over walls (originally one which escaped into common property, i.e. the scattald). [N. *aalmark*: land shared by the community in common]

A'm I am. *A'm no hed me denner yit.*

ammerswak (amerswakk) (n) state of agitation or unrest. [from N. *ama-*: to push on; to set in motion; O.N. *amask*: to trouble oneself; and N. *-kvekkr*: to be startled; Fær. *kvökka*: to be startled]

amp (n) state of anxiety. *He was in sic an amp aboot gaan tae da doctor.* [Fær. *ampi*: trouble; unrest; haste; N. *ampe*: bother; trouble]

an aa (adj) as well. *I telt him an aa.* [Sc.]

anaeth (prep) beneath. [Sc.]

anker (n) liquid measure – 8⅓ imperial gallons (a third of a barrel). [old European measure for wines and spirits]

anns (n) residue of chaff left behind when winnowing. [O.N. *agnar, agnir*: husks; L.Sc. *awns*: beards of corn]

anse (ans) (v) to obey; to heed. [O.N. *ansa*: to notice; care about]

ant (v) to heed. *Never ant his atfirts*; (also **ent**). [O.N. *enta*: heed; care about]

anterin (adj) occasional. [orig. uncertain cf. O.Sc. *aunter*: chance]

anunder (prep) under. *I niver took up anunder it* (I paid no attention). [L.Sc. *anunder*: lit. 'in-under']

anyatwart (annehwart) *anya*-twart (adj) awkward in nature; contrary; unpredictable, esp. of weather. *He's bön blaain anyatwart aa dis ook.* [O.N. *annarhvarr*: every second one]

anyister (annester, annister) *an*-yister (n) maiden ewe, one which has not had a lamb. [O.N. *annars vetrar*: of the second year]

anyoch an-*yoch* (adj) enough. [O.Sc. *aneuch*]

apo (prep) upon.

appearance (n) suggestion; indication. *Der an appearance o snaa idda sky.*

apper (aper) (v) to put off; detain. *Du man apper him if du can.* [O.N. *aptra*: to pull; take or keep back; call back]

applöse (v) offer; make available; make known. [orig. uncertain, poss M.E. *apleyse*: to please; gratify]

ard (n) stone ploughshare commonly found on archaeological digs or uncovered when cultivating a field. [O.N. *arðr*]

ard (haard, hoord) (N. Yell) (n) a scar; scratch; a sore caused by chafing; (adj) scarred. [O.N. *arr*; D. *ar*; Eng.dial. & L.Sc. *arr-id*]

argie-bargie (n) tedious argument; quarrel. [Sc. *argie-bargie*: to argue tediously; Fr. *arguer*]

ark (n) a large meal-chest; anything large of its kind. *Dat in feth! Yun's a graet ark o a staig.* [O.N. *ork, arka*: chest; case; L.Sc. *ark*: chest]

arl (arel) (v) to crawl or creep. [Sc. *harl(e)*: to feebly drag or draw oneself along]

article (n) a naughty or tricky person. *Dat is wan article.* [Sh. variant on E. *article*: item]

arvi (n) chickweed (*Stellaria media*). [N. & D. *arve*; O.N. *arfi*]

as (conj) than. *Hit's a lok bigger as de last een du cam wi.* [Sc.]

ask (n) haze; mist; drizzly rain; (also **shask**). [O.N. cf. *hoss*: greyish; *aska*: ashes; E. *haze*]

asoond a-*soond* (adv) unconscious. [O.E. *gesund*: sound 'swoon'; *aswoon*]

asticle (n) a glazing bar in a window. [Sh. variant on E. *astragal*]

asundry (adv) asunder. *A'm hed ta tak de hale ting asundry ta fix it*; (also **sindry**). [O.Sc. *sindry*; M.E. *sundar*; O.E. *sundrum*, *syndrig*]

as wiz wi (as wiz be) phrase used in expressing something after the manner of another. *As wiz wi Robbie, hit's a lokk a hellery*. [equiv. phrase in E. *As Robert would say…*]

at (rel pron) that; who. *Yun's aa at I hae*; *Ony een at wants t spaek hes ta pit up his haand*. [O.N. *at*: conj. that; also O.Eng. & L.Sc.]

atfirts (atferd) *at*-firts (n) antics; manner of behaviour. [O.N. *atferd*: behaviour; manner of proceeding]

athin (prep) within. [Sc.]

athoot (prep) without. [Sc.]

atraholla (adj) said of weather which is alternating between wet and dry. [O.N. *annarhvárr*: every other]

atteri (etri) (adj) bitterly cold, as weather. [O.N. *eitr*: venom; *eitrkaldr*: freezing cold]

atween (prep) between; **atween da bed an da fire** (adv phr) in a state of semi-invalidity.

auld man idda daek (n) bearded lichen (*Cladonia portentosa*).

aurrie (arrie) (n) the space or area down the middle of churches, between the rows of seats; aisle – *aurrie o' kirks*; a section or stripe; *tak anidder arrie* – said of painting or tarring. [L.Sc. *aurrie*: aisle; open space]

ava a-*vaa* (adv) at all. *Dir nae wirk ava*. [Sc. used as in Eng. *at all*]

aye (i) yes. *Aye, du's right*. [E. *aye*, archaic except in dial. and voting in The House of Commons; Sc. *ay* = yes, *aye* = always (see below); O.N. *ei*: eh! ha!]

aye, aye (i) (Westside **yae, yae**) yes, yes – a common form of greeting; an expression of agreement though may convey some reservation or scepticism, depending on tone of voice, especially if followed by *I hear dee*. [E. formal response to a naval command]

aye (adv) always. [Sc. *aye*: always; ever]

ayre *air* (n) a beach or sandy headland. [O.N. *eyrr*: sand or gravel bank]

ax (axe) (v) ask. '*We ax for what we want*' – slogan on Guizer Jarl's Seal on **Up-Helly-A'** Proclamation. [O.N. *œskja*: ask]

aze (es) *ayz* (n) blaze. [O.N. *eisa*: to rush on violently (occas. of fire); glowing embers]

azin *ay*-zin (adj) blazing.

B

baa (n) 1) a sunken or partially submerged rock. [O.N. *bodi*: a hidden shoal in the sea] 2) a ball; egg yolk; pupil of the eye; (v) to lullaby a child. [Sc. *ball, baw*]

baagie (bagi, baki) (n) great black-backed gull (*Larus marinus*) (also **swaabie**). [deriv. of O.N. *bak*: back]

baak (bak) (n) 1) hen's perch. [O.N. *bjālki*: a beam] 2) head-rope in fishing-lines and nets. [O.N. *balkr*; N. *line-balk*]

baak-high (adj) highly excited. *He göd baak-high at da news.* [Du. *balk*: girder]

baand (n) tether used to tie a cow to a **veggel** in a byre; a rib in a boat; a twist of straw used to bind a sheaf; a gathering of people; used derogatorily – *For sic a baand!* [O.N. & E. *band*: bunch; bundle; two objects tied together; boat ribs]

bachus (n) revelry (generally involving drink). *Boy hit wis a total bachus at Willie's dastreen* (Whalsay). [prob. deriv. of *Bacchus*: Roman god of wine; E. *bacchanal*: a drunken reveller]

backaboot (adj) isolated; out of the way. *He's a backaboot place dir in.* Also applied to an old-fashioned person; out-of-date.

back-brack (n) 'back-break', excessive fatigue.

back-brackin (n) a job requiring great effort.

back-burden (n) heavy load carried on the back.

backdraa (n) sharp intake of breath, or smoke, as in a chimney. *Yun shimley's gotten a right backdraa* (when smoke is drawn back into a room owing to atmospheric inversion).

backlins (baklins) (adv) backwards. *Shö fell backlins idda burn.* [N. *baklengjes*]

back-owre (adv) *He's back-owre* – he is in the back (of the shop, back yard, room, etc.).

bad (n) principal article of clothing; a suit of clothes. [DSL '*bit and baid*': food and clothing; S.dial. *pade*: cloak; overcoat]

badly (adj) unwell; ailing. *I'm bön badly wi da caald.*

baess (n) cattle. [O.F. *beste*; E. *beast*]

baess-maet (n) cattle-fodder (lit. 'beast-food').

baet (bait, bet, bate) (n) plaited stalks of dried **floss** (common reed) or **gloy** (straw) used for making **kishies** (baskets) or **simmens** (straw ropes); a bundle of flax or straw used for thatching; (v) to beat. [O.Sc. *beit*]

baff (n) a blow; a struggle. [L.Sc. *baff*; also cf. *buff, buffet*]

baffel (n) a struggle; also **baff** (v) to struggle; **baffin** (adj) struggling. [see above]

baid (n) both (also **baith**). [E. *both*; L.Sc. *baith*; D. *baade*; O.N. *bádir*]

bain (n) thick leather used for soles of shoes. [Gael. *bian*: skin, hide]

bairn (n) child. [O.Sc. *barne, bairn*, O.N. *barn*: child]

bairndom (n) childhood.

bairns (n) folk (colloq). *Weel, bairns, is dis dee? Come du in.*

bal (baal) (n) a ball; (v) to throw. [O.N. *bella*: to hit]

baldin (baldung) (n) halibut (*Hippoglossus hippoglossus*); turbot (*Scophthalmus maximus*). [O.N. *baldinn*: powerful; head-strong; defiant]

bamp (v) to nag or harp on about something constantly. [cf. O.N. *bamba*: drum (to make a drumming noise)]

bang (v) to rush; a sudden action; to spring. [O.N. *banga*: to knock; hammer]

bank (n) the section of moor from which peat is cut; working face of a peat-pit. (Each croft has its own designated peat bank from which the tenant may obtain fuel.) [Fær. *bakki*]; (v) to cover a fire with ashes, etc., in order to make it burn more slowly. [Sc. bank]

bank(s) steep coast; cliff face. [O.N. *bakki*: edge]

banks flooers (n) thrift; sea pinks (*Armeria Maritima*). [O.N. *bakki*: edge]

banks-gaet (n) path along cliff-top or way up or down a cliff. Used fig. to describe a difficult undertaking. *He'll be him a banks-gaet* (It will be a difficult job). [O.N. *bakki*: edge + *gata*: a road; path]

banks girse (n) scurvy grass (*Cochlearia officinalis*) or any grass growing in or on cliffs. [O.N. *bakki*: edge]

banks-sparrow (-sporrow) (n) rock pipit (*Anthus spinoletta*); also **tang-sparrow** so named for its shore-line habitat, as opposed to **hill-sparrow** the meadow pipit; (lit. '*banks-sparrow*'). [see **bank(s)**]

bannock (n) scone (*not* oatcake). [O.E. *bannuc*, O.Sc. *bannok* – usually a flat oatcake cooked on a griddle]

banstickle (n) stickleback (*Gasterosteus aculeatus*) a small, spiny backed fish. [L.Sc. *bane* (bone) -*stikkell*]

barber (n) cold mist rising from freshwater lochs and streams; freezing sea-mist. Known also in Halifax, Nova Scotia (DOST). [orig. obs.]

bard (n) a steep headland; promontory; common in placenames, e.g. Bard o Bressay. [O.N. *barð*: brim; edge]

barflog (v) to beat one's hands crosswise around the body to keep warm (also referred to as 'baetin de skarf' – see **skarf**). [O.N. *berja*: to flog; *berja flóka* in same sense as Shet. *barflog*]

bark (n) tormentil (*Potentilla erecta*) used in tanning process. [cf. Fær. *börka*: root of tormentil (*börkuvisa*)]

barmin (adj) frothing; fermenting, as yeast; seething with rage. *Shö wis fairly barmin* (frothing at the mouth). [O.E. *beorma*: yeast]

bass (n) a fiercely blazing fire. [Sw.dial. *basa*: to warm; to heat]

bassel (n) a struggle; (v) to struggle (see **baffel**).

bat (n) a light puff of wind; a gust (not so strong as a **flan**); (pt of) bite. *De dug bat him.* [LSc. *bat*: a stroke or blow]

be-aest (prep) to the east of; similarly **be-nort, be-sooth, be-wast**. '*Oot bewast da Horn o Papa, rowin Foula doon.*' (Vagaland).

bear (v) to build up in a drift, as snow driven by the wind.

be dat (adv) with that; at that moment. *Be dat, he göd awa fram*; (see also **be noo**).

bedral (**beddrel**, **bedrill**) *bed*-ral (n) a bedridden invalid. [O.Sc. *bedlare*]

bee (n) common or house-fly (*Musca domestica*) (esp. Yell), as opposed to bluebottle (*Calliphorida*), the blowfly; however, many Shetlanders call all flies bees – *muckle bees, peerie bees, a yellow-coloured bee, a sharny bee*, etc.

bee-bo (n) a triviality. [colloq. O.E. *bee*: a whim; a caprice; a fanciful idea; cf. 'a bee in the bonnet']

beek (v) 1) to bathe; wash. [cf. O.N. *bekkr*: a brook]; 2) to bask. [O.Sc. *beke*: to expose body to warmth]

beest (n) first milk of a newly calved cow which when boiled resembles fresh cheese. [O.E. *bēost*; Ger. *biest*]

beetle (v) to strike a heavy blow. [O.Sc. & O.E. *bitel*: a flat round piece of wood used by dyers and washerwomen to beat clothes; *bittle, beetle*, from *beat*]

beetlin (n) a thrashing. [see above]

begöd (v) (pt of begin) began.

begrutten (adj) tear-stained. [O.Sc. *begrete*: to beweep (see **greet**)]

begunk (n) a drawback, let-down or disappointment. *He wis gotten a right begunk whin shö never cam*. [Sc. *begunk*: to trick; to cheat; to jilt]

be hed (v pp) have had. *Du'll be hed dy denner afore we come.*

bein (v) a person; a human being – commonly *pör bein*; (also **body**).

bell (v) to fester. [Sc. *bele, beil*, O.E. *belgan*: to swell out]

bellin (adj) festering; swollen. *I'm gotten a bellin toom* (I have a swollen thumb). [see above]

below (v) lower; demean. *I widna below mesel ta be seen wi dem.* [N.Yell equiv. of E. lower]

Beltane (n). first day of May. One of the old Scottish 'quarter-days' on which rents and stipends were paid – Hallomas (1st Nov); Candlemas (2nd Feb); Beltane (1st May) and Lammas (1st Aug). [Gael. *Bealltainn*: an ancient Celtic festival marked with bonfires]

Beltane ree(s) (n) seasonal stormy weather associated with Beltane; also referred to as *Da gabs o May* (see **gabs**). [beltane + O.N. *hrí*: a spell of bad weather]

ben (n) the inner or better room in a cottage, as opposed to the **but** or kitchen end; also **ben-end**. *Come awa ben* (Come through to the best room). [Sc. *ben*: the inner or better rooms of a house; O.E. *binnan*: within]; **but-n-ben** two-roomed cottage (see **but**).

bend (n) the entire harness of a peat-pony; (v) to harness a peat-pony. [Sw.dial. *bänne* (*bende*): a hamper which is girt on a pack-horse]

ben (n) bone. [L.Sc. *bane*; O.N. *bein*]

beni-plukkins (**-pluckins**) (n) wool plucked from a dead sheep; inferior wool. *Hae ye ony beni-pluckins at I could get a hair o' it?* (Vagaland '*Hae ye ony moorit oo?*'); (also see **ali-plukkins**). [O.N. *bani*: bane; death + *plukka*: to pluck; to pull]

benkle (**benkel**) (n) a dent; (v) to dent. [Fær. *bongla*: a dent; N. *bungla*: to dent something]

be noo (adv) by now (see also **be dat**).

benon (adv) as well; on top of; over and above. [O.E. *anon*]

benwark (**benwerk**) (n) muscle pain; gouty pain; aching joints. [O.N. *beinverkr*: pain in the legs; L.Sc. *bane-*: bone-]

berg (n) a prominent rock on land or sea. [O.N. *berg*: mountain; rock; rocky soil]

better 1) (adv) more. *Tak da table better in tae dee*. [usage more in accordance with Norse than English – N. *drinka beter*: to drink more]

better 2) (adj) get better; recover. *Did he better fae de feerie?* **betters** gets better. *Yun's a bad feerie du hes, I hope du shune betters*. [Sh. variant on E. *better*]

bick (**bikk**) (n) a bitch; female dog. [O.N. *bikkja*]

bid (v) to invite; (pt) **bade**; (pp) **bidden**; (see **fiddler's bid**).

biddable (adj) obedient; compliant. [of E. *bid* – *able*, willing to accept an invitation]

bide (v) to reside. *He bides in Scallowa*; wait; stay. *I canna bide lang*. [Sc. *bide*, esp. as *to bide one's time*: await a favourable moment]

bidey-in (n) [colloq] one who co-habits with a member of the opposite sex.

bide you! (exclam) Just wait!

bigg (v) to build; make a nest. *De starns begöd ta bigg idda daek* (The starlings began to build in the wall); used in placenames, e.g. Biggins. [O.N. *byggja*: to build; *bygd*: a village]

bigg (n) barley (now commonly *bere*); used in placenames, e.g. Buggerslit (Papa Stour); a rig name *Byggrhlaut*, the barley plot, apparently owing to the nature of the soil being unsuitable for growing oats. [O.N. *bygg*: barley]

biggin(s) (n) a dwelling or a cluster of houses. Da Biggins. [O.N. *bygd*: a village; L.Sc. *biggin*: building]

bill (n) Up-Helly-A' proclamation, traditionally posted at the Market Cross, Lerwick during the annual festival and comprising humorous comment on the previous year's events. [Sc.]

billie (n) a fellow, commonly used disparagingly in Shetland. *He's a muckle billie*. [S. *billy, billie*: a close friend]

bing (n) a pile, mound or heap. [O.N. *bingr*]

birker (n) a spell of excessively cold weather. [orig. uncertain cf. N. *bjert* and *birt*: applied to weather, biting cold with occasional showers]

birl (v) to whirl rapidly, as in a dance. [N. *burla* (v) of air or water: to whirl; bluster; L.Sc. *birl*: rolling or whirring sound; (v) to revolve rapidly]

birler (n) one who birls. [see *birl*]

birlin (verbal n) whirling around. [see *birl*]

birr (n) a whirring sound, e.g. as a spinning wheel in motion; a passion, rage. [L.Sc. *birl*: rolling or whirring sound]

birse (**birst**) (n) bristles; hair. [O.N. *burst*: bristle; hog's hair]

birsie (**birsi**) (adj) angry; peeved; ill-tempered; keen, sharp – applied to weather. *He's a birsie day*. [N. *bysten*: choleric; fierce; harsh; Sc. *birsie*: hot-tempered; keen (of weather)]

B

birze (v) to squeeze. [L.Sc. *birse*, *birze* (n): a bruise; (v) to bruise; injure by pressure; O.E. *brýsan*: to crush]

bismar (bismer) (n) a 3 ft. long steelyard or wooden counter-balance, used at one time for weighing goods. [O.N. *bismari*: steelyard]

bister (n) dwelling; farm; a collection of farms, e.g. Fladdabister, Symbister. [O.N. *bólstadr*: farm; an area divided into farms]

bit (adv) only. *Dey wir bit de twa o wiz at göd*; (prep) but. *Bit whit aboot de idder een.* [E. *but*]

bittel (bitel, botel) (n) an abnormal tooth. [N. *bitel*: small, solitary tooth]

bitter-aks (n) dandelion (*Taraxacum officinale*) (also **eksis girse**). [O.N. *bitr*: keen; bitter + *ax*: ear; seed-cluster]

bitterness (n) cold, stormy weather. The word appears to be a variation on **bittersie** [see below]

bittersie (n) very cold. *Siccan a bittersie o wadder wir had*; stormy weather. [E. *bitter* + (s)ie]

bizzie (bisi, bissi) (n) litter on floor of a barn or for cattle in a stall; the stall itself. [O.N. *báss*: a stall; N.dial. *bos*: litter; straw]

bizzie-wappit (adj) felted hair that looks like a bizzie (see above). [N.dial. *bos*: litter; straw + Sc. *wap*: to wrap or wind]

blaa (v) to blow; (pp) **blaan**. [Sc. *blaw*]

blaand (n) sour whey. [O.N. *blanda*: milk (whey) mixed with water]

black-fantin (adj) extremely hungry (see **fantin**); note: **black** is commonly used to indicate extremes – *black-affrontit*, black benighted. [L.Sc. *fant*: weak, feeble]

black calm (adj) said of sea or loch lying mirror-calm. [Fær. *bilk*: very still and calm weather; *bilkastilli*: calm (sea); dead calm]

blae (n) a blemish. [O.N. *blá-r*: blue; livid; black]

blaegit (blaget, bleget) (adj) said of a sheep which has dark spots in its fleece. [Sw.dial. *blaga*: to spot with dirt; Icel. & Fær. *blettur*: a spot]

blashy (adj) scudding rain; wet and windy. [Sc. imitative of scudding rain]

blashy blinks (n) sudden flashes of lightning generally associated with the **hairst** (harvest). [Sc. (see above) + *blink*: a moment]

blate (blaet) (adj) shy; retiring; timid. [L.Sc. *blate*, *blait*, *bleet*: poss. from sound of a sheep – hence 'sheepish']

blatter (n) the flapping of a sail, clothes on a line or similar; (v) to flicker, as a naked flame or human breath. [O.N. *blaka*, *blakra*: to flap; flicker]

bledder (v) to prattle; talk nonsense; talk foolishly or at length. [O.N. *bladra*: to utter inarticulately; N. *bladra*: to babble; O.Sc. *blether*, *blather*: to stammer; Sc. *blether*: to talk nonsense]

bleddick (n) buttermilk. [O.Sc. *bladdoch*, *bladoch*, Gael. *blàthach*: buttermilk]

blen (blan) (n) a light breath of wind. [O.N. *blása*: to blow]

blett (n) a spot; blemish; a piece of ground of a distinct colour – a *möldi-blett* is a place from which peat-mould was gathered for bedding cattle. [Fær. *blettur*: a spot]

blibe (n) bubble; small blister. [L.Sc. *bleib*: to cause the face to swell with weeping; used of tea – a weak, watery portion]

blink (n) a moment in time; a wink; (v) to extinguish a light. [L.Sc. *blenk*, *blink*: a glance; a look; short, sudden gleam of light; a moment]

blinkie (n) a battery torch. [appears to be exclusively Shetlandic]

blinnd (n) a glimmer of light; in ref. to sleep – *to blinnd de een*. [O.N. *blindr*: blind; *blundr*: a wink of sleep]

blinnda (n) a mixture of inferior grains. [prob. from L.Sc. *blendit bear* (bere): a mixture of rough bere with barley]

blinnders (n) stove lids – presumably because they hide the light from the fire. [see above]

blinnd hoe (ho) (n) lesser spotted dogfish (*Scyliorhinus canicula*). [O.N. *hár*, N. *haa*, D. *haj*: a shark]

blinnd(in) moorie (n) a snowstorm so severe as to reduce visibility to zero. [O.N. *blindr*: dark; dense + **moorie**; N. *mjoll*, *mjell*: dry, newly fallen snow, cf. Fær. *murrukavi*: thick and fine frosty snow]

blissit (bleset, blessit) (adj) said of an animal having a white blaze down the forehead. [O.N. *blesóttr*: blazed]

blot (blott) (n) the first water in which clothes are washed; dirty soap suds. [O.N. *blautr*: wet; soaked]

blöd-freends (n) family; (blood) relations. [O.N. *blæda*: to bleed; L.Sc. *blood-friend*]

blöd-fastin (adj) having fasted all day. [see above]

blöd-spring (adj) with great speed; 'a rush of blood'.

blöv (v) originally to perish or die, now spoken in the sense of 'to faint'. [Du. *bliven*, *blijven*: to perish]

blue doo (n) rock dove (*Columba livia*). [Fær. *bladugva*]

blue-finsket (adj) affected with a bluish mould resulting from being kept in a damp place (see **finnet**). [Fær. *-finska*: to become musty]

blue hoe (ho) (n) spurdog (*Squalus acanthias*). [O.N. *hár*, N. *haa*, D. *haj*: a shark]

blue-litt (n) indigo dye (also **litt**). [O.N. *litr*: colour; complexion]

blue-melt (blumelt) (n) a bruise. [Fær. *blódmelta*]

blue-meltet (v pt, adj) bruised. [as above].

blue-niled (nildet) (adj) as **blue-finsket**. [Sw.dial. *knäll*: damage]

blugga (n) marsh marigold (*Caltha palustris*). [Fær. *blödka*: leaf of certain plants]

bluntie (n) disappointment. [cf. L.Sc. *bluntie*: a dull-witted fellow; a reproof]

blurtin (n) blocked nasal passages. [L.Sc. *blirt*, *blurt*: to cry; to weep; burst into tears; prob. imitative]

bluster (bluester) (n) coarse, mossy peat, originally *bluester*; inferior peaty soil of a blueish colour. [O.N. *blástr*: rising; swelling]

blyde (blide) (adj) glad. [O.N. *blidr*; L.Sc. & E. *blythe*]

blyde-maet (n) (lit. 'glad-food') first meal taken by a woman after childbirth.

blydeness (n) gladness; happiness.

blyde-spokken (adj) said of one who speaks well of others.

boady (n) physical body; a considerable quantity; a mass. *Yun's a boady o fish du's gotten de nycht*. [E. *body*; O.E. *bodig*]

boags (n) insects. [prob. *bugs*]

boannie (boany) (adj) good looking; attractive. [Sc. *bonny, bonnie*]

board (jumper-board) (n) an adjustable wooden frame on which to stretch or shape a finished knitted jumper or cardigan to correct size; also used to reconstitute an old garment which may have shrunk, or to prevent shrinkage; (see **jimp**; also **dress**).

bocht med (lit. 'bought made') *Did du mak yun shair deesel? Na, hit's bocht med*; (see **bowt**).

boddam (n) bottom; the sea-bed; (v) to ground a boat or touch the sea-bed. [O.N. *botn*; E. *bottom*]

body (n) a person (also **bein**). *Pör body*. [E. *body*]

boky (boakie) (n) a bogeyman; a supernatural being; also applied in fun of an oddly-dressed person; thick discharge from the nose – **taatie-boky**. [O.E. *bogy*: a goblin; spectre]

bombaze (v) to astonish; confound; bewilder; stupify. [O.Sc. *bumbase, bumbaize*: to confuse; cf. E. *bamboozle*]

bonfrost (n) a severe frost, when water freezes to the bottom. [O.N. *botn*: bottom]

bong (n) a loud knock or bang. [O.N. *bang*: hammering; knocking; clamour; noise (imitative)]

bonhoga (bonnhoga) (n) childhood home; spiritual home. [O.N. *barn-*: child & *-hagi*: a pasture]

bonxie (bunksi, bonksi) (n) great skua (*Megalestris catarrhactes*). [O.N. *bunki*: thick-set; heavily clad; corpulent; lumpy]

boo (n) bow of a boat; (v) to bow. *Boo dee heid gyaan in de door*. [L.Gr. *boog*; Du. *boeg*]

boo o wadder (n) continuation of a particular weather pattern. [orig. somewhat confused, cf. N. *budvedr*: 'long heavy rains, confining one to the booth' (*búd*)]

booce (v) work with vigour. [cf. N. & Sw.dial. *busa*, D. *buse*: to dash; rush]

boocin (adj) energetic and constantly on the move. [see above]

booel-cramp (n) colic. [O.F. *buel*; Sc. *buel* + cramp]

booel-rivin *bull-ryvn* (n) a large, hearty meal (lit. a tearing out of the bowels through overeating). [O.N. *rífa*: to tear]

boof (n) a dull thud. [imitative sound, E. *buff, buffet*]

boofel (v) to pound; pummel; beat repeatedly. [O.F. *buffe*: a blow, esp. on the cheek]

book (buk) (n) robustness; body. *Dir nae muckle book in him* – said of something worn-out or feeble. [O.N. *búkr*: abdomen; body; trunk]

bool (n) crescent-shaped handle of kettle or pail. [O.Sc. *boull*: bowed; bent; Sc. *boul*: a curved handle]

boolin (v) to jump through surface of water. *Da sillocks wis boolin*. [Icel. *bulla*: to bubble or boil; swirl like boiling water]

boolik (n) a pimple. [cf. Ger. *beule*: an inflamed swelling; a boil]

boo-stane (n) foundation stone of a building – one fixed in the earth. [cf. O.N. *bú*: abode + *steinn*: a stone]

booster (n) pillow. [L.Sc. *bouster*, E. *bolster* – properly the long cushion placed under a pillow]

bore (n) hole in a boat's gunwale for sheet, shroud or tack. [O.N. *bora*: hole; opening]

borrowin days (n) last three days in March. [according to O.Sc. folklore supposed to have been days borrowed by March from April, and to be especially stormy. The Spanish version of the borrowing days tells of a shepherd who promised March a lamb if he would bring soft winds to suit the flock. After his request was granted, the shepherd reneged on his promise and in revenge March borrowed three days from April in which to send fiercer winds than March ever delivered]

bosie (n) the bosom. [O.Sc. *bosie, bosey*]

boss (adj) hollow (also see **toom**). [O.Sc. *bos*: hollow; concave]

bost (n) a short spell of bad weather. [N. *bausta*: to rush violently]

bowe (n) 1) a buoy. [Sc. *bow*, cf. Du. *booi*]; 2) a boll, as of meal (6 imp. bushells – 140lb). [O.Sc. *boll*: measure of grain (amount varied between 2 and 7 bushells); O.N. *bolle, bolli*: a bowl]

bowt (bocht, boucht) (pt of) buy (also **bowten**).

böd (n) a fisherman's bothy or hut; a store used for fishing requirements. [O.N. *búd*: booth; tent]

böddie (bodi) (n) a basket made of straw or dockens, having a band for carrying over the shoulder, commonly used as a fishing creel; a smaller type of **kishie**. [cf. Icel. *byda*: wooden tub; Fær. *bydi*: milk pail]

böl (n) a shelter or wind-break for animals; a resting-place, extended in jest to a person's bed. *I doot he's no wun oot o his böl yit*. [O.N. *ból*: resting place; abode; farm]

bölliments (n) bits and pieces; odds and ends of possessions. [der. of N. *bala*: to heap up and *bøla*: to fill; stuff (esp.with worthless objects)]

bön (v) been. [E. *been* (sometime *bin*)]

bördly (adj) strong; robust. [E. *broadly*]

börep (n) 1) a boat's bow-rope; 2) buoy-rope for a fishing line; (lit. '*bow-rope*'); (also **burrop**).

böst (n) a small, oval, wooden carrying-box. [L.Sc. *boist, boyst, buist*, O.F. *boiste*: a small box used for containing ointment, spices, etc.]; (aux v) had to; must.

böt (n) boot. [L.Sc. *buit*]

braa (adj) fine; grand; splendid. [L.Sc. *braw*, variant of *brawf* (brave): fine; elegant; beautiful; excellent]

braaly (adv) fairly; very; rather. *Du's lookin braaly plaesed wi deesel*. Also used to mean reasonably well. *Foo is du de day? Braaly weel*. [orig. *braw* (see above)]

braand (n) burning or partly burned piece of peat. [O.N. *brandr*]

braander (n) cross-piece supporting a wooden frame, as spacer between legs of a chair. [O.N. *brandr*: stock; beam; post]

braand-iron (n) a gridiron. [Sc. *brander*: a gridiron]

brace (n) mantelpiece. [L.Sc. *brase, brace, bres(s)e*: the breast or arch of a chimney; mantelpiece]

brack (brak) (n) a break or fracture; the breaking of sea on a shore; (v) to break; (pt) **brook**; (pp) **brocken**. [Sc. *brack*]

B

brack da bröd (v) to form a pathway for the first time; metaphorically, to do something for the first time. [L.Sc. *brack*: break + O.N. *braut*: an open way]

brack on (v) to break up sod in digging.

brack oot (v) to bring fallow land under cultivation; begin ploughing. [O.N. *broti*: a piece of old meadow ploughed up]

brack up (v) to raise a subject in conversation. [E. *bring*]

brae (n) the brow of a hill; a road with a steep incline. [Sc. *brae*: a hill slope; O.N. *brá*: eyelid, cf. E. *brow*; O.E. *brü*]

bran (n) the calf of the leg. [L.Sc. & O.E. *brawn*: fleshy part of leg or arm]

bran(d) (n) drudgery in work. *Foo is du getting on boy? A'm joost brandin on.* [Icel. *brana*: to burst (boldly) out]

branks (n) 1) the mumps; 2) a halter, having a leather nose-piece studded with nails to prevent a calf from sucking from its mother. [1] orig. obs. but cf. O.F. *bernac*: a barnacle, from fact that disease causes swelling of glands; 2) O.E. *branks*: scald's bridle; cf. Du. *pranger*: a fetter]

brash (n) an ailment or sickness, frequently undefined – *Hit's just a brash*; (also see **spendin brash**). [Sc. *spean*: to wean + *brash*: an attack or illness]

brat (n) apron. [L.Sc. *brat*: a poor or ragged garment; an apron, cf. Gael. *brat*: a mantle]

breek-baand (n) waistband of trousers. [O.E. *brēc* + O.N. *band*]

breeks (breekses) (n) trousers. [E. *brēc*]

breenge (v) to rush. [cf. Frisian *brinzgje*: to brawl]

breer (breid) (n) the first shoots of a crop; (v) to sprout, as seed. [N. *brydda*: to sprout, of corn, grass]

breid (n) bread; baker's goods in general, including cakes (see **fancies**). [E. *bread*, but with additional meaning in Shetland]

brennastyooch (brima-skodd, brimasteuch, brima-stew) (n) fine spray rising from sea breaking on a shore; spindrift. [O.Sh. *bräim*: spray from the surf; O.N. *brim*: surf and L.Sc. *stew*: dust; vapour, cf. N. *støv*: dust]

bretsh (brest) (n) the breaking of waves on a shore. [O.N. *bresta*: to burst; crash; crack]

bridder (n) brother. [Sc.]

brieder (n) brothers. [Sc.]

brig (n) bridge. [O.N. *bryggja*: bridge]

brigdi (bregdi) (n) a basking shark (*Cetorhinus maximus*) (also **hobrigdi, sulbrigdi**). [cf. N. *bregda*: to alter; shift; move quickly; O.E. *bregdan* (note: the shark's habit of basking on the surface of the sea does not seem to equate with the meaning of *bregda*)]

briggistanes (brigstens) (n) footpath of flagstone stones laid in front of a house. [O.N. *bryggja* + *stein*]

brimasteuch (see **brennastyooch**)

brimtud (brimtod) (n) sound of breaking sea on the shore. [N. *brimtot*: sound of waves breaking against rocks]

brind *brinnd* (short *i*) (v) to copulate, in animals, esp. of cats; to be on heat. *De cat is brindin.* [O.N. *brundr*: rut; sexual desire]

brismak (n) young torsk (*Brosme brosme*) – North Atlantic, white-fleshed fish of the cod genus having a single dorsal fin; otherwise known as **tusk**. [O.N. *brosma*]

broag (n) bradawl. [L.Sc. *brog, brogue*: a bradawl; a boring instrument]

broch (borg) (n) 1) Pictish ring-fort; Iron Age circular stone tower, e.g. Clickimin Broch, Mousa Broch; 2) a luminous ring round the moon. [O.N. *borg*: fort] Distribution of brochs is mainly confined to northern Scotland, with Shetland having the greatest concentration (over 150 listed sites) and Mousa Broch being considered the best preserved in Britain. The prime purpose of these buildings has never been satisfactorily established.

brochen (n) a hot drink containing oatmeal, cream of tartar and sugar, used as a cure for chill or high temperature (also **pirr**). [Gael. *brochan*: porridge]

brods (n) board covers for books. [L.Sc. *brod, broid, brodd, etc*: board]

broddit (adj, pp) covered by a lid, as a pot. [L.Sc. (n) *pot-brod*: a wooden lid or covering for a pot]

brølek dreet (coarse slang) nonsense; humbug; bull; (see **brølek** fishermen's tabu word – addenda). [O.N. *baula*: a cow – from *baula* (v): to bellow + **dreet (drit)** O.N. *dreit, dritinn*: excrement; E. (coarse slang) *bullshit*]

brongie (brongiskarf) (n) immature cormorant (*Phalacrocorax carbo*) (also see **loren**). [O.N. *bringa*: breast + *skarfr*: cormorant]

broo (n) forehead; the brow of a hill or slope; (also see **brug**). [L.Sc. *broo*: brow]

broog (brug, brugg) (n) a small, flat-topped mound; the edge, as of the shoreline. [N. *bru*; Sc. *broo*; E. *brow*]

brook (n) a heap of seaweed on a beach; (v, pt) broke; (pr t) **brack**; (pt) **brook**; (pp) **brocken**; [O.N. *brúk*: a heap]

broon (adj) brown. [Sc.]

brooncaidies (n) bronchitis. [Sc. *broonchadis*]

brootsh (brotch, britj) (v) to crush; squash; to strike. [O.N. *brytja*: to cut up; Sw.dial. *britsa*: to strike; Sc. *broche*: a kind of chisel; *brocher*: to indent with a chisel]

brose (n) a dish made by pouring boiling water or milk on oatmeal and seasoning with butter and salt. [Sc. *brose*, cf. O.F. *brouez*: broth]

broucht (browt) (v) (pt of) bring.

browdened (broser) (adj) brazen; forward; presumptious. [Sc. *browden*: intent upon; eager; possibly originally from same word as *brosek*: bold; quick; clever; and, in the sense of a pretentious person, N. *brøsen*: well built; clever; stout]

browst (n) a brew of tea. [O.Sc. *brawst, broust*: brew]

brö (n) the water in which any kind of food has been boiled; gravy – *mutton brö*; *kaill brö*. [Sc. *bree*: brew]

bröd (n) a path or breach (see **brack da bröd**). [O.N. *braut*: an open way]

bröl (n) bellow; (v) to bellow, as cattle. [cf. N. *braula*: to bawl; D. *brøle*]

brönnie (brøni) (n) a round, thick oatmeal scone; a barley or oatcake baked on a grid-iron. [cf. Sw.dial. *bryn*: to roast; N. *bryne*: a piece or slice of bread]

bröski (n) gristle; cartilage, as in the nose. [O.N. *brjósk*: gristle]

bruck (n) rubbish. Anti-litter slogan – '*dunna chuck bruck*' (don't litter); (v) to crush (also **bruckle**). [O.N. *brúk*: a mass; a multitude; heap]

brucks remains of; dregs. *De brucks a Yöl* – drop left in the bottle after Christmas celebrations; *da brucks a da helly* – what is left of the weekend. [see above]

bruckly (adj) easily broken; friable. [cf. Du. *brokkelig*: crumbly]

brunga wheedie (brongikwidin, brungi-) (n) cormorant (*Phalacrocorax carbo*). [O.N. *bringa*: breast + *hvit*(e): white]

brunklet (n) butterfish (*Pholis gunnellus*). [prob. from *brunket* an obsolete Sh. word meaning brownish; having a brown tint and corresponding to the colour of the fish; N. *brunka*, Fær. *brúnka*: to dye slightly brown; N. *brunke*: the act of dying brown; brown spot]

brunt (v pt, pp) burned. [E. *burnt*]

brunt rift (n) heartburn (also **hertscad**). [E. *burnt* + Sc. *rift*: to belch]

brust (n) turn of the tide; (v) to turn (of tide). [cf. N *brusta*: to force one's way or to push forward]

bucht (bugt) (n) a coil of fishing rope of variable length (40-50 fathoms). [O.N. *bugt*: a bend; curvature; in the sense of inside bend of the elbow-joint and therefore perhaps representative of the method by which rope is commonly coiled]

buckle (v) to entangle, as a tethered animal; to wrap up ineptly. [Sc. *buckle*: a tussle; (obs. to join in marriage)]

bucky (buckie) (n) common whelk (*Buccinum undatum*); any mollusc; (also see **wylk**). [O.Sc. *buckie*, *bukky*: shell of a whelk or other mollusc; orig. obs. cf. L. *buccinum*]

buggie (bogi) (n) bag made from skin of sheep after the wool has been removed. [cf. Sw.dial. *bög*: leather sack]

buggiflay (bogi-flay) (v) to skin a sheep, maintaining the skin in one piece in order to make a **buggie**. [cf. N. *bægfletta*]

buggiflooer (bogiflooer) (n) sea campion (*Silene vulgaris*, *subsp. maritima*). [originally from the bladder shape]

buks (v) to walk or trudge heavily, as going through snow. [O.N. *byxa*: to jump; to walk smartly or run with jumping, swinging movements]

bulder (n) loud noise; gurgling of water; (v) to blunder clumsily. [N. & D. *bulder*: rumble]

bulderit (adj) clumsy; headstrong. [same root meaning as above]

bullits (bolleti) (n) small, round stones; beach pebbles (esp. Westside); in placename Bullits Ayre (Westside). [O.N. *bolli*: globular; round; Sc. *bullet*: a round stone (dim. of Fr. *boule*: a ball]

bult (n) a butt, as from a ram; (v) to butt, as a ram. [cf. S. *bulta*: to knock; beat]

bulwaaver (n) to become lost; go astray; wander aimlessly. [O.Sc. *bulwaver*, *bellwaver*, poss. from 'bell-wether': the sheep others follow; the one which roams at will]

bulwaand (n) mugwort (*Artemesia vulgaris*). [O.Sc. *bulwand*, *bulwint*, from *bull* (big) and *wand*]

bummel (n) floundering, esp. in water; (v) to make heavy weather of a subject, as in speaking; to flounder. [cf. N. *bumla*: to splash; dabble]

bummer (n) a bulky thing or person. [cf. N. *bumba*: a woman with a bloated figure]

bungle (bungel) (n) a big clod of earth. [cf. N. *bungl*, Fær. *bongla*: bump]

burd (bord) (n) a nestling; a young bird. [O.N. *burðr*: bearing; the act of giving birth; fetus; offspring; descent; L.Sc. *burd*: offspring]

burgie (n) glaucous gull (*Larus hyperboreus*) in juvenile plumage. [cf. Du. *grote burgemeester*]

burn (n) a small stream. [Sc. *burn*, O.E. *burna*: brook]

burra (bora) (n) heath rush (*Juncus squarrosus*). [cf. O.N. *borða*: a long, narrow leaf]

burra toog (-tueg) (n) a tuft of heath rush. [see above + O.N. *túfa*: a mound]

burrop (n) (see **börep**)

bursin (v pp) of burst; (pt) **burstit**; (adj) breathless from exhaustion. [Sc. *bursen*, *bursten* (for breath)]

bursten (burstin) (n) meal made from bere (barley) dried in a kettle over fire or rolled between hot stones; a dish of that name made by mixing the toasted meal with sour milk or cream. [orig. uncertain, probably from ears of grain bursting when roasted]

busk (n) the beard of a fishing fly; (v) to dress up or embellish; to put the busk on a fishing hook. [cf. N. *busk*: top; tassel; copse; O.N. *búask*: prepare oneself]

buss (n) the bedding of a nest. [N. *bus*, *bos*: straw for bedding]

but-end (n) outer family room, or kitchen end of croft house; as opposed to **ben-end** the inner or more formal room. [M.E. *boute*, *bute*: outside; outer part or end of a house]

by *bi* (prep) beside; close to; near; (adv) in usages: *up by*, *doon by*, *owre by*; past and done with. *Hit's aa by wi noo.*

byelsit (bjelset) *be-el-sit* (adj) having a white ring round the neck, as a sheep. [Fær. *hölsutur*: with a stripe of another colour round the neck]

byoags (bjog) (n) collar made of three pieces of wood set in triangular fashion and placed round the neck of a sheep to prevent it breaking through fences (also see **hems**). [O.N. *baugr*: ring]

byock (bjock) (v) to retch, as in vomiting. [prob. imitative. O.Sc. *bok*, *bock*: belch]

byre (n) a cow-shed, where cattle were housed in inclement weather, frequently for weeks on end (croft houses and byres were usually interconnecting). [Sc. *byre*: a cowhouse]

byurg (bjørg) (n) a rocky hill. [cf. Fær. *björg*; O.N. *bjarg*]

C

C

Note: The Norn alphabet did not include the letter 'c' (to this day Norwegian language has very few 'c' words and most are to accommodate English words like 'computer' and 'cyberspace'). Assuming the following 'c' words which appear in blue are in fact Norn, they would all originally have been spelt with a 'k', however most contemporary wordlists favour spelling them with a 'c' and so we have maintained this practice. Lovers of the old language will be pleased to note there are still more than 90 'k' Norn words in this dictionary along with 43 more in the Fishermen's Tabu List at the back.

caa (n) a drive of cattle or sheep; a whale-chase; (v) 1) to muster sheep or cattle. *Wir bön caain de sheep aa day for de rooin*; 2) to abuse; to call names. *He caad him for de föl he wis*; 3) to drive in a nail. *Caa yun twae pieces o wid ta haad doon de lid*; 4) to knock into. *Dunna caa de heid apo de lintel*; 5) to keep in motion, e.g. churning butter. *Come an caa de handle.* [E. *call*: urge on]

caa canny (v) go cautiously; proceed warily; don't overdo it. [L.Sc. *ca canny*]

caain-time (n) the time of year for mustering sheep from the **scattald**.

caain whaal (n) long-finned pilot whale (*Globicephala melas*), (lit. 'driving whale'). [see **caa**]

caa-tö (n) a disturbance. [orig. unknown]

caald (**kald**, **cauld**, **cowld**) (n) common cold; (adj) cold. [Sc. *caald*]

caald-rife (**kald-rif**) (adj) very cold; said of a luke-warm reception. [Sc. *caald* + O.N. *rífr*: abundant – thus the opposite to normal Shetland hospitality]

caav (**kav**) (v) to eat greedily; also the driving of snow (see **caavie**). [O.N. *ákafi*: hastiness; eagerness]

caavie (**kavi, kava**) (n) a blizzard (see **moorie-caavie**). [cf. Fær. *kavi*: snow; O.N. *kaf*: depths (of the ocean); Icel. *kafi*: dense smoke; heavy dew or rain]

cabbi-labbi (**kabbi-**) (n) an outcry; uproar; a racket caused by several people speaking at the same time; a rowdy gathering. [E. *gabble*, Du. *kibbelen*: to wrangle]

caddel (**kadel**) (n) a coloured thread tied round the neck or through the ear of a sheep for the purpose of identification; (v) to attach a thread as described. [O.N. *kadall*: a rope]

caddie-lamb (**kadi-**) (n) pet lamb. [O.N. *kid*: a kid]

caerd (n) card; fine-toothed implement for carding wool; (v) the act of carding wool. [Fr. *carde* from L. *cardus*: thistle – originally teasel-heads were used for carding]

caerdin (n) a group of women gathered for the purpose of carding wool. [see above]

caff (**kalf**) (n) chaff; the innermost soft part of rushes. [cf. Sw. *kalf*, *calf*]

calafine (n) a pencil. [orig. obs. cf. Sc. and N. Eng.dial. *keely-*, *keeli-*, *kylevine*; Galloway and Cumberland have *callevine*, *calavine*, *guillivine* = black-lead, graphite pencil; *keel* = red-ochre, once used for marking sheep, etc.; *vine* = cedar-wood; black-lead was called *killow* in Cumberland and therefore *keel-i-vine* may be a corruption of *fine killow*]

caloo (**kallu**) (n) long tailed duck (*Clangula hyemalis*). [probably an onomatopœic word associated with the bird's call – *ka-ka-kalu*]

cam o da kind of a kind; having certain inherited qualities.

camshious (adj) contrary; perverse. [O.Sc. *camschoch*: crooked; deformed; perverse; cf. Gael. *cam*: crooked and O.E. *sceolh*: wry; oblique]

Candlemas (n) 2nd February. One of the old Scottish 'quarter-days' on which rents and stipends were paid – Hallomas (1st Nov); Candlemas (2nd Feb); Beltane (1st May) and Lammas (1st Aug). [O.E. *candelmæsse*: a Christian festival on which candles are blessed and carried in celebration commemorating the presentation of Christ in the temple and the purification of the Virgin Mary]

cangle (**kings or kingsa**) (v) to quarrel; dispute. [N. *kjangl*: quarrel]

canna (v) cannot; do not. *Whaar's dee ram geen? I canna keen.* [Sc. *canna*, contraction of *cannot*; the second meaning is exclusively Sh.]

canna can (adj) unable. *Get yun howe doon aff a de twartbaaks. I canna can ta, A'm ower peerie.* [Sh. variant on Sc. *canna*]

canny (**kani**) (n) stern compartment in a Shetland rowing-boat, esp. the skipper's seat in a sixern where he sat with the helm over his shoulder. [cf. Icel. *kani*: something projecting on an object, the beak of a boat]

canny (adj) shrewd; knowing. [Sc. *canny*: from can; able]

cant (**kant**) (n) 1) humour; spirits; 2) an affected style of speech – such as the way in which Shetlanders pronounce standard Eng. words, e.g. *face* becomes *fiss*; (v) to veer away; turn. *I took a cant aroond de shops whin I wis in Lerook.* [E. obs and dial. also N., D., Sw. *kant*: edge; angle – hence good or bad cant, as of a boat]

canty (adj) lighthearted; cheerful. [(see above) Sc. *canty*: cheerful; lively; presumably at a good angle; L.Ger. *kantig*]

cappie (**kappi**) (n) sinker on a fishing line; a small bowl, esp. wooden. [N. *kapall*, *koppul*: a round stone]

carvy-seeds (n) caraway seeds. [Arabic, *karwiyā*: seeds of carum carvi plant]

case-alaek (adj) all the same (lit. 'case-alike').

cassen (**kasen, kassen**) (adj) tainted; sour; beginning to decay; stale, esp. of fish. [N. *kasen*: sourish; beginning to decay]

cast (köst) (n) 1) skilful way of working; technical ability. *Hit's no taen her lang ta fint de cast o yun job*; 2) mannerisms. *He's blissed wi de cast o his faider* (cast in the mould of); 3) a sheep or cow which has been culled; one which has fallen and become 'cast', unable to get up; (v) to dig peats; (pt) **cöst**; (pp) **cassen**. Phrases: **ta cast** to cull from a flock; **ta cast aff** reduce stitches or finish off knitting; take off clothes; **ta cast by** to discard; **ta cast on** lay up stitches to begin knitting or add more stitches to a pattern; **ta cast oot** to quarrel, to reject; **ta cast up** to taunt by raking up the past. *Dey'll laekly cast yun up til her a time or two*; **cassen awa** lost at sea. [O.N. *kasta*: to cast; to fling in order to shift from one place to another]

castin (köstin) (n) a season's supply of peat; an amount of peats cut from a bank.

cat-aet (n) state of excitement. [origin uncertain, cf. *catticloo* (see below)]

catmoagit (kattmoget) (adj) said of a sheep having light-coloured body with dark-coloured belly. [O.N. *mogóttr*, Icel. *mögóttur*: having the belly of another colour; the prefix 'cat' – O.N. *kattr* – appears to be likening the 'moagit' sheep to a cat of similar appearance]

catticloo (kattaklur) (n) a rowdy mob. [N. *kattarklor*: cats scratching]

caution (n) a character; a person with an amusing, droll or astonishing personality. [colloq. Sc. L. *cavēre*: to beware]

chug (shug, sogg) (n) thick clumps of grass, esp. wilting grass (also see **foggage**). [cf. Fær. *sugga*: a disorderly heap; L.Sc. *sow*: an untidy heap; a haystack]

claa (n) physical setback resulting from illness. *Da feerie is gien him a nesty claa*; (v) to claw.

claag (klag) (n) noisy speech; (v) to cackle. [O.N. *klaka*: to voice; cry; cackle; twitter; cluck (esp. birds); also appl. to people – to jabber]

claes (n) clothes. [Sc. *claes*]

claed (cled, kled) *cledd* (adj) clothed; dressed. [O.N. *klæda*: to dress oneself; put on clothes; L.Sc. *cled*; E. *clad*]

clag (klag) (n) a sticky mass or clod of dirt; (v) to stick together. [D. *klag*: mud]

clair (klar) (adj) in a state of preparedness; ready. [N. *klar*: ready – the meaning coming from nautical usage developed from the meaning of 'clean']

clamp (klamp) (n) a patch; (v) to patch. [N. *klamp*, D. *klampe*: block; wooden patch esp. on a boat]

clap (v) pat; stroke gently; flop down. *He clappit him doon idda shair*. [O.N. *klappa*: to pat; stroke gently; also L.Sc]

clash (n) idle talk; chatter; gossip. [O.E. *clashe*: imitative sound]

clash (klask) (v) to strike; to give a dull blow. *I'll gie dee a clash at de side o de head*. [cf. D. *klask*: a smack]

clashmelt (kleks) (n) in a dirty state. [Sc. *clash*, *clatch*]

clashpie *clash*-pee (n) a person who tells tales or divulges secrets (also **clipe**). [cf. M.E. *clepian*: to call]

clatch (klass) (n) a sticky or glutinous deposit; a large, clumsy person; (v) to besmear. [N. *klessa*: soft mass; Icel. *klessa*: a splash of mud; N. *klassa*: to stick; to soil with something sticky]

clatter-benns (n) originally bones rattled together as castenets, now used proverbially to describe a gossip or chatterbox – *a voice lik de clatter-benns o a duek's erse*. [Sc. *clatter-banes*]

clave (kliv) (n) a steep slope. In placenames De Klivens; De Clave o Urafirth. [Fær. *kliv*: a steep place; a brink]

cleek (n) a hook. [L.Sc. *cleke*, *cleik*, *cleek*: a metal hook]; (v) to fasten or hang from a hook; to get a grip of. [M.E. *cleke*: act of clutching]

clegsie klek(si) (n) horse-fly (*Tabanidae*). [O.N. *klegge* – root *kli-*: to stick]

clert (v) to paste or smear (also **clester**, **clatch**). [deriv. *clag* (see above)]

clester (v) to paste or smear. [see above]

clever (adj) quick. *Du's owre clever wi dee tongue*. [Sc.]

clew (n) a ball of wool. [cf. L.Sc. *clew*, obscurely related to claw]

clewball (clewbing) (n) a tangled mass. *De kittlin gotten yun worsit in a clewball*. [see above]

click (v) to snatch; seize or filch. [L.Sc. *cleke*, *cleik*: to catch or snatch]

clime (klem) (v) to smear; to spread, as with butter; (also **kline**). [O.N. *klína*: to smear]

clink (v) to rivet; to clinch. [form of E. *clinch*]

clinkin (adj) superb; splendid. [Sc. & E. (slang) *clinking*: excellent]

clipe (clype) (n) a telltale (also **clashpie**). [M.E. *clepian*: to call]

cliv (kliv) (n) a hoof. [O.N. *klauf*: a cleft hoof]

clivmett (n) a cow's or cloven animal's footprint. [as above + Sh. *met*: a mark; footprint, cf. Icel. *mat*: measure; mark]

clivgeng (klivgeng) (n) sound of hooves; metaphorically, a procession. *Dey wir a clivgeng o fok gaan alang de street dastreen*. [*cliv* (see above) + Sc. *geng*, *gang*: to go]

clock (n) a beetle (see also **hointiclock**, **hundiclock**, **witchie klokk**). [O.S. *clok*: a beetle; S.dial. *klocka*: a beetle]; (v) to brood, as a broody hen. [imitative sound]

clockin *klawkin* (adj) broody. [O.Sc. *clok*, *clock*: to cluck; hatch]

clocks-midder (n) hen with chickens. [*broody* (see above) + Sc. *mither*: mother]

clod (klod) (n) small lump of hard peat. [cf. N. *klot*: lump; M.E. *clod*, *clodde*: a lump of earth]

cloo-bing (n) a bundle, esp. of clothes. [Sc. a combination of *cloot*: cloth and *bing*: bundle]

clooky (adj) cunning; tricky; artful. [O.N. *klókr*: wily, merged with L.Sc. *cleuch* in same meaning]

cloor (klur) (v) to claw or scratch. [O.N. *klóra*: to scratch]

cloot (n) cloth; dish-cloth; sail of a boat (fisherman's language); (also see **swab**). [cf. O.N. *klútr*: a clout; Sc. *cloot*: a cloth; **clootie-pudding** a suet pudding containing dried fruit, steamed in a cloth]; (v) to clout; cuff. [L.Sc. *clout*: heavy blow]

clooter (n) the sound of noisy footsteps. [imitative of clatter, noisy]

closs 1) (n) a narrow lane or alley between houses (esp. Lerwick), e.g. Greig's Closs, Jamieson's Closs; (adv) near. *Cuddle du closs t me*. [L.Sc. *clos*, *close*, *closse*: an enclosed space; a narrow space between buildings and permitting access to them]

closs 2) (adj) sultry; airless. [E. *close*, in same meaning]

clowe (n) a clove. *Dunna say clowe* (Don't say a word). (DOST – J. Gray *Lowrie on Eddication Needs* [Shetland Times 1926-28] '*Naebody can say clowe*' (No one can say a word or interfere)). [L.Sc. *clow*, M.E. *clowe*: clove – possibly originally from likeness to a nail]

clump (klump) 1) (n) any large object. *A clump a aert*; a big clumsy person. *A great clump o a boy*; 2) (v) to walk noisily. [1] N. *klump*: a lump; 2) N. *klumper*: a kind of wooden shoe]

clumpse (klums) (v) to render speechless. [N. *klumsa*]

clunk (klunk) (v) to swallow a drink rapidly; to gulp. [N. & Sw. *klunka*: to drink greedily with a gurgling sound]

clushit (klosset) (adj) clumsy. [deriv. of N. & Sw.dial. *kloss*: a) a lump; b) a corpulent, clumsy person]

coag (kog) (v) to peer, to look out cautiously. [O.N. *kaga*]

coarn (n) oats; a small quantity; a bit. [Sc. *coarn*: a grain; a morsel; as E. *corn*]

cob on (n) mood, esp. a bad mood. *Shö's got a rycht cob on da day*. [orig. obs. cf. L.Sc. *cob*: to beat; strike; therefore *in a mood to lash out*]

cockie (v) to defecate. [slang obs.]

cockies (n) excrement. [as above]

cog (kog) (n) a small wooden vessel. [O.Sc. *cog*, *coggie*: a wooden bowl; O.N. *kaggi*: a keg or cask]

cole (n) a conical pile of hay; a haycock; (v) to build haycocks. [orig. uncertain, cf. Fr. *cuellir*: gather; O.N. *kollr*: the top; covering of a haystack]

coll (koll) (n) a burning piece of fuel esp. peat. [N. *koll*; E. *coal*]

collcoomed (adj) burned to ashes (lit. 'coal-coomed'); overcome with hot stuffy atmosphere; (see **coom**).

coll-slock (koll-slock) (n) a fire gone out. *We cam hame till a coll slock*; (v) to extinguish, as a fire. [N. *koll*: coal + O.N. *slokva*: to extinguish]

colly (see **kolli**)

collyshang (kallishang) (n) a rowdy dispute. [N. *kalle*: call]

come (v) in normal English usage but with additional idiomatic meanings as follows: **ta come at** 1) to befall or happen. *Is du feard o what might come at dee?*; 2) to come to one's senses. *Lat him be an he'll shune come at*; 3) to improve. *Laeve him be, he'll come at by and by*; 4) to touch. *Dunna come at da dug wi yun stick*; 5) to come on; to develop; to become of. *What's tinks du will come o aa dis?* **ta come aboot** to take a new tack in sailing; **ta come awa** to grow, as seed; **come du** invitation to enter a house; come along. *Come du in*; *come awa in*; *come dee wis in trowe*; **come dee wis** hurry up; **come till** to revive; recover. *Laeve him be, he'll shune come till*.

condamned (v) a combination of condemned and damned. *Dat is wann condamned thing*. [O.Sc. *condamne*: condemn]

condingly con-*dingly* (adv) entirely; fittingly; deservedly (esp. N.Yell). [O.Sc. form of E. *condingly* in similar meanings]

condwined (adj) hateful (see **dwine**). [cf. O.Sc. *dwyne*: to decline; wither]

coo (n) cow; (pl) **kye** [Sc.]

coom (koom) (n) 1) dust or small particles; 2) sloping ceiling esp. in an attic. [1] O.Sc. *cowm*: soot; grime; O.N. *kám*: grime; a film of dust; 2) Sc. *coom (ceiling)*: inside ceiling sloping from the wall]

coorse (adj) of weather – inclement; stormy. *He's bön a coorse day*. [Sc.]

coose (køs) (n) a heap. *Coose de lemm* (wash (pile up) the dishes); (see **laem**). [O.N. *kos*: a heap]

cootch (n v) to coat with preservative, as fishing nets. [orig. uncertain cf. E. *coat* as coat of paint; cover]

corbie (n) raven (*Corvus corax*); harsh, guttural manner of speaking, as a raven; (v) to speak with exaggerated rolling of the letter 'r'. *Yun aald wife corbies dat wye du'd tink shö wis crexin*. [O.F. *corb* or *corbin*; L.Sc. *corby*, *corbie*]

corp (n) a corpse; the raven's call (see above). [L.Sc. *corp*, false singular formed from M.E. *corps*]

cose (kos) (v) to trade; exchange or barter. [orig. uncertain cf. O.N. *kostr*: sustenance or duty payable in kind; tax in kind]

cosh (adj) friendly. [Sc. *cosh*: cosy; close]

cotts (n) skirts. [from E. *coats*]

coup (v) to tilt; upset; heel over. [O.Sc. *coup*, *cowp*: to turn up; to upset]

couple (n) a pair of rafters (or one of these) supporting roof of a house. [O.Sc. *cupple*, *coupill*]

cöl (kul) (v) to cool. [O.N. *kæla*: to cool; *kul*: a cool breeze]

cöllie (v) to appease; mollie-coddle; make a fuss of. [O.Sc. *culze*, *cuille*: to caress; fondle, cf. Fr. *cueillir*: to gather]

cöllik (kollek) (n) a clam; sound of a gull (onomatopæic). [O.N. *kollr*: top; head; *kúla*: knob]

cösh (kuss, kusj) (interj) shoo! a word used to drive away cattle or hens. [cf. N. and D. *kyss*! as a shout to scare away cats]

cöst (kast) (v pt) see **cast**.

cöt (n) the ankle. [L.Sc. *cute*, *cuit*]; also localised pronunciation of **cud** – *cow showein da cöt*; to dwell on unpleasant incidents or experiences – *ta showe bitter cöt*.

cöttikin (n) ankle-sock. [L.Sc. *cuitikin*: cloth gaiters]

craa (n) hooded crow (*Corvus corone cornix*). [L.Sc. *craw*, *crau* – includes other genus of crows not found in Shetland; note: the Faroese call the rook *Hjalta kraka* (Shetland crow) because it first arrived in The Faroes from Shetland]

craaheid (n) chimney head (where crows like to roost). [Sc.]

craa peel (n) small mussel (*Mytilus edulis*). [Icel. *krakuskel*: mussel; lit. 'crow shell' owing to the fact crows eat the flesh, carrying the shells into the air and dropping them on rocks]

craa's tread (n) small hen's egg about the size of starling's, frequently the last of a clutch, indicating the end of the laying season for the hen which produced it. [orig. of – *tread*, obs.]

craatae (n) meadow buttercup (crowsfoot) (*Ranunculus acris*). [so named for the seed-corm's appearance to a crow's foot]

crabbit (adj) bad tempered. [L.Sc. *crab*, *craib*: to annoy; irritate; orig. *crab* – crustacean assoc. with *crab-apple* – sour wild apple]

crachtless (krak-) (adj) powerless. [O.N. *krakki*: a thin and spare limbed person; N. *krakk*: a poor wretch]

crack 1) (n) a yarn; light-hearted conversation, hence (v) to crack a joke; 2) (n) hearty laughter; (v) to laugh heartily. [L.Sc. *crak(e)*, *crack* (16th cent.): a talk or gossip]

craetir (n) creature; a person, commonly used in commiseration. *A pör aamos craetir*; (see **aamos**). [Sc. *crater*, *craiter*]

craig (krag) (n) neck; throat; **craig-stoopit** fell headfirst. [O.N. *kragi*: the collar of a coat (this meaning now obs.); L.Sc. *crag*, *craug*: the neck]

craigs (n) rocks along the foreshore; a rocky outcrop; rock-fishing. [Sc. *craigs*]

craigsaet (craigstane) (n) a suitable rock for fishing from. [Sc. *craig-*]

cram (kramm) (v) to claw or scratch, as a cat. [N. *krama* and *kramsa*: to grab; snatch; *kramsa*: also to scratch. *Da cat kramms or klurs (is krammin or klurin) to da wast* – considered to indicate the wind is going to be westerly (Jakobsen)]

crammicks (krammeks) (n) cat's claws. [O.N. *hrammr*: bear's paw (but see above)]

cramper (n) a character; a show-off. [L.Sc. *cramper*: to strut or swagger]

crang (n) a carcase; the dead body of an animal. [extension of O.E. *crang*: carcase of a whale]

crappin (krappin, crawpeen) (n) a dish comprising fish-livers mixed together with meal and/or flour, seasoned with salt and pepper, stuffed in the head of a large fish and cooked in boiling water; **crappin muggies** the same dish cooked in the stomach of a fish. [the word is a merging of L.Sc. *crappit head*: head of haddock, stuffed with oatmeal, suet, etc., from *crap*: to fill; stuff]

creeks (kreks) (n) muscle pain brought on by excessive walking (also **hansper**, **spaigie**). [N. *kreks*, *kreksa*: a crooked object]

creeksit (krekset) (adj) infirm; in poor physical condition. [originally applied to animals, esp. foals or pigs, having feeble, crooked and stiff legs; cf. N. *kreksa*: a crooked object (a branch)]

creepie (n) a small three-legged stool. [L.Sc. *crepie*, *creepie*: a low stool; M.E. *crepe* (n): to creep or crawl; assoc. with penitents stool in churches]

creesh (n) grease. [imitative sound]

creeshy (adj) greasy.

crex (see **kreks**)

crim (v) to cough or clear the throat as a sign of disapproval (ahem!). [imitative; poss. development of L.Sc. *crim*: to purse the mouth and prob. same root as E. *crimp*: to wrinkle]

crimp (krimp) (adj) tight-fitting; skimpy. [N. *krympa*: to squeeze; D. *krympe*: to shrink]

cring (kring, cringle) (n) two lambs tied together with a cringle, a halter – *a cring o lambs*; (v) to tie two lambs together with a cringle. [O.N. *kringja* and *hringja*: to encircle; surround]

cro (kro) (n) (not to be confused with **crö**) a nook or boxed off space for storage – *a paet cro*; *a tattie cro*. [L.Sc., O.N. *krá*: a nook; a corner]

croft (n) a small-holding, originally rented from an estate but now increasingly freehold. [Sc. *croft*: a small farm]

crofter (n) someone who lives on or operates a croft. [see above]

crooels (n) running sores, usually tubercular. [F. *écrouelles*: scrofula (tuberculosis of lymph glands)]

croog (see **crug**)

crook (kruk) (n) a hook (usually attached to a chain or **crook baak**) from which pots were hung over an open fire; a sheep's ear-mark; a corner or nook. [O.N. *krókr*: a bending, winding; a hook; a nook or corner]

crook baak (n) a beam horizontally fixed above open fire from which links and crooks are hung.

croon (n) a crown; top of the head. [O.N. *krúna*: a crown; wreath; the crown of the head; E. *crown*]

croon ida lift (n) the zenith (lit. 'crown of the sky'); (see **lift** – sky).

crooner (n) gurnard (*Eutrigla gunardus*) species of fish which makes a grunting noise when taken from the water. [L.Sc. *crointer*, *croynter*, E. *grunter*: gurnard]

croose (adj) cheerful; in exp. *dunna du craa sae croose* – said to someone being too boastful and therefore courting disaster. [O.Sc. *crouse*: lively; cheery; merry]

croppened (kroppend) (adj) misshapen; shrunk or twisted. [O.N. *kroppinn*: bowed together; crooked]

crö (kru, krø) (n) sheep-fold, usually built of stone. [Icel. *kró (lambakró)*: a fold (sheepfold); O.Sc. *crue*]

cröl (krøl) (n) a hump on the back. [N. *kryl*: a hump]

crub (krubb) (n) a small circular drystone enclosure, usually without an opening, for growing cabbage plants (also referred to as a **crö** or **planticrö**). [N., Sw., Fær., *krubba*: a crib; a box for holding fodder]

crubbit (krubbit) (adj) restricted in space. [N. *krubben*, *krubbutt*: narrow; confined; pinched for room]

crug (krug) (v) to crouch; to hunch down in taking shelter; to huddle. *De lambs wis cruggin in ahint de yowes*; (also **skrug**, **skyug**). [O.N. (Icel) *kroka*: to bend oneself; to huddle oneself up (against bad weather)]

crugset (krugset) (v) to drive an animal into a confined space in order to catch it. *De dugs hae de sheep weel crugset*. [N. *króksetja*: to put into a corner]

crump (krump) (v) to crunch, as ice or snow when impacted by tramping on. [cf. N. *krumpa*: to crush (between the teeth)]

cruttle (krutl) (n) a low gurgling sound; (v) to gurgle. [N. *krusla*, *krutla*: to simmer]

cry (n) hysterics. *Shö wiz cryin at da hert whin da news cam*; (v) 1) to call. *Cry de bairns tae dir denner*; 2) to read the banns of marriage in church; 3) about to give birth to a child. *Shö's aboot ta cry*. [O.Sc. *cry* (all of above meanings); F. *cri* (*cri de cœur*: a cry from the heart)]

cry-rek (n) within calling distance (cry-reach). [N. *rekkja*: to stretch out]

13

cuddie (kuddi) (n) a small basket; **saat-cuddie** small basket for holding salt, often hung on a nail or hook near the fire. [L.Sc. *coodie, cudie*: a small tub; N. *kudde*: a nest]

cuddy (n) used in the expression 'up in his cuddy' to mean elated. [orig. obs., cf. E. *cuddy*: place in a boat where the steersman stands; in larger vessels, the officers' cabin under the poop deck]

cuffey (kufi) (n) quahog – edible clam (*Arctica islandica*). [O.N. *kúfóttr*: (adj) convex; Icel. *kúfr*, N. *kuv*: rounded top]

cuggle (kugl) (n) wobble; unbalance. [N. *koklutt*: lumpy; uneven; L.Sc. *cogglie*: moving from side to side; unsteady and apt to be upset]

cuggly (adj) in a state of unbalance.

cuids (køds) (n) grilled coalfish to which extra livers have been added. [O.N. *kød*: a small fry; N. *kjøda*: a young trout]

cummel (kuml) (v) to overturn. [O.N. *hvelfa*, N. *kolva, kolve*: to turn a hollow object bottom up]

cürious (kürious) (adj) not as E. 'curious', but anxious, willing.

curl(ie)-dodie (n) early-purple orchid (*Orchis mascula*); any genus of orchid. [*curl-doddy* (round headed) in Sc.; *Ribwort plantain* but applied to various round-headed plants]

curn (n) currant. [Sc.]

curn-loff (n) fruit loaf (also see **hufsi**). [Sc.]

curny pudding (n) fruit pudding – one in which *curny duff* is stuffed into an intestine for cooking. [Sc.]

currie (kori) (adj) lovable. [poss. O.Sh. *kokr, kukr*: to talk gently; to fondle; caress; E. *cocker*: to pamper; to fondle; to indulge; O.N. *kærr*: dear, in sense of *my korri* – my dear]

curry-raag (n) dealings. *We dunna hae curry-raag wi dem.* [orig. obs.]

cussie (kussi) (n) pet name for a calf or a cow. [O.N. *kussa*: a heifer; cow; a term of endearment]

cut (n) a substantial part; a 300yd length of yarn, also known as a **hank**. [Sc.]

cutty (n) a small, short-stemmed tobacco pipe, originally made of clay. [O.Sc. *cutty*: a short clay pipe]

cuttanoy (n) a disturbance; an annoyance. *He's joost a cuttanoy.* [orig. obs.]

D

d (short *d*) (def. article) the – *d sooth boat*. (more generally written as **da** or **de**, the short **d** is the most common spoken sound and occasionally favoured in writing, esp. poetry)

da (short *d*) (def. article) the – *da sooth boat* (also see **de**).

da (de) moarn (n) tomorrow.

daa (da) (n) grandfather; occas. father (see also **auld daa**).

daachen (v) of wind – to lull or abate. [N. *daka*: to go slowly]

daal (dal) (n) a dale; a valley. [O.N. *dalr*, Sw. *dal*, E. *dale* (O.E. *dæl*), of same extraction]

daalamist (dalamjork) (n) valley mist which gathers at night. [O.N. *dalr*: dale + *mjorkvi*: dense fog]

daamish (v) to tire with endless talk. [L.Sc. *dammish*: to stun; to stupefy]

daander (n) a gentle walk; (v) to amble; saunter. [O.E. & Sc. *dander*, *daunder*, orig. obs.]

daa nettle (n) hemp nettle or day nettle (*Galeopsis tetrahi*); also ascribed to (*Lamium*). [O.Sc. *dea-nettle*; O.N. (*akr*)*dai*]

dad (n) a solid lump of something – *a dad a butter*; a heavy blow; (v) to strike; to slam, as a door; to plod; trudge. [Sc. with Sh. extensions in meaning 'to plod; trudge']

daddery (dadderi) (n) tiresome, exhausting work; drudgery. [see **daddit**]

daddit (daddet) (adj) exhausted; weary through overwork. [Sw.dial. *datta*: to tire; exhaust]

daek (n) dyke; wall; new-cut peats built like a wall to dry; **innadaeks** within bounds; **ootadaeks** outwith the confines of boundary walls. [Sc. *dyke*, *dike*: drystone wall without mortar; O.Sc. & M.E. *dyk(e)*, *dik(e)*: a ditch]

daek-end (n) end of a drystone dyke where it merges with contours of the hill or at the seashore. [see above]

dael (n) loose planks. [L.Sc. *dale*, *dail*: a deal or plank]

daev (dev, deave) (v) to deafen; irritate by excessive noise or persistent talk. [cf. O.N. *døyfa*: to deafen; deaden; Sc. *deave*: deafen; worry; bother]

daffik (n) small wooden bucket for carrying water. [L.Sc. *daffok*: a tub or vat; Gael. *dabhach*: a vat]

dag (dagg) (n) thick mist or light drizzle; mitten (rarely, but see fishermen's tabu list – addenda). [N. & Sw. *dogg*: (dew) also drizzle]

dan (adv) then; at that time. *Dan we göd hame*.

dan-a-days (adv) in those days. *Aa wir fok göd tae da paets dan-a-days*.

dang pushed; hit; (v) (pt of) **ding**; (pp) **dung**). [O.N. *dengja*: to beat or thrash]

dart (v) to strike a foot on the ground or floor in an expression of anger. [N. *darta*: to walk with a tripping gait; Icel. *dark*: heavy gait and *darka*: to walk clumsily]

dark-advised (dark-a-vised) (adj) having a dark-complexion; having dark hair and eyes. [L.Sc. *dark-a-vised*; *black-a-vised*; O.F. *á vis*: of the face; appearance]

darknin (n) the twilight.

dastreen (de streen) (n) last night. [E. *yester-even*, *yester-e'en*; O.Sc. *yistrene*, *the strene*]

da street (de street) (n) Commercial Street, Lerwick. *Dir datn uncan fok alang de street dis days*.

dat (pron) that (interchangeable with **yun**); (adj) *Dat boy!*; (adv) *Aa de fok wir spaekin dat fast I couldna twig da jist o it*.

dat! dat! (interj) I told you so! What can you expect!

dat in feth! (interj) That in faith! i.e. Good Heavens!

dat in traath! (interj) Yes, truly!

datn (datna) (adj) so; such. *Shö's bön datn a göd peerie ting wir laek ta keep her*.

dayset *day*-set (n) nightfall; dusk

de (short *d* as *di* in E. *did*) (def. article) the – *de sooth boat*. (The preferred rendering in this dictionary although the spoken word frequently indicates a need for variation – see introductory chapter; (also see **da**). [cf. Sw. *de* (*den*) definitive article: the]

dead man's mittens (n) autumn gentian (*Gentiana amarella*).

dead-traa (n) death throes. [O.E. *-thrahes*, *-thrawes*, Sc. *-throe*: spasm, cf. Sc. *thrawn*: twisted]

debaetless (adj) exhausted; feeble. [cf. O.Sc. *debait* – said when one has eaten his fill. *I'll debait noo* – in the sense of having exhausted one's capacity]

dee (pron) (second person singular) you (used in familiar sense). *Dee* (thee) *an me*; *Du can geng deesel* (thyself); (also see **du**). Compatability of adjoining words dictates when to use **dee** instead of **du**, thus: *I'll gie dee dis if du gie's me dat* (reversing the highlighted words inhibits the speech flow). [O.E. *thee*, *thy*, *thou*, N. *de*: you (they, them)]; (v) to die. [Sc. *dee*: die]

deer (v) to impress. *Du'll no deer him whatever du says*. [L.Sc. *deer*: to harm; injure]

dell (v) to dig. [E. *delve*]

dellin (n) the portion of a field or garden allocated for a certain crop – once commonly for a neighbour who had no land of their own or was no longer able to tend a crop. *We aye hey a dellin o tatties and neeps to aald Jeemsie i wir rig*.

demaloorie (adj) dull and drab; out of sorts. [O.N. *dimma*: slight darkness + (*luri*) N. *luren*: faint; drowsy]

dem (pron) them. [Sh. form of E. *them*]

demmel (deml) (v) to fill a vessel by dipping into water. [N. *demla*: to splash = *damla*: to fill a vessel by pressing it down into the water]

demlane (pron) themselves alone. [*dem*: as above + Sc. *lane*: lone]

demsels (pron) themselves. [*dem*: as above + O.Sc. *sel*: self]

denkie (denki) (n) a hollow in the ground. [cf. O.N. *dokk*: a depression; hollow]

D

depooperit (adj) at the last gasp; exhausted. [O.Sc. *depauper*: impoverish; reduce to poverty; O.F. *depaupier*; Americanism *pooped*: out of breath; exhausted]

der (poss adj) their. *Among der ain fok*; (adv) there; (also **dir**). [Sh. & Ork. form of E. *their*; *there*]

der (dere) contraction of *dey wir* (there is/are). *Der a strenge boat doon at de pier*.

der bön there has/have been. *Der bön mair fok at de Hairst gadderin dan we lippened*.

dere's a loss! (interj) What does it matter! Who cares!

dereeshion d-*ree*-shin (n) a stupid person; an object of ridicule; an idiot. [E. *derision*: cf. Psalm 79 v 4 '*We have become a reproach to our neighbours, a scorn and derision to those who are around us*']

ders (pron) theirs. *Yun's ders, no wirs*.

dess (des) (n) stack of hay; hay-rick. [O.N. *des*: stack; hay-stack, also cf. Sw.dial. *dös*: stack of straw or hay; L.Sc. & N.Eng. *dass*: a stack; heap of corn]

deuk (dyook) (n) a duck. [O.Sc. *duik*; O.E. *dūce*] (not to be confused with Duke – see introduction)

dey (pron) they; also used as emphatic (negative) interjection. *Did de fokk gaaf at de concert? Dey!* [Sh. & Ork. equiv. of E. *they*]; (adv) there; (also see **dir**). [Sh. equiv. of E. *there*]

dey wid there would. *Dey wid a bön seeven o wis dere*.

dey wir there was/were. *Dey wir a murge a fok at de roup*.

dibe (däib) (n) one who dips; (v) to dip in water; to strive and toil. [O.N. *djúp*: deep; *dúfa*, *deyfa*, *deypa*: to dip]

dicht (dycht) (v) to wipe; to clean; to dust; to make tidy. [L.Sc. *dicht*, *dight*, *decht*: to put in good order; clean]

digel (djigel, diggle) (v) to stamp or trample something down. *A'm ay bön diggled doon bi ithers* (I'm constantly put upon by others); to shake. [cf. N. *diga*: to tremble; shake; swing; also *dika*: to rock; move slightly to and fro. In its current meaning the word has probably been influenced by E. *jiggle*]

dight (v) to clean; gut, as a fish. [Sh. variant on Sc. *dight* (see **dicht**)]

dill (v) digest. *Let dee denner dill doon afore du gengs fur a swim*; to die down, esp. of wind, or a lull in the weather; to hang still. *De claes is dillin apo de line*; settle. [E.dial. *dill*: to soothe; die down; become quiet]

dill-bells (n) lumps of matted, soiled wool hanging from the rear end of sheep; pendulous dewlaps of a goat or other animal. [from N. *dingle*: to dangle; swing to and fro]

dilse (n) seaweed; the common dulse (*Palmaria palmata*). [Gael. *duileasg*: dulse; the edible seaweed; L.Sc. *dils(e)*, *dilce*]

dim (dimm, also dimmer) (n) dusk; twilight; a long time; (see **simmer dim**). [O.N. *dimma*: (slight) darkness]

dimriv (n) dawn. [O.N. *dim(m)*: (slight) darkness + N. & Fær. *riva*: to tear (of weather); to clear up]

dimsket (adj) downhearted; dispirited – fig. usage of **dim**. [see above]

dine (poss pron) yours. *Dis is mine, yun's dine*; (also **dines**). [O.E. *thine*]

ding (v pt) to beat or strike; to knock over; to drive, as nails; to drive into the mind. [O.N. *dengja*: to beat; thrash; L.Sc. *ding*: to beat or strike]

dingle (dingel) (v) to wander aimlessly; to potter. *He's gyaan dinglin aboot*. [cf. E. *dingle-dangle*: swinging to and fro (cf. *dangler*: a person who dangles about after others); from O.N. *dingla*]

dink (v) to clothe; decorate. [L.Sc. *dink*, *denk*: fine; dainty]

dip (v) to sit down. *Dip dee aside wiz a peerie start and gie wiz aa dee news*. [in a similar sense N. *dyppa*]

dipple (v) to plant potatoes using a dibble. [E. *dibble*: a pointed tool used to make holes for planting seeds or plants]

dipplin-tree (n) a dibble. [see above]

dir (poss adj) their. *Among dir ain fok*; (also **der**). [Sh. & Ork. form of E. *their*]

dirl (n) a blow or knock; state of haste; (v) vibrate or shake. *Hear du de wind dirlin idda lum*. [N. *dirl*: something dangling or swinging; Sc. *dirl*: thrill; vibrate]

dirr (v) to vibrate. [influenced by associated words, *dird* and *dirl*, cf. L.Sc. *dird*: a stroke]

dirri du (doo) (n) storm petrel (*Hydrobates pelagicus*). [onomatopœic lit. 'vibrating dove'; N. *dirla*: to vibrate + L.Sc. *doo*: a dove]

dirt (n) nonsense; rubbish talk. *He jöst spaeks a lok a dirt*. Also applied to bad weather. *He's bön a day a dirt*. [E. *dirt* (with similar meanings)]

dis (disn) (pron) this; (adj) these. [Sh. & Ork. form of E. *this*; *these*]

disjaskit (adj) debilitated; exhausted; worn out. [O.N. *dasast*: to become weary; exhausted; also cf. O.Sc. *daisket*: exhausted; *jaskit*: jaded; worn out]

distress (n) extreme harshness of weather. *Pity dem oot in siccan a distress o wadder*. [from O.Sc. usage – bad, stormy weather]

dittie (ditti) (n) a small bag for keeping trifles in; also a **ditti-box** – a small box carried by fishermen in which they kept bits and pieces to carry out minor repairs at sea. [cf. N. *dytta*: to potter; busy oneself with trifles]

divvish (v) to adorn; to put in order; to prepare food for the table; to complete a set piece of work; commonly used in sense of *ill-divvished* (badly prepared). [cf. E. *devise*: to plan; in sense of prepare, make ready]

djuk (jouk) (v) to duck; stoop; jerk one's head away to avoid a blow. *He djukkit de straik*. [Sc. *jouk*]

dochter (n) daughter. [O.N. *dokka*: girl; O.Sc. *dochter*, *dochtir*]

docken (n) dock (*Rumex-*) – coarse weed, the leaves of which are used to alleviate nettle stings; note: docken stems are used to make **böddies** – open-work baskets commonly used for carrying fish. [L.Sc. *dokkan*, *docken*]

docken sparrow (n) corn bunting (*Emberiza calandra*) (also **trussie laverek, shurl**). [Sh]

doely (dowly) (adj) doleful; plaintive; mournful, as a piece of music. *Yun's an aafil doely soond*. [cf. O.N. *daufligr*: dull; dismal; lonely]

doggit (adj) harassed; (n) intense anxiety; anxious waiting. [E. *dogged*]

dog's pennies (n) yellow rattle (*Rhinanthus minor*).

doit (v) to be confused in mind. [O.N. *dottr*: a dull, incapable, careless person; O.Sc. *doit*: a fool; numbskull]

doitin (adj) mentally befuddled; senile. [see above]

doork (n) jaunt. [orig. obs.]

doo (du) (n) pigeon. [O.N. *dufa*, Sc. *doo*: a dove]

dook 1) (n) a dip; a bathe. [L.Sc. *douk*]; (v) to duck, as under something; to plunge in water. [Sc. *dook*; Du. *deuvik*; E. *dowel*]; 2) (n) a wooden wall plug to which a nail may be driven.

doon-by (adv) nearby; further down. *He's joost geen doon by*. [E. *down*; Sc. *doon-*]

dooncome (n) a disappointment; a comedown. [Sc.]

doondrappin (n) state of collapse (lit. 'dropping down' from exhaustion). [Sc.]

doontak (n) taunt; humiliation (lit. a 'take down' – a degradation). [O.N. *nidrtaka*: pulling down]

doontöm (n) a heavy fall of rain. [Sc. *doon*: down + O.Sc. *teme*, *tume*: to empty]

doon upon it (adj) depressed.

doose (dus) (n) a blow; (v) to strike; dart, as in dancing. [N. *dus*: a blow; stroke; O.Sc. *douss*]

doot (v) to suspect in a negative way. *I doot he's gyaan ta come a gale de nycht*; *I doot du'll no fin dee böts dere*. Also (contrary to E.) affirmative in some uses. *I doot du's rycht* – meaning agreement. [Sc.]

dorro (n) a handline, having several hooked lines attached, used in catching mackerel, coalfish, etc.; the act of fishing using such a line. [O.N. *dyrgja*: to fish with a trolling line]

dort (v) to sulk (see **frimse**). [Sc. *dort*, orig. unknown]

dorts (n) the sulks. *Ta tak da dorts* (to take offence or sulk); also **dorty** (adj) sulky.

dose (dos) (n) a substantial quantity. *Der a dose a fish i da shott*. [O.N. *dys*: a cairn; stack of straw or hay; O.E. *dass*: a stack]

doven (v) to numb; deaden. *He wis doven we de caald*. [O.N. *dofna*: to become dull; slack; feeble or insensible]

dov (v) to doze. *Yun peerie lass is doverin owre*. [O.N. *dovi*: indolence; slackness]

dowe (dølos) (v) to droop; wither. [O.N. *dygdarlauss*: incapable; useless]

dö (v) to do; (v pp) **dön**.

döl (dool) (n) grief – in exp. *less an döl* (alas what sorrow). [L.Sc. *dool(e)*, *doull*, *dowll*: grief; sorrow; mourning]

döless (dolos) (adj) lazy; lacking in drive. [O.N. *dádlauss*: lacking in deeds (good capacity, energy of action, ability)]

dön (v pp of **dö**) done; (adj) physically incapable. *Shö's a pör dön body*.

dörkable (adj) equable, as weather, i.e. tolerable for outside work even if overcast. [deriv. O.N. *drýgja*: to make to keep longer; *drjúgr*: to augment]

draa (n) draw; **boat's draa** a place on the shore where a boat is drawn up. [O.N. *drag*]; (v) to infuse tea; to **draa on** to pull on, as socks; move a kettle from the back of a stove to over the heat; **draa me till** I will go there; to **draa up** to progress toward, as in the passage of time. *Hit's draain up tae wir denner time*; **draa in** take a chair in to the table; to become shorter. *De days draa in at hairst-time*. [cf. E. *draw*]

draacht (n) the drawing of an implement, especially a harrow. [O.N. *drag*: to draw; to pull slowly; however in pronunciation now more related to O.Sc. *draucht*, *drawcht*, with same meaning]

draatsi (dratsi) (n) (sea) otter (*Lutra lutra*). Originally fishermen's tabu language (see addenda) but now commonly in dialect. [deriv. from *drats* (now obsolete but see **drittle**): to move heavily and slowly; to shuffle along; cf. O.N. *drattla*, Icel. *drattast*: trudge; plod; move with a heavy, slow gait; O.Sc. *dridland*]

draig (dreg) (n) a dredge, one used by fishermen for collecting **yoags** (large mussels); (v) to trawl a fishing line; cause a fishing line to be kept in constant motion in the water. [O.N. *drega*: to draw; also O.N. *dyrgja*: to troll]

drang (v) to knot tightly. [O.N. *drengja*: to draw together; to tie firmly]

drave (v) (pt of) drive. *We drave back de idder wye*. [O.Sc. *drave*: a drove, of sheep or cattle]

dreach (n) nourishment; sustenance. [cf. Sc. *dreach*, Gael. *dreach*: appearance; shape; beauty]

dree (v) to endure; suffer (pain, misfortune, etc.). *What I'm hed t dree wi dis*. [O.Sc. *dree*; O.E. *dréogan*]

dreel (v) to speedily remove; to drive out. [cf. E. *drill*, in sense of work done speedily and efficiently]

dreep (n) an ineffectual person; (v) to drip. [L.Sc. *dreep*, with same meanings]

dreeple (n) a small trickle of water; drizzle. *Dir joost a dreeple comin oot a de tap*. [L.Sc. *dreeple*]

dreich (adj) cheerless; dismal; dreary. *He's gey dreich company*. [Sc. *dreich*: long drawn out; tedious; wearisome, cf. O.N. *drjúgr*: lasting; substantial]

dreid (n) fear; regard with awe; (v) apprehend; dread; suspect something will undoubtedly happen. *I dreid du's begun some spaekalation wi yun news*. [E. dread; L.Sc. *dreid*]

dress (v) prepare a newly made article of knitting in readiness for sale or wear by washing, rinsing and shaping on a frame to dry (see **board**). [spec. meaning of E. *dress*: to prepare or make ready; O.F. *dresser*: to prepare]

drib (v) to beat; thrash; scold. [cf. variant of E. *drub*, N.dial. *dribba*: thump; strike against something]

dribes (dribs) (n) the last drop or dregs; said of someone who has been taken advantage of: *Dey took the dribes oot a him* (They bled him dry). [archaic E. *drib* – now only as 'dribs and drabs'; L.Sc. *drib*: the last drop or dregs]

drintled (driplet) (adj) spotted; speckled; having small irregular spots. [N. *driplutt*, *droplutt*: variegated, having small dots]

drit (dritten, dreet): (n) excrement; of something unsavoury or disagreeable. *Dat be dritten*; (see **brølek dreet**). [O.N. *dreit*, *dritinn*]

drittle (drintel) (v) to walk slowly; to drag one's feet; to dawdle. [N. *drunta*, *drynta*: to idle; dawdle]

drocht (drought) (n) drying, breezy weather. *I needna pit de claes oot, der nae drocht*; (also see **sook**). [L.Sc. *drocht*, *drucht*; E. *draught*]

dronj (droin, dronn) (v) to grumble in a low, moaning sort of way. *He wis dronnin on*. [N., Icel., Fær. *drynja*: to low softly, prolonging the sound]

D

droo (n) sea lace or dead man's rope (*Chorda filum*) (also **drooie-lines**, **lucky lines**). [cf. O.N. *drauch*: dead man]

drook (v) to soak (also **drookle**). [L.Sc. *drouk*, *draik*: to saturate; drench, cf. O.N. *drukna*: drown]

drookin (n) a soaking; (pa p) **drookit (drookled)** soaked. [as above]

drooth (n) 1) a drunkard; 2) lack of rain; said of *wadder heads* (cloud formations): *nort-sooth is a drooth*; *aest-wast fur a blast*. [E. *drought*, and therefore in the case of *drunkard* having the same sense as 'a soak']

drukken (adj) drunk; intoxicated; (v pp of) drink. [O.N. *drukkinn*; L.Sc. *drucken*]

drult (drölt) (n) a large clumsy person. [N. *drult*, *drulta*: stout, clumsy person]

drummie-bee (n) bumble bee (*Bombus*). [imitative – droning or drumming sound. D.dial. *drum*: a hollow sound; song; booming or drumming sound]

drush (droosh) (n) small worthless fragments; fine rain; (see also **raag**, **shug**). [N. *drusla*: to sprinkle (drizzle); to strew].

druttle (n) thin or watery butter-milk. [partly imitative of 'dribble']

du (pron) the informal form of 'you', used by parents to children, old people to young, but not *vice versa*. Also used between equals (although some couples will use 'you' to signify their special relationship); (v) to address familiarly. *Hit's wrang t 'du' your elders* – i.e. you must not be overly familiar in addressing your elders; (also see **dee**). [O.N. *pú*, N., Sw., D. *du*: thou. The introduction of *you* to English in place of *thee* and *thou* brought about the distinction between formal and informal usage, a distinction which still exists in a number of other languages i.e. French – *vous* (formal and singular), *tu* (informal singular)]

dub (dwog) (n) a bog or small muddy puddle. [O.Sc. *dub*: a small, stagnant pool, cf. N. *tvaga*, *tvagla*: to soil; splash]

duddered (adj) seedy and dilapidated. [cf. Sc. *doddered* (fr. E. *dodder*): feeble with age]

dukkie (dokki) (n) a doll. [O.N. *dokka*: girl; D. *dukke*: a doll]

duff (n) soft, mossy peat unsuitable for burning, used sometimes as bedding for animals (see **möldie-coose**). [L.Sc. *duff*, E.dial. *doaf*, *doof*: dough]

dulskit (dolsket) (adj) sluggish and lethargic. [cf. O.N. *dælskr*: foolish; silly; with O.Sc. *dulse*: dull; heavy]

dumba (n) dust; the residue from corn husks floating in the air after winnowing. [O.N. *dumba*: dust, esp. dust resulting from threshing corn]

dumbit (adj) (of animals, esp. sheep) dusty-coloured, greyish; (of clothing) dull, shabby. [N. *dumbutt*: dusty; Icel. *dumbóttur*: dull of colour; of a dusky hue]

dumpised (domsket) *dum*-pis-ed (adj) despondent; downhearted. [deriv. of O.N. *dumbr*: dumb; speechless (with paralysed senses), cf. E. exp. 'in the dumps']

dunder (n) a loud noise; (v) to make a sound like thunder. [N. & Fær. *dundra*: to thunder; rattle; bang]

dungeon (n) said of someone with a wealth of knowledge. [O.Sc. *dungeon*: in sense of a deep repository of knowledge]

dunt (n) a heavy blow; a thud; (v) to strike. [O.N. *dyntr*: a din; heavy fall; push]

dunter (n) eider duck (*Somateria mollissima*). [imitative of the bird's action – cf. Icel. *dynta*: to bob lightly up and down]

duss (v) to take down a sail. [N. *dusa*: to fall, tumble down; E. *douse*: to take a sail down quickly]

dwaam (n) a swoon; a senseless state; a fool; (v) to faint. [N. *dorm (durm)*: a nap, a light sleep; L.Sc. *dwaum*: a swoon]

dwang (n) a short, wooden cross-member fixed between two upright timbers as a support; (v) to fix the above in position. [L.Sc. *dwang*: a short traverse piece of timber; to subject to pressure; Du. *dwang*: compulsion; restraint; O.N. *pvengr*: a strap; latchet]

dwine (v) of persons or animals, to waste or pine away; to fail in health or strength; esp. used as a curse. *Dwine dee!* (Confound you!) [M.E. *dwyne*, *dwine*; O.E. *dwínan*]

dy 1) (poss pron) your (thy). *Is dis dy coo?*

dy 2) (n) a wave (see **moder dy**). [O.N. *dý*: quagmire, with extension of image to the sea and the idea of underlying motion; O.Sc. *die*, *däi*]

dycal (n) boat's compass. [O.Sc. *diacle*, *daikel*: a small compass (prob. from *dial*)]

dysel (pron) yourself. [O.E. *thyself*]

E

ean (pron) one (also **een**, **wan**). [O.E. *einn*; L.Sc. *ane*]

eans (eens) (pron) (pl) ones. *Du can gie me yun eans* (You can give me those ones). [see above]

ebb (n) the area of foreshore exposed by the going back of the tide. [cf. O.N. *fjara*: partly ebb (as English) partly foreshore, dry at ebb]

ebb cock (n) redshank (*Tringa tetanus*).

ebb fool (n) sanderling (*Calidris alba*) (lit. 'ebbfowl').

ebb-sleeper (n) dunlin (*Calidris alpina*). (Some confusion with ebb-snippek – a) turnstone; b) dunlin; c) sandpiper; and also ebb-picker – purple sandpiper) [Jakobsen names the dunlin a *sklattiskre* or *skrattiskre* – see **sclaterscrae**]

edder (conj) either. [E. *either*; O.Sc. *uther*; O.E. *ōer*]

ee (n) the eye. [E. *eye*; O.N. *auga*]; (adj) one. [Sc. *ane*; E. *one*]

ee-breer (n) the eyelash (also **ee-wharm**). [*eye-* and O.Sc. *breer* (*breard*): to sprout; to shoot]

eel-towe (n) a line laid inshore for catching eels for bait. [E. *-tow*: a rope or line]

eela (ila) (n) rod (**waand**) or handline fishing in the sea, mainly for **piltocks**, from small boats. [O.N. *ili*, N.dial. *ila*: stone used as an anchor, with extension in meaning to inshore fishing from an anchored position or within that sphere]

eemage (n) a person – generally **pör eemage** – an expression of commiseration in reference to one in poor health or of weak constitution. *Yun pör eemage sood be taen ta de doctor.* [E. *image*, with the meaning of 'a pale reflection of former self']

een (n) eyes; (numeral) one. *Een, twa, tree…*

eence (adv) a single time; at a former time; once. [L.Sc. *aince*: once]

eence a errant (adj) for the sole purpose. *As du aye laekit smok-ed fish A'm come eence a errant wi some tae dee.* [L.Sc. *aince* + *errand* = for the one and only purpose; the sole reason]

eenoo (adv) just now; for the time being. *Cheerio eenoo*; in a moment. *A'm comin eenoo.* [O.Sc. *eenoo*: lit. 'even now', 'just now']

eeraster (iraster) (n) a flayer; a scourge; metaphor for a tyrant. [N. *rasa*: to scratch the skin]

eeskit (isket) (adj) mottled; of animals having a skin of different colours. [N. *hysjutt*: mottled in different shades]

eetch (n) an adze. [O.Sc. *eche*, *eitch*: an adze (prob. from *edge*)]

eetimtation (n) very small amount; an iota. [O.Sc. *eetemtation*: a small, puny creature; cf. E. *item*]

eever (ever) (n) something of an unusually great size (also **wheefer**). [cf. O.N. *ærinn*, *yfrinn*: excessive; abundant; very large; also S.dial. *övra*: to increase in vigour and growth]

ee-wharm (-hwarm) (n) the eye-lash (also **ee-breer**). [E. *eye-* + O.N. *hvarmr*: the eyelid]

eft (adv) aft; in the stern section of a boat or ship; (adj) belonging to the stern part. [E. *aft*]

efter (adv) after; left over. *Haes du ony loff efter?* (Have you any bread left?); (prep) as heir to. *Shö's weel aff noo efter her uncle Wullie.* [O.N. *eptir*: after]

efterklaps (efterkast) (n) result; outcome; sequel. [N. *etterkast*: after-clap]

eident (idint) (adj) industrious; always busy. [O.N. *idinn*: assiduous in work]

eight o'clocks (n) mid-evening snack and cuppa (not necessarily at 8pm) – a substantial repast and something of an institution in bygone years. *Du'll stay an tak dee eight o'clocks wi wiz.*

ekkelgirse (n) common butterwort (*Pinguicula vulgaris*) (also see **yirnin girse**). [prob. from O.N. *ax*: ear of corn; L.Sc. *girse*: graze – hence grass]

eksis girse (n) the dandelion (*Taraxacum officionale*) (also **bitter-aks**). [*eksis* – originally *exi* – is probably from O.N. *ax*: ear of corn; L.Sc. *girse*: graze – hence grass]

elbuck (n) the elbow. [O.Sc. *elbok*: elbow]

ellis (eelist) *eh-lis* (n) reluctance; timidness; disinclination. *Shö's an ellis craitur* (She wouldn't say boo to a goose). [N. *ulyst*: distaste; disinclination]

ellishon (n) a shoemaker's awl (also **yarken ellishon**). [O.N. *alr*: awl + L.Sc. *shoon*: shoes]

elsk (v) to love. [O.N. *elska*: to love]

elska cry (ilska-cry) (n) death cry. [O.N. *illska*: a) ill-will; malice; b) enmity; hatred; c) mischief; misfortune; in Fær. the word is also used in the sense of indisposition or illness]

elt (v) 1) to make dirty. *Da bairns wis elt wi coom efter playin ida laft*; 2) to stroke or pet excessively, as a young animal; 3) to work toil at a dirty job; to rake up the ground. *Du'll fin him eltin ida byre.* [originally to knead dough – O.N. *elta*: to squeeze; press; knead; to drive; chase. (The sense of making dirty appears to be as a result of 'eltin')]

em (ame) (adj) infested; crawling with maggots or lice. [N. *eima*, *ema*: to steam; reek; smoulder]

emmer gös (n) great northern diver (*Gavia immer*). [L. *immer*: to dip; to plunge + *goose*]

emmers (emers) (n) embers. [O.N. *eimyrja*: embers]

emskit (adj) of a dark, bluish-grey colour. [N. *imutt*: of animals – having dark-greyish stripes]

end (n) 1) a waxed thread used by a shoemaker. [E. *shoemaker's end*: a waxed thread ending in a pointed bristle]; 2) breath. [O.N. *andi*: breath]

end on (ende) (adv) continually. [Icel. *ennpá*, Fær. *enntá*: yet; still; even now]

enk (n) the setting aside of a young domestic animal to a child or friend. It would generally remain on the croft but be considered the property of the recipient who would receive the produce – milk, wool, eggs, etc.; (v) to carry out the above process. [O.N. *eigna*: to transfer something to someone]

E

ent (v) pay attention; heed; (also **ant**). [O.N. *enta*: to heed; care for]

eredastreen (n) the night before last night. [O.E. *ere*: before + **dastreen**: O.E. *yester-even*, *yester-e'en*; O.Sc. *yistrene*, *the strene*]

erne (n) white-tailed eagle (*Haliaeetus albicilla*). [O.N. *örn*]

errands (n) groceries; provisions; the shopping. [O.N. *eyrindi*]

erse (n) (slang) arse; buttocks; backside. *Du's gotten yun erse aboot face*. [E. (slang) *arse*]

ert (n) direction. [L.Sc. *airt*, Gael. *aird*: quarter of the compass]; (v) to irritate; tease. *Dunna ert fornenst de faider*. [O.N. *erta*]

ess (n) ash; ashes. [E. *ash*, but cf. O.N. *eisa*: intense fire]

essibucket (n) ash-bucket. [see **ess**]

essi-bin (n) rubbish bin. [see **ess**]

essikert (n) council garbage truck. (Note: as peat fires produce a lot of ash, its collection became one of the primary purposes of the garbage truck when Shetland Islands Council instigated the service – hence the nickname '*essikert*'.)

essimidden (n) dunghill or rubbish heap where ashes are deposited (see **midden**). [E. *ash* + archaic Sc. *midden*: a dunghill; O.N. *myki*, D. *mög*: dung]

eterskap (**aeterkepp**) (n) devil's coach horse beetle (*Staphylinus olens*). When disturbed the beetle lifts its tail and emits a foul-smelling liquid – hence *eters*. [O.N. *eitr*: venom]

etterscab (**aeterkepp**, **etterskab**) (n) ill-tempered or troublesome person. [O.N. *eitr*: venom; also bitterness; enmity]

ettersome (adj) bitterly cold weather; freezing cold with sharp wind. [O.N. *eitrkaldr*: freezing cold]

every (adj) each. *Wan in every haand*. [poss. deriv. from E. exp. *each and every*]

F

faa (n) 1) fall; the act of falling; (pt) **faan**. [Sc. *fa*]; 2) the intestines of a slaughtered animal. [N.dial. *fall*: carcase of slaughtered animal minus the entrails]; (v) become. *He's faan an aald föl*; used idiomatically in several forms besides the recognised English expressions such as: *faa (fall) in wi(th)* – meet; *faa (fall) aff* – doze, etc.; **faa afore** to occur. *Hit faa's afore me wir taen de wrang rod*; **faa asoond** faint; **faa awa** fall away; abate, as wind; **faa upon** become sour or decayed, as food; come across. *Du'll laekly faa upon wir sheep ida park*; **faa by** collapse; fail to continue; **faa owre** to drop into sleep; **faa tö** commence labour in childbirth; tuck in to food. [Sc. *fa*, O.S. *fall*: to become]

faader (n) God. *My Faader! For sic an onkerry*; (also see **faider** for distinction between God and man). [O.N. *fadir*: father]

faase (adj) false.

faase-face (n) false-face; mask.

faat (n) injury; that which injures; hurt; harm. *Hit'll dö him nae faat t keen de truth*. [E. *fault*, *flaw*]

fack (n) fact. *A'm tellin dee hit's a fack*. [E. *fact*]

faddom (n) fathom; (v) to fathom; also used in expression **faddomin da skroo** – an old Hallowe'en ritual in which a young woman measured or 'fathomed' a stack of oats with her outstretched arms and subsequently was given a vision of her future husband (see **skroo**). [Sc. form of E. *fathom*: the reach of outstretched arms (6ft or 1.8metres); to comprehend or get to the bottom of]

fadmal (fedmel) (n) a fat, corpulent woman. [O.N. *feitr*: fat]

fae (prep) from; of place, motion or time; (conj) from that; (also **frae**); (adv) since. *A'm no spoken tae her fae last week*. [Sc. *fae*, *frae*; O.S. & O.N. *fra*]

fael (faells) (n) a sod or turf. [O.Sc. *fayle*, *faill*]

faelly-daek (n) a wall (dyke) made of turf blocks. [Sc.]

faider (feder) (n) father. *Waakin up dee faider afore he misses de news*. Note the different spelling – **faader** – and pronunciation when referring to God. [O.N. *fedir*: father]

fain (fen) (v) to show delight and pleasure at one's coming; receive with approval. [O.N. *fagna*: to welcome]

fair (adv) completely; absolutely. *De sicht o it fair scunnered me*. [Sc.]

faird (adj) afraid. [L.Sc. *feart*]

Fair Isle (n) the distinctive patterned knitting of Shetland so named for the island of Fair Isle where (it is supposed) the women first perfected the style and created many of the patterns, popularised and made famous by the Prince of Wales in 1930s. [O.N. *Frjóey*: Fair Isle]

fairntickle (n) a freckle. [Sc. & O.E. *ferntickle*: freckle – owing to its resemblance to spores on the back of ferns]

fairlie (n) a marvellous occurrence; a wonder. [LSc. *farly*, *fairlie*; also *ferly*: strange; wonderful; O.N. *ferligr*: monstrous; dreadful]

fairy's caird (n) fern; bracken (*Pteridium aquilinum*); (also **feeri-caird, trowies caird**). [Sh. & Ork. deriv. from folklore; the 'caird' being an implement for carding wool and used by fairies; also used by the witch **lucky-minnie**]

faize (v) to untwist; fray, as a rope. [L.Sc. *faize*, O.E. *feaze*: to unravel; fray]

faks(in) (n) long, high, foam-crested wave; (v) waves breaking to form ·'white horses'. [O.N. *fax*: a mane, which in N. *faks* can also denote a fringed border]

fams (n) excessive fuss. [E. *foam*: excessively angry, as in 'to foam at the mouth']

fan (v) found; (pr t) **fin**; (pp) **fun**. [O.N. *fann*: found; E. *find*]

fancies (n) any kind of baker's small cakes and iced biscuits. *Wir browt a box o Malcolmson's fancies fur dee eight o'clocks*. [Sh. abbrev. of E. *fancy cakes*: iced or decorated cakes]

fann (n) a drift of snow. [O.N. *fonn*: a heap of snow; a drift]

fant (v) to starve; to be very hungry (see **black-fantin**); also **fanteen** (to fast). [L.Sc. *fant*: weak; feeble]

fantation (n) in a state of extreme hunger. [see above]

far (n) a boat; ship. [O.N. *far*: conveyance; vessel]

farlin (n) large wooden trough to hold herrings while being gutted by hand – from the practice of four women working two on either side of the box. [E. *fardel*: a fourth part; Sc. *farl*: the quarter of a round cake of flour or oatmeal]

fasgerd (n) the strip of plaited straw round the rim of a kishie. [O.N. *fastgardr*: a stronghold]

fash (v) to bother. *Dunna fash deesel wi yun eenoo*. [Sc. *fash*: to trouble or bother; Fr. *fâcher*]

fast (n) mooring rope for a boat. *Ta mak fast* – tie up; (also **fasti**). [O.N. *festr*: a rope (fastened or by which something is fastened)]

fastibaand (n) a cross-beam running under the thwarts of a boat to hold the frame (also **haddibaand**). [O.N. *festa*: to fasten + band]

fastin hert (adv) without breakfast (lit. 'fasting heart').

fecht (n) fight; struggle; (v) to fight. [L.Sc. *fecht*, *feght*]

fedder (n) feather; the thin (feather-like) cutting edge of a **tushkar**. [E. *feather*]

feeky (fik, feekerie) (adj) over-concerned with trivialities. [N. *fika*: to bustle about with trifles; D.dial. *fige*: to hasten (to desire; aspire); the 'k' ending is probably due to O.Sc. and not to be confused with. Sc. *feck*: value; worth & O.Sc. *fek*]

feelin-herted (adj) sensitive. [Sc.]

feerie (firi) (n) contagious ailment; epidemic, frequently involving diarrhoea. [cf. Sw.dial. *far*, N. *farsott*: epidemic]

feespin (fispen) (adj) light and nimble despite being rather feeble, esp. of elderly people. [cf. N. *fjappen*: light; nimble]

feet (n) footwear. [Sc.]

feetiks (fikek) (n) unruly tufts of hair hanging over the face. [cf. N. *fiklast*: to become entangled]

feevil (fivl, fivel) (n) a light fall of snow. [O.N. *folva (fölva)*: a thin covering of snow; Fær. *følv, felv*: a thin layer of snow; of butter on bread]

feeze (fis) (v) to press through an opening. *He could hardly feeze his fit intae yun shoe.* [deriv. of air or fluid being forced out; O.N. *fisa*: to fizzle; puff]

feft (adj) bespoken; promised. [variant of E. *feoff*: to put in legal possession; cf. *fief*: something over which a person has rights or exercises control; a *fiefdom*]

fegs (n) (interj) used as an expression of surprise or emphasis. *Fegs! Du gluffed me.* [L.Sc. *fegs, faigs*, a shortening of *faikins*: faith (see **feth**)]

fendy (adj) seaworthy, as a boat capable of fending off waves. [L.Sc. *fendie*: able to look after oneself (and therefore a seaworthy boat)]

ferdie-maet (ferdimet) (n) food for a journey, esp. a fishing trip. [*ferdar-matr* – O.N. *ferd*: journey + *matr*: meat]

ferri-caird (n) fern (*Pteris aquiline*) (also **fairy's caird, trowie-caird**). [Sh. & Ork. deriv. from folklore; the 'caird' being an implement for carding wool and used by fairies; also used by the witch **lucky-minnie**]

fetch (v) to gasp for breath. [prob. a combination of L.Sc. *fecht*: to fight; to struggle and *pecht*: pant for breath]

feth (n) faith, in exp. *Feth, I doot dat!* (By jove, I expect so!). *Dat in feth!* [O.Sc. form of E. *faith*]

fettle (fetel) (n) a rope or strap for carrying something over the shoulder (originally made of twisted straw); (v) to secure; tie up; overpower. [O.N. *fetill*: a strap with which something may be carried over the shoulder]

fey (adj) bewitched; slightly mad; otherworldly; able to see the future. *Du's no fey yit!* said ironically of someone who appears to have all their wits about them. [O.E. *fāege*: doomed; O.N. *feigr*: on the point of death; O.Sc. *fey*: doomed]

feyness (n) a feeling of impending doom; a general atmosphere of death. [see above]

fiddler's bid (n) a late invitation to a wedding (see **bid**).

fidge (n) a restless person. *Haad still. Du's a rycht fidge*; (v) to fidget. [L.Sc. *fidge*: fidget]

fiels (n) hill grazing. [L.Sc. *fiel*: field]

fierdy (ferdi) (adj) able to work; (of a boat) **sea-fierdy** seaworthy; in good condition. [cf. N. *ferdig, ferdug*: brisk; hale; L.Sc. *feirdy*: strong; active]

filska (n) high-spirited; flighty behaviour. [O.N. *fiflska*: folly; *fólska*: foolishness; N. *villska*: wildness; cf. L.Sc. *flisk*: to move in a frolicsome way; to caper; frisk]

filsket (adj) high-spirited; frisky. [O.N. *fiflskr*: silly; foolish]

fim (n) a light covering or thin layer of frost, snow, powder, etc. [N. *fim*: a thin layer]

fin (v) 1) to find; (pt) **fan**; (pp) **fun**. [O.N. *fann*: found; E. *find*]; 2) to feel. [O.N. *finna*: to feel]

fingerin (n) worsted spun '2-ply jumper-weight' woollen yarn (standard 4-ply). [O.Sc. *fingering* (originally from a technique involving the spinning of the yarn)]

finnet (finsk) (n) a layer of mould or dust (see **blue-finsket**). [Fær. *-finska*: to become musty]

fir (fur) (conj) until. *We stayed in Lerook fir de sooth boat göd;* because. *I couldna win dastreen fur I wiz at de eela.*

firbye (prep) besides. *Du'll hae ta pit on mair claes firbye yun wi dis wadder.* [Sc. *forby(e)*: besides]

fire (n) fuel. *Pit on some mair fire an gie wis a bit a het*; (v) to oven-bake (oatcakes, etc.); to throw. *Fire yun trash idda essi-bin.*

first (adj) first in sense of new, not until now; a recent event (esp. Unst). *Wir horse first died on Försday.* [O.N. *fyrstr*, D. *først nu*, Fær. *nú fyrsta*: I'm first come]

first fit (n) the first person to enter a house on New Year's Day; (v) to enter a house as **first fit**. [L.Sc. *fut(e), fuit, fit*; Sc. *first foot*: a New Year's tradition involving entertainment and the bringing of good luck]

firsmo (v) to diminish or lessen; to fall from grace; said of someone who is showing off: *He'll get a firsmo* (a downfall). [O.N. *fyirsmá*: contempt – but used in Shetland in original meaning of 'to reduce, lessen the value of']

firyat (v) forgot.

fishy-flee (n) blue-bottle fly (*Calliphora*) sometimes used for fishing bait. [Sc.]

fismal (firsmo) (n) a small quantity; a trifle of little value. [O.N. *fyrirsmán*: contempt]

fit (n) foot. [L.Sc. *fut(e), fuit, fit*]

fitch (fidge) (v) to fidget; move restlessly. [O.Sc. *fidge*: to be restless; to fidget]

fitless (adj) unsteady; apt to stumble. [L.Sc. *fitless*; E. *footless*]

fitlinn (n) a stretcher in the bottom of a rowing boat for the oarsman to brace his feet against. [O.Sc. *fit*: foot + O.N. *hlunnr*: a wooden runner]

fit-rig (n) the unploughed section of ground at the end of a field on which horses or tractor turn with the plough; the foot of the rig; (see **rig**). [Sc.]

fit-stramp (n) a footstep. [Sc. *fit*: foot + O.Sc. *stramp*: to tread]

fitty (fittie, futi) (n) a short sock covering foot only. [cf. N. *fötla*: a stocking-foot; O.Sc. *fittie*: a foot]

fjask (adj) nimble; fit; sprightly. [N. *fjasa* (v): to puff; over-hurry oneself]

flaa (fla) (n) a piece of heather turf used for thatching; turf cut off top of peat bank prior to **casting**; (see **flae**). [Fær. *flag*, O.N. (*moldar*) *flaga*: thin covering or layer of earth or mould; cf. O.Sc. *flauchter*: to cut turf (see **flaachter-spade**)]

flaacht (n) a flash; lightning flash. [O.Sc. *flaucht, flacht*: a burst of flame; a flashing of lightning]

flaachter (v) to flutter. [Sh. & Ork. – also *flochter*; cf. O.N. *flohte (flótte)* – related to O.E. *flyht*: a flutter]

flaachter-spade (n) spade for cutting **flaas**. [O.Sc. *flauchter*: to cut turf; *flauchter-spade*: tool used for cutting turf]

flaag (v) to flap loosely. [N.dial. *flak*: a flap; Icel. *flaka*: to hang loose; *flogra*: to flutter]

flae 1) (v) to cut turf from the surface of a peat-bank prior to **casting**. [O.N. *flaga*: thin covering or layer of earth or mould]

flae 2) (v) to skin; to peel off. *Du's broken de clock boy, he'll flae dee alive*; (see **buggie-flae**); (pt) **flaed**; (pp) **flen**. [O.N. *flä*: to skin]

flakki (n) a straw mat, over which corn was winnowed. [O.N. *flaki*: a raft]

flan (n) a sudden squall or down-draft of wind. [Icel. & N. *flana* (v): rush on blindly; tumble; gad about]

flatsh (flatj) (v) to flatten. [O.N. *fletja*: to level; stretch out]

flatshie (flatsi) (n) a temporary bed, originally of straw, made on the floor. [O.N. *flatsæng*: a bed made on the floor]

flech (n) a flea – used figuratively to describe a small insignificant person or thing. [O.Sc. *flech*: a flea]

fleckit (flekket) (adj) white, with large black or brown spots, as a cow. [O.N. *flekkóttr*: flecked; spotted]

flecky (flekka) (n) a pet name for a spotted cow. [O.N. *flekkr*: a fleck; spot]

flee (n) a fishing fly. [O.Sc. *fle*, E. *fly*: the insect; a fishing fly]

fleet (n) a set of nets or lines carried by a boat; a set of flies on a **dorroo** used to catch mackerel. [O.Sc. *flete*: to float; 'fleeting' being a variation on sweep-netting for fish]

fleeter (n) a flat-edged wooden utensil for skimming a pot of liquid (see also **scoomer**). [E.dial. *fleet*: to skim]

fleg (flegg) (n) a fright; (v) to frighten. [Sc. *fleg*: a fright; O.E. *fleegan*: to put to flight]

flenk (v) flirt. [O.Sc. *flink, flenk*: to walk jauntily or nimbly; N.dial. *flingsa*: to run; gad about; flirt]

flesh (n) meat – mutton, beef, etc., as opposed to **maet**, which is food. [L.Sc. *flesch*: meat]

flickament (n) state of excitement. [same root meaning as **flenk** (see above)]

flipe (flype) (n) a turn-up on a garment; (v) to turn up a sleeve, trouser, or skirt end in order to shorten it. [Sc. *flype*: to strip back; to turn partly outside in; D. *flip*: a flap]

fliss (n) a flake; a thin sliver; short, light shower of rain; (v) to peel off. [O.N. *flis*: a chip; splinter; N. *flysja*: a thin slice]

flit (v) to move from one house to another; to move a tethered animal to fresh grazing; to fetch or carry peats home from the hill. *De bairns hed a holiday fae skule for de peat-flittin*. [O.N. *flytja*: to move; transport; O.Sc. *flit, flyt*: to transport]

flit-boat (n) a small boat used to ferry goods ashore from a larger vessel. [O.N. *flytja*: to move; transport]

flite (v) to scold; (pt) **flet**; (pp) **flitten**. [L.Sc. *flyt(e), flite*, O.E. *fliten*: to wrangle violently; to scold]

flittin-stane (n) stone used for knocking down an animal's tether. [see **flit**]

floamie (faloamie, flomi) (n) something wide, flat and spread out. *A muckle floamie o a cott flung aboot his shooders*; a spate of words. [Icel. *flæmi*: something wide, large, extensive; flat surface or space]

floss (flos) (n) the common rush (*Juncus conglomeratus*); poss. denoting something frayed, scaled or peeled off – pith from the *Juncus* rush used to be used for wicks in open oil-camps (**collies**). [N. *flasa*: peel off in large, long flakes]

flör (n) floor. [E. *floor*]

fluke (n) flounder (*Platichthys flesus*). [Sc. *fluke*; O.E. *flóc*; cf. O.N. *flöke*]

flukker (v) to flap; flutter, as a bird (of *flukner*, originally a fishermen's tabu word for hen – see addenda). [O.N. *flognir*, from *fljúga*: to fly]

flukra (flukkra) (n) snow falling softly in large flakes. ('...*a peerie, roond clew as white as da flukkra snaa.*' – *Da Kokkilurie*, James Stout Angus) [Fær. *flykra*: snowflake]

flunkset (adj) said of wide (unbecoming) clothes: *Du's no gyaan oot in yun flunkset froak, is du?* [poss. cognate with N. *flange*, in same meaning]

foally (n) a prank; light-hearted mischief. *Wir Jeemsie wiz aye wan for foally*. [L.Sc. *folly*: a prank]

fock (fok) (n) people; the public; population – *aa de Shetlan fok*; members of one's family – *wir fok*. [E. *folk*]

foggage (n) grass that grows after crops or hay has been cut; rank grass used as winter grazing; (also see **chug**). [O.Sc. *fog, fogage*]

fogrie (fogri) (n) a mackerel (*Scomber scombrus*), (mainly fishermen's tabu language but sometimes heard elsewhere). [O.N. (*hinn*) *fagri*: the fair one]

follow (v) to accompany someone on a journey or to see them home. [L.Sc. *follow*, with same meaning]

fommis (fimis) (n) confused state of mind; trembling; (see **virmish** for related etymology). [N. *fume*: confusion; Icel. *fum*: confused state; O.N. *fimr*: nimble; agile]

foo (adv) how. *Foo is du?* (How are you?); (adj) full; intoxicated. [O.Sc. *fou, fow*: full]

fool (ful) (n) a bird. [O.N. *fugl*]

foolakavi (fugle-ca') (n) a dense flock of birds. [O.N. *fugla*: a bird + Icel. *kafi*: dense (smoke)]

footer (n) a pottering, aimless person. *He's joost an aald footer*; (v) to fiddle about with something. [Sc. *fouter* (v): to mess around aimlessly; (n) a worthless person; L. *futuere* (of a man): to have sexual intercourse]

footh (n) a large quantity. [O.Sc. *fouth, fowth, fulth*: an abundance; E. *full*]

forby (prep) as well as. *We hed taaties an neeps forby maet*; (adv) as well. *Shö wrowt at de skule forby*; near, in front of. *Hit's rycht forby dee neb*. [Sc. comb. of *for* and *by*, besides]

fore (tae da fore) of persons still living – *still tae da fore*.

foregeng (n) premonition. [N. *fyreferd*: foreboding]

foremist (adj) at the front; first in place. [E. *foremost*]

forenön forenoon. [E. *forenoon*: morning; before midday]

fore owre (adj) toward the front. *Come fore owre an tak dis ropp*; forward. *He fell fore owre apo de rodd*.

foreroom (forum) (n) the compartment in a sixern (6-oared boat) immediately for'ard of the mast. [O.N. *fyrirrúm*: frameroom; fore-hold in a boat]

foreside (n) the front side; the time just before. *Dey göd de foreside a denner*.

foretaft (n) the for'ard seat in a boat, next to the bow. [O.Sc. *forethaft*, i.e. fore + *thaft*: a rower's seat; a thwart]

forfochen (adj) exhausted. [O.Sc. *fauchinless*: weak; without strength]

forgie *for-gie* (v) to forgive. [E. *forgive*]

forkietail (n) earwig (*Forficula auricularia*) (see also **spurrytail**). [Sc.dial. *forkit-tail*: earwig – owing to its forked tail]

forlegen (adj) without hope; lost; extremely exhausted. [N. *ferlodin*, Fær. *firilagstur*: to become weakened, exhausted]

fornenst (prep) in front of; opposite to. *Hit's right fornenst dee beak!* (It's right under your nose!). [Sc. *fornent*: right opposite to (in position)]

forrard (for'ard) (adj) in the front, esp. of a boat.

forro (adj) (of a cow) not pregnant but has been milking for over a year; farrow. [Sc. *farrow*]

forsmo (n) a snub; cold-shoulder. [N. *forsmaa*, O.N. *fyrirsmá*: to disdain; despise]

fourareen (four-ærin) (n) a four-oared boat. [O.N. *ferærr*: four-oared]

fower (n) four. [Sc.]

foy (n) in the days of **haaf** fishing, a feast held by a boat's crew at the close of the season, later applied to a party or celebration to mark any special occasion (see **Johnsmas Foy**). [O.Sc. *foy*: a farewell feast; an entertainment given to mark a parting; O.F. *voie*; L. *via*: a journey]

fozie (fosen) (adj) soft and sapless; spongy; porous. [O.Sc. *fozie*, Du. *voos*: spongy; porous]

föl (n) a fool; (adj) foolish. [Sc. *fule*]

Försday (n) Thursday. [O.Sc. *Fuirsday*, O.N. *Thōrsdagr*: Thor's day]

föshin (n) power; vigour; fortitude; hence **föshinless** (see below). [O.Sc. *fushion, foison*: strength; vitality]

föshinless (adj) weak; feeble; tasteless; (see **föshin**). [Sc. *foisonless, fushionless*: weak; feeble]

föti (fosti) (adj) mouldy. [L.Sc. *fustie*, O.F. *fust*: cask – of wine smelling of the cask]

fracht (n) a load; consignment of freight; a burden. [O.Sc. *fraucht*: a load; freight – esp. a ship's cargo; M.Ger. *vracht*: carriage by sea]

frad (n) a fart; (v) to break wind; to fart. [O.N. *fretr*, (v) *frata*]

frae (prep) from (also **fae**). *Yun gimmer is no frae wir flock.* [O.Sc. *frae, fae*: from; O.N. *frá*]

fram (adv) out to sea. ('*De faider is comin awa fae fram*' – *Minnie o Shirva's Cradle Sang*); (adj) far off; further out (to sea). [O.N. *fram*: forwards; seawards]

freend (n) a blood relative; a kinsman. *Lowrie's a far-oot freend o wirs*; (also see **sib**). [Sc. *friend*, with same meaning, contrary to E. *friend* which is specifically someone *not* related; O.N. *frændi*: blood-relative]

freksit (frumset) (adj) peevish; fretful. [the word appears to have become confused with **fræk**: a feeble, delicate person; or is ironical opp. use of O.N. *frakk*: clever; active; brave; also cf. N. *frynsa*: to turn up one's nose; to sulk]

fremd (n) stranger; outsider. *I kenna wha dey ir, der aa fremd*; also used with the def. art. **de fremd** (strangers); (adj) unfamiliar; strange. [N. *framand*; Sw. *främmande*; D. *fremmed*]

frimse (n) a display of peevishness; a flounce; (see **dort**, **frums**). [orig. obs., cf. E. *frumps*: sulks]

froch *frohh* (adj) brittle; soft, as rotten wood. [O.Sc. *freuch*: frail; brittle]

froad (frod) (n) foam. [N. *froda* (v): to froth; foam]

frugal (adj) open-handed; generous; ample, e.g. in being liberal with hospitality. *He's aye frugal wi the bottle, dir's no half-measure wi him.* [opposite meaning of E. *frugal*: economical]

frumset (adj) peevish; fretful; moody; offended without cause. [N. *frynsa*: to turn up one's nose; to sulk]

frush (fross) (n) abundance, as of heavily bearded. [N. *fruns*: tassel; bristling tufts of hair]; (v) to spit and splutter, as one in a rage; to spurt. [O.N. *frýsa*: to snort; splutter; gush; N. *frøsa*: to splutter; emit froth]

fry (n) a small quantity of fish (or other food), sufficient for a meal. *A'm been tae de craigs an gotten a fry.* [Sc. *fry*, in same meaning, esp. when presented as a gift]

fun (v) (pp of) **fin** (find); (pr t) **fin** (find); (pt) **fan** (found); (pp) **fun** (found). [E. *found*]

fun(s) (n) entertainment; jollity; a jest. *Can du no tak a fun?* [cf. E. *make fun of*; *in fun* – as a joke]

furr (n) a furrow; (v) to make a furrow. [O.Sc. *for(re)*, O.E. *furh*: a furrow]

furt (adv) out-of-doors. [E. *forth*: in the open]

fyaana (fjana) (n) a small act of celebration, in the sense of a bit of devilment. [O.N. *fjandinn*: the devil]

fyaarm (fjarm) (v) to gratify; flatter; to butter up. [N. *fjarma*: to talk softly; to seem gentle and kind; to fawn]

fyach (feech, feich, fych) (interj) an expression of disgust, esp. associated with a foul smell. *Dunna touch yun, hit's fychie*; (also see **teesh**). [L.Sc. *feech*]

fyunk (funk) (n) thick smoke; the stench associated with smoke. [Sc. & E. *funk*: a strong unpleasant smell, usually associated with smoke]

G

gaa (ga) (n) 1) gall; bile. [E. *gall*]; 2) a luminous circle or halo caused by the sun's rays being reflected off ice crystals in the atmosphere – a parhelion – regarded as an omen of impending bad weather. [D.dial. *gall(e)*: gall; fragment of a rainbow; cf. E. *gall*: a sore or swelling]

gaa-bursen (adj) breathless with extreme effort (lit. 'gall bursting').

gaa-girse (n) stonewort (*Chara vulgaris*), so named because the plant was boiled and given to cattle as a cure for liver diseases.

gaan (gawn) (v) to gape; gaze open mouthed. [O.N. *gana*: to gaze; stare; S.dial. *gana*: to stand gaping]

gaase (v) to force; cause; compel. [var. on E. *cause*]

gaat (galti) (n) a castrated boar. [O.Sc. *gaut, galt*: a boar or hog; O.N. *galti*: a hog]

gab (gabb) (n) the mouth; however, the expression *hadd dee gab* hopes for a closed mouth with the accompanying cessation of chatter; (also see **gob**). [orig. N. & Sw.dial. *gapa*: to chatter; cf. Sc. *gab*: mouth; M.E. *gabben*]

gabbleation (n) noisy speech. *Hear's du de gabbleation a dat crood a fokk.* [imit. of E. *gabble*]

gabbord (n) the board in a boat adjacent to the keel. [E. *gar-board*: plank next to ship's keel; obs. Du. *gaarboard*]

gabs (n) stormy weather round the beginning of May – *de gabs a May* (see **Beltane rees**). [Sc. *gab*: mouth, opening = fig. *opening*]

gadder (v) to gather. [M.E. *gader(e)*, O.E. *gaderian*: to assemble or bring together a number of people in one place; O.Sc. *gader, gadder*]

gadderie (n) a gathering of people; an assembly. [see above]

gadge (gyaad) (interj) an exclamation of disgust; yuk!

gae (v) (pt of) give. *I gae it till him dastreen.* Can also be present tense. *A'm gyaan ta gae ta Lerwick efter denner.*

gaed by (v) collapsed; died. *Shö nearly gaed by hersel gaffin.*

gaep (gep) (n) gossip. [O.N. *gap*: tattle; gossip]

gaepshot (gebshot) (adj) having the lower jaw protruding beyond the upper jaw. [Orig. obs. cf. O.S. *gape, gaip*: the act of gaping]

gaeslin (geslin) (n) gosling. [O.N. *gæslingr*: a gosling]

gaet (n) a footpath; a way; a journey. *He wis gyaan de sam gaet so we göd tegeddir.* [O.N. *gata*: a road; a path; Sc. *gate, gait*]

gaevil (gavel) (n) gable. [Sc. *gable, gavel*: triangular section of exterior wall of house between top of side-walls and roof slope; O.N. *gafl*]

gaevalos (gevlos) (adj) having weak or clumsy movements; powerless. [O.Sc. *gaive, gaivel*: to move about in a clumsy fashion; poss. N. *geifla*: to speak indistinctly]

gaff (gaaf) (n) orig. loud laughter; a guffaw; now laughter in general; (v) to laugh. *Dey wir gaafin an haein a fun.* [O.Sc. *gawf, gaff*: a loud laugh]

gag (gagl) (n) mire; mud; porridge-like mass. [O.N. *gogli*: mire; mud; L.Sc. *gag*]

gaggit (adj) irritated; annoyed. [E. *gagged*: in sense of choked back]

galder (n) a loud, penetrating voice; a boisterous laugh. [O.N. *galdra*: to bawl; cry]

galdery (n) a large, open building. [prev. assoc. with O.N. *galandi* (howling wind) with the meaning of an empty building through which the wind blows, but now principally from E. *gallery*]

galley (n) replica Viking longship built and burned each year at **Up-Helly-A'** festival.

gammy (adj) lame; injured. *I'm gotten a gammy leeg.* (Yell) [E. *game*: injured; crippled]

gandigooster (gandigo) (n) a noisy dispute; blustering talk; loud complaint; strong squall of wind and rain. [N. *gau(d)*: a barking; bawling + O.N. *gustr*: a gust; a blast]

ganfer (n) the apparition of a living person, considered to be an omen of their impending death. [Sw. *genfärd*, D. *genfærd*: a ghost]

ganselled (adj) exceedingly fed-up. [O.Sc. *gansel*: a sour, ill-natured person]

gansey (n) a jersey. [O.Sc. & E.dial. *gansey* (orig. *garnsey*): a woollen jersey, esp. one worn by fishermen; originally a garment of the sort from the island of Guernsey]

gant (v) to yawn. [O.Sc. *gant, gaunt*: yawn; gape, cf. **gaan**]

garron (n) a large, square-headed nail. [O.Sc. *garron*: a length of squared timber; large nails or spikes such as used to fix a cart-garron to the axle; hence *garron-nails*]

garl (garel) (v) to dredge; to stir or gather together. *I'll laekly hae t garl up some maet for wir denner.* [of *vatsgar*: a watery mixture of oatmeal; O.N. *vatr*: water + *gar*: mire; mud]

gauvenliss (gavlet, gevlet) (adj) powerless; limp in one's movements; feeble-handed; mumbling indistinctly; clumsy; slack. [N. *gievla*: to speak indistinctly]

gavern ga-*vern* (v) to control; manage (esp. N. Yell). [E. *govern*: direct; control]

geddek (giddek) (n) lesser sandeel (*Ammodytes tobianus*); greater sandeel (*Hyperoplus lanceolatus*) also known as **saandi eel**; any of several eel-like fish that bury themselves in wet sand at ebb-tide. [L.Sc. *geddeck* – of *ged*: a pike; O.N. *gedda*]

geel (gil) (n) an eddy or ripple on water. [O.Sc. *geel, gill*; orig. O.N. *gil*: fermenting beer; now a tidal eddy round a sunken rock or similar. (Jak. 'greenish, bluish foam') presumably in the appearance of fermentation wort]

geng (gang) (n) a passage or thoroughfare; a row of stitches in knitting; (v) to go; to walk; (pt) **göd**; (pp) **gien**; (pr p) **gyaan**; to fit, as clothes. *Yun'll niver geng owre dee head.* Also used in a number of phrases: **geng aboot** change course, as a boat; **geng dee ain gaet** go your own way; please yourself; **geng dee wis** go your ways; **gyaan aboot** on the go, as an epidemic. [O.N. *ganga*: to go; to walk; inter alia, to flow; stream; Sc. & O.E. *gang* but modern English now only in the form of *gangway, gangplank*]

G

genner (n) a gander. [L.Sc. *ganner*]

geo (n) a cleft in a rock, esp. on a rocky coast; a ravine into which sea-water flows; (also **gyo, gjo**). [O.N. *gjá*: a cleft in the landscape]

gertan (n) a garter. [O.Sc. *gartan*]

gey (adv) great; considerable. [O.Sc. *gey*: (of quantity) considerable; good-sized]

gie (n) elasticity; stretch; (v) to give; (pt) **gied, gae**; (pp) **gien**. [O.Sc. *gie*: give]

gien at constant persistence (lit. 'gone at'). [Sc.]

gien in shrunk (lit. 'gone in'), as reduced in size. [Sc.]

gimmer (n) a yearling ewe. [O.N. *gymbr*; Sw. *gimmer*]

gird (girdeen) (n) a barrel hoop; a child's play hoop; a girth; a rope to gird or bind something; (v) to put hoops on a cask. [O.N. *gyrda*: a girth; hoop of a cask]

girn (n) a snarl; a complaint; (v) to complain in a peevish manner; to screw up one's face in a grimace. [O.Sc. *girn*, *gyrn*: to show the teeth in rage; to snarl; E. *grin*]

girnal (n) a large chest for storing grain. [O.Sc. *garnale*, *garnell*: a large chest or space for storing grain; E. *garner*]

girny (girnie) (adj) childishly cross or fretful. [see **girn**]

girse (n) grass. [O.Sc. *girse*; E. *grass*]

girsy (girsie) (adj) grassy. [as above]

gizzen (gisen) (v) to dry up; to become leaky due to shrinking, as in a wooden boat. [N. & Fær. *gisna*, D. *gistne*: to become leaky by shrinking]

glaar (n) a mess; mud. [O.Sc. *glaur*: mire – orig. unknown]

glaep (n) a glutton; one who swallows greedily; (v) to gulp; to swallow greedily. [N. *glop*: in the sense of a glutton]

glafterit (adj) frolicsome; boisterously jolly. [Sw.dial. *glaffs*: a person behaving unseemly; N. *glaffsa*: to be frolicsome and impetuous]

glaiket (adj) half-witted; irresponsible. [N. *glaffsa* (see above) with additional meaning – to gape]

glans (glansin) (v, adj) twinkle; sparkle. [N. *glansa*: to shine; glitter]

glant (n) jollification. [N. *glant*: jest; mirth; frolicsome pleasantry]

glebe (n) land assigned to a parish minister in addition to his stipend. [Sc. *glebe*]

gleer (glir) (n) sunshine through clouds or haze. [N. *glir*: a blinking; gleaming; Sw.dial. *glira*: a ray of light; a sunbeam (between clouds)]

gleers (n) merriment. [cf. E. *glee*]

gleg (adj) perceptive; mentally alert. [O.Sc. *gleg*: quick in movement or perception; O.N. *gleggr*: clear-sighted; clever; clear; distinct]

glegness (n) perceptiveness; cleverness. [see **gleg**]

glerl (n) a sheet of ice. [O.N. *gler*: glass]

glerlit (gleret) (adj) glazed; wall-eyed. [see above]

gligg (n) pop-hole in a henhouse; a hole in a wall or byre for admitting air and light. [O.N. *glyggr*: a gap; a window bay]

glim (n) a gleam; a faint streak of light. [N. *glima*, Sw. *glimma*: to glimmer; to light; to flash; to twinkle; E. *gleam*]

glinder (glir) (v) to peer with half-closed eyes. [N. *glire*: to blink; to peer; Sw.dial. *glira*: to blink]

glink (v) to glint. [O.Sc. *glink*: to shine; to gleam; variation of *glint*]

glisk (n, v) a glimpse. [N.dial. *glisa*: to gleam; flash; glisten; *glis*: gleam of light]

gliv (n) glove. [L.Sc. *gluive*; O.Sc. *gluve*, *gloove*]

gloor (glur) (n) a glimmer; insufficient light. [variation on **gleer**, N. & Sw.dial. *glora*, Icel. *glóra*: to gleam; glitter; stare; gaze]

gloup (n) sea cave or cavern, the top of which has fallen in at the landward end. [N. *glup*: glop; chasm; gulf; hollow or deep mountain fissure]

glowerit (adj) excessively bright, as of a dress; lurid, as a fiery sunset. [N. *glorete*: flashy; gaudy; O.Sc. *gloweret*: (of the sky) lurid]

gloy (n) undamaged, clean, straight straw used for making **kishies** or in thatching; also used for making guizers hats in 19th and early 20th cent. [O.Sc. *gloy*: clean, unbroken straw carefully selected for making baskets; M.E. *gloy*, O.F. *glui*: straw]

glöd (gloder) (n) a glow of heat or light. *Shö wis glödin wi excitement* (figuratively). [O.N. *glitr*: to glitter; shine; cf. O.N. *glód*: red-hot embers]

gluff (n) a fright; a scare; (v) to frighten. *Dunna gluff de bairn*. [O.Sc. *gluff*: a sudden fright; a scare; cf. N.dial. *glufs*: a gust of wind, in the sense of being unexpected]

glumse (n) an abrupt, ill-mannered reply; (v) to reply abruptly. [N. *glufsa*, *glupsa*: to snap with one's mouth; to yelp]

glunsh (glons) (v) to wolfishly swallow food. [N. *kluns*, D.dial. *kluns*: a large knot; a lump – hence Shet. *glons*: to swallow (in large lumps)]

gly (v) to squint; to look sideways. *Lik a gös glyin at thunder*. [O.Sc. *gley*: to squint; to cast a sidelong glance; M.E. *glēzen*: to squint]

glyed (adj) squint-eyed; sometimes **gly-eyed**. [see above]

gob (n) a mouth, esp. a large or ugly one. [O.Sc. *gob*: a mouth; a beak]

gob-smacked (v) to be taken aback; amazed; lost for words. [as above]

gock (n) a simpleton; a fool; (v) to gape; to drift around aimlessly. [O.N. *gaukr*: a cuckoo; also a fool]

gogar (goger) (n) anything large of its kind. [O.Sc. & O.E. *gogar*: originally a large fishing hook, needle or knitting needle, extended to mean anything large of its kind; Icel. *goggr*: an iron hook used by fishermen]

gogie (n) a louse (also see **gunnie**). [O.Sc. *gunni, gonni*: a bogie; a bugbear; humorously applied to a louse; Sw.dial. *gonnar*: elves; goblins]

gointek (gongtag, gongtak) (n) the strap or rope by which a girth is fastened to a pony's pack-saddle. [O.N. *gangtak*: a strap which fits into the opposite side of the girth, in order to fasten it]

gomeril (n) a fool. [O.Sc. *gomerel*: a fool; a stupid person; *goam*: gaze about vacantly]

goom (n) gum. [O.Sc. *goom*, O.N. *gómr*: the gums; palate]

goosel (gosel, gosen) (n) a variable, gusty wind. [interconnected words variously relating to sharp, contrary wind or drying wind include – Fær. *gos*: current of air; draught; O.N. *gjósa*: to gush; stream; N. *gusa*: to blow gently]

gooster (gouster, guster) (n) a sudden, strong gust of wind (also see **gandigooster**). [O.N. *gustr*: a gust; a blast]

gord (n) a wall; dyke; an enclosure; used in placenames, e.g. Kergord [O.N. *gardr* – now obsolete as an independent word but preserved in composite usages]

gori (interj) *My gori!* – a mild form of oath. [E. *glory*]

gorstie (gordsta) (n) a ridge of untended ground (the remains of an old dyke) left uncultivated as demarcation between two plots of arable land (also see **strodie**). [O.N. *gardstadr*: a place in which there is or has been a fence; Sw.dial. *gärdsel-sto*: traces of an old fence; O.Sc. *gersty*]

gorstie-girse (n) grass growing on a ridge, as described above.

gotna got none; did not get. [Sc.]

gotten got. *Wir gotten a new telly. Is du gotten a cowld?* [archaic Sc., O.E., U.S. *gotten* (re-appearing in E. grammer, esp. Aust.)]

gowan (n) marsh ragwort (*Senecio aquaticus*), though probably given to many other species of yellow wild flowers as elsewhere in Scotland. A simile to denoting yellowness. [O.Sc. *gowan*: a daisy]

gowl (gjol) (n) a cry or howl; (v) to weep; to howl. *Whin he gied me a row I begöd t gowl.* [O.N. *gaul*: howling]

gowster (gouster, guster) (v) to speak in a domineering or threatening manner. [O.N. *gusta*: to blow; N. *gausta*: to speak loudly in a threatening or scolding manner]

gowsterit (adj) domineering and blustering. [see above]

göd (pt of) go; (p) **go**; (pp) **geen**. [O.Sc. *gaed*: went]

gödably (adj) barely; almost; easily; without hindrance. [O.Sc. *guidably*: good + ably, as in probably]

göd claes (n) best clothes. [O.Sc. *guid-claes*: (good) best clothes]

gödless (adv) used to reinforce an adj. *His language wis gödless coorse.* [*God-less*, in the sense of base, morally lacking]

göd man (de) (n) God (euphemism – lit. 'the good man').

göd place (de) (n) heaven (euphemism – lit. 'the good place').

göd's mak (n) God's creation.

gölbröl (göl) (n) a very loud bellow or roar; (v) to bellow or roar loudly. [O.N. *gaula*: to howl]

gölgriv (golgrav, golgref) (n) an open drain used to carry manure from a byre to a midden; liquid manure, as found in this drain. [poss. N. *gul*, O.N. *gulr-*: yellow + O.N. *graf*: ditch; trench]

gös (n) a goose. [Sc. *guse* (of E. *goose*)]

göt (n) threshold. [O.Sc. *gat(e)*]

gözren (n) the gizzard. [Fær. *kjós*: the gizzard; E.dial. *gizzern*]

graav (gref) (n) muddy ooze on the sea bed; the sea bed itself. [O.N. *graf*: a pit; N. *grov* (also of a peat-pit, *torvgrov*) (see **greff**)]

graim (grem) (v) to gripe; complain. [N. & Fær. *gremja*: to grieve; complain]

grain (n) a small quantity; a morsel; a little bit. [E. *grain*: one seed; the smallest unit of weight and therefore a minute amount]

gravit (graavit) (n) a scarf or muffler. [E. *cravat*, F. *cravate* (Croatian *hŕvāt*) from the scarf worn by Croatian mercenaries in France during the Thirty Years War]

gree (n) grease, esp. the fat removed from the boiling of fish or fish livers. [O.Sc. *gree*: grease, with *grese* being the plural]

greek (n) dawn. [O.Sc. *greiking*: daybreak; first glimmer of light]

greemik (grimek) (n) a rope halter. [N. & Fær. *gríma*: a halter]

greemit (grimet) (adj) said of cattle having a white face with dark stripes or spots; of humans, having a greyish or dirty face. [Fær. *grimutur*, N. *grimutt*: dirty or having dark stripes in the face]

greenbowe (n) a scouring condition caused by moving sheep to green pasture direct from the heathery hill. [prob. *green-bowel*]

green paek (n) first shoot of grass in spring. [*green-pick*]

greest (grist) (n) a spell; the deprivation of will by means of hypnotism. [N. *grust*: harsh authority; fear caused by domineering; N. *grusa*: to force one's way]

greet (grot) (v) to cry; (pr t) **greet**; (pt) **gret**; (pp) **grutten**. [O.N. *gráta*: to weep; Sc. *greet*]

greetie-gowlie (grotsi-gjolie) (n) derogatory term given to a child who is always crying; a 'cry-baby'. [O.N. *gráta*: to weep + *gaula*: to howl]

greety (greetie, grotsi) (adj) prone to crying. *Shö aye wis a greety bairn.* [O.N. *grátr*: a weeping; N. *graassen*: inclined to weep]

greff (n) the bottom of a peat-bank. [O.N. *graf*: a pit; N. *grov* (also of a peat-pit, *torvgrov*)]

greht *gret* (adj) Shetland variant on E. *great*.

grein (v) to yearn, particularly for food. [O.Sc. *grene*, *grein*: to desire earnestly; to yearn; O.N. *girna*]

gremster (grefster, grimster) (n) an exceptionally low ebb-tide. [O.N. *greftr*, *greptr*: a digging up; a burial; Fær. *grefstur*: a digging; deep waves hollowing down in a strong gale as if rooting up the sea]

greth (n) urine. [O.Sc. *graith*: stale urine, formerly used for washing clothes, esp. blankets and in dyeing]

grethy-cloots (n) baby's napkins. [(see above) *graith* + *cloots*: cloths]

grethy-pot (n) chamber pot (also **pish pot**). [once used esp. to collect urine for washing clothes when it was called a **greth-kettle**]

grey gös (n) greylag goose (*Anser anser*).

grice (gris) (n) a pig. [O.N. *griss*: a pig]

grice ingan (n) vernal squill (*Scilla verna*). [O.N. *griss*: a pig + O.Sc. *ingan*: onion]

grice mites (n) very small potatoes suitable only for pig food (see **grice**).

grice mooreks (n) (disparagingly) of very small potaotoes. [O.N. *griss*: a pig + *mura*: silverweed – which has an edible root bulb]

grind *grin-d* (short *i*) (n) a gate. [O.N. *grind*: a barred gate; a frame (filled in with lattice-work); lattice door; wicket fence]

grinndin *grin-din* (n) the purring of a cat. *Hear du yun peerie cat grindin efter takkin her mylk.* [imitative of grinning and grinding]

grit (adj) great; large; bulky. [E. *great*]

groff (adj) gruff; rough textured; harsh and raucous, as a strident voice. [O.N. *grófr*: coarse; large]

groff-siv (n) a large-holed sieve. [O.N. *grófr*: coarse; large + E. *sieve*]

groint (gront) (n) a grunt; (v) to grunt. [N. *grumta*, *grymta*: to grunt]

grop (n) drizzle, though originally said of rain falling in big, heavy drops, and still used in this sense in parts of Shetland. [N. *grop*: granular mass; coarse grain]

grottie-buckie (n) European cowrie (*Trivia monacha*). [L.Sc. *groatie buckie*: originally *John o' Groats buckie* due to John o' Groats being a place where the shells (buckies) were found in abundance]

grovel (gravel, grøfel) (v) to grope around in the dark. [O.N. *grufla*: to grovel]

gröflins (adv) prostrate; on hands and knees. [O.N. *falla á grúfu*: to fall face downwards]

gröt (n) sediment of oil from fish-livers; by association any thick, liquid mess. [Icel. *grútr*]

grötti-barrel (n) a barrel for holding fish-liver oil. [see above]

gruel (n) porridge; any messy mixture. [Sc. *gruel*: thin porridge – from O.F. *gruel*: groats]

gruel-tree (n) wooden stick for stirring porridge (see **gruel**).

grulik (grølek, gruli) (n) a guizer; a masked person; one in fancy dress and disguise esp. at Halloween. [Fær. *grýla*: a masked person]

grumlie (adj) said of muddy water, full of sediment. [Sw.dial. *grum*: sediment; dregs]

grummel (grumset) (v) to cause water to become muddy; (adj) of turbid or muddy water. [deriv. of *grum* (see above)]

grund (n) ground; soil. [O.N. *grund*]

grunds (n) sediment; dregs; tea-leaves or coffee-grounds. [E. *grounds* (pl): remains of coffee beans after brewing]

gub (n) froth; spume; lather; (v) to lather. [form of *gob*: spittle]

guddick (godek) (n) a riddle; phrase; (v) *To lay up guddicks* – to ask a series of riddles. [O.N. *gáta*: a riddle]

gue (gu, gju) (n) a two-stringed fiddle, a Norwegian musical instrument once played in Shetland. [O.N. *gigja*: a fiddle; a stringed instrument]

guff (guf) (n) a strong smell of something, usually unpleasant; puff or whiff of smoke or wind; (v) to puff, as smoke. [Fær. & Sw.dial. *guva*, N. *gova*: to steam; smoke; fume; blow]

gufset (adj) noisy and rough in behaviour; incapable; blundering; oafish. [N. *gofs*: an impetuous, violent person; cf. Sc. *goff*: a fool – fr. *goffe*: dull-witted; lumpish; coarse]

guggle (gogl) (v) to foul; soil; make a mess of. [O.N. *gogli*: mire; mud]

guideship (n) usage; handling; treatment. [O.Sc. *guide*, *gyde*: to control; to manage; *guideship*: management]

guize (v) to attend a **foy**, festival or party in disguise; to act as a guizer. [O.F. *guise*]

guizer (n) an individual or member of a troupe disguised in costume and taking part in a festival such as **Up-Helly-A'**, **Hallowe'en**, Christmas or **Hogmanay**. [O.Sc. *gyse*, O.F. *déguiser*: to disguise oneself]

guizer jarl (n) the designated Viking chieftain or Earl at **Up-Helly-A'** festival; the leader of the principal group of guizers at that event. [O.N. *jarl*: earl]

gulbröl (v) bellow (see **gölbröl**).

gulder (golder) (v) to speak angrily. [N. *golder*: a strong gust of wind; a hard (really noisy) blast]

gulmoget (golmoget) (adj) having a dark body with a light breast or belly, as a cow. [O.N. *gulr*: yellow + *mogóttr*: of a certain colour on the belly]

gulsa (n) jaundice. [O.N. *gulusótt*: jaundice]

gulsa girse (n) marsh trefoil or bogbean (*Menyanthes trifoliata*). When infused the liquid was given to cattle as a cure for jaundice. [O.N. *gulusótt*: jaundice + O.Sc. *girse*; E. *grass*]

gundy (n) home-made toffee consisting of sugar, butter and treacle or syrup and flavouring. [Sc. *gundy*: prob. candy]

gunnie (n) a louse (also see **gogie**). [O.Sc. *gunni*, *gonni*: a bogie; a bugbear; humorously applied to a louse]

gurblottit (adj) badly washed, as clothes. [N. *gor*: dirt; mud + *bløte*: to soak; steep; O.Sc. *gurblot*: to wash badly so that the dirt is only partially removed, cf. M.E. *blot*: stain; also O.Sc. *goor*, *gurr*: slimy dirt or filth of any kind]

gurl (v) to work amongst filth, e.g. liquid manure or fish offal. [O.N. *gor* (n): mire; mud]

gurm (gorm) (v) to be employed in dirty work. [N. *gurma*: to make muddy; stir up; Sw.dial. *gorma*: to stir up dirt; to do work badly]

gurmullit (adj) having a face (path, floor, etc.) covered in a layer of dirt. [N. *gor*: dirt; mud + Fær. *mullittur*: having a snout or muzzle of a different colour]

gurr (n) rheum gathered in the corners of the eyes. [O.Sc. *goor*: slime; mucus; waxy matter]

gutriv (n) the anus of a fish. [Icel. *gotrauf* – from *got*: spawn + *rauf*: slit]

gutter (n) mud; any muddy mess. *Dunna gutter up de flör.* [Sc]

gyaad (interj) an expression of disgust. *Gyaad, yun pheesic is nasty.* [deriv. of E. *gad*: a mild oath]

gyill (n) a ravine; a narrowing in the head of a valley; a steep-sided hollow. [Sc. *gill*, *ghyll*: a small ravine; a brook]

gyo (gjo) (n) a steep-sided cleft or creek esp. one on a rocky shore; a deep ravine into which seawater flows; (also **geo**). [O.N. *gjá*: a cleft in the landscape]

gyola (n) thin or watery buttermilk (also **druttel**). [N. *kjore*: curdled milk]

gyoppm (gjomek) (n) an amount of anything which can be gathered up in both hands (also **gyoppmfoo**). [cf. Fær. *keymur* (from orig. *kaumr*) and *kjómur*: both hands held cupped together]

gyurd (gjord) (n) a gift. [O.N. *gjord*: (doing; carrying out) in the sense of duty; contribution]

H

haa (n) a laird's house or substantial dwelling that at one time was a laird's house. [Sc. *ha*: the main dwelling of a farm; E. *hall*: manor-house]

haaf (haf) (n) the deep sea outside of coastal waters; deep-sea fishing as operated during 18th and 19th century and carried out 30-40 miles offshore in open boats (**sixerns**). Note: while the common spelling of this word is *haaf*, the pronunciation follows the Norse (*short a*) *haf*. [O.N. *haf*: the open sea]

haaf fish (n) grey seal (*Halichoerus grypus*) – associated with the **haaf** (also **sylkie**). [see above]

haaf-man (n) a fisherman engaged in deep-sea fishing. [see above]

haagless (haglos) (adj) remorseless; boundless; excessive; illimitable. [O.N. *haga*: to manage; arrange]

haandigrips (n) physical blows; close grappling. [O.N. *handgrip*: wrestling with the hand]

haandless (adj) clumsy with hands, though originally without hands. [O.N. *handalauss*: wanting both hands or arms]

haands turn (n) a stroke of work.

hackit (n) (of the skin) chapped; (v) to chop. [N. *hakk*: a mark left by hacking]

hadd 1) (v) hold; (pt) **höld/held**; (pp) **hadden**; continue in same direction. *Hadd on till du sees d haa dan geng rycht*; to observe a celebration. *We aye hadd a foy at Johnsmas*; wait, stop. *Hadd dee a peerie while an he'll be hame*; (n) hold. *Hadd yun gimmer till I vass it.* Phrases: **hadd aff** keep off; **hadd at** continue; **hadd awa** keep away, esp. in instruction to a working dog. *Hadd awa oot owre!*; **hadd for** make for; **hadd in** to keep close to. *Hadd in aside me*; **hadd oot** persist; **hadd oot a langer** to entertain. *Wir blyde ta dee comin alang ta hadd wiz oot a langer*; **hadd dee wheesht!** keep quiet; **hadd sae** (v) pause a moment. *Hadd sae till de idders catch up*; **hadd up** remain fine, as in weather. 2) (n) an animal's lair. *Der a otter's hadd up yonder*; a **trow's** den. [1] O.N. *hald*: hold; grip; 2) L.Sc. *hald, hauld*: a place of stay; a dwelling; refuge]

haddibaand (n) the cross-beam under a thwart which secures the frames of a boat (also **fastibaand**). [O.N. *hald + band*: a plank across the bottom of a boat; ribs of a boat]

hae (v) have; (pt) **hed**. [Sc. *hae*]

haet (n) heat; (v) to make hot; (pt) **haetit**. [E. *heat*]

haethenous (adj) cruel; severe. *Dir a haethenous feerie gyaan aboot eenoo* (There's a severe sickness going about just now). [of E. *heathenish*]

hag (n) moderation; limit; state; management. *Dir nae hag wi wir Magnie* (There is no moderation, limit…); *Du's made a poor hag o yun* (You have made a poor job of it); (also **hog**). [O.N. *hagr*: state of things; management; moderation; N. *hag*]

hagmark (n) a boundary stone or mark between two hill pastures. [O.N. *hagi*: pasture + *mark*: a boundary mark; Fær. *hagamark*: boundary-mark in the hill]

hail (n) a catch of fish. *A göd hail*; (v) haul; to haul in fishing lines. [O.Sc. *hale, haill*: to draw or pull; to drag or haul]

hailin kabe (n) the thowel-pin over which a fishing line is hauled (see **kabe**). [*hail* (see above) + O.N. *keipr*: a rowlock]

haily-puckle (n) hail-stone (see **puckle**). [O.Sc. *hailpuckle*: a hailstone; O.Sc. *pickle, puckle*: a grain of seed; a small amount]

hain (v) to use economically; to be thrifty; (of rain) to ease off. [O.S. *hain*: to fence in; to save; from O.N. *hegna*: to hedge; protect]

hair-riven (n) a fight, esp. one involving hair-pulling. *Dir been naethin bit hell an hair-riven*; (lit. 'hair-tearing'). [O.N. *riv* (v): to rive; tear; pull]

hairse (adj) hoarse. [O.Sc. *hairse*: hoarse]

hairy-möldit (hairy-nildet) (adj) covered with hairy green mould. [O.N. *-mygla*: mould; fungus growth]

hairst (n) the harvest; autumn; work associated with that season. [O.Sc. *harvist* – from 1456, *hairst, hayrst*]

hairst-blinks (n) summer lightning. [Ork. & Sh. only]

hairst-rig (n) any section of a field where harvesting is taking place. [harvest + O.N. *hyrggr*: a ridge]

hairst mön (n) harvest moon.

hakk (n) a hack; mark or scar. [N. & Sw. *hak*: a notch; N. *hakk*: a mark left by hacking]

hale (n) the complete amount. *He bowt de hale consignment*; (adj) whole; in good health – 'hale and hearty'; undamaged. [O.N. *heill*: whole; sound in body; in good health; Sc. *hale*]

hale-an-hadden (see **hell-an-hadden**)

half-gaets (adv) halfway. [*half* + O.N. *gata*: a road; a path]

half-oot-afore (n) a sheep earmark in which a piece is cut out of the front side of the ear ('*half out before*').

half-oot-ahint (n) a sheep earmark in which a piece is cut out of the back part of the ear. ('*half out behind*')

halliget (halltott) (adj) behaving preposterously; wild and unrestrained behaviour. [metaphorical of O.N. *hallr*: sloping; cf. Fær. *høllur*: unevenness; a lump in worsted yarn]

hallo (n) a bundle of straw; a feed-lot for cattle. [N. *halge*: a bundle of eight sheaves of straw; *holge*: wisp of hay; great bundle of straw]

Hallomas (n) 1st November. One of the old Scottish 'quarter-days' days on which rents and stipends were paid – Hallomas (1st Nov); Candlemas (2nd Feb); Beltane (1st May) and Lammas (1st Aug). [E. *Hallomas*: the feast of All Saint's Day (All Hallows)]

halvers (n) a half share. *I'll geng halvers wi dee*; (adj) applied to stock held co-jointly. [Sc. *halvers* (interj): used in claiming half a find]

hamar (n) a rocky hill – specifically a steep projection of rock in a hillside. [O.N. *hamarr*: stone; a steep rock; rocky wall]

hame (n) home; (adv) at home. [Sc. *hame*]

hame-aboot (adj) homely; within the family circle; spoken of things belonging to or produced at home. *Hame-aboot eggs*, as opposed to shop-eggs. [Sc.]

hamefarin (hamefir) (n) home-coming celebration; festival held at irregular intervals (1960, 1985, 2000, 2010) to welcome home expatriate Shetlanders from throughout the world; any party held to celebrate a Shetlander's home-coming, esp. a bridal couple. [*hamefarin* is a coined expression first used in 1960; the older word *hamefir* may arise out of O.N. *heimfred*: 'home-peace']

hame-trowe (hame-trod) (adv) towards home. *We'll better mak hame-trowe afore de mirknin.* [*home* + *trowe* (*trod*) from O.N. *troō*: a tread; footsteps]

hank (n) 1) the section of a boat where the side plank turns towards the stem or stern; commonly in plural, *eft hanks*, *fore hanks*. [N. *hanka*: to fasten together]; 2) a skein of yarn, approximately 300 yards in length, also known as a *cut*. [E. *hank*: a coil or loop of yarn, rope, etc. (Note: when referred to as a unit of measurement for worsted yarn, E. is 560yds compared to the Shetland measure of 300yds); N. *honk*, *nystehonk*]

hansel (handsel) (n) a gift to commemorate a new event or inaugural occasion, i.e. the launching of a boat, birth of a child, a new home or enterprise – coupled with the idea of conferring luck by doing so; (v) to give such a present. [Sc. *handsel*; O.N. *handsal*: transference of a right, bargain, duty to another by joining hands]

hansper (ansperr) (n) muscle pain brought on by excessive walking (also **creeks**, **spaigie**). [Fær. *andsperri*]

hantle (n) a considerable amount. [orig. obs. cf. O.Sc. *hantle*, *hantill*, poss. orig. *hand* + *tale*: what one could count on one's fingers]

hanvaegin (v) putting off time; but originally sauntering about idly; (adj) doubtful; hesitant; a slight impression of something. [Jak. has **hanvag**, **hanvagin**, cf. O.N. *andvaka*: sleeplessness; *andvaki*: sleepless – the development of the word thus being somewhat obscure]

hap (n) knitted shawl; stole or wrap; (v) to wrap up, as with a shawl; to cover. [Sc. & E.dial. *hap*: a wrap; a covering]

hap-lace (n) border of a knitted shawl. [Sc.]

hap-yarn (n) yarn used for knitting a **hap**, generally standard 2-ply worsted-spun Shetland wool. [specif. Sh]

happer (v) to hinder; to obstruct; (see **apper**). [O.N. *aptra*: to pull; take or keep back; call back]

hard darknin (n) the last remnants of daylight. [archaic E. *hard by*: close to, thus 'close to dusk']

hark (v) to whisper. [Sc. *hark*: to listen; to whisper]

hark (v) to hawk; clear the throat of phlegm. *He harkit oot o his trot.* [N. *harka*: to make a rattling sound in the throat]

harl 1) (n) rough-cast; (v) to apply rough-cast (cement mixed with crushed stone) to an exterior wall. [Sc. *harl*: rough-cast];

harl 2) (v) to walk slowly or feebly. [N. *harla*: to walk with a jerking gait]

harlibens (n) a thin, skeletal person or animal (also **rinklabens**). [cf. N. *harla*: to walk with a jerking gait]

harned (adj) hardened. [O.Sc. *hardin*, *hardyn*: to become hard]

harnpan (n) skull. [O.Sc. *harnpan*, lit. 'brain-pan' (see **harns**)]

harns (n) brains. [O.Sc. *harnis*: the brains; O.N. *hjarni*: brain]

harpey (n) scallop of *Pectenidae* family. [Icel. *hqrpu (skel)*: harp shell – owing to shape/appearance]

harr (n) hinge of a door or gate; the upper of the two pieces of a wooden hinged door. [O.N. *hjarri*: a hinge; O.Sc. *herre*: hinge; note: *harrabel* was the name given to a type of hardwood imported from Norway and used for making harrow-beams and door frames]

harsk (adj) harsh; coarse; unpleasant, as rough weather. [N. *harsk*: somewhat gruff; harsh]

haslock (halslokk) (n) the wool under a sheep's neck which is the softest and finest micron wool in a fleece, once kept for hand-spinning to make **haps**. [O.N. *hals-*: neck + *lokkr*: a lock of hair; O.Sc. *haslock*, from *hause*: the neck; throat + *lock*: a tuft of hair; a wisp of wool]

hass (n) the throat; specif. the windpipe, in exp. *geen in de wrang hass*. [O.N. *hals*: neck; O.Sc. *hause*]

hassens (n) the strakes of a boat next to the garboard. [cf. O.N. *hals*: neck, in sense of the forepart of a boat next to the stem]

haste dee (v) hurry up; get a move on. [E. *hasten* + O.E. *thee*]

hatter (v) to harass; torment; treat roughly. [O.Sc. *hatter*: to batter or bruise; knockabout – imitative of 'batter'; 'clatter'; N.dial. *hatra*: to persecute]

haver (v) to talk foolish nonsense. [Sc. & N. Eng.dial. *haver*: to talk nonsense]

havr (n) oats (now commonly *aits*). [O.N. *hafre*: oats – from which the E. word haversack is derived]

he (pron, n, adj) used colloq. to refer to weather – *He's some storm. A doot we'll no weather him*; *He's a braaly coorse day*; and frequently of objects – *He's a boannie dress du haes.*

head (heid) (n) a measure of (Shetland) yarn comprising eight x 25gram hanks in both lace and jumper-weight wool. [Sc. *head*: a measure of yarn]

headicraa (heidi-) (n) a somersault; (adv) head-over-heels. [cf. poss. deriv. from N. *-krugga*: raised; humped back, in the sense of required hunched position to perform a somersault]

headlite (heid-) (adj) giddy; light-headed.

headlins (heid-) (adv) headlong. [O.Sc. *heidlingis*: headlong; precipitately; E. *headlong*, from earlier *headling*]

head-rig (heid-) (n) the section of land at the end of a field where horse (or tractor) and plough are turned during ploughing (the head-rig is subsequently ploughed crosswise when the rest of the rig is completed). [O.N. *hryggr*: a ridge – in the sense of land cultivated in ridges]

heads ta traas (heids-) (adv) 'head-to-toes' – said of two or more articles or people, laid side by side and facing in opposite directions. [orig. obs. cf. O.Sc. *tras(e)*: to inter-twine; interweave]

H

hear (v) heed; listen with a degree of disbelief or amazement – *I hear dee*; to listen to – *ta hear apon*. [Sc.]

hearin (n) a report or piece of gossip, heard with incredulity. *For sic a hearin. Is du ever heard da lik?* [Sc.]

heck (kek) (n) crutch. [O.N. *hœkja*: a crutch]

heckle (kek) (v) travel laboriously; to walk jerkily; to walk with a crutch. [see above]

hed (v) had; (pt of) **hae**. *It laekly hed ta be* – fatalistic expression. [Sc.]

hedder-kowe (n) a clump of heather. [heather + Sc. *knowe* (*knoll*): a hillock; a mound]

hedderkindunk (hederkandunk) (n) seesaw; anything bobbing up and down; nickname for eider-duck (**dunter**). [Edm. gives 'heather-cun-dunk'. This seems unlikely. The eider-duck's characteristic bobbing action suggests 'hedderkin-dunk' – *hedderkin* being the act of *heading* or *nodding* cf. O.N. *hoppa*: to jump; with the last part deriv. from N. & Sw. *dunka*, or D. *dunke*: to thump (with a muffled resound)]

hedimoo (hedemu) (n) heat mirage. [O.N. *hiti*, N. *hite*, *hete*: heat]

heeld (n) the latter part of the day, when the sun is *heeldin tae de wast*; (v) to heel over; lean; to overturn. [E. *heel*: to tilt to one side; O.E. *heildan*: to lean]

heesie (hisi) (n) an exhibit of powerful action or impetus. *Shö's gotten a heesie dis time* (She has been sent packing). [N. *heisa*: to sprout too quickly; N. & Sw. *hissa*: to hoist; D. *hisse* – with assimilation to L.Sc. *heis*: the act of lifting]

heeze (v) to heave; to hoist; to raise up. [see above – but also L.Sc. *heis* (*heeze*): the act of lifting up; a heave – cf. sailor's chant when lifting or hauling]

heezie-up (adj) lift up; hoist; a leg up. *Gie's a heezie-up.* [see above]

heft (n) a handle; a valued possession; (v) to fit with a handle. [O.N. *hepti*, Fær. *hefti*, also Sc. *heft*, E. *haft*: handle]

hegrie (hegri) (n) heron (*Ardea cinerea*). [O.N. *hegri*, N. *hegre*: a heron]

heicht (n) top. [O.Sc. *heicht*: height]

heksi (n) a witch. [D. *heks*, N. *heksa*, Ger. *hexe*: a witch]

hell-an-hadden (heel-, hale-) (pron) everything. *He's taen de hell-an-hadden* (He's taken the lot); (adj) well in body and soul. *Ir du aa hell-an-hadden?* (Are you whole (well) and continuing in that way?). [L.Sc. *hale*: whole + *hadden*: hold; holding]

hellery (n) rubbish; nonsense. *Yun's jist a lok o hellery du's spaekin*; a great many; a lot. *Dey wir a hellery o stirlins idda gairdin*. [prob. variation on O.Sc. *heller*: an obstreperous troublesome person and *hellish*: in the manner of hell]

hellick (hellek) (n) a large, flat rock, such as may serve for a landing-stage at the sea's edge. [O.N. *hella*: a flat stone or rock]

hellisom (adj) good-natured; winsome; aimable. [cf. E. *wholesome*]

helli-möld (n) burial ground (lit. 'holy earth'). [O.N. *helgr*, *helgi*: holiness; the day or time to be kept holy + *möld*: earth mould]

hellsest (adj) awful. *I hed de most hellsest teethache de streen*. [Sh. variant on E. *hellish*]

helly (helli) (n) the weekend (Saturday & Sunday) but originally 'holy-day' – the period between Saturday and Sunday evening; series of holy-days; festival. [O.N. *helgr*, *helgi*: holiness; the day or time to be kept holy; N. *helg*, esp. of the interval between Saturday evening and Sunday evening]

helsin (n) the act of welcoming. *Du'll aye git a helsin in der hoose*. [O.N. *heilsan*: a greeting; salutation; congratulation]

helyer (n) a sea-cave into which the tide flows. [O.N. *hellir*: a cave; cavern]

hems (n) a wooden, triangular device placed round a sheep's neck to prevent it going through fences (see also **byoags**). [O.Sc. *hem*: a horse collar]

hench (heench) (n) the hip; haunch. [O.Sc. *hench*, *hensh*, *hanch*, M.E. *hanche*: the haunch]

hench-ben (heench-bane) (n) hip-bone. [as above + O.Sc. *bene*, *bane*: bone]

hench-head (n) top of hip. [see above]

henk (hinkl) (v) to walk with a limp (of same derivation as **heckle**, **hek**). [N. *hinkra*: to limp; O.N. *hœkja*: a crutch; M.L.Ger. and M.Du. *hinken*: to limp; falter]

hent (v) to gather; reap; collect. [O.N. *heimta*: to fetch; bring home; N. *hemta*: to gather; pluck; pick up]

hentins (n) gleanings. [see **hent**]

hentilagets (n) tufts of wool shed from a sheep's back and gathered up by hand. By extension, bits and pieces. [*hent* (see above) + *laget*; O.N. *lagdr*: a tuft (of wool or hair); a lock]

heogue (n) a hillock. [Sc. *heuch*: a crag; ravine or steep-sided valley; O.E. *hōh*, E. *hoe*: promontory or projecting ridge]

herald (herald deuk) (n) red-breasted merganser (*Mergus serrator*). [Sc. *herald duck*; Fr. *harle huppé* (borrowed from Gr. *har*, imitative of harsh call of the bird); through folk etym. the word came to be associated with Orkney and Shetland, changing through **earl duck** to **herald deuk**]

herlane (her lane) (pron) by herself; her alone.

herra (n) an inhabited district – preserved in placenames (Yell, Tingwall). [O.N. *herad*: an inhabited part of the country; village; district]

herrin hog (n) applied to several species of whale and dolphin but commonly minke whale (*Balaenoptera acutorostrata*).

hersel (pron) herself; also used in phrase *by hersel* – out of her mind; mentally stressed. *Shö wis gien by hersel wi worry.*

hert (n) heart; stomach. [Sc. form of E. *heart* – but with additional meaning of stomach]

hert-holl (n) the centre; the heart of the matter. *De hert-holl i de nycht* (midnight to early hours). [Sc.]

hertscad (n) heartburn (also **brunt rift**, **watter traa**). [O.Sc. *hert scaud*: heart + scald]

hesp (n) a skein of yarn ready for spinning, from 400-500 threads according to their thickness. Proverb: *a reffled hesp ta redd* (a tangled situation to sort). [O.N. *hespa*: a skein of yarn (also a hasp; fastening)]

heth (interj) a mild oath. [O.Sc. *haith*, prob. a euphemistic alteration of E. *faith*]

hicksi (hiksti) (n) hiccups. [O.N. *hixti*: hiccough; hiccoughing]

hidder an didder (adv, phrase) hither and thither. [a good example of the Shetland adherence to the O.E. or O.N. *edh* – see introductory chapter]

hiddle (v) to hide. [O.Sc. *hiddillis*, *hidlis*: hiding places]

hide (n) human skin. *Laid ta da hide* (soaked to the skin). [an extension of E. *hide*: the skin of an animal]

hidmost (adj) last in line; hindmost; the last one. *Yun's my hidmost neep*. [O.Sc. *hindmaist*: hindmost]

hill-gaet (n) path through the hill or to the hill (also see **sheep's gaet**). [E. *hill* + O.N. *gata*: a road; a path; Sc. *gate*, *gait*: a way or road]

hill-grind (n) gate between **toon** and **scattald** (i.e. between enclosed arable land and common hill grazing). [E. *hill* + O.N. *grind*: a barred gate; a frame (filled in with lattice-work); lattice door; wicket fence]

hill moose (n) field or wood mouse (*Apodemus sylvaticus*). [Sc.]

hill-sparrow (sporrow) (n) meadow pipit (*Anthus pratensis*) (also **teetik**).

himlane (him lane) (adv) by himself; him alone. [Sc.]

himst (hims, himset) (adj) silly; touchy; capricious or foolish in manner. [N. *himsa*: behave in a silly way; making wild gestures; D.dial. *hjamsk*: half-witted; silly]

hinder (v) prevent. Used idiomatically – *Du'll no hinder him in gyaan his ain wye*.

hing (v) to hang. [L.Sc. *hing*]

hingin widder (n) earmark in a sheep – a slanting cut or strip cut off. [O.N. *hanga*: to hang + *fidrdr*: feathered]

hinny (n) darling; sweetheart. [O.Sc. *hinnie*; E. *honey*]

hinny-spot (hinnispot) (n) the three-cornered piece of wood joining the gunwales of a boat to the stem. [cf. O.N. *hyrni*: a corner; angle + Icel. *spotti*: a fragment; piece; also cf. Fær. *enni-spónur*: in a similar meaning to Sh. *hinny-spot*]

hinnywar (n) dabberlocks – edible seaweed (*Alaria esculenta*). [**hinny**: honey (sweet) + Sc. *ware*, *ore*, *oarweed*: seaweed; O.E. *wār*]

hint (v) to steal in and out unobtrusively; to flit; to vanish suddenly. [cf. N. *himta*: to glance; to brush past]

hintet (adj) said of a person who is peculiar, not right in the head – the outcome of being *hintet by de peerie-fok* (spirited away by fairies and bewitched); shy; secretive eccentric. [synonymous with **hint** – see above]

hip (v) to omit; to skip over. [O.Sc. *hip*, M.E. *hippe*: to skip; pass over]

hiplin (n) cormorant (*Phalacrocorus carbo*) when in adult plumage and showing the white thigh patch. [O.N. *hypplingr*, Fær. *hiplingur*, a contraction of *hvithypplingr*: the white hipped bird]

hipp (hepp) (v) to earth; to heap earth. *A'm gyaan ta hipp de tatties*. [N. *hypja*, Fær. *hyppa*: to hoe or earth (potatoes); E. *heap*, but in sense of 'earth up' or build up earth around potatoes to improve cropping]

hipp (interj) gee up! [D. *hyp*: gee-up]

hippen (n) a baby's nappy. [Sc. *hippen*, *hippin*: a baby's nappy (wrapped around the hips)]

hird (v) to herd animals or gather crops; to harvest. [O.N. *hirda*: to mind; care for; to bring into safety (to secure hay or corn; to tend cattle) thus E. *herd*]

hirdet (adj) harvested. [see above]

hirda (herda) (n) confusion; smithereens; untidiness; of things broken by a storm. [cf. N. *hære*: husks; refuse of corn]

hirnik (n) a corner; a hidey-hole; a small portion. [O.N. *hyrna*: a corner; angle]

hirple (v) to limp; hobble along. [Sc. *hirple*, E.dial. *hirplin*: limping; lame; poss. from obs. E. *hip-halt*: lame in the hips]

hiss-hass (v) to be in a state of confusion and unrest; also associated with (interj) *huss*, *hoss* – to shoo animals. [N. *hussa*: to frighten; chase away]

hit (pron) it; also used as emphatic (negative) interjection. *Hit! Du keens better!* [O.Sc. & O.E. *hit*: it]

hit (v) to strike; to throw; to pitch; (pt) **hat**; (pp) **hitten** to throw. [Sc. *hit*]

hitsel (pron) itself. [Sc.]

hivvet (heved) (n) a knob; a swelling; a lump. [O.N. *hofuð*: the head; an object like a head]

Hjaltland (prop n) Shetland. The name given to the islands by the Vikings when they colonised them around the end of the 9th century. [O.N. *hjalt*: hilt or crossguard of a sword and representative of the shape of the island group. As the local language evolved the *ja* became *je*, following which the combination of the letters *hj* became *sh* – hence *Sh-je-land* – later to be spelt Zetland through mispronunciation and to appear as such on all official printed matter until the latter part of the 20th century] While the above is the popularly accepted etymology of **Hjaltland** there is compelling evidence for *Hjaltr* or *Hjalti* being common bynames in Shetland at the time of the Viking invasion and thus leading to the islands being designated the land of the *Hjalti* – *Hjaltiland* (*Cultural Contacts in the North Atlantic Region: The Evidence of Names*: Ed. Peter Gammeltoft, Carole Hough, Doreen Waugh; NORNA, Scottish Place-Name Society and Society for Name Studies in Britain and Ireland. 2005).

hobrand (hobrin) (n) the blue shark (*Prionace glauca*). [N. *haabrand*: a big, ugly fellow]

hobrigdi (n) basking shark (*Cetorhinus maximus*) (also **brigdi**, **sulbrigdi**). [cf. N. *bregða*: to alter; shift; move quickly; O.E. *bregdan* (note: the shark's habit of basking on the surface of the sea does not seem to equate with the meaning of *bregða*)]

hobs (n) in exp. *Wan tae de hobs*; *de hobs a hell* – a mild oath. [E. *hob*: flat surface beside a fire or removable ring on a stove where pots or kettles are laid to keep hot]

hoch (n) the hollow at the back of the knee; the ham; (sometimes) the back of the thigh; the thigh itself. [not as O.Sc. *hoch*: hock or heel (O.E. *hōh*: heel) but E. *hock*, O.Sc. *how*: back of knee-joint; the ham]

hochbend (v) to tie a rope round an animal's hoch (hock – see etymology) to restrain it and prevent it kicking – sometimes applied to a restless cow when milking; (n) the cord so used. *Pit a hochbend apo her an she'll quieten*. [contrary to *hoch* etymology above, here *hoch-* refers to lower leg or *hock* + E. *bend*: a knot]

H

hock (v) to dig; to poke around. *He's aye hocken aboot in yun kist.* [Sc. *howk*; O.Sc. *holk*]

hockin (hoken) (adj) very hungry. [N. *haaken*: ravenously hungry]

hoe (ho) (n) any dogfish but commonly lesser spotted dogfish (**blinnd hoe**) (*Scyliorhinus canicula*) or spurdog (**blue hoe**) (*Squalus acanthias*). [O.N. *hár*, N. *haa*, D. *haj*: a shark]

hoe-moothed (adj) having an under-developed lower jaw, like a dog fish (compare **swine-moothed**). [see above]

hog (n) a castrated male sheep. [not as E. *hogget*, or L.Sc. *hog*: a yearling sheep, not yet shorn]

hog (n) moderation; limit; (see **hag**).

hogmanay (n) the last day of the year, New Year's Eve. [O.Sc. *hagmonay*; Fr.dial. *hoginane*, from 16th c. Fr. *aguillanneuf*: a gift given at the New Year]

hoid (v) to hide. [E. *hide*]

hoidie-holl (n) a hiding-place. [Sc. *hidey-hole*]

hoilter (holgin) (n) a bulky or clumsy person. [L.Sc. *hulter*: a large boulder; fig. anything clumsy or unwieldy; N. *holt*, Sw.dial. *hult*: a rough, stony hill]

hointiclock (honnklokk) (n) the great winged beetle (also **hundiclock**, **witchie klokk**). [O.N. *hyrndr*: horned; having horns + Sw.dial. *klocka*: a beetle]

hol (n) a hole; (v) to make a hole in. *Dunna du hol dee breekses.* [O.N. *hol*: a hole; *hola*: to make hollow]

holm (n) small island. [O.N. *hólmr*: an islet; an isolated meadow on the shore]

holtry (adj) very rough; (of ground) uneven, potholed. [O.N. *holt*: dry, barren, stony ground rising to a higher level than the surrounding surface; N. *holt*, Sw.dial. *hult*: a rough, stony hill; a slope]

hooch (hōōhh) (interj) an exclamation of enthusiasm akin to *Hey! Hurrah!* given when engaged in a country-style dance or reel; (v) to utter such a shout. [Sc. *hooch*: a Highland dancer's shout]

hoodie maa (n) black-headed gull (*Larus ridibundus*). [E. *hooded* + O.N. *mar*; N. *möke*; Icel. *máfur*; M.E. *meue*; O.E. *mēu*]

hooenever (adv) however. [L.Sc. *hooanever*]

hookers (n) the haunches; bended knees. [O.N. *húka*: bended knees]

hoorkle (hurkle) (v) to crouch; walk in a bent position. [O.Sc. *hurkill*, cf. N. *horkla*: to drag oneself along]

hooro (horro) (n) a hubbub or uproar. [N. *hurra*: whirling and rushing speed; (v) to hum; whirl]

hoosamilla (hoosamilli, husamilla) (adv) to go from house to house (originally gathering news or gossip). [N. *husamillom*, Fær. *húsa midlun*: from one house to another]

horroration (adj) extreme anger (esp. Unst). *He banged intil a horroration lik a sauvage.* [see **hooro**]

hoosomever (adv) notwithstanding; nevertheless; however. [L.Sc.]

hoose (n) house. [Sc.]

hoot (interj) expressive of disagreement or dissatisfaction, commonly accompanied by 'toot'. *Hoot, toot, du's spaekin rubbish!* (also see **toot**). [Sc. hoot – imit. of a snort of disgust]

hooter (v) to silence by threats. [poss. deriv. of O.N. *hætta*: to cease]

horn (n) the top of stem or stern of a boat. [from E. *horn*: a pointed projection]

horn-towes (n) cow's tether in byre. [*horn* + O.Sc. *tow*: a rope]

horrid (adv) very; used contrary to English, to convey an intensity of approbation. *Yun pictur is horrid boannie.* [O.Sc. *horrid*, with same meaning; cf. E. *awful*, *odious*]

horse-gock (n) snipe (*Gallinago gallinago*). [O.N. *hrossagaukr*, N. *rossegauk*, Sw. *horsagök*, D. *horsegøg*: snipe]

hosiery (n) collective noun describing all knitted woollen goods. [E. *hose*, *hosiery*: socks and/or underwear]

host (n) cough; (v) to cough. [O.N. *hósta*, O.Sc. *host*: cough]

houb (hub) (n) a small, shallow lake at the head of a voe. [O.N. *hópr*: a small, landlocked bay]

howdie (n) a midwife; at one time applied to untrained local women who attended at childbirth or sickbed. [obs. O.Sc. (1700) *howdie* (with same meaning) poss. a nickname]

howe (n) a hoe; (v) to hoe. [E. *hoe*]

höld (v) held. [Sc. *helt*; E. *held*]

hömin (n) the faint light after sunset (also see **simmer dim**). [O.N. *húm*: twilight]

höv (v) (pt of) heave; (pp) **höved**. *He höv oot de soor mylk yesterday.* [O.N. *hefja*: to throw; fling]

hövi (n) an open-work basket woven from straw or dockens, used for carrying bait or fish. [O.N. *háfr*, N. *haav*: a basket with a long handle (a landing net) by means of which small fish are scooped out of the water]

hubbelskyu (humelsku, hobbastju, habbleshue) *hubble-skew* (n) an uproar; an untidy upheaval. *De place wis in a humelsku.* [Several related Sc. words include **hubble** bustle; confusion; **skew** to move to the side obliquely; **skew-whiff** (**wheef**, **quieff**); also **skave** off-centre; squint; **ajee** ajar; at a rakish angle; O.Sc. *hubbilchow*, *hobbleshow*: tumult; hubbub]

hubbit (v) blamed in an unfair way; driven out because of an accusation. *Dey hubbit him as a tief.* [O.Sc. *hub* (*hubbed*): suspected; accused]

hufsi (n) any home-made cake (or bread) which has risen in baking and uses ingredients to hand; a large, round oven-baked bannock with **curns** in it and including a raising agent such as baking powder or yeast. [cf. O.N. *ofsa*: to exaggerate; do to excess; but in fig. sense of to cause to swell up, as bread]

huggistaff (hoggistaf) (n) a gaff; a stout-handled implement with a large hook on the end, used for landing large fish; (pl) **huggiestaaves**. [O.N. *hogg*: a blow + O.N. *stafr*: staff]

huker (v) to crouch with bended knees. [L.Sc. *hunker*, cf. N. *hokra*: to go bent]

hull (v) to hollow out. [O.N. *hol*; O.Sc. *hull*: a hole]

hulter (holter) (n) a large boulder; beach boulder; a very big wave. Used in placenames. [O.N. *holt*, Sw.dial. *hult*: rough, stony hill or slope]

humlibaand (homliband) (n) a loop of rope fixed to a boat's **rooth** and serving as a rowlock. [O.N. *hamla*, *homluband*: a grommet]

hummel (v) to chip or remove the edges from something; said of old tools: *Du can fairly see whaar dir hummeled.* [O.N. *hamla*: to mutilate; L.Sc. *hummel*: to remove the bearded ears from bere]

humpigumpi (n) rump. [comb. of N. *hump*: knoll; piece of flesh; rump and O.N. *gumpr*: rump]

hund (n) a dog; (v) to chase off. [O.N. *hundr*: a dog; E. (v) *hound*: to pursue; harass]

hundiclock (n) a beetle (see **hointiclock, witchie klokk**). [O.N. *hyrndr*: horned; having horns + Sw.dial. *klocka*: a beetle]

hundihol (n) the widest, deepest part of a stream where whelps were drowned. [O.N. *hundr-*: a dog + O.N. *hol*: a hole; *hola*: to make hollow]

hunkle (honkl) (n) a shrug; (v) to raise or shrug the shoulders. [N. *honkla*: to move unsteadily; to stumble]

hunkse (hunk) (v) to lift or heave up, generally onto the shoulders; hoist. [extension of N. *honkla* (see above)]

hunnik (honnek) (n) stern compartment of a boat (also see **kannie** and **shot**). [of O.N. *horn*: in sense of the conical shape; a nook or corner]

hunse (hons) (v) to hunt for; ransack; rummage. [deriv. N. *handska*: to grab; shake; pull; Sw.dial. *handska*: to catch]

hurd (n) a big boulder on the seashore. [O.N. *urd*, N.dial. *urd*: a heap of stones]

hurda (herda) (n) corn husks; pieces of broken crockery. *Shö laid de jug in hurda.* [N. *hære*: husks; refuse of corn]

hurl (n) a ride in a wheeled vehicle; a rattling sound in chest/lungs caused by conjestion. *Dey wir an aafil hurl in his breest*; (v) to push, as a wheelbarrow; to drive; to trundle. [O.Sc. *hurl(e)*]

hurl-borro (n) a wheelbarrow. [O.Sc. *hurl-barrow*]

hurless (adj) debilitated; exhausted. [N. *hurra*: whirling and rushing speed – hence *hurless*, a lack of the same]

hurr (n) rough breathing; (v) to make a whirring sound, as a spinning wheel; imitative of the sound. [N. *hurra*: whirling and rushing speed]

hush (n) 1) the sound of a comparatively calm sea breaking on the shore [imitative of the sound]; 2) a large number or quantity; a surfeit. [Icel. *urör*: a great quantity]

hushie-baa (n) expression used to pacify a child and lull it to sleep (lit. 'hush-baby').

hwal (n) a whale. [O.N. *hvalr*; L.Sc. *whaal*]

hwar (kwar) (adv) where. [O.N. *hvar*: where; whither]

hwenk (hwink) (v) sudden, jerky movement associated with turning the head while looking sideways (also **kwenk**). [Icel. *hvima*: to move quickly and unsteadily; to look round slyly; N. *kvisma*]

hwimble (hwuml, hwumel) (v) to capsize; overturn; (also **whummel**). [O.N. *hvelva*, N. *kvelva*: to turn a hollow object bottom up; Sc. *quhemle*]

hyocklebane (n) shoulder-blade. [O.N. *holka*: to hollow out + O.Sc. *bane*: bone]

hyook (n) 1) a sickle; 2) a fish hook. [O.Sc. *hook, huke*: a reaper's hook; a sickle]

hyst (v) to hoist. [E. *hoist*]

H

I

i (*short i*) as *it, if* (prep) in. *Da boat's i de noost*; compare usage of **i** and **o** in connecting a person to his place of abode – *Robbie o Dale*; *Willie i Setter* – Robbie is 'of' Dale while Willie is 'in' Setter, the latter being the Norn usage; also compare **idda, inna**. [O.N. *inni*: in; *inn i*: into]

Iceland skorie (n) glaucous gull (*Larus hyperboreus*) in juvenile plumage. [O.N. *skári*, N. *skaare*: a young gull].

idda (**ida, i de**) (prep) in the. *Dir mair tae idda pot*. [O.N. *inni*: in]

idder (adj) other; different. *Haes du ony idder kind a tatties?* [Sc. form of E. *other*]

idders (pron) others. [as above]

idle-sit (n) idleness; laziness; circumstance in which no work is being done or can be done. [L.Sc. *idleset* – of O.Sc. *idleseat*]

igg (v) to urge on; incite. [O.N. *eggja*, from *egg*: an edge]

ill (n) moral wickedness; evil; (v) to do evil; to deal harshly with; (adj) bad. *Hit's no sae ill* (It's not so bad); *Ta tak ill wi* (to take offence at); *I tout ill aboot yun* (to feel sorry for). [O.N. *illr*: bad; ill; evil; wicked]

ill aff (adj) badly off; poor; needy; having limited choices. [as above + O.N. *af*: off]

ill-best (n) best of a bad lot; in phrase *ta mak de ill-best o* (to make the best of a bad job); (adj) the least bad of several poor alternatives. [cf. O.N. *ills-bestr*; Fær. *ill-bestur*; O.Sc. *ill-best*]

ill-bistet (**ill-birstet**) (adj) angry; awkward. [*ill-*: as above + N. *bysten*: hasty; *busta*, Sw.dial. *illbyste*: a hot-tempered and cross being]

ill-döer (n) one who does ill to others; one who behaves badly. [Sc.]

ill-faared (adj) ugly. [O.Sc. *ill-faurd*: (of looks) ill-favoured; ugly; uncomely; from E. *ill-favoured*]

ill helt (interj) ill health, extended to become an expression of annoyance. *What da ill helt is yun?*; the devil. *He ran lik da ill helt*. [O.Sc. *helt*: health, however in Sh. *ill-helt* euphemistically refers to the devil; Ork. *helty*: the devil]

ill-laekit *ill-laek-it* (adj) ugly; unpopular; (v) disliked. [Sc. *ill-liket*]

ill-luckit *ill-luk-it* (adj) unlucky. [Sc. *ill luck*: bad luck]

ill-makin (adj) creating trouble; mischief-making. [Sc.]

ill-mou (n) vile language; an abusive tongue. [Sc.]

ill-named (n) having a bad reputation. [Sc.]

ill-naitered (adj) ill-natured; irritable; bad-tempered. [Sc. *ill-natured*: bad-tempered; spiteful]

ill-pairted *ill-pair-ted* (adj) unfairly divided and distributed. [Sc.]

ill-plaesed (adj) annoyed with or at someone or something. [Sc. *ill-pleased*]

ill-set (v) of clothes, badly fitting. [Sc.]

ill-spaekin (adj) given to malicious talk; (v) to slander. [Sc. *ill-spoken*]

ill sunse (n) bad luck; used as a curse – *Ill sunse apo him for yun*; (also **ill-trift**). [O.Sc. *sons*: good luck or fortune; Gael. *sonas*: good luck; prosperity – and therefore *ill-sons* = bad luck]

ill-trickit (adj) full of tricks. [O.Sc. *tricket*]

ill-trift (n) same meaning and usage as **ill sunse** [O.Sc. *thrift*: good fortune – therefore ill-thrift denotes the opposite]

ill-trivven (adj) undernourished. [N. *treve*: small rag; tatters; Fær. *trevsutur*: frayed; ragged]

ill-vaandit (adj) disagreeable; having unattractive manners; with bad awkward behaviour; said of a job badly or carelessly carried out. [Icel. *illa vandadur*: carelessly carried out]

ill-vicket (adj) malicious; wicked. [N. *vik*: small bend; Icel. *vik*: slight movement, thus metaphorical in Sh. *inclining or turning of the mind (towards evil)*]

ill-willied (adj) bad-tempered. [Sc. *ill-will*: unkindly feeling]

ilska cry (n) death cry. [O.N. *illska*: ill will; malice; enmity; hatred; mischief; misfortune; in Fær. and N. the word is also used in sense of indisposition, illness and of exasperation, anger]

ime (**im**) (n) soot coating the outside of a cooking utensil. [O.N. *im*: dust; a coat of dust; dirt]

immense (n) a large number or quantity. *I'm made an immense o tattie soup ta feed dem aa*. [Ork. in same meaning – E. *immense* (adj): vast in extent or degree; F. from L. *immēnsus*]

imna (v) am not. *I imna gyaan ta do it*. [Sc. *amna*: am not]

imper (v) to make a cursory remark; to murmer; barely a squeak by way of comment. [O.N. *impa*: to set in motion; N. *impra*: touch up; hint at; Icel. *ympra á*: to touch upon; mention]

inbi (adv) in from the door; towards the fire; (lit. 'in by').

inbiggit (ppl, adj) intractable; morose; sullen and uncommunicative. [cf. 'built up', 'closed in' and therefore poss. a depreciatory use of N. *innebugga*: well provided]

inbös (n) a welcome; hospitable reception, though generally used in a negative way. *Dere's little inbös ta be hed fae him*. [N. *innboð*: an invitation]

incomer (n) someone other than a native-born Shetlander who has taken up residence in the islands (also **sooth-moother**). [L.Sc. *incum(m) er*: a new-comer]

incomin (adj) in the designated time shortly to come. *De cooncil elections ir dis incomin week*. [L.Sc. *incum(m)ing*: shortly to come]

infield (n) all that piece of land nearest to dwellings, generally the most productive and therefore kept tilled and manured, as opposed to **ootrun**. [O.Sc. *infeild*]

inhad (n) barely enough; just sufficient to sustain life. [O.Sc. *inhaud, inhad*: to hold in; barely enough]

inna (**inna i**) (prep) inside. *He wis inna (de) hoose*. [O.N. *inni*: in; *inni í*: inside]

innadaeks (adv) within the confines of the township dykes. By extension, near home. [*inside* + Sc. *dyke*, *dike*: drystone wall without mortar, lit. 'within the walls']

inside claes (n) underclothes. [Sh., Ork., Caithness, Aberdeen]

intil (prep) in; into, in the sense of understanding. *Ir de police gotten intil yun mysterious disappearance yit?* [Sc. *intil*, *in til*: into; in]

ir (pl. of (v) to be) are. *Dey ir boannie flooers.*

irg (erg) (v) to aggravate or annoy; to incite. [N. *erga*: to vex; irritate]

irp (erp) (v) to complain incessantly; to harp on. [Fær. *erpa*, *erpa saer*: to turn up one's nose]

is (aux v) instead of *has* or *have* – *Whaar is du bön?*; also *are* – *Is du gyaan ta da picturs da nicht?*; (pron) us (Westside). *Yun's nae ös ta is.*

ise prop. I sall (I shall). *Ise gie dee a skelp aroond dee lugs!* [L.Sc. *I'se*]

ita (prep) in – generally rendered **ita de** in the. *De kye ir ita de coarn*; (also **ida**). [Sc. *intae*, *inta*, in sense of 'within']

ithoot (ith-oot) (prep) without. *Ithoot a doot, du's rycht* (Without a doubt, you're right). [O.Sc. '*ithoot*: without; also *athoot*]

itil (prep) into. [see **intil**]

J

jaa (jaw) (adj) said of an egg that is infertile. [O.Sc. *jaw*: (of water) splashing; surging, as waves – thus a *jaw-egg* is infertile or addled, having only liquid contents that make a splashing sound when shaken]

jalin (yally) (n) heavy clouds associated with rain. [cf. O.N. *él* (n): a shower]

jalouse (v) to have doubts or suspicions; to suspect. [O.F. *jalouser*: to regard with jealousy; Mod.Fr. *jaloux*: jealous]

jamp (v) jumped; (pt of) **jimp**; (pp) **juppm**. [Sh. & Ork. form of E. *jump*]

jander (v) said of a female animal in heat. [E. *gender*: to breed; copulate]

jantry (n) gentry. [E. *gentry*]

jap (n) a choppy sea. [orig. obs. cf. D. *hjappe*: to jabber, thus metaphoric; also *jaup*]

japple (v) to paddle and splash in water. [prob. imitative; also *jabble*; O.Sc. *jaup*: (of water) to dash; splash]

jarl (n) principal guizer at **Up-Helly-A'** festival (see **guizer jarl**). [O.N. *jarl*: earl]

jarl's squad (n) the principal group of **guizers** at **Up-Helly-A'**, led by the **guizer jarl**. [see above]

jee (v) to move slightly; to shift out of alignment. [Sc. *agee*, O.Sc. *jeed*: awry, squint, shifted out of normal position]

jeely (n) jam. [Sc. *jelly*: jam]

jeely-jar (n) jam-jar. [see above]

jimp (v) 1) to jump; (pt) **jamp**; (pp) **juppm**. [Sc. form of E. *jump*]; 2) to shrink. *Me ganzie jimpet becis he wizna pitten on a board* (see **board**). [Sc. *jimp*: (of clothes) close-fitting]

jocktaleg (n) a large pocket-knife. [O.Sc. *jockteleg*: a large clasp or pocket-knife (*jock*: knife – *tae*: to – leg); apparently some 17th cent. pocket knives had handles carved to represent a human leg]

Johnsmas (n) June 24th (Midsummer's Night). [The midsummer pagan festival-date was appropriated by the Christian church to celebrate a mass (St John's Mass) commemorating the birth of St John the Baptist; O.N. *Jónsmessa*: Midsummer's Day (24th June)]

Johnsmas Foy (n) the celebration which used to be held by Dutch fishermen before the Shetland herring fishing commenced on 24th June. Now a summer festival in Shetland (see **Johnsmas + foy**).

Johnsmas flooer (Johnsmas-girse) (n) ribwort plantain (*Plantago lanceolata*). [see **Johnsmas** + Sc. *flooer*: flower. An old superstitious custom is attached to this plant in connection with St John's Eve, since an omen of the future was taken from the jutting stamens of the plant to determine whether one was to marry one's true love. In Fær. *Jóansøkugras* denotes the same plant and the same custom was attached to it on St John's Eve]

jokkel (jokl, yokkel) (n) shoulder, commonly *jokkel benn* (shoulder bone); placename for a crag or shoulder-like protuberance in a hillside. [O.N. *oxl*: the shoulder; a crag]

joob (n) originally a deep place in the sea, now deep mud or mire. [O.N. *djúp*: a deep place; the deep sea]

jookerie-packerie (jookerypackery) (n) trickery; scallywag behaviour; deception. [O.Sc. *joukerie*: deceit; roguery; trickery + *pauk(erie)*: a trick]

joopie (n) a woollen shirt or singlet. [O.Sc. *joup*, *jawp*, *jupe*: a kind of jacket worn by men; a tunic; a bodice worn by women]

jorum (n) entertainment. [cf. Sc. *jorum*: a large drinking vessel and therefore linked to partying, poss. imitative of O.Sc. *jorum*: a thunder-crash]

joy (n) a term of endearment. *Du's granny's peerie joy, is du no*. [Sc. *joy* – linked to *jo*: sweetheart]

julk (v) to squelch. [poss. imitative; cf. Fær. *dalka*: to soil with moist filth]

julter (n) edible sea-urchin (*Echinus esculentus*) (also **yulter, scaddiman's heid**). [Icel., Fær., N. *igulker*]

jumper-board (board) (n) an adjustable wooden frame, also referred to as a **woollie-horse**, on which to stretch or shape a finished knitted jumper or cardigan to correct size; also used to reconstitute an old garment which may have shrunk, or to prevent shrinkage; (see **jimp**; also **dress**). [Sh. & Ork. – produced in a number of patented designs the jumper-board appears to be a Shetland innovation although the concept of dressing knitted garments in this manner is now universally acknowledged as desirable for certain yarn types]

juppm (pp of **jimp**)

K

kaam (n) a mould in which lead weights for fishing, etc. were once cast. [O.Sc. *calm*, *caum*: a matrix or mould]

kabe (n) the thowel-pin of a boat. [O.N. *keipr*: a rowlock]

kabbilabbi (n) (see **cabbi-labbi**)

kail (kale, keel) (n) cabbage; *A kail runt* – cabbage stem (see **runt**). Used in expression *caald kale het ageen* – yesterday's leftovers re-heated for consumption; – an old sermon being preached anew. [Sc. *kale, kail*]

kail flea (kale-) (n) cabbage butterfly (*Pieris brassicae*). [Sc.]

kaitrins, white (n) grass-of-parnassus (*Parnassia palustris*). [*kaitrin* being Shetland dialect for Catherine (from Greek meaning 'pure') so named for the delicate white flower of this plant]

kall *caal* (*as pal*) (v) call; in placename Kalliness (the promontory from where the ferry-boat was called across Weisdale Voe). [O.N. *kall*: a calling; shouting]

kalliflakk (n) the shrill crying of gulls. [O.N. *kall, kallan*: a calling; shouting + Sc. *flack*: to flap; make a flapping noise]

kame (kamb, kaim) (n) a comb; a ridge of hills; used as a placename, e.g. The Kaim – Foula's highest cliff; (v) to comb. [O.N. *kambr*: a comb; a crested ridge of hills]

kan (n) capability; skill; knack. [O.Sc. *can*: ability (*canny*)]

kannie (kani) (n) stern compartment of a boat (also see **hunnik** and **shot**). [N. *kane*: a bowl; Icel. *kani*: a small wooden vessel; Ger. *kahn*: a boat]

kapp (n) wooden bowl. [O.Sc. *caup*]

karm (n) soiled or wet, as of clothes. A child coming in covered with mud from play might be met with *For sicca karm du's in*. [Fær. *karmur*: a drenched suit of clothes; wet clothes (on one's body or thrown in a heap)]

karrant (karr-*ant*) (n) high jinks; great fun. [O.Sc. *carrant*: a revel; social gathering; a frolic; escape; Fr. *courante*: a dance from 16th and 17th cent. performed with a running step]

kassen (adj) sour. [N. *kasen*: sourish; somewhat decayed; Icel. *kasadr*: beginning to decay by having lain in a heap]

kastik (n) stem of cabbage. [O.N. *kálstokkr*: cabbage stem; M.E. *caule stok*]

kattikloo (n) common bird's-foot-trefoil (*Lotus corniculatus*). [D. *katteklo*: trefoil; O.N. *kló*: claw]

kattyuggle (kattyuggla, kattool) (n) owl – various species (*Strigidae*) (also **ul, yuggle**). [N. *katugle*, dial. *kattula*: tawny owl; *katt*: cat + *ula*: owl; O.N. *u(g)la*: owl]

kavvel (v) to extract the hook from the mouth of a large fish by means of a stick with a notch at its end. [O.N. *kafli*: cylinder; stick]

kavvelin-tree (n) the stick used for the above operation.

kecksie (keksi) (n) hogweed (*Heracleum sphondylium*) or wild angelica (*Angelica sylvestris*). [poss. deriv. from O.N. *keikja*: to bend the upper part of the body backwards; N. *keika*: bend back; to dislocate (a member or joint) – and therefore figurative of the bent joints in the stem of this plant]

keek (v) to peer; to peep through fingers. [O.Sc. *keik*, Du. *kijken*: to peep]

keel (n) the spine of a person or animal; the hollow of the back. [N. *kjøl*: elevated line or ridge]

keel-dracht (n) covering of iron to protect a boat's keel when it is being drawn over a beach. [N. *drag*, *kjøldrag*]

keeng (king) (v) an old method of mending broken crockery by using metal clasps, usually of pewter. [N. *kjenga*: to fasten with a clamp]

keest (ksst) (interj) shoo! be off! used to scare off or threaten a cat. [N. *kjest! kist! kyss!*]

keetchin (n) a savoury additive to make plain food more tasty; (v) to add relish; to render palatable. Proverb: *Better a moose ida kale as nae keetchin*. [O.Sc. *kichin*, *kechin*: kitchen – with the inference of provisions]

kefsi (kefset) (v) unhandy; awkward; clumsy. [N. & Sw.dial. *kava*]

keggle (kegl, kegel) (v) noisy, argumentative commotion. *Stop de kegglin*. [N. *kjegla*: to spin; Fær. *keglast*: to wrangle; brawl; quarrel]

keita (n) halibut (*Hippoglossus hippoglossus*). [N. *kveita*: halibut]

kemp (v) to vie; to strive to be first. *Stop kempin fornenst dee sister*. [O.Sc. *kemp*: to strive; to struggle]

ken (v) to know. [O.N. *kenna, kenna á sér*: to have a feeling of]

kenk (v) to twist; bend. *He kenkit his cöt* (He twisted his ankle); (also see **kwenk**). [Icel. *hvima*: to move quickly and unsteadly; to look round slyly; N. *kvisma*]

kenno (v) don't know. *I kenno whaur dey guid;* (lit. 'ken not'). [Sc. *ken*: know]

kendlin (n) kindling such as live coals, pieces of wood or other material used for lighting a fire. [E. *kindling*]

kennin (n) a very small quantity; previously a feeling, a sensation, and thus the expression, 'a sensation' enough to taste. [O.N. *kennin*: knowledge; acquaintance]

kent (adj) known.

kep (n) a cap; (v) to intercept; to keep from doing something. [O.Sc. *kep*: to catch; intercept]

kepsweevil (v) overturn. [Sh. variant and combination of E. *capsize* & *swivel*]

kerrel (kerl) (n) originally a crone, now a big woman. [O.N. *kerling*: (old) woman; cf. L.Sc. *carl*: a man]

kettle (v) (of a cat) giving birth to a litter of kittens. [N. *kjetla*; E.dial. *kittle*]

kettlin (n) a kitten. [O.N. *ketlingr*: a kitten]

key (n) mood. [E. *keyed*: excited; nervous; tense]

key (v) to lock or fasten with a key. *Key de door afore du goes*, as opposed to **lock** which means close. [O.E. *cæg*: key – though obs. usage elsewhere in Britain]

khoik (n) cake (Whalsay).

kiarr (kior) ki-*arr*, ki-*or* (n) form of English *coir*; rough fibre for making ropes. [Tamil or Malayalam *kāyar*: coconut fibre used for making rope and matting]

38

kibby (adj) eager; willing; anxious. [N. *kipen*: restless from merriment; frolicsome]

kilt (v) tuck up skirts to bare legs. [Sc. *kilt*: to tuck up (skirt)]

kin (n) family relatives. *Coontin kin* – establishing one's family-tree; (also **sib**). [O.N. *kyn*; O.E. *cynna*]

kind (n) inherited characteristic. *Shö cam o da kind*.

kinda (adj) sort of (lit. 'kind of').

king-cum-a-lay (n) children's chasing game. [Also called *king-cum-ali*; *keeng kumalay* – one form of the game in Shetland involves a 'king' (chaser) standing in centre of playground and calling king-cum-a-lay (king – come-all-o-ye?). The players, lined up at one end of the ground, then run to other end trying to avoid being caught by the 'king'. Captives help as catchers as the game progresses until all are caught]

kirk (n) church; Sunday morning worship – *de kirk*, as opposed to *de **meeting*** (more informal evening service); a common prefix to placenames where churches once stood – e.g. Kirkigarth, Kirkidale – frequently denoting the former site of pre-reformation churches. [O.N. *kirkja*]

kirk folk (n) church-goers. [O.N. *kirkjufólk*]

kirk-mark (n) hare-lip. [orig. obs.]

kirkin (n) ceremonial church attendance of, for example, newly elected council.

kirknin (n) first attendance at church of couple after their wedding.

kirk-skailin (n) the dispersal of a church congregation after a service (see **skail**).

kirn (n) a churn; a milling crowd of people; (v) to churn milk or cream; to stir up, as trouble. [O.N. *kjarni*: a churn]

kirnin (n) the act of churning; sufficient milk for churning; the complete task of churning from start to finish. *Dey ir a kirnin ta dö afore du goes*. [O.N. *kirna*: to churn]

kirn-korse (kirn-kors) (n) the two pieces of wood fixed crosswise at the end of the churn-staff. [O.N. *kjarni*: a churn + *kross*: a cross; cross-pin]

kirn-mylk (n) curds; buttermilk.

kirr (v) to scare away, esp. hens. [N. *kjørra*: to quieten; to frighten; check]

kirr-mirr (n) a noisy commotion (also **tirri mirri**). [see above]

kirr-mirren (n) pleasing sensation. [N. *kjørra*: to quieten + N. *mirra*: to tingle]

kirsen (adj) fit and proper; passable; satisfactory to eat or wear. [O.Sc. *kirsin(e)*, *cristin*: Christian]

kishie (kessi) (n) straw basket or creel designed to be carried on the back. [O.N. *kassi*: a basket; N. *kjessa*: an osier-basket]

kishie-baand (n) rope attached to kishie and used for carrying it over shoulders. [O.N. *kassi*: a basket + O.N. *band*: bundle; bunch]

kishie-foo (n) such as will fill a kishie. *Bring wis a kishie-foo o paets*. [O.N. *kassi*: a basket + O.Sc. *fou, fow*: full]

kist (n) a chest, trunk or coffin; (v) to lay a dead body in a coffin. [O.N. *kista*: chest]

kist (interj) used to scare away cats; be off! [N. *kjest! kist! kyss!*]

kistin (n) the laying of a dead body in a coffin. [O.N. *kista*: chest]

kist-neuk (n) corner of a chest or trunk where valuables may be stored. [O.N. *kista*: chest + O.Sc. *neuk*; M.E. *noke*; E. *nook*]

kit (n) a wooden tankard or bowl for holding milk, butter, etc. [O.Sc. *kit*: a jug; tankard; wooden tub; M.Du. *kitte*: a hooped container for beer]

kitti (kittie) (n) pet name for a hen. [cf. Sw.dial. *kytta*: a girl]

kittle (v) to tickle. [O.N. *kitla*: to tickle]

kittly (kittelsom) (adj) ticklish. [O.N. *kitall*]

kläip (claipe) (v) to pinch; squeeze; of an emaciated animal – *Hits sides wis kläipit tagidder*; to cling; of clothes wet by a person falling in the water – *His breeks wir kläipit tae his legs*. [N. *klypa*: to pinch; squeeze]

klair (adj) ready. [O.Sc. *clair*: clear; Du. *klaar*, but with additional meaning of ready which originates in nautical use having developed from 'clean']

klapp (n) a tap; a light blow. *A'll gie dee a klapp anunder de lug*. [O.N. *klapp*, D. *klap*: a tap]

klebber (klaeber, kleeber) (n) steatite (soapstone). [N. *klybberg*: steatite]

klep (clip) (n) a hooked tool (gaff) used for landing fish. [O.N. *kleppr*: a staff, supplied with an iron hook, by which large fish are hauled into a boat]

klett (n) a lump of stone. [N. *klatt*: a lump; a mass]

klevi (klavi) (n) a trampled pathway or track. [Fær. *kleyva*: to trample; O.N. *klauf*: a cloven hoof]

klibber (clibber) (n) wooden pack saddle (also used in Orkney and Caithness) made from two boards (one each side of pony) with two projecting wooden 'horns' crossing each other and fastened with a bolt or pin. Creels or **kishies** are hung from the horns – one each side for balance. [N. *klyvbere*, *klyf*: a pack; *bera*: to carry]

kline (v) to smear; to spread, as with butter, jam, etc.; to strike a blow. *A'll gie de a kline at de sides o de heid*; (also **clime**). [O.N. *klína*: to smear]

kling (cling) (v) shrink, as *Da paets kling as dey dry*. [O.Sc. *clyng*; M.E. *clinge*; O.E. *clingan*]

klip (v) to cut. *Shö haes a tongue dat could klip cloot*. [O.N. *klýpa*: to squeeze; pinch; *klippa*: to cut]

klipet (adj) of a person who is sharp tongued or niggardly – *Dat's a klipet craiter*; (also **nippet**, **snippet**). [N. *klypen*: stingy; miserly]

klondyker (n) an Eastern European factory ship; crew member of such a ship. [E. *klondyke*: a very rich source of wealth, deriv. of Alaskan/Canadian goldrush (1896) when miners working the Klondyke River (a tributary of the Yukon River) were termed *klondykers*]

klonger (n) dog rose; the wild brier (*Rosa canina*). [O.N. *klungr*: brier]

klurmose (n) clamour; hullabaloo; noisy outcry. [prob. deriv. O.N. *klóra*: to scratch]

knab (nabb) (n) a knoll; a rocky promontory; a headland, e.g. placename The Knab, Lerwick. [O.N. *nabbr*: projecting knoll or point; N. *nabb (nebbe)*, Sw.dial. *nabb*: a peg; nail; point of land]

K

knap *k-nap* (v) to speak English; to talk 'proper' – *Du canna ös wir hameaboot wirds wi him. Du'll hae ta knap*; sometimes also used in a derogatory reference to a Shetlander speaking in an affected way – *He cam back fae sooth knappin.* [M.E. *gnap*: to bite in a snapping fashion; Du. *cnappen*: to crack; to snap – thus Sc. *knap* in the sense of speaking ('southern' English) in a snapping, mincing or affected manner. '*King James of Scotland hearing one of his subjects knap suddrone,* (*southern*) *declarit him a trateur*' (Hamilton 1581)]

knaw (knav) *k-naw* (v) to gnaw; to go at something *lik a dug wi a bön.* [N. *knavla*]

knep *k-nep* (v) draw together, as the mouth of a bag; purse lips; (also **nyep**). [O.N. *kneppa*: to press; squeeze; pinch]

knockit *k-nockit* (n) ground in a **knockin-stane** – a large stone with round hollow in which bere was pounded with a **mell** (wooden mallet) in the manner of a large scale mortar and pestle; (v) to grind. [O.Sc. *knokit-bere*: barley bruised or burst by *knokin*]

knock-soe *k-nok-so* (n) limpets that have been mashed by pounding them in a hole in a rock. Half-boiled, chewed or mashed limpets were thrown or spat out on the sea to produce an oily matter on the surface in order to attract fish. [O.N. *sád*: that which is sown (spread), as seed]

knoilt *k-noilt* (n) a sharp blow; a rap with the knuckles. [N. *knolta*: to push; *knultrust*: to buffet each other]

knowe *k-nowe* (n) hillock. [Sc. *knowe*, E. *knoll*, O.E. *cnoll*: a round hillock; Ger. *knollen*: a knob; lump]

knuckle (n) a linear measurement – the length of the second finger from tip to knuckle. [O.Sc. *knuckle* (with same meaning)]

koillet (adj) polled, as a cow without horns or one which has had its horns removed. [O.Sc. *coll*: to clip; to take the top off; O.N. *kollóttr*: polled; N. *kolla*: a cow without horn]

kokkaloorie (kokkeloori) (n) common daisy (*Bellis perennis*). [cf. N. *kokul*: a cluster + N. *lur*: a nap; doze; – in the sense of the flower curling into a dozing lump when out of the sun; also cf. N. *kokkelur(e)*: pine-cone (seed capsule: *kokul*); *kukkelur(e)*: snail-shell]

kokkasødi (n) manx shearwater (*Puffinus puffinus*) (also see **leerie**). [onomatopœic of the bird's call]

kolli (collie) (n) a small open iron lamp with a wick floating in fish oil. When obsolete, the name was transferred to the small paraffin lamps that replaced it. [O.N. *kola*: a small, cup-shaped, open lamp]

köli (kölli) (v) to fondle; caress. *Du man köli de peerie ting whin shö's greetin lik yun* (You must caress the little one when she's crying like that). [L.Sc. *culye*]

krampis (krampi, krampies) (n) a dish made of fish livers and **burstin** or oatmeal which has been kneaded into a dough with melted fat then boiled. A variation on **krappen**. [N. *krumpa, krympa*: to press; squeeze; knead]

kransit (kranset) (adj) having the head, or face, a different colour from the body, especially in sheep; originally partly white faced esp. around the eyes and with white neck. [O.N. *krans*: a ring; garland; crown]

krappen (n) fish livers and oatmeal mixed together and seasoned, then stuffed into a fish head and boiled. [N. *krumpa, krympa*: to press; squeeze; knead; O.Sc. '*crappit head*' – from (v) *crap*: to fill; stuff; cram]

kreks (crex) (n) the sound of clearing the throat; (v) to clear the throat; to hawk. [O.N. *hrækja*: to spit; N.Sw.dial. *kraaks*: to hawk; cough; cough up]

kring (n) two lambs tethered together. [O.N. *kringr, hringr*: a circle; ring]

krolkit (adj) crooked. [N. *krylt, kryl*: a hump on the back]

kröl (n) small oatmeal scone. [N. *kryl*: a hump; N.dial. *krult*: something rolled up; Sw.dial. *krøl*: a shaped piece of dough]

krom (kröm, krön) (v) to complain; to whinge or fret while ailing. [N. *krauna, krøyna*: to shrink from; to whimper; complain]

kroppm (v) pp of creep – crept; crawled. [O.N. *kroppin*: crept – pp of *krjúpa*: to creep]

krummick (n) a small measure, such as can be held between the tips of four fingers and the thumb. [E. *crumb*, O.E. *cruma*: a small amount]

krus (n) originally a small earthenware vessel, now a mealy dough with fish-livers in the centre, baked in a cup-shaped vessel. [O.N. *krús*: a jug or tankard, properly of stone or earthenware]

kukker (kokr, kjukker) (v) to cheer up; revive. [N. *kokra*: to fondle; talk gently to]

kunki (kjonki) (N. Yell) (n) an attack of illness; a severe chill. *Du's gotten dee a kunki. Du'll catch dee kunki* (equiv. to E. *You'll catch your death (of cold)*) [cf. Sw.dial. *kyng*: a sudden violent attack of illness; N. *kyng*: a gust; rush; sudden noise; downpour]

kurrip (kurrop) (n) croak; imitative of a frog or crow – *de kurrop o de craa.*

kurry-raag (n) dealings; friendly relations; rapport. [prob. merging of O.N. *kærr*: a term of endearment and *korr, kurr*: murmer + E. *rag*: in sense of banter; horse-play; wrangle]

kwaak (kwak) (v) to quiver; shiver. [O.N. *kvikna*: to quicken; come to life; poss. also connected to E. *quake*]

kwar (hwar) (adv) where. (esp. Westside) [O.N. *hvar*: where; whither]

kwarkabus (kwirkipus) (n) a disease of sheep characterised by an oedema in the throat. [O.N. *kverk*: the throat + N. *pus*: a swelling filled with pus; Sw.dial. *pusa, pusna*, D.dial. *puse*: to tumefy]

kwenk (kwink) (v) sudden, jerky movement associated with turning the head while looking sideways (also **hwenk**). [Icel. *hvima*: to move quickly and unsteadily; to look round slyly; N. *kvisma*]

kwilk (kwolk) (v) to swallow with a gulp. [Sw.dial. *kulka, kolka, kålka*, D. *kulke*, Fær. *kulka*: to gulp; to drink in high draughts]

kwiss (quiss) (v) to husk; consume entirely. *Kwiss de bens* (suck on fish or mutton bones to remove all the flesh). [O.N. *kvista*: to lop off twigs]

kyaandit (v) counted.

kye (n) cattle, (pl. of cow). [Bible, *kine*; Sc. *kye*]

K

kyemp (v) to compete; to fight. [N. *kjempe*: to contend; N.E., Sc. *kemp*: a fighter; a champion]

kyittims, **playing da** (v) gambolling and frolicking. [of O.N. *ketlingr*: a kitten]

kyoab (n) a gift, usually given in expectation of some personal recompense. [O.N. *kaup*: compensation; payment]

kyoder (kjoder) (v) to caress or show favour. [orig. obs. cf. O.Sc. *cuiter*, E.dial. *couther*: to comfort with refreshment and warmth]

kyucker (kukker, koker) (v) to invigorate; revive. [N. *kokra*: to fondle; to talk gently; Sc. *cocker*: to pamper; fondle; indulge; O.F. *conqueliner*: to dandle]

kyufset (kefset) (adj) untidy. [N. *kafsa*: to grab; to move one's hands continually; to stir something about]

kyunnin (kaninchen) (n) a rabbit (*Oryctolagus cuniculus*). [O.Sc. *coning*, O.F. *conyn(g)*, *connin*, L. *cuni*: rabbit + *culus*: an underground passage]

kyunnen hadd (n) rabbit hole. [coning (see above) + L.Sc. *hald*, *hauld*: a place of stay; a dwelling; refuge]

K

L

laaber (v) to thrash; to cultivate ground; (also **ledder**). [E. *leather*, *leathering* – a belt or leather strap being the most commonly used method of administering punishment]

laaberin (n) a thrashing. [see above]

laach (lach, laachter) (n) a laugh; (v) to laugh; (also see **leuch**). [O.Sc. *lauch*: laugh]

laachter (lachter) (n) a litter of puppies, or other animals; (v) to breed. [O.Sc. *lachter*: originally a hatch or brood of chickens and later extended to other animals; cf. O.N. *látr*: the lair of an animal, from *lag*: to lay]

laad (n) a boyfriend; lover. [Sc. *lad*]; (v) breathe one's last. [O.N. *hlada*: in the expression *hlada einhverjum*: to slay; to kill someone]

laag (lag) 1) (n) a handful of wool. [O.N. *lagðr*: a tuft (of wool or hair); a lock; N. *lagd(e)* is also a tuft of grass]; 2) (v) to pull a boat up the beach in short stages. [N. *lagga*: to move slowly and steadily]

laalie (lollie) (n) a toy or plaything; by extension, a young child, so spoiled as to be likened to a toy. [Icel. *lalli*: a little child not quite able to walk; (v) *lalla*: to begin to walk; to toddle]

laamer (n) amber, as in *laamer-beads*; (adj) of amber colour. [O.Sc. *lammer* (*lamber*), O.F. *ambre* (*l'ambre*): amber]

laar (lar) (n) a slight breeze; a puff of wind. [D. *laring*: a slight breeze; Icel. *lar-* in *laradr* (adj): faint; weak; exhausted]

laav (v) to hover, as a bird of prey. [O.N. *lafa*: to hang dangling]

lackie (n) manyplies, the third stomach of a ruminant animal. [O.N. *laki*; Fær. *lakki*, *rukkulakki*]

lae (n) a wave. [O.N. *lá*]

laebrack (le-break) (n) surf; the breaking of waves on a reef or beach. [O.N. *lá*: a wave; the line of the shoal water along the shore, edged by surf + (see) **brack**: break]

laekin (v) at one's liking; to be or seem likely to. [Sh. form of E. *likely, liking*]

laekly (n) exact resemblance; 'the spitting image of'; appearance; probability. *Dere a laekly o shooers in yun cloods*. [Sh. variant on E. *likeness, liklihood*]

laem (lemm) (n) a half-loft or mezzanine made by laying planks over crossbeams of house or barn. [O.N. *hlemmr*: a loft floor; N. *lem*: wooden floor resting on cross beams at the top of the house]

laem (leem) (n) dishes; crockery. (**laem-pig**, see **pig**) [L.Sc. *leem*: earthenware; china; O.E. *lam*: clay]

laer (ler) (n) learning. *He's full a laer*. [N. & Fær. *læra*; L.Sc. *lare*]

laerned (pt of teach) taught. *Shö laerned me ta write*; (also see **teached** and **towt**). [this is acceptable Shetland grammer based on Norse idiom]

laeve (v) leave. [Sh. variant on E. *leave*]

laeverek (n) skylark (*Alauda arvensis*). [Sc. *laverock*: lark]

laft (n) top storey of a house or barn, commonly used as a storage area. *Wir pitten aa yun bruck ida laft*; (v) to ascend; rise. [Sc. form of E. *loft*, Ic. *lopta*: to lift or to be lifted]

laich (n) low; lower floor or basement (the prison in Scalloway Castle is called the **laich vault**); a stretch of low-lying ground – *Da Laich Ness* – the low, flat part of Dunrossness. [O.Sc. *laich* (poss. *lech(e)*): a stretch of low-lying ground; common in placenames]

laith (adj) reluctant; unwilling. [Sc. form of E. *loath*]

laks (n) a salmon (*Salmo salar*); esp. in placenames, e.g. Laxafirth. [O.N. *lax*: salmon]

lamb (n) a term of endearment. *Yis, dat's rycht lamb*. [O.N. *lamb mitt*: my lamb – the mitt ending now being lost]

lambiehoose (n) outhouse for lambs. [Sc.]

Lammas (n) 1st August. One of the old Scottish 'quarter-days' on which rents and stipends were paid – Hallomas (1st Nov); Candlemas (2nd Feb); Beltane (1st May) and Lammas (1st Aug). [Sc. *Lammas*: originally a harvest festival for consecration of the new bread; O.E. *hláfmæsse*: 'loaf-mass']

Lammas-speet (n) heavy fall of rain in autumn. [Sc. lit. 'Lammas-spit']

lane (adj) alone. *I göd fishin on me lane de streen*; (also see **nain**). [Sc.]

lanerly (adj) lonely. [Sc. form of E. *lonely*]

lang (adj) long. Used in following expressions: *ta mak a lang airm* – invitation to guests to help themselves at the table; *at da lang an da lent* – eventually; *tink lang* – long for. [Sc. *lang*: long]

langband (n) piece of timber fixed across roof-rafters as additional support; a purlin or cross-beam. [Icel. *langband*]

lang-bed (n) a temporary bed (originally of straw) made up on the floor to accommodate overnight visitors (see **flatchie**). [Sc.]

langer (n) boredom. [deriv. of O.Sc. *langsome*: tedious]

lang-lippened (adj) long expected or awaited. [Sc. *lang*: long + O.Sc. *lyppyn*: to expect; O.N. *líta*: to look to]

lang-nebbit (adj) 'long-nosed'; of words having many syllables 'long-winded'. [Sc. *lang*: long + *neb*: a beak or bill; nose]

lang sin syne (adv) long ago. [Sc. *syne, sith(en)*: since; *lang-sin-syne*: lit. 'long since since']

langsome (langsom) (adj) lazy; shiftless. [N. *langsam*; L.Sc. *langsum*]

lap-a-midder (n) a wet nurse. [prob. from O.Sc. *lap*: to enfold a person or clasp to one's bosom – hence a lap-mother]

lapper (lappir) (v) to congeal or curdle; to lap gently, as water. [O.Sc. *lapper*, M.E. *loper*: to curdle; O.N. *hløypa*: to curdle milk]

lapple (n) flap or fold in clothing; ear lobe. *A'll cut aff de lapple o me lug if I'm wrang!* (N.Yell exp.) [E. *lapel* (dim. of *lap* in sense of clothing flap); Sc. *lap*: ear lobe]

lapstane (n) a flat stone on which wet leather was beaten to soften it for making half-soles for shoes. [N. *lappe*, D. *lap*: a patch; O.N. *leppr*: a small piece (a patch)]

lass (n) applied to a female of any age. *I'm tellin dee, lass…* [note: the Sc. diminutive 'lassie' is not used in Shetland dialect]

last (n) an old measurement of land. (In Shetland a 'last of land' was a unit of land, the area being that which had an annual rent and tithe value of 18 marks and was based on the productivity of the soil; one mark (**merk**) was worth 13 shillings and 4 pence.) [O.N. *lest*: a certain quantity of goods, about 4000lb or 12 barrels]

lat (v) allow; permit; let; (pr t) **lat**; (pt) **löt**; (pp) **latten**. [Sc. form of E. *let*]

lat on (v) to reveal; divulge; 'let on' [Sc.]

lavilugget *lavi-luggit* (adj) having drooping ears, esp. a sheep. [N. *lava*: to hang; to dangle; Icel. *lafeyrdur*, N. *lavøyrd*, having hanging ears]

lawting (n) old Shetland supreme court held on the 'Ting-holm' in Loch of Tingwall before being moved to Scalloway under Earl Patrick (also **ting**). [O.N. *logting*: the public court of law]

lay (n) mood; curb; subdue. *Lay de wind* – ease, abate. Phrases: **lay aboot** to turn, as a boat at sea; to turn back. *I forgot me money gyaan tae de shop an hed ta lay aboot*; to flail or strike in all directions. *I laid aboot me*; to place in close contact; **lay aff** tongue-lash; talk volubly; measure out a piece of land or peat bank; moor a boat out from the shore; take off, e.g. clothes. *Lay aff dee jacket*; damage. *Hit laid aff de fence post*; **lay aff till** wait. *Lay aff till denner time*; **lay afore** to come to mind. *Hit lays afore me wir bön dis wey afore*; **lay apo** to beat or thrash. *A'll lay apo dee*; **lay at** to work energetically. *Tak dee sokk an lay at*; **lay athin** place inside of. *Lay some denner athin dee*; **lay awa** lay away; put by. *Lay awa yun book eenoo*; to bury someone. *Dir bön ta lay awa Jeemie*; **lay back** drink with relish. *He's laid back nae want a drink in his time*; **lay ben** place in the ben room; **lay by** to make unfit; store or save up. *Du better lay by twartree pound for yöl*; **lay caald** stun; knock out; **lay doon** lay down; snow heavily. *He's fairly layin him doon*; incapacitate through illness. *He wis laid doon wi a feerie*; cease to refer to. *Dey niver laid it doon til him*; **lay fae** to hit out all round; put energy into. *Tak de fiddle an lay fae dee*; **lay in** plant potatoes (see also **set**); to stock up; put in store; build a reserve; unship the oars in a boat (eating no more and placing fork and knife on the plate might lead to the observation *I see du's laid in dee oars*); **lay in bruck/coom/akker, etc**. break into pieces; damage. *Du'll lay yun plate in shallmillens*; **lay on** organise. *Shö's gyaan ta lay on a concert*; to foster an animal, esp. a lamb or calf. *Du'll hae ta get a lamb ta lay on* (an act which involves taking the skin of a newly dead lamb and placing it over the back of the one to be fostered by the mother of the dead one); fall heavily, as snow; **lay on a aamos** promise a reward with luck attached; **lay oot** knock out; **lay oot for** abuse; speak harshly of. *Shö laid oot fur him nae want*; **lay ower** place or knock something on its side. *Watch oot or du'll lay ower dee cup*; lie down. *A'm gyaan ta lay me ower a start*; **lay pockie** the ovarium of a hen. *De hen has shot her lay pockie* (prolapsed); **lay till** be in close proximity. *De cat laid till de fire*; apply the mind to. *Lay dee mind till it*; **lay till a side** put aside [N. *tilsideesette*: disregard,

ignore, neglect]; **lay tö** close; **lay up** cast on stitches for knitting; to ask a series of **guddicks** or riddles; place in a safe place; be incapacitated. *I doot yun bad leg'll lay him up*; **lay up aside** commence to live with, esp. without proper legal standing. *Shö's geen an laid her up aside him*; **lay warnins on** warn. [O.N. *leggja*: with corresponding meanings]

lear (n) learning. [O.Sc. *lere*: to teach; to learn]

ledder (v) to thrash (also **laaber**). [Sc. form of E. *leather*, *leathering* – a belt or leather strap being the most commonly used method of administering punishment]

ledderin (n) a thrashing. [see above]

lee (n) a lie; a steep slope; (v) to lie. [Sc. form of E. *lie*]

leeir (n) a liar. [O.Sc. *leyer*: a liar]

leek (n) a corpse; dead body (archaic). [O.N. *lik*]

leek-stane (n) (archaic) stone on which a corpse was rested while waiting for a boat to provide transport over a waterway to burial ground (an example may be found in Wester Quarff where there is no burial ground and all burials used to take place on Burra Isle) (also see **leek-strae**). [O.N. *lik*: a corpse; dead body + Sc. *stane*]

leek-strae (**lik-strae**) (n) (archaic) straw on which a corpse has lain on the deathbed and traditionally burned during the funeral. [O.N. *lik*: a corpse; dead body + O.Sc. *strae*: straw]

lee-lang (adj) livelong. [Sc.]

leep (n) a state of extreme warmth; (v) to parboil; to become exceedingly hot. [O.N. *hleypa*: to curdle (milk) by heating it; cf. N.dial. *løypa*: to half-roast food]

leepit (adj) parboiled. [see above]

leerie (**liri**) (n) Manx shearwater (*Puffinus puffinus*). [O.N. *liri*, N. *lira*: the shearwater]

leesh (v) to work with vigour. [O.Sc. *lesche*, *leich*: lash – in the sense to work with great vigour and speed]

leet (v) to heed. *Dunna leet him*; to reveal; make known. *Never leet du keens*. [O.Sc. *lete*: to pretend, to declare; also *lat*: to allow, let out]

leggin (n) the angle formed by sides and bottom of a hooped vessel, as a bucket or tub – usually in plural form. [O.N. *logg*: a groove in the bottom of a cask]

leid (n) diligence; perseverence. [O.N. *hlít*: sufficiency; Fær. *lít*: zeal (in the executing of a work)]

lem (n) earthenware; crockery; (also **löm**). [O.Sc. *leem*: earthenware vessel; dishes; crockery]

lemminder (n) a cripple. [O.N. *lami*, Fær. *lamin*: lame; crippled; O.Sc. *lamit*, *laymet*, *leamit*: lamed; cripple]

lempit (n) a limpet. [O.Sc. *lempit*]

lempit-cuddy (n) a basket in which limpets are collected. [O.Sc. *lempit* + L.Sc. *coodie*, *cudie*: a small tub; N. *kudde*: a nest]

lemse (**lems**, **lemsket**) (adj) limp; feeble; powerless. [Sw.dial. *lamsen*, N. *lemster*: stiff; numb]

len (n) a loan; (v) to loan. [O.Sc. *len*, *lane*]

lent (n) length; way; the distance. *If du's de lent o de shop du'll meybe fetch me de pipper*; full length; at length; *At da lang and da lent* – eventually. [Sh. form of E. *length*; *at length*]

lep (v) to lap up liquid. [N. & Icel. *lepja*, Sw.dial. *läppja*, Fær. *leppa*: to lap]

lepp (n) a small amount, esp. a small amount of tea left in the bottom of a cup. [see above]

ler(a) (n) a stretch of clayey soil or a muddy shore; placenames: Lera, Larigeo, Lerwick, also Lerik. [O.N. *leir*: clay]

less (interj) equiv. to Eng. 'alas'; used in a number of forms: *Less pör ting* (Alas, poor thing); *O less aless…* (Alas, alas…); *O less an döl* (Alas, what sorrow); (prep) except; (conj) unless; (also **aless**). [Sc. *less, aless*]

lest (n) ability to last; (v) to last; to hold out. [E. *last*]

lett (n) a small amount of liquid. [L.Sc. *lite, lyte*: a small part or portion; Sw.dial. *lyta*]

leuch (v) (pt of) **laach**; (pp) **laached**. [O.Sc. *lauch*: laugh]

levin (n) dough. [O.N. *hleifr*: a loaf (not as E. *leaven*)]

ley (n) fallow ground that has returned to grass; (adj) fallow; **ley-croft**; **ley-rig**. [O.Sc. *ley, lea*: land left untilled for some time and allowed to return to grass; O.E. *lēah*]

lib (v) to castrate. [O.Sc. *lib*: castrate; M.E. *libben*, M.Du. *lubben*: to geld]

libbet (adj) castrated. [see above]

licht (lycht) (n) light; illumination. [O.Sc. *licht*; E. *light*]

licht til (v) to attack physically or verbally. [colloq. E. & N.Amer. *light into*: to attack (someone)]

lichtenin-tree (n) the wooden beam in a water-mill which raises or lowers the upper grinding stone in order to adjust the fineness of the meal being ground. [N. *lettetre*: a wooden lever or apparatus by which a millstone can be raised or lowered]

lichtsome (adj) uplifting; cheerful; good-natured. [Sc.]

lie (v) to stop; to become stilled; in phrases: **lat it lie** let the matter rest; **lie in** *If du banks de fire right he'll lie in till de moarn*; **lie on** to batter, as rough weather; to be exposed to. *Yun gale's lyin on wir byre door lik ta brack it doon*; **lie apo** to spend a lot of time in one place. *He's joost lying apo yun fok every day.* [Sh. variant on E. *lie*]

liefalane (adv) all alone (also **löf-alenn**). [O.Sc. *lief-alane*: entirely alone]

life-tinkin (adj) showing signs of recovery from illness; reasonably fit. [in this sense probably originating from O.N. *lif*: a living being; poor creature]

lift (n) 1) the sky; the heavens. [O.Sc. *lift*, O.E. *lyft*: the sky]; 2) swell in the sea. [O.N. *lyfta*: to lift; raise; to move; stir]

liftit (adj) high-spirited. [E. *lift*: to boost one's spirits]

lifteen (verbal noun) a cow was considered to be *lifteen* when it was too weak to rise unaided to its feet after a winter in the byre with little food; any animal too weak to rise was '*in lifteen*'. [O.Sc. *a lifting* – said of a debilitated animal, lit. one requiring 'lifting' to its feet]

limmer (n) a brazen hussy; a loose or worthless woman. [Sc. *lymmar*: a rogue; a rascal – often implying a thief; a loose woman; a prostitute]

limmerik (limrek) (n) bog asphodel (*Narthecium ossifragum*). [the word derives from *limb* + *break* owing to folklore which maintains the plant made the legs of sheep brittle; Du. *beenbreck*; Ger. *beinbrechgras*]

lin (v) to cease; (pt) **lint**; (pp) **lint**; to rest. [O.N. *linna*: to cease; to stop]

ling (n) heather (*Calluna vulgaris*); common in placenames, e.g. Linga. [O.N. *lyng*: heather]

link (n) chain which held a pot-hook or crook suspended over an open fire. [Sc. *link*, with same meanings]; (v) to apply a link; to move in a frolicsome manner; to dance. [N.dial. *linka*: to toss or bend the body; to fling; to throw about]

links (de) (n) rope used to hold down thatching on a roof or haystack and weighted by **link-stanes**.

links (n) joints of the body; used in colloquial phrase *apo da links o his neck* – as in threat of hanging. [O.Sc. *links*, in same expression]

linn (n) a runner, i.e. one of several pieces of wood laid on the beach, over which a boat is drawn (whale bones were also used at times). [O.N. *hlunnr*; Fær. *lunnar*]

lintie (n) twite (*Acanthis flavirostris*). [Sc. *lintie*: a linnet]

lip (n) a mere taste; (v) to sip or take a morsel to taste. [colloq. E. *lip*: to touch with the lips; to taste]

lippen (v) to expect; look forward to. [O.Sc. *lypnyns*: trust; *lyppyn*: expect; O.N. *líta*: to look to]

lipper (n) a disparaging description of a person. [E. & Sc. *leper*: a spurned person; O.F. *lepre*: leprosy]; (v) to be full to overflowing. [O.Sc. *lipper, lipperin ower*: brimming]

lirk (n) a crease; (v) to crease or wrinkle something. [O.Sc. *lirk*: a wrinkle; N. *lyra*: protruding crease or fold of skin]

lisk (n) a tuft of hay or wool; a wisp. [N. *lusk*: forelock]

lispund (n) a 15th cent. weight of grain or butter, approx. 12lb Scots (16.3lb avoirdupois) but gradually increased by extortionate lairds and merchants through 16th and 17th cent. until it reached over 30lb Scots in the 18th century. [O.N. *lispund*: a weight – properly 'lifsk pund' Livonian pound = 24 marks; D. *lispund* = 12 skålpund; N. & Fær. *lispund* = 16 skålpund]

litel (little, litl) (adj) little; small; note: the common dialect word for little is **peerie (piri)** however the Norn *little* continues in placenames, e.g. Papa Little, Little Asta. [O.N. *litli, litla*, used in exp. *sommere litla* – the little summer or short Indian Summer]

litesome (lichtsome) (adj) cheerful (of people or places). [Sc. *lightsome*: light; gay; lively; cheering]

lith (n) joint or segment of the body; figuratively *I ken every lith o his rigg* (I know him thoroughly); (also **tivlik**). [O.N. *lidr*: a joint of the body; a curvature; a bend; Sc. *lith*, O.E. *lith*: a member]

litt (n) originally any colour, now indigo dye (**blue-litt**). [O.N. *litr*: colour; complexion]

little wirt (adj) feeble; insignificant; (lit. (of) 'little worth').

liver (n) said of a jelly-like pool of mud, a consistency found in the **greff** of peat banks at times where the **möld** has become sodden: *Hit's in a liver*. [E. **liver**, as in the consistency of]

liver-drink (n) a fatal blow. Originally a last drink taken on the death-bed. [cf. O.N. *lifsdrykkr*: life-giving drink – which has taken an opposite meaning in Shetland]

liver-head (n) the head of a fish, usually cod or ling, stuffed with fish-livers and cooked in boiling water (see **krappin**, **liver muggie**), (one of several Shetland specialities using fish-livers).

liver muggie (n) a dish using the stomach of a fish (**muggie**) into which diced and seasoned fish liver is packed. After tying shut with string the muggie is placed in boiling salted water to cook. [N. *mage*, O.N. *magi*: the stomach]

loash (loashie) exclamation of surprise, wonder; sometimes **loash mercy!** [Sc. *losh*: deformation of *Lord*]

lob-lilly (n) someone (esp. a boy) who is at everyone's beck and call; odd jobs person. [origin obscure]

lock (v) close, as opposed to **key** which means lock. *Lock de door an du better joost key her too*. [Sh. variant on E. *lock*]

lock (lok) (n) a lot; a substantial quantity; an abundance. [Sc. *lock*: a small quantity – however, possibly through mispronunciation, in Shetland the word has come to mean the opposite]

lod (lade) (n) a load, esp. sea cargo. [O.E. *lod*: a load]

lodberrie (n) a house built with its foundations in the sea which combines a pier or gantry where vessels can load or unload merchandise, e.g. The Lodberries, Lerwick, which date from 17th cent. and are said to have had smugglers' passages underneath them leading into the old town. [O.N. *hladberg*: a flat rock on the seashore where boats can lie alongside for loading or unloading]

lodge (n) fisherman's bothy at haaf fishing station where men rested between spells at the haaf-fishing (see **haaf**). [O.Sc. *loge*: a bothy]

lodigrut (n) a whimpering sound. [O.N. *lát*: a sound; whimpering + *grátr*: a crying]

longie (longvie) (n) guillemot (*Uria aalge*) (see **loom**). [O.N. *longve*, N.dial. *longve*, *lomvi*: guillemot]

loo (adj) tepid. [E.dial. *lew*: lukewarm; N. & Sw. dial. *lya*: to warm; to soften; to make lukewarm]

loobit (adj) of **loo** (see above) though commonly used in a disparaging way. *Loobit tae an loobit helsin* (Lukewarm tea and lukewarm welcome). [E.dial. (Cornish) *looby*: warm; damp and sultry]

looderhorn (n) a cow's horn made into an instrument to sound a warning from one boat to another during foggy weather; a fog-horn. Used figuratively to describe a very loud voice. [O.N. *látr*: to emit a sound; note: one of the **haaf** fishermen's words for a preacher or clergyman was **loder**]

loodie (n) loud, noisy behaviour. [O.N. *lát*: a sound; N. *laat*, *læta*: a sound; a complaint]

loom (n) sometimes confused with **longie** – guillemot (*Uria aalge*), but properly the red-throated diver (*Gavia stellata*). [O.N. *lómr*: the loom or red-throated diver. Jakobsen comments on the erroneous designation as applying to only some parts of Shetland]

loop (n) a stitch in knitting. *Lay on twartree mair loops*. [E. *loop*, but with specific meaning in Sh]

loor (n) very brief and deceptively fine spell of weather. [N.dial. *lura*: to doze; be drowsy; to lull; to abate (of a storm); also cf. N.dial. *ljor*: an opening in the clouds]

loord (adj) said of a lowering, threatening sky. [E. *lour*, said of weather which is becoming dark and gloomy]

loren (lorin, lorn) (n) great cormorant (*Phalacrocorax carbo*) (see also **brongie**). [O.N. *lár*: the thigh. Breeding birds have conspicuous white patches on their thighs (absent in winter)]

loren shön (n) (archaic) shoes, as opposed to boots. [orig. obs. cf. haaf fishermen's tabu word **ler** – a sea-boot; O.N. *ledr*: leather + O.Sc. *shoon*: shoes]

loup (v) to jump or spring; run in long bounding strides. [O.N. *hlaupa*; N. *laupa*, *lope*; Sw. *löpa*]

lowe (n) a flame; a blaze; (v) to burn brightly. [Sc. *low*, *lowing-hett*]

lowrie-towe (n) (nautical) a tow-rope, esp. a line or rope, with a hook at the end, used for hauling heavy objects. [E.dial. *lurry*: to drag; to pull + tow]

lowse (v) 1) to loosen; to unfasten an animal. [O.N. *løysa*: to break; to burst]; 2) the onset of rain. [N. *løysa*: (to loose) in sense of to commence]; 3) to break out, as in anger. [O.Sc. *lowss*: to break out]; 4) to begin to perspire; 5) (adj) loose. [E. *loose*]

lö (v) to listen attentively. [O.N. *hlýda*: to listen; give ear]

lö-cup (loa-diet) (n) a snack between meals, usually taken furtively. [cf. N. *lysmør*: tiny lumps of cheese in the cream during churning]

löd (n) a mood; a song. [both meanings deriv. from O.N. *hljód*: a sound; tone; silence]

lödi-pipe (luli-pipe) (n) a primitive pipe or whistle made from reed-grass or straw. [cf. Fær. *látupipa*: a whistle; Icel. *hljódpipa*]

löf (n) the palm of the hand. [O.N. *lófi*; L.Sc. *lufe*, *luif*]

löf-alenn (adj) all alone (also **liefalane**). [O.Sc. *lief-alane*: entirely alone]

löm (n) a dish (also **lemm**). [O.Sc. *lume*, *lome*: a dish; vessel]

löm (lüm, lümie, lumji) (n) shiny appearance on surface of water caused by oil or other greasy substance. [O.N. *ljómi*: brightness; radiance]

lönabrack (n) sea breaking on the shore – originally with calm sea further out. [N., Fær., Icel., *lygna*: a calm; a calm spot on the surface of the sea – hence *lönabrack*: the breaking of the calm]

lör (n) the pollack (*Pollachius pollachius*). [O.N. *lýrr*; N. *lyr*]

lörabub (lirigob) (n) sea-spume, especially thick foam piled in a narrow space by heavy sea. [O.N. *laudr* or *leydr*: sea-foam; Icel. *leydra*: to foam; to wash]

lubba (n) coarse, boggy vegetation of any kind, usually associated with mossy ground, e.g. cotton-grass. [O.Sc. *lubba*: leaves of the heathrush; any similar coarse boggy vegetation; cf. Icel. *lubbi*: shaggy tousled hair; *lubbalegar*: (of hair) shaggy; matted; unkempt]

luck (lukks) (n) entice; coax. *Shö luckit de kittlin fae ahint da cooch wi a saacer o mylk*. [O.N. *lokka*: to allure; to entice]

lucky-lines (lukki-lines) (n) long (up to 8 metres) sea lace or dead man's rope (*Chorda filum*) which grows in shallow sea, attaching itself in the sea-bed by means of a disc-shaped holdfast (also **droo**, **drooie-lines**). [O.N. *lykkja*: a loop; coil; winding. Jakobsen suggests **lukki-lines** may derive from Loki, the mischievous giant in Norse mythology who murdered Balder. Loki's enemies hunted him down and after killing his sons Narfi and Váli, they bound him to a rock with Narfi's entrails, leaving him there until Ragnarök – The Doom of the Gods]

L

lucky minnie's oo (lukka-) (n) bog cotton or cotton grass (*Eriophorum augustifolium*). [*Lukki-minni* was a witch in Shetland and Orkney folklore. She lived in the hills and gathered the 'oo' (wool) from the bog cotton which she then carded on a **ferri-caird** or fern. She also went to sea in an egg-shell, using **lucky-lines** (see above) to secure her 'boat'. *Shetland Traditional Folklore*, Jessie Saxby p.185. Both 'lucky' and 'minnie' are O.Sc. for mother, or grandmother, so *lucky-minnie* may have been a variation on the wicked step-mother]

lug (n) ear. [colloq. Sc. *lug*: ear]

lum (n) chimney (also **shimley**). [Sc. *lum*: a chimney; cf. Welsh *llumon*: chimney]

lunder (v) to beat severely; hit hard. [O.Sc. *lounder*, *lunder*: cuff]

lunderin (n) a thorough beating. [O.Sc. *lundering*: cuffing]

lundilag (londilag) noisy commotion. [N. *lund*: a melody; tone + *laga*: to talk nonsense]

lungasott (n) lung-disease (in cattle and sheep). [O.N. *lungnasott*: lung-disease]

lungie (longi) (n) the long gut (colon) of a sheep's intestines, used for making sausages (**puddins**). [Icel. & Fær. *langi*: the long (gut)]

lunk (v) to walk with a dipping or bobbing action; to heave. [N. & Sw. *lunka*: to go leisurely; to jog]

luraferdi (N. Yell) (n) a 'curious' illness; an exaggerated or feigned illness. [N. *lureferd*: stealthy or sly practices]

lurgit (lorkji) (n) a large quantity of something. [N. *lyrgja*: loosely tangled mass]

lurk (n) a big, clumsy person. *A great lurk o a boy*. [N. *lurk*: a stout and heavy person]

lyoag (ljog) (n) a small hollow or depression in the landscape, commonly swampy. [Fær. *låg*: a hollow or depression]

lyrie (n) pollack (*Pollachius pollachius*). [O.N. *lýrr*; N. *lyr*]

lythe (n) pollack (*Pollachius pollachius*). [O.N. *lýrr*; N. *lyr*]

L

M

maa (n) seagull, esp. herring gull (*Larus argentatus*). [O.N. *mar*; N. *möke*; Icel. *máfur*; M.E. *meue*; O.E. *mēu*]; (v) to reap; mow. [E. *mow*]

maal (n) mall; mallet. [E. *mallet*]

maallie (n) fulmar (*Fulmarus glacialis*). [also *mallimot*, *mallimoke*, *mall-ducks*; Du. *mallemok*, from *mal*: foolish + *mok*: a gull]

machtless (adj) impotent; powerless; without strength. [M.E. (13th cent) *maght*, Sc. *maught*, *micht*: might; strength – thus *michtless*: lacking in strength]

maddrim (madrim) (*mödrim*) (n) fun; hilarity. [cf. O.N. *móðr*: excitement; (excited) state of mind]

maed (n) maggot. [O.N. *madkr*, M.Du. & Ger. *made*: maggot]

maedit (adj) infested with maggots. [see above]

maeger (magerdom) (n) in a state of exhaustion or weakness; a feeling of misery or depression. [O.N. *magr*: meagre; lean]

maegins (n) the central part of a period of time; the heart or depth of something. *De maegins o de nycht*. [O.N. *megin*: the main part of a thing; *vetramegins*: the depth of winter]

maeshie (mesi, meshie) (n) a net designed for carrying hay or corn on the back or for attaching to a pony's pack-harness for similar purpose. [O.N. *meiss*: a basket; N. & Sw.dial. *meis*: a wicker basket for transport by a pack-horse]

maet (n) food, as opposed to **flesh** which is meat; (v) to feed. *Maet de kye ida byre afore du maets deesel*. [O.E. *mete*: food]

maet-hale (adj) healthy; having a good appetite. [O.E. *mete*: food + *hāl*: whole – a variation on 'hale and hearty']

mairch (mark) (n) the demarcation line between two properties. [O.N. *mark*: a mark (boundary-mark)]

mairch-stane (mairch-sten) (n) stone marking a property boundary (see **mett**). [O.N. *mark*: a mark + Sc. *stane*: stone]

maistlins (adv) mostly; almost. [O.Sc. *maist*: most + *-lins*, *lings*: 'in the direction of']

mak (n) a match; an equal. [O.N. *maki*]

mak (v) (pt **med, made** to make; produce (in weather terms). *He's makkin a göd sook da day* – said of a day that produces a drying wind; knit; **mak a, mak o** make of. *Whit can du mak a dat?* **mak aandoo** make headway, as in walking, esp. against wind. *I couldna mak aandoo* (fig. of **aandoo** to row a boat); **mak a better o** do something better. *I couldna mak a better o it* (I couldn't do it better, couldn't help it); **mak a hakk o** make a botched job of. *Du's makkin a hakk o pentin yun door*; **mak aff** scamper away. *I mighta kent du wid mak aff*; complete a knitted garment; suppose; believe. *Du'll be home fae de sea I mak? I made it ta be Robbie shö wis spaekin aboot*; depart (also **mak awa**). *We better mak aff fur de toon*; **mak apon/apo** knit a garment; **mak apo** gather up. *Dir a mak apo de baa* (wave about to break

over a sunken rock); **mak at** charge at. *De tup med at de grind*; **mak awa** depart. *Hit's late so A'll hae ta mak awa*; dispose of. *Dunna mak awa wi yun book*; **mak awa wi aen's sel** commit suicide; **mak a head wind; mak heavy weather** to stagger from drunkeness; **mak a wark** make a disturbance. *Du's makkin a wark finnin somthin ta wear*; **mak a wark wi** romp with. *Shö med a wark wi him at de dance*; **mak back** return. *Whan does du tink du'll mak back?* **mak back fur** return to. *I hed ta mak back fur hame*; **mak back ower** fall backwards. *Sit apo de fower legs a de shair or du'll mak back ower*; **mak fae** come from, as wind or tide. *He's makkin fae de sooth*; leave, depart. *We'll hae ta mak fae de hill*; **mak fast** tie up a vessel or object; **mak fur** move towards, with aggressive intent. *De dug med fur de cat; Mak fur de shop*; prepare for. *He's makkin fur rain*; **mak maen** moan; lament [O.N. *meina*: to hurt]; **mak nae odds** make no difference, does it matter. *He's wearin his faider's socks bit it maks nae odds*; **mak o** to make much of; **mak on** pretend; **mak oot** extricate oneself. *De coo couldna mak oot a de gutter*; discern. *I couldna mak him oot in de mirkin*; ascertain; understand what is being said. *He spak saft an I couldna mak him oot*; **mak redd apon/apo** sort out. *A'll mak redd apon it de nite*; **mak til** go forwards; **mak troo wi** finish, conclude. *I wiss I cud mak troo wi dis darg*; **mak owre/ower** go towards. *Mak ower tae de idder side*; assign. *He's gyaan ta mak ower de hoose tae wis*; **mak up** arrange; travel upwards. *Mak up fur Setter* (similarly **mak doon**); prepare for. *He's makkin up a rainy sky*; **mak up wi** catch up, overtake. *I wis tryin ta mak up wi dee*; **mak watter** to urinate; **mak wye** break, come apart; begin a journey. *A'm gyaan ta mak wye fur Scalloway*. [Sc. version of E. *make*, however the sense behind some of the expressions is rather more Scand.]

makadö (n) pretence; sham. [corruption of E. 'make do']

makkin (n) knitting; a gathering of women for the purpose of knitting. *Der a makkin at aald Leezie's de nycht*; a brew of tea. *Wait du, I'm pitten on a makkin o tae*. [Sh. variant on Sc. *mak*]

makkin on (v) filling the load of peats and lifting the **meshies** on to the **klibbers**. [Sh. variant on Sc. *mak*]

makker (n) knitter. *Shö's an excellent makker*. [Sh. variant on Sc. *mak*]

makkin waers (n) knitting needles; double-ended steel needles used for knitting Shetland yarn. [Sc. *mak* + Sc. *wire*: a knitting needle; O.Sc. *weir*]

mallivoag (v) to sort out. [orig. obs. cf. O.Sc. *mullyo*: harvest gleanings; *mullyoed*: to form gleanings into small bundles]

mam (n) mother (also **mammie, midder**). [E.dial. *mam*; Sc. *mither*]

man (v) expressing necessity; must. (p) *What man be man be* (What must be must be). [Sc.dial. *man, maun*: must]

man-body (n) adult man; (pl) **men-fokk**. [Sc.]

mankit (manket) (adj) exhausted. [N. *manga*: to decrease in strength and condition]

man man (min min) an exp. of surprise. *I hear shö geed aff wi di postman. Man man!*; also an exp. of disapproval when used in a more drawn out way. **Minn minn**, *dunna tramp ower me neeps laek yun.*

manna (v) must not. [Sc.dial. *maunna*]

mant (n) a stammer; (v) to stammer. [O.Sc. *mant*; Sc. & Ir. Gael. *manntach*: lisping; stammering]

manyugilti (manyuggilty, manjuggelti) (n) originally to perform magic art, juggling tricks, now a piece of trickery or deceit; underhand activities. [O.N. *magna*: to strengthen – esp. to make strong by witchcraft + Fær. *gykl, gygl*, D. *gøgl*, Sw. *gyckel*: juggle]

mar (n) the sea. [O.N. *marr*: the sea]; (v) to confuse; distract; (also see **mer**). [Sc. *mer*: to confuse; O.E. *mearrian*: to go astray].

mara (n) nightmare; the fearful subject of a bad dream. [O.N. *mara*]

mareel (maril, marelde) (n) phosphorescence which appears on the sea. [O.N. *marr*: the sea + *eldr*: fire; O.N. *mörueldr*; Icel. *maurildi*; N. *moreld*; D. *morild*]

marlek (marlok, marl) (n) eel grass (*Zostera marina*). [N. *marlauk*: seaweed; grass-wrack; sea-onion]

marlet (marglit) (adj) mottled. [Icel. *marglitr*: variegated; L.Sc. *marled*: partly mottled; partly chequered]

marool (marul) (n) angler or monkfish (*Lophius piscatorius*) (also **masgoom**). [O.N. *morulfr*: the angler fish; N. & Sw.dial. *marulk*]

marshum (n) empty egg cases of common whelk (*Buccinum undatum*). [Fær. *marsoppur*]

Martinmas (n) 11th November. A Scottish 'term-day' (the other being Whitsun on 15th May) when rents, annuities, etc. are payable; the feast of St Martin of Tours.

masgoom (marsgum) (n) angler or monkfish (*Lophius piscatorius*) (also **marool**). [O.N. *marr*: the sea + *gumi*: a man. Jakobsen also has **murgab** with -*gab* from O.N. *gap*: an opening]

masheeve (v) to do bodily harm; to injure; to receive a cut or wound. [O.Sc. *mischieve*: to bring to destruction; to do bodily harm]

mask (v) to infuse tea. [O.Sc. *mask, masc*: steep, as malt brew, etc.]

mask (n) the mesh of a net; (v) to catch in a net. *De troot wis maskit.* [O.N. *moskvi*; N. *moske*; D. *maske*]

matchie (madgie); (n) immature female herring, one with roe not fully developed. [Du. *maatjes*: herring; cf. M.L.Ger. *madikes-herink*, both from L.Ger. *mädeken*: a maiden]

matlo (n) the blue-bottle or 'maggot fly' (*Calliphora vomitoria*). [N. *maggafluga*: bluebottle; O.N. *madkr*: a maggot]

maugerment (magerment) (n) strength; substance, esp. of food being tasteless or insipid. *Dey wir nae maugerment ta de soup.* [O.Sc. *macht*: strength; power; O.N. *máttr*]

mayflooer (meyflooer) (n) primrose (*Primula vulgaris*), so named because it flowers during the month of May.

meesery (n) emaciated. [Sh. variant on E. *misery*]

meeting (n) semi-informal low-church gathering for evening worship, as opposed to **de kirk** (the more liturgical form of worship service held on Sunday mornings). *We aye hae Sankey hymns at de meeting.* [Sc.]

meid (meed, mid) (n) a prominent landmark which, when lined up with a second one, enables fishermen to confirm direction or maintain a fixed position at sea. Fishing grounds located by the above procedure. [O.N. *mida*: to mark a place]

meldie (meldi) (n) corn spurrey (*Spergula arvensis*). [N. *melde*: small seeds of grass or weeds among the corn]

mell (n) a wooden mallet used in conjunction with a knockin stane (see **knockit**). [E. *mall*: mallet]; (v) to mix. [O.Sc. *mell*: mix; mingle]

mellishon (n) a curse; the devil; said of someone going at speed: *He wis gyaan lik de mellishon.* [O.E. *maliso(u)n*; E. *malediction*]

mell-moorie (mellmurin) (n) violent flurries of fine, powdery snow (see **moorie, moorie-caavie**). [Fær. *murrukavi*: finely drifting, choking snow; N. *mjoll, mjell*: dry, newly fallen snow]

mention (n) a modicum; a shade. [Sc. *mention*: a fraction; particle; modicum]

mer (merr) (v) confuse. *Dunna mer me*; distract; (also **mar**). [Sc. *mer*: to confuse; O.E. *mearrian*: to go astray]

mercy (n) an exclamation. *Gude mercy!*; a blessing. *Hit wiz a mercy shö wan hame.*

merk (n) an old Scots monetary sum equal to 13s 4d on which land rentals were based. [see **last**]

merky-bane (mergie-bane) (n) marrow-bone. [O.N. *mergr*: marrow; O.Sc. *merch, mergh* (corrupted to merkerin) + O.Sc. *bane*: bone]

mert (n) an animal fattened for market. [O.Sc. *mart*: an ox or cow fattened for slaughter]

meshie (n) (see **maeshie**)

mester (n) a master; schoolmaster; (v) to accomplish. *A'll mester it yit.* [E. *master*]

mett (n) mark; a boundary mark (stone). [O.N. *met*: the weight of a balance; O.Sc. *mett*: measure]

micht (mycht) (n) might. [O.Sc. *micht*; E. *might*]

michty (mychty) (interj) exclamation of astonishment or surprise. *Michty me!* [Sc.]

midden (n) manure pit; muck-heap. [archaic Sc. *midden*: a dunghill; O.N. *myki*, D. *mög*: dung]

midder (n) mother (also **mam**); in exp. **midder's blissins** (n) white spots on finger nails – signs of good luck; **midder-nakit** (adj) stark naked; **midder-wirsom** (n) the core of an abscess; **midder wit** (n) common sense. *Dat boy haes nae midder wit.* [Sh. variants of Sc. *mither*]

middlin (adj) reasonably well; so-so. [Sc. & E. *middling*: indifferent; mediocre; fairly good; moderately well]

millin (n) a tiny particle; a speck; (also see **shalmillens**). [N. *myl*: a particle]

milsprinda (melspindra, millspindra) (n) alpine lady's mantle (*Alchemilla alpina*). [orig. obs.]

mindin (n) used in phrase *aa my mindin* (as far back as I can remember).

mines (poss. pron) mine; my property. *Dis is mines, no dines* (This is mine, not yours). [Sc. form of E. *mine*]

minkie (adj) small (also see **mootie, peerie**). [Sc. *minikin*: a diminutive or undersized person or thing]

minnie (n) grandmother. [Sc. *minnie*: pet name for mother or grandmother]

mirackle (mirakill) mir-*ackl* (v) to severely injure. [the etymology of this word has evolved from E. *miracle* – a spectacle, a thing to be wondered at – to the old Shetland meaning of a ridiculous sight, an oddity, a physically disabled person and finally the act of injury itself; as such, the word is a good example of evolution in language]

mird (mirj) (n) a swarm; a throng; (also **murge**). [O.N. *mergd*: multitude; plenty]

mirdin (adj) teeming. [see above]

mire-laid (adj) bogged down. *De ploo is mire-laid ida boddam o de rig.* [E. *mire*: mud]

mirk (adj) dark. [O.N. *myrkr*, E. & Sc. *mirk*: dark]

mirkabrod (n) light, variable wind; orig. a mist covering the hill-tops, followed by wind. [O.N. *myrkvi*: (darkness) fog]

mirken (mirker) (v) to grow dark. [O.N. *myrkna*: to grow dark]

mirknen (n) the evening twilight. [N. *myrkning*: twilight]

mirl (v) to quiver; to shimmer; to tremble; deriv. of **mirr** (see below); (also **pirm, pipper, titter, vimmer**). [N. *mirra*: to tingle; prick; itch]

mirr (n) a blur; vibration; trembling; (also see **simmer mirr**). [see above]

mirry-begyit (n) an illegitimate child (lit. 'merry-begat').

mirrie dancers (n) (*mirry-*) (Sc. *merry dancers*) aurora borealis (also **pretty dancers**). [N. *mirr (myrr)*: tingling; itching; trembling; quivering. Note: as aurora in vicinity of the polar regions is characterised by a shimmering, tremulous motion, the Shetlandic '*mirrie*' is a better description of the phenomenon than the Scottish '*merry*']

misackered (adj) badly injured. [see **mirackle**]

misanter (n) a mishap; an accident. [E. *mishandled*: ill-treated; roughly handled]

miscaa (v) to slander or speak ill of. [O.Sc. *misca*; E. *miscall*]

misfare (v) (pt) **misför**; (pp) **misforne**; to come to grief; experience a calamity or mischance. [O.N. *misför*, *misferd*: miscarriage; accident]

miss (n) to lose by death. *Did du miss mony sheep wi de snaa?*; a loss through death. *Shö'll be a miss.* [O.N. *missa*, Fær. *missur*: a loss]

misskenn (v) to mistake one person for another; (pt) **miskent**. [O.N. *miskenna*: mistake one person for another]

mitten (v) to grasp; take a hold of. [O.Sc. *mitten*: to grab; catch hold; E. *mitten*: glove (with or without fingers) with additional meaning 'to glove' (to take hold of something)]

moarn (n) used with definitive article **de moarn** tomorrow; **de moarn's morn** tomorrow morning. [E. *morn, morning*]

moch (n) moth. [M.E. *moch, moghe* & E. Sc.dial. *moch*: a moth]

moch-aeten (adj) infected with moths (lit. 'moth-eaten'). [see above]

moder (n) older form of 'mother' (see below). [O.N. *módir*]

moder-dy (moder-däi) (n) an underlying swell of the sea which experienced seamen were said to be able to detect and use to steer by as it always set landwards irrespective of wind or the state of the sea; every 9th wave (lit. 'mother-wave'). [O.N. *módir*: mother + *dý*: quagmire, with extension of image to the sea and the idea of underlying motion; cf. N. *grunnmoder*: undercurrent]

moget (adj) of animals having a belly of darker colour to the body. [O.N. *mogóttr*; Icel. *mögóttur*]

mogie (n) stomach of an animal or fish (also **muggie**). [N. *mage*, O.N. *magi*: the stomach]

Monenday (n) Monday. [Sh. variant on E. Monday]

moniment (n) a foolish person. [O.Sc. *moniment*: monument – fig. of a person who is prominent in making a fool of themselves]

monn (v) to moan. [E. *moan*]

mooed (adj) said of sheep having a mineral deficiency. [O.N. *moedi*: weariness; exhaustion]

mool (n) 1) a headland (also **mull**); 2) mouth or snout. [N. *mule*, O.N. *múli*: muzzle; mouth (upper lip in animals)]

mool-baand (v) to muzzle, though generally said in sense of restraining someone. *He's a wild een, du'll laekly hae ta mool-baand him.* [N. *mule*: muzzle + *band*]

moor (mura) (n) peaty soil. *paet-moor.* [Icel. *mór*]; (v) heavily falling snow that is drifting. [O.N. *mor*: dust; dregs; mud; Sw.dial. *murjog*: thick; dim; hazy (of weather); however, see **moorie-caavie**]

mooratoog (muratug, möratu) (n) ant (*Formicidae*), though more correctly an ant-hill; a mound (see **toog**). [O.N. *maurr*: ant + *tug* – O.N. *þufa*: a mound; D. *myretue*: ant-hill]

moorek (n) silverweed (*Potentilla anserina*), also vernal squill (*Scilla verna*). [O.N. *mura*: silverweed]

moorie (n) a blizzard. [see below]

moorie-caavie (murkavi) (n) blinding snowstorm or blizzard (older renderings include *mellkavi, mellmurin*, all related to heavy snowfall) (see **mell-moorie**). [Fær. *murrukavi*: finely drifting, choking snow; N. *mjoll, mjell*: dry, newly fallen snow]

moorit (adj) brown, most commonly used to describe a Shetland sheep with brown wool, or spun yarn of that colour. [O.N. *móraudr*, N.dial. *moraud*: reddish, yellow-brown (of sheep and wool), lit. 'moor-red']

moose (n) house mouse (*Mus musculus*) (also see **hill moose**). [O.N. *mús*; L.Sc. *moose*]

moose-wub (n) a cobweb. [O.Sc. *mousewab (-wob)* – 'wab' being woven fabric or a spider's web]

mooskit (adj) mouse-coloured; grey. [O.N. *mús*: a mouse; O.Sc. *moose*]

moot (mutt) (n) a mite; a small creature. [properly a *mite* or *moth*; O.N. *motti*: a moth]

mootie (muti) (adj) very small – commonly used as a term of affection. *Peerie mootie lamb.* [see above; also **alamootie**]

mooter (v) to decay. *Hit joost mootered awa.* [N. *muten*: to grow musty; N. *mott*: (thick) must]

mooth (n) a mouthful of food; a morsel. [Sc.]

mooth-liftin (n) a bite to eat; a morsel. [Sc.]

morless (adj) matchless; not matching, as of odd socks. [*marrow-less*, *match-less* (see below)]

morrow (**morro**, **marrow**) (n) an equal; a match. *Du'll no fin his morrow fur strent*; (v) said of cats mating: *De cats is morrowin*. [M.E. *marrow*: mate; partner; equal; match; O.E. *marwe*: a fellow; companion]

mortal (n) intoxicated (one of hundreds of expressions used to describe a state of drunkenness, lit. 'mortally drunk' i.e. 'dead drunk'). [see **paloovious**]

mott (n) a mote; a particle. [O.N. *motti*: a moth (see **moot**)]

motty (adj) covered with or full of small particles. [see above]

moy-foy (**moifoi**) (n) mischief; capers. [N. & S. *maafaa*: absurd conduct; nonsense]

moyenless (**moinlos**) (adj) enervated; lacking energy. [O.N. *magnlauss*: weak; feeble]

möld (n) earth-mould. [O.N. *mold*: mould]

möld-drocht (n) a state of near-death when the dying person drank copious quantities of liquid before expiring (lit. a 'death-drink'). [*möld* (see above) + E. *draught*, O.E. *dracht*: the act of drinking]

möld-rich (adj) lit. 'filthy rich'. [see **möld**]

möldie-blett (n) a bare patch of hill-pasture from which peat-mould has been gathered for **möldie-cooses** (see below). [O.N. *mold*: mould + Icel. & Fær. *blettur*: a spot]

möldie-coose (**möldikjos**) (n) a quantity of peat-mould used as bedding for cattle. [O.N. *mold*: mould + O.N. *kos*: a heap, pile, thrown together]

mön (**monin**) (n) the moon. [O.N. *máni*: the moon]

mön-broch (n) a luminous ring of light round the moon, purported to foretell windy weather. [O.N. *máni*: the moon + O.N. *borg*: fort]

möni (n) the spinal cord. [O.N. *mæna*, Icel. *mæna*: spinal marrow]

mös (v) to be bewitched; benumbed. [orig. obs. cf. *mölos* – O.N. *mállaus*: speechless; dumb]

muck (n) cows' manure; dung; (v) in exp. *muck oot* – to remove dung from byre or other animal housing. *I'll need tae muck oot de byre*. [O.N. *myki*, D. *mög*: dung]

muck haak (n) a tool for pulling dung from the back of a cart to form piles along a **rig** prior to spreading. [*muck* (see above) + O.Sc. *haik*: drag forth]

muckify (v) to make dirty. [O.N. *myki*: dung]

muckle (adj) (of quantity or size) large; much; *muckle de sam* – little changed. [O.N. *mikill*: great; large; much; E.dial. *mickle*, O.Sc. *muckle*: much]

muckle kokkeloori (n) sea mayweed (*Matricaria maritima*). [so named for its appearance to a cockle-shell when closed; N. *kokkelur(e)*: pine-cone (seed capsule – *kokul*); *kukkelur(e)*: snail-shell]

muckle skarf (n) cormorant (*Phalacrocorax carbo*). [*muckle* (see above) + O.N. *skarfr*]

mud (v) to lightly dig, rather in the manner of hoeing; to loosen up soil before setting potatoes or planting seed. *Tattie mold* was mudded – the spade seldom being 'heeled', as in deep digging. [N. *modda*: to root about in straw or hay]

mudjick (**mujek**, **midjick**) (n) a midge. [O.N. *mý*: a gnat; E. midge (*Chironomidae*)]

muggie (n) the stomach of a fish (also see **mogie**). [N. *mage*, O.N. *magi*: the stomach]

mulder (v) to reduce to dust. [Sw.dial. *mullta*: to smoulder under the ashes]

mummie (n) small fragments. [N. *molma*: a soft, granulated mass; E.dial. *muimmy*: a soft, shapeless mass; a pulp]

munt (n) a month. [Sh. version of E. *month*]

murg (**morg**) (n) a mess. [N. *morke*: a mass; a mixture; Sw.dial. *mörja*: damp or dirty mass]

murgadge (**morgadge**) (n) a mess or muddle; untidiness. [N. *myrja*: a mass; mixture + N. *gysja*: mud; filth; a great mass]

murge (**morg**, **mirge**) (adj) an overwhelming number (also **mird**). [N. *morke*: a mass; mixture]

murken (**morken**) (v) to become mouldy or musty, esp. hay. [N. *morken*, Icel. *morkinn*, S. *murken*: somewhat decayed; rotten; mouldering; O.N. *morkna*: to wither, die or waste away]

murn (v) to weep. [O.Sc. *murne*: to mourn]

murnin (adj) weeping. [see above]

murr (n) tiny particles; small things of their kind. [O.N. *mor*: small particles; dust; dregs; N. *murke*: chips of wood]

mutch (n) a woman's close-fitting cap, frequently having a frilled border. [O.Sc. *much*: a night-cap; M.Du. *mutse*: a covering for the head]

mutchkin (n) a liquid measure, approx. 1 pint. [Sc. *mutchkin*: a measure equal to ¼ old Scots pint or ¾ imperial pint]

myaatless (see **machtless**)

myl-gruel (n) porridge made with milk instead of water (lit. 'milk-gruel').

mylk (n) milk. [Sh. variant on E. *milk*]

mylk-an-mell (n) a drink made of oatmeal mixed with hot milk. [Sh. (Sc.) lit. 'milk and meal']

N

na (adv) no; negative – with a tendency to iterate. *Na, bairns!* – an expression of incredulity or disbelief. [Sc.]

naaber (naber) (n) a miser; an avaricious person; (adj) mean; miserly. [O.N. *knappr*, Icel. *knappr*, *hnappr*, N. & S. *knapp*: scanty; spare; mean; cf. Biblical character 'Nabal' who was notorious for his avarice (Jak.)]

nackers (n) the testicles. [E. (slang) knackers]

nae (adj, adv) no; not any. *Nae doot* (without a doubt). [O.Sc. *nae*]

nain (adj) own; my own. *I göd fishin on my nain destreen*; (also see **lane**). [O.Sc. *nain*: deriv. from wrong division of 'mine ain' as 'my nain']

name-faider (n) the man after whom one has been named (lit. 'name-father').

nane (pron) none. [O.Sc. *nane*; E. *none*]

nasems (n) sexual intercourse with women. [N. *nossa*: to enjoy oneself]

nattek (n) an ill-tempered, troublesome child. *Du is wan nattek*. [Sw.dial. *knatte*, *knatt*: something stunted; a small being]

naverspell (n) a piece of birch-bark found washed ashore, at one time burned as a source of light. [O.N. *næfr*: birch-bark + *speld*, *spjald*: a tablet; slab; flake; slice; also *spila*: a thin, narrow slice]

nearbegyaan (adj) mean; miserly. [see **naaber**]

near-haand (adv) close by (lit. 'near to hand').

neb (n) a bird's beak; nose. [O.N. *nebb*: the nose; beak of a bird; projecting point]

nedder (nedderen) (conj) neither. [E. *neither*]; (adj) lower; under, as in *nedder-regions*; in placenames, e.g. Nedder Tun; (also **nedmost**). [E. *nether*]

nedfallsott (n) epilepsy (lit. 'down-fall-sickness'). [an obscure Norn word, rarely used and deriv. of Fær. *nidurfallsott*: a composite word created to describe the Eng. word epilepsy]

nedmost (n) lowermost. [O.N. *nidr* (adv): down]

neeb (nib) (v) to be drowsy; nod with sleep. [O.N. *hnipa*: to hang the head; to droop]

neebit (nibet) (adj) sickly. [O.N. *hnipinn*: disheartened; sad; prop. drooping; hanging the head]

neebour (neebir) (n) neighbour; one of a pair. *My joopie's de very neebir o dines*; (adj) neighbouring. *Shö's a neebour tae wis*. [Sc. *nebor*, *nibor*, etc.]

neebrid (n) neighbourhood. *He wiz raikin trow de neebrid*. [of Sc. (see above)]

neep (n) turnip. [O.Sc. *neip*; L. *napus*]

neer (nir) (n) a kidney. [O.N. *nýra*, O.Sc. *neir*: kidney]

neer spikk (n) fat from around the kidney. [O.N. *nýra* + *spik*: blubber]

neesik (nisik) (n) harbour porpoise (*Phocaena phocaena*). [O.N. *hnisa*: the porpoise]

neest (nist) (n) a spark of fire. [O.N. *gneisti*: a spark]; (adj) next. *Neest munt*; (adv) next. *Pit de kishie neest de shair*; (also **neist**). [O.Sc. *neste*; O.N. *næst*]

neester (n) a creaking noise; (v) to squeak or grate, as an unoiled hinge. [O.N. *gnista*: to produce a penetrating sound – deriv. N. *gnistra*: to creak; whine]

neeve (v) to succumb to (an illness). [D.dial. *knøvle*: to get the upper hand of; to vanquish]

neeze (n) a sneeze; (v) to sneeze. [O.N. *hnjósa*, N. *njosa*, *nysa*: to sneeze; to snort]

neist (adj) next (also **neest**). [O.Sc. *neste*; O.N. *næst*]

ness (n) a headland or promontory. [O.N. *nes*; D. *næs*; Sw. *näs*]

nev (n) a fist; clenched hand. [O.N. *hnefi*: the fist; Fær. *nevi*; S. *näve*; O.Sc. *neive*]

nevfoo (n) handful. [*nev* (see above) + Sc. *foo*: full]

news (n) gossip; information; chat. *Shö aye gengs owre ta Leezie's for her twal an t hae a news*; (v) to chat. [Sc. variant on E. *news*]

Newerday (n) New Year's Day. [Sc.]

nibbie (nibi) (n) a projecting knob. [O.Sc. *nib(bie)*, *neb*: a beak or knob]

nicht (nycht, nite) (n) night. [O.Sc. *nicht*]

nidd (v) to chafe with the teeth, such as horses, cats and dogs do to massage muscles or relieve an itch. [cf. O.N. *gniða*: to rub]

nigg (v) to nag or carp. [cf. N.dial. *gnigga*: to rub; drudge; *nyggja*: to fret; also E.dial. *niggle*]

nildet (adj) mouldy (see **blue-niled (-nildet)**). [Sw.dial. *knäll*: damage]

nile (n) a boat's bilge-plug. [N. *nygla*, O.N. *negla*: a bilge-plug]

nile-hol (n) a small hole in the bottom of a boat for draining bilge water. [N. *nyglehol*: nile-hole (see above)]

nipp (v) to break with a quick movement or jerk. *Du'll faa an nipp dee neck*. [N. *nippa*: to snatch; pull; cut off (pinch off) with a smart nick]

nipp (n) a steep slope. *He's a nipp up ta Houll*. [Sc. in same meaning as E. *pinch*: a place of difficulty or steepness]

nippet (adj) 1) close-fitting, as of clothes; pinched. [O.Sc. *nippit*]; 2) sharp-tongued (also **klipet**, **snippet**). [O.N. *knippen*: somewhat harsh and short in words and deeds]

nipsiccar (nipp-sicker) (adj) bitter; satirical; scathing. [O.N. *knippen*: somewhat harsh and short in words and deeds]

nirls (n) chickenpox. [O.Sc. *nirrilis*: measles – from *nirls*: festering sores]

nirt (n) small particle. [N. *nerta*, Sw.dial. *narta*: to give scant measure; to be stingy]

nitter (v) to shiver and shake with cold. [O.N. *gnotra*, *notra*: to clatter; rattle]

njarg (njirg, sjarg) (v) to constantly grumble; to harp on. [Sw.dial. *narg*: clamour; grumbling; wrangling; Fær. *knarra*, N. *knarka*: to grumble]

no (adv) not. *He'll no shenge his mind*. [Sc. *no*, *na*]

nochtify (v) to belittle; to speak ill of. [O.Sc. *nocht*: nothing – hence *naughtafee*: to disparage; deprecate; speak slightingly of]

nonie (noni) (n) a very small person or animal; used in phrase *Du's a nonie* to imply mild reproof or censure. [L. *nanus*: a dwarf]

noo (adv) now. [Sc. *noo*]

noo an sae (adj) so-so; middling. [Sc.]

noo dan hello. *Noo dan, is dis dee?* (Hullo, is this you?); (lit. 'now then').

noodel (njudl, nudl) (n) to hum or sing low to oneself. [Sw.dial. *nunna*: to hum]

noost (noust, nust, naust) (n) a natural hollow or scooped out trench (sometimes walled) at the beachhead, into which a boat is drawn up and secured; a boat-shed. [N.dial. *naustr*, O.N. *naust*: a boat-shed; dock]

nordert (adv) to the north. [O.N. *nordan*: from the north; on the north side]

norderly (adj) northerly; a northerly wind. [see above]

norie (nöri) (n) puffin (*Fratercula arctica*) (also **tammie-norie**). [onomat. owing to the call being a purring sound; N. *knurra*; D. *knurre*]

Norn (Norröna) (n) the Old Norse language which survived as the native tongue of Shetland and Orkney until the 17th century and from which words shown in blue in this dictionary are, on balance, most likely to have derived their etymology. [O.N. *norræna*: Norn language]

nort aboot (n) northern district. *He wis born nort aboot.* [see below]

nort-boat(s) (n) any of the ro-ro passenger ferries plying between Aberdeen and Lerwick (also **sooth-boat**). [Sc.]

nort by (adv) towards the north. *He geed nort by wirs at denner time*; also **nort ower/owre** *I saa her comin nort ower dis mornin*. [O.N. *nordan*: from the north; on the north side]

noup (nup) (n) a steep headland. [O.N. *gnúpr*: a high and steep mountain with overhanging top]

nön (nün) (n) a soothing hum; (v) to hum. [Sw.dial *nunna*, *nynna*; D. *nynne*]

nug (nugg) (n) a nudge; (v) to nudge; to rock, as a cradle. [O.N. *hnoggr*: a push; a blow]

numskolt (n) a stupid fellow. [N. *skolt*: the forehead; cranium; skull]

nurr (nyrr) (v) to purr, as a cat. [L.Sc. *nerr*: to snarl; growl; N. *knurra*]

nyaaf (njaf) (n) an insignificant but pretentious person; (v) talk nonsense. [O.Sc. *nafferel*: a good-for-nothing; an insignificant person; also *nyaff*: to talk in a senseless, trifling or snappish way – probably originally imitation of a small dog barking; Sw.dial. *naffa*: to snap; nibble]

nyaag (njaf, knagi) (n) nagging ache; (v) to ache. [O.N. *knaga*: to gnaw]

nyaarm (njarm, jarm) (n) the bleat of a sheep or lamb (also **yaarm**). [O.N. *jarma*: to bleat; Fær. *mjarra*: to whimper; mew; bleat]

nyarg (njarg) (n) a nagging person; (v) to nag; to constantly grumble or complain. [Sw.dial. *narga*: to gnaw; chew – thus, to wrangle about trifles]

nycht (n) night. [O.Sc. *nicht*]

nyep (nepp) (v) to clasp the hands or purse lips; to firmly tie the mouth of a sack; (also **knep**). [O.N. *kneppa*, *hneppa*: to squeeze]

nyepkin (n) a headsquare; a handkerchief. [O.Sc. *napkin*: handkerchief; neckerchief; O.F. *nappe*: a cloth + dimin. *-kin*]

nyiff (adj) 1) nimble. [O.N. *næfr*: clever; skilled]; 2) a malodorous smell. [Sc. & E. slang *niff*: an unpleasant smell]

nyig (v) to tug; to jerk. [prob. of **nyiggle** – see below]

nyiggle (nigl) (v) to cut (ineffectively), as with a knife. [E.dial. *niggle*: to gnaw; to nibble; also to cut with a blunt instrument]

nyim (nimm) (interj) a variation on 'yum, yum', said in response to a pleasant taste or to encourage a child to eat. [altered form of Sc. *nyum, nyum*, cf. variant of *nyamff*: hungry]

nyirg (see **nyarg**)

nyitter (n) constant nagging; a crabby complaining person; (v) to chatter endlessly in a complaining manner. [variation on colloq. Sc. *natter*, but influenced by Sw. *gnata*: carp; nag; nibble; O.N. *gnotra*: to chatter; rattle]

nyivvel (nivl) (v) to squeeze or manipulate with the fingers. [N. *knefla*: to squeeze; knead]

nyoag (njog) (n) a moan; (v) to moan. [N. *naukra*: to complain; moan]

nyook (n) a nook; corner or recess; a recess where peats are stored in a house. [E. & Sc. *nook*]

nyuggel (njuggel, njugl) (n) the legendary water-horse in Shetland folklore associated with lochs, burns and mill-dams and not to be confused with **tangie**, the sea-horse. [O.N. *nykr*: a water-spirit. Nyuggels were especially associated with mischief around mill-ponds and mill-wheels (dangerous places for small children to play and therefore to be discouraged by any means possible)]

nyuggelben (n) a projecting bone, esp. hip bone, e.g. of a cow. [O.N. *hnykill*: a swelling; protuberance; bump]

nyurl (njurl) (v) to whimper; complain. [O.N. *gnollra*, *nollra*: to yelp; N. *gnöldra*: to murmer; grumble]

N

O

o (prep) of – commonly used to link a person with his place of abode. *Andy o Baakhoose*, however, see **(i)** and the more correct Norn usage of *Andy i Baakhoose*; (also see **a**). [Sc.]

oag (og) (v) to crawl. [O.N. *aka*: to move; in N. & Fær. also to draw oneself forward]

object (obshikk, obshick) (n) a person in a pitiable state through illness or age. [O.Sc. *object*: a person who is deformed, diseased – commonly a 'poor object']

obleegement (n) a favour; a charitable act. [E. *obligement*]

obstropolous (obstropulous) (adj) noisy; unruly. [E. *obstreperous*]

öbdee (adj) out towards. [etymology obs. cf. *öb*: as ebb + *di*: for (the purpose of)]

ocht (n) anything; (v) ought. [Sc.]

odious (adv) extremely; similar to the informal usage of 'awful' in English; awfully nice. [E. *odious*: hateful; offensive]

oil-cloth (n) linoleum; vinyl floor covering. [E. *oil-cloth*: oil treated cotton used as table and shelf covering]

oiler (oller) (n) the open drain behind cattle in a byre which connects to a **runnick** and from hence to a **midden**. [N. *aale*: urine of cattle; liquid manure from byres]

okrabung (ekrabung) (n) tuberous oatgrass (*Arrhenatherum bulbosum*) which grows as a weed in cultivated land; grass weeds generally. [O.N. *ekra*: land ploughed up; cultivated land; a field + Sw.dial. *bynke*: weeds in the field]

okregord (okregert) (n) properly a fence surrounding cultivated fields (*okra*: corn and *gord*: enclosure); used in the expression *slip* [O.N. *slepp*] *de okregord* (open the gate(s)), thus permitting hill animals access to stubble pasture at the end of the harvest season. [idiomatic Shetland (esp.Yell) but deriv. of O.N.]

olick (ollek) (n) a ling (*Molva molva*); used in plural – *Is du comin wi wis t da olicks?* – to indicate fishing for **olick**. [O.N. *áll*: eel; N. *vallonga, vollaange*: a small ling almost cylindrical in shape – from O.N. *volr*: cylinder; rod; stick]

ölg (n) steamy; oppressive heat, as in muggy weather. *He's an ölg a haet*; steaming sweat. *A'm in a ölg a sweat*. [N. *ulka*: mustiness; mould; *ulken* (adj): close]

ölger (olga) (n) filth from a drain; liquid manure in a byre. [N. *aale*; D. *ajle*]

öliklörum (illek + arm) (adj) sickly; of an ugly, sickly appearance. [**illek** = O.N. *illiligr*: frightful; abominable + **arm** = O.N. *armr*: poor; unhappy]

on-draw (drawin) (n) a garment worn only on certain occasions or to go outdoors (lit. a garment 'drawn on' over the top of others). [Sh. variant on E. *draw* (cf. O.N. *draga*) + *on*]

onkerry (n) a carry-on; a disturbance. [O.Sc. *oncairry*: a to-do; rowdy behaviour]

on-laek (adj) of good appearance – commonly used in the negative. *Yun breeks is no on-laek*. [cf. N. *anselig*]

onlay (n) a heavy shower or fall of snow. [O.Sc. *onlay*]

onlookin (adj) presentable; fit to be seen. [see **on-laek**]

onn (n) a section of field or **rig**, cultivated by a single spade, as opposed to one cultivated by a **geng**, and by extension a set task; an enterprise. *Shö hed ta dö her wark in onns* (She had to do her chores in piecemeal fashion). [Sw.dial. *von, ån*: a small piece of field or meadow falling to a single labourer to reap]

onstaandin (onstandin) (adj) obstinate; persistent. [O.N. *standa á*: to stand on; insist on; persevere in]

ontack (n) a heavy undertaking; (v) to become excited; to shout or scold. [O.N. *átaka*: a taking hold of]

ön (ond) (n) sultry; stuffy atmosphere. [prob. originally O.N. *ond*: breath from which a breeze, current of air, has developed and subsequently *orna*: to warm; to get warm. Sw.dial. *orna*: to be spoiled by heat; to become musty; also cf. **ölg**: oppressive heat; N. *ulka*: mustiness; mould]

oo (n) wool; sheep's fleece, as opposed to **wirset** or **yorn** (the spun fibre used for knitting). [O.Sc. *oull* (sometimes *woo*)]

oob (n) a plaintive sound; (v) to moan; to wail. *Oobin an takkin on*. [O.N. *óp*: a shout; a cry; wail]

ooen (adj) woollen; made of wool. [see **oo**]

ooie (adj) woolly. [see **oo**]

ook (n) week. [Sh. variant on E. *week*]

ool (v) to mope. *Shö's bön oolin aboot aa day*; to be depressed as result of illness. *An oolin body*. [E. *ail*: unwell; however, cf. *owl* (of birds) popularly represented in fable as moping, complaining and solitary; thus *oolin*: behaving like an owl (see **ul**)]

oolet (ulet) (n) a brat; a difficult, troublesome or annoying child; a peevish person. [N. *ulæta*: cry; unpleasant sound – hence a whimperer. Icel. & Fær. *ólæti*: bad manners; rude behaviour; noise]

oonawaars (unawaars) (adv) unaware. [L.Sc. *unawar*]

oonbemmed (adj) unacclimatised. [E. *un*- + Ork. *beamed*: accustomed to; ready for; *beam*: to warm a teapot before putting in the tea]

oonhaandy (unhaandy) (adj) awkward; not skilful; not convenient. [Sc. *unhandy* – in similar meanings]

oonlippened (adj) unexpected. [E. *un*- + O.Sc. *lypnyns*: trust; *lyppyn*: expect; O.N. *líta*: to look to]

oonmik (umak, oomik) (n) a very small quantity. [the prefix 'oon-' signifies 'un-' in English, meaning the opposite of the action specified, however, as **oonmik** is a noun, it is likely the prefix is a mis-spelling of 'um'. Jakobsen has *umak(ie)* as an adj. meaning very small, and *umek*, a small sheaf of very short corn. Other similar words relate to very small objects suggesting (Jakobsen) that **umak** is developed from the meaning of the word for child; N. *umage*: a person not fully grown; a child]

oonmoaderate (adj) boisterous; over-active; uncontrollable.

oonsaired (adj) unserved. [E. *un*- + O.Sc. *saired*: served; O.Sh. *sare*: serve]

oonteelie (ontili) (adj) unlucky; ill-omened. [*un-tili* deriv. from *utili* with the anglicized negative prefix being added later; Icel. *ótidlegur*: untimely]

oor (n) hour; (v) to be miserable; ailing. [O.Sc. (n) *oor*, *ooer*: hour; (n) variant of **ool**]

oorie (adj) eerie; strange. [O.Sc. *oorie*, poss. E. *eerie* but more prob. *oolie*: owl-like; cf. dim. of (v) *oor*, *ool*]

oorick (urek, oorack) (n) a small person. [Ork. *orri*: diminutive – *a peedie orri ting*; cf. *oor*, *ool*]

ooril (url) (v) to work slowly; to potter about. [deriv. of **ur**: to move slowly; to doze; cf. N. *ora*: to doze; Icel. *óra*: to dream – leading to the expression '*to geng urin*']

ooster (ouster) (v) to act or speak in a domineering manner. [O.N. *austr*: the act of baling out bilge-water; thus metaphorically an *ouster*: one who takes control and dominates]

ootadaeks (adv) beyond the hill-dykes (**daeks**) thus **ootadaeks** – in the open; **innadaeks** – within bounds. [Sc. *oot*: out(side) + *dyke, dike*: drystone wall without mortar; O.Sc. & M.E. *dyk(e)*, *dik(e)*: a ditch]

ootbaits (n) grazing area beyond the hill-dyke; patches of pasture in the scattald. [O.N. *útbeit*: out pasture]

ootburg (n) peats that have been laid out on the turf beyond the **daek**. [O.N. *útburdr*: a bearing out; unloading; also *útborg*: outwards]

ootdön (adj) tired out (lit. 'done-out'). [E. *done-in*]

ootliers (n) animals without a roofed shelter. [O.Sc. *outlier*, *outlair*: an animal which is not housed but lives outside in winter]

ootmaagit (adj) worn out; exhausted by hard work. [O.N. *má*: to wear out; make blunt from use]

oot owre (adj) out beyond; a distance away; on top of. *Tak dee cot t wear oot owre if hit gets caald*; (lit. 'out-over').

ootrun (n) the section of land attached to a croft which contains rough grazing (seldom cultivated) and bordering on the **scattald** wall. [Sc. *outrun*: a piece of outlying grazing on an arable farm. Shetland crofts commonly comprise a small acreage of arable land together with outrun and a share of the scattald or common grazing in the hill]

ootset (n) a piece of undeveloped ground in the **scattald** or common grazing leased to a tenant who then had to build a house on it and bring the rough pasture into cultivation. [cf. O.N. *sætr*, N. *sæter*: mountain pasture; dairy land]

oot-tack (uttak) (n) of lasting quality; durable. [O.N. *úttaka*, said of something that has lasting quality or quantity]

oot-waelins (n) rejects; that which is culled out; (see **wael**). [O.N. *val*: choice; selection; O.Sc. *waile*: to choose – thus *outwale*: that which is selected for exclusion or rejection]

opstropolous (adj) rowdy (also **upstropolous**). [Shet. version of E. *obstreperous*]

orm (n) a dense shoal. *De silleks wis ormin at de craigs*; (v) to crawl or creep. *De crang wis ormin wi maeds* (The carcase was crawling with maggots). [N. *yrja*, *urja*: to swarm; teem]

ormal(s) (ormel) (n) remnants; a particle; a scrap. [O.N. *ørmul*: ruins; remnants; N. *aarmole*: remnant; fragment]

ort (urt) (n) a clutch of eggs; a brood. [O.N. *verpa* (v): to cast; to lay eggs]

osmil (adj) odd-looking; sinister; dark; dingy. [N. *ysmen*: dark; hazy]

ös (n) use. *What ös is yun?*; (pt) **ösed**. *Dey ösed aa de mylk.*

öswal (adj) usual.

öt (v) ate; (pt of) **aet**; (pp) **aetin**.

ötna (n) smithereens. [Jakobsen – *øtna*: destruction; to destroy; lay waste; Du. (Irel.) – but etymology unconfirmed]

overly (overli) (adj) given to extremes or excess. *He's dat overly wi de bairns*. [O.N. *ofrliga*: excessively; E. *overly*: to an excessive degree]

owld (adj) old (also **aald**, **auld**). [Sc. *auld*]

owre (ower) (prep) over. *De gimmer göd owre de daek*; (adj) too. *I widna geng owre closs tae yun dug*. [O.Sc. *our*: over; too; in excess; Sc. *o'er*, *ower*]

owre by (adv) across; over beside. *Shö's owre by dellin ida rig*; (also see **back owre**). [see above]

owre-end (adj) over-excited; irritable. *Dunna tak aff de dug or he'll geng owre end* (Don't tease the dog or he'll become over-excited); stiff, as hair standing on end. [O.Sc. *owerend*: tip over; turn topsy-turvy]

owre-geen (adj) unruly; beyond management; over-run, as with weeds. [O.N. *ofrgangr*: going beyond all bounds]

owre göd (adj) all right; satisfactory. *Foo is du de day? A'm owre göd*; (also **owre weel**).

owre muckle (adj) too much. *Gie me nae mair, yun's owre muckle*. [Sc. *ower* + O.N. *mikill*: great; large; much; E.dial. *mickle*, O.Sc. *muckle*: much]

owre-steer (owre-storr) (adj) boisterous; given to outrageous behaviour. *Dey aal göd owre-steer eftir twartree drams*. [*over* + *storr*, N. *styrja*: to make a stir; *størta*: to incite; urge on]

owre true (adj) true enough. *Hit's owre true, du's rycht*. [Sc.]

owre weel (adj) reasonably well; ok healthwise. *I'm owre weel, foo's deesel?* [Sc.]

owse (ous) (v) to bale out a boat; to pour out; said of rain falling in torrents – *He's owsin some*. [O.N. *ausa*: to bale]

owsen (n) oxen. [O.Sc. *oussin*: oxen]

owse-room (n) the bilge of a boat. [see **owse**]

owskerri (ouskerri) (n) a boat's baling scoop. [O.N. *aus(t)ker*: boat's scoop (not connected to Out Skerries which is a group of islands NE of Whalsay)]

oxter (n) the armpit; (v) to carry under the arm. [O.Sc. *oxter*, deriv. O.E. *ohsta*: armpit]

oy (n) a nephew. [O.Sc. & Sc. *oy*, *oye*: a grandchild, (nephew or niece); Gael. *ogha*, *odha*]

öyger (oger) (n) a huge wave. [Icel. *ægja*: to flow; flood; E.dial. *eagre*: tidal wave]

P

paal (v) 1) to drag one's feet; to prop or brace a foot, as against a door to prevent it being opened; press against. [O.Sc. *paal*: to move forward at a slow pace; go wearily; drag one's feet; N. & Sw.dial. *pata*: to trot along or walk slowly; Sw.dial. *palla*: to trip; to walk softly]; 2) to puzzle. [cf. N. *por*, *pora*: a roguish trick; Sw.dial. *pula*: to make fun of]

paand (n) a curtain valance. [O.Sc. *pand*, *paund*: a valance; F. *pendre*: to hang]

paap (n) a nipple. [E. *pap*: a nipple]

packie (n) 1) a hawker; a pedlar; door-to-door salesman. [O.Sc. *pack*: a pedlar's pack – hence a *packie*]; 2) a bundle of fishing lines, sometimes referred to as *a packie a towes*. [O.N. *pakki*: a pack; bundle]

paddel (paidle) (n) the lump-fish or lump-sucker (*Cyclopterus lumpus*). [orig. obs. cf. O.N. *padda*: a toad; O.Sc. *padill*, poss. from *paidle* (n): an oar, owing to its shape]

paddock-stöl (paddik) (n) a mushroom. [Sc. *puddock*: a toad or frog; O.E. *pade*: a toad; frog; O.N. *padda*: frog + E. *stool*]

paek (n) a snippet; a small quantity of grass; a bite. [E. *peck*]; (v) to work slowly but steadily; having climbed a steep slope or carried out a strenuous task one might say *He wiz a paek*. [O.Sc. *pech*: to pant; puff (due to exertion)]

Paesday (n) the Monday after Easter Day. [O.Sc. *Paschday*: Easter Day (also Easter Monday), the day on which **paes-eggs** were rolled; M.E. *Passe Day*; O.F. *pashe*: Heb. Passover]

paes eggs (n) decorated hard-boiled eggs collected by children going from house to house on **Paesday**. [see above]

paes-wisp (pes-wisp) (n) an entangled or ravelled mass of lines or threads. [Fær. *pes*, *pesja*: old tangled wool on sheep (adj. *pesjutur*: tangled) + N. *vopsa*: entanglement, esp. threads; also cf. L.Sc. *wisp*, *wusp*: a rope or cord made of twisted straw, heather, etc.]

paet (n) peat, the semi-carbonised material under moorland, cut in blocks and dried for burning as fuel; also **paet-bank** the turf from which peat is cut; **paet-castin** the act of cutting peats; **paet-borro** large-wheeled barrow for transporting peats across the moor; **paet-möld (paet coom)** the crumbled remains of peat used as bedding for cattle; **paet-neuk** a recess by the fire where peats are stored; **paet-reek** pungent smoke from burning peats; **paet-roog** a roughly made pile of peats in the hill or at the roadside ready for bringing home prior to building into a weatherproof **paet-stack**. [Anglo-Latin (13th cent.) *peta*: peat]

paloovious (adj) inebriated; very drunk; (also see **mortal**). [orig. obs. cf. N. *påvirket*: inebriated]

pampero (n) a violent gale (esp. N.Yell). [S.Amer. *pampero*: a strong SW wind over the pampas or vast treeless plains of South America. (This is an example of a word being taken up by whalers who travelled to the southern Pacific region in the 19th and early 20th cent. and subsequently adopted into local usage)]

panfry (n) a state of agitated excitement (also **panshite**). [E.dial. *pansheet*, *panshite*: state of excitement or rage; cf. *panshard*: a potsherd or fragment of pottery and the practise of breaking and throwing pieces of pottery into houses on Shrove Tuesday in W.Eng]

pantan (n) a slipper, esp. one with a wooden sole. [O.Sc. *pantonis*, O.F. *pantoufle*: a slipper]

park (n) enclosed grazing within a croft; a meadow or field; (also a **toon** or **tun**). [L.Sc. *park* (in same sense)]

partan (n) a crab; common edible crab (*Cancer pagurus*). [O.Sc. *partan*]

parteeklar (adj) very fine; excellent. [E. *particular*: attentive to detail]

pat (v) put; (pt of) **pit**; (pp) **pitten**. [Sc. form of E. *put*]

pattel (pattle) (v) to push; poke; rake in something. (*Essypattle* is the name given to Cinderella in Shetland's version of the well-known story – see **ess**) [Sw. *pittla*: to poke; pick]

pay (v) to smack. [O.Sc. *pay*: fig. to undergo punishment]

pech (n) a wheeze; (v) to puff and pant. [O.Sc. *pech*, E.dial. *peff*: imitative of the act of puffing and panting]

Pecht (n) a Pict. [Sc. & E. *Pict*: ancient inhabitants of northern Britain (including Shetland) associated in folklore with a dwarfish race of underground dwellers. Believed to have painted or tattooed their bodies – hence *Pict*, from L. *picti*: painted people]

peeg (n) a peek; a glimmer. [cf. *peek*: glimpse; N. *pikke*: little; Sw.dial. *pykke*: a trifle]

peegset (peegsin, peegin) (adj) weakly; ill-looking. *He's a pör peegset craitur*. [cf. above]

peel (n) a small quantity; a single grain or blade of grass – *a peel a girse*; a small mussel (also called a *cra peel*). [N. (E.Nor.) *peele*, *pæle*: a small lump; clod]

peen (n) a pane of glass. [orig. of L. *pannus*: cloth; rag]; (v) to throw at. [orig. obs]

peenie (n) apron. [Sc. *pinny*: short for pinafore]

peerie (piri) (adj) small. [orig. E., Sc., now only Shetland] In the following expressions: **peerie-breeks** (n) nickname for a small child or person with short legs; **peerie haak (hawk)** (n) merlin (*Falco columbarius*); **peerie-hoose** (n) child's play-house; **peerie-start** (n) a short period of time. *Bide du a peerie-start and we'll hae coarn a tae*; **peerie little** (as above); **peerie swaabie** (n) lesser black-backed gull (*Larus fuscus*); **peerie whaap** (n) whimbrel; species of small curlew (*Numenius phaeopus*); **peerie-winkie** (n) little finger or toe; **peerie wyes** (adv) softly; gently; cautiously. *Geng peerie wyes (ways)*. [Ork. *peedie*, origin uncertain; cf. N.dial. *piren*: niggardly; sickly; feeble; thin; Sw. *pirug*: slender; little; N. *piir*: a young, frail creature; *perr*, *pir*: a small fish; E.dial. *pirrie*, *perry*: a light (little) breeze]

peester (pister) (v) to utter a faint sound; to squeak. [N. *pist*: a small person; a whimperer; a gnome; *pist(r)a*: to squeak; whimper]

peety aboot dee ironical expression used to suggest *serve you right*! (lit. 'pity about you').

pell (peel) (n) 1) a pail or bucket. [E. *pail*]; 2) a disreputable person. [O.Sh. *pell*: skin or hide (pelt) extended to matted or tufted hair and hence a *pell* or *pjoli(man)*: a scruffy reprobate]

pellet (pellit) (adj) ragged; patchy and peeling off, as animal hair or fleece in summer; *a pellet röl* – a pony that is shedding its coat as new hair begins to grow from underneath. [see above]

pells (n) ragged clothes. [see **pell**]

pen (n) a feather. [Sc. *pen*: a large feather – at one time used as a writing quill (pen); O.E. *penne*, from L. *penna*: feather]

penga (n) money. [O.N. *pen(n)ingr* – contracted to *pengr*: (property) penny; money; coin]

pengle (v) to struggle at a job or work laboriously, as in knitting. [Sc. *pingle*: to strive; struggle with difficulties; O.Sc. *pingill*, Sw.dial. *pyngla* to work in a trifling way; to be busy in small matters]

penk (pink) (v) to dress up; to decorate; having an air of superiority. *Shö wiz gyaan penkin aboot.* [N. *pinka*: to point; shape neatly]

penshins (n) the part of cow's stomach from which tripe is made. [O.Sc. *penche*: paunch – that part used for tripe]

pernickety (pernitret) (adj) fussy; hard to please. [D. & Sw. *pertentlig*: very finical; fastidious; E.dial. *pernickety*; Sc. *perjink*]

pernyim (adj) prim and proper. [O.Sc. *pernim*: saucy; cheeky; pert]

perskeet (adj) fastidious; over particular; hard to please. [L.Sc. *pershittie*: precise; punctual; formal]

pew (pja) (adj) last gasp; to barely show signs of life; (also see **pyaa**). [N. *paesa*: to pant; to breathe hard; Fær. *pøsa*: to exhaust]; (n) a puff of smoke. *Dey wirna a pew o reek fae de lum.* [O.Sc. *pew*: a puff of smoke; wind, etc.]

pex (v) to proceed with effort. *He wis comin pexin up da hill.* [imit. (see **pech**)]

pexins (n) punishment. [O.Sh. *pilk*: to thrash; to beat; cf. N. & Sw. *pilka*, D. *pilke*: to pick; scrape; stick]

pey (v) beat; thrash; punish. *A'll pey dee bum*; also said in fun when teaching a child to clap – the adult will demonstrate saying *pey, pey, pey*. [O.Sc. *pey*]

pheesic (n) medicine. [O.Sc. *feesick*, Sc. form of E. *physic*: (to dose with) medicine]

pick (pikk) (n) a tap, as on a door; (v) to tap; knock lightly. [O.N. *pikka*; Sw. *pikka*; D. *pikke*]

pickit (adj) very dirty; pocked. [cf. O.Sc. *pokkit*: infected with pocks]

picky (pikki) (n) a children's game played around the corn-stack in autumn, similar to tag. [cf. the game *pikki-hoggi* – A taps B after which B has to catch A; N. & Sw. *pikka*: to pick; to tap; O.N. *hogg*: a blow; a stroke]

pie-holl (n) a hole in leather or fabric through which a lace is passed. [cf. O.Sc. *pie-hole*: the steam hole in a pie]

piece (n) a sheep's ear-mark involving the removal of a piece; a distance. *Wir paets are a piece fae de rodd*; a length of time. *A'm a piece fae feenishin dellin de taaties.* (In time and distance both are usually long rather than short). [Sc. in similar usage]

pig (n) an earthenware bottle, esp. one used as a hot-water bottle (also see **laem, laem-pig**). [O.Sc. *pig*: earthenware vessel shaped like a pig when viewed side on]

pikka maa (n) common gull (*Larus canus*). [L.Sc. *pick-maw*; N. *pikka-*]

pikkatari (n) (collective) terns (*Sterninae*). [see above]

pikket (adj) filthy. *Whit's du been doin bairn, du's joos pikket!* [poss. cognate with Sc. *pick*: pitch; tar]

pillie (n) penis. [O.Sc. *pillok*; O.E. *pilkok*; N.dial. *pill*]

piltie (n) a little child. [O.N. *piltr*: a boy; Fær. *piltur*: a lad; small boy]

piltek (piltock) (n) a coalfish 2-4 years old (*Pollachius virens*) (also see **sillek**). [O.N. *piltr*: a boy – with the extended meaning of 'small-fry', a sprat; N. *pjakk*: a young salmon; O.Sc. *pelltack*]

pin (v) 1) to move quickly. [O.Sc. *pinnin*: moving with speed (using one's pins (legs) to advantage]; 2) to pack. [O.Sc. *pin*: to plug up holes in masonry or a dry stone wall, using small stone wedges or 'pins']

pinger (n) a small haddock. [O.Sc. (esp. Aberdeen) *pinger* (also *ping-pong*): a small haddock]

pinnish (pinnis) (v) to endure extreme cold. [O.N. *pina*: to torment]

pinnishin (n) an excessively cold bout of weather. [see above]

pintle (n) the penis. [E. *pintle*: a bolt or pivot on which an eylet (esp. a rudder) turns; O.E. *pintel*: penis]

pipper (de) (n) *The Shetland Times. Is du gotten de pipper yit?* (Have you got *The Shetland Times* yet?) [E. *paper*: (newspaper)]

pipper (n) a state of nervous excitement; (v) to shiver or shake; (also see **mirl, pirm, titter, vimmer**). [O.N. *pipra*: to quiver; tremble; Fær. *pipra*]

pirg (v) to nag. [N. *pirke*: to prod; poke]

pirl (n) pebble-like dung, e.g. of sheep, rabbits, mice, etc.; (v) to void excrement of the sort. *Wir pet rabbit is aye pirlin.* [N. *perle*: a lump; gritty excrement]

pirm 1) (v) to tremble; shake with anger. *He wiz pirmin wi rage*; (also see **mirl, pipper, titter, vimmer**). [D.dial. *pirme*: to be restlessly busy]

pirm 2) (n) a spool or bobbin; a reel of cotton. [O.Sc. *pirn*: a weaver's spool]

pirm treed (n) cotton thread. [Sc. (see above)]

pirn (v) to shrivel up; waste away. [N. *piren*: ailing; thin; frail; *piir*: a young, frail creature; cf. **peerie**]

pirr (n) a light breeze. [O.N. *byrr*: a fair wind; O.Sc. *pirle* (of wind), E.dial. *pirrie, perry*: a light breeze]

pirr (n) a hot drink containing oatmeal, cream of tartar and sugar used as a cure for chill or high temperature (also **brochin**). [L.Sc. *pirr*: to fizz (action of the drink when stirred)]

pirrie (pirri) (adj) quick tempered; touchy; easily annoyed; (v) an exclamation of annoyance – *Oh pirrie!* [cf. L.Sc. *pirr*: a fit of rage; a sudden temper; a 'fizz']

pirvok (v) provoke. [Sh. variant on E. *provoke*]

pish (n) urine; (v) to urinate. [Sc. variant on E. *piss*: to urinate; O.Sc. *pisch*]

pish pot (n) chamber pot (also **grethy pot**). [see above]

pisk (n) a cheeky or naughty child. [Sw.dial. *pyske*: a dwarfish person; a gnome]

pit (v) to put; (pt) **pat**; (pp) **pitten**. [Sc. version of E. *put*; D. *putte*; Sw. *putta*]

pit apun (v) to dress (lit. 'put upon').

pitna (v) put not. *Pitna dee guttery bots yunder*. [negative version of Sc. *pit*: put]

pit-on (n) a pretence. [E. *put on*: assume another character; pretend]

pitten aboot (adj) distressed. [O.Sc. *pit aboot*: put out; distressed]

pjöfl (v) to whistle softly – more blowing than actual whistling. [orig. obs., poss. onomatopœic]

plag (n) a garment, though generally one that is ragged or well-worn. [O.N. *plagg*: equipment; N., Sw. & Fær. *plagg*: a garment; material or cloth]

planticrub (plantikrobb) (n) a circular dry-stone enclosure (usually without an entrance and accessed via a stile) for growing cabbage plants, frequently found in the **ootrun** of a croft and sometimes on the **scattald** (also a **crub**, **crö** or **planticrö**). [E. *plant* + N., Sw. & Fær. *krubba*: a box for holding fodder; also Icel. *kró*: an enclosure; a fold (esp. a sheep-fold)]

platsh (plut, pluts) (v) to trudge, in a flat-footed way, over wet ground. [prob. imitative. cf. D.dial. *plutte*: to splash]

platt (adj) perfectly smooth (of sea or loch); calm. (N. Yell uses the exp. *platt malli calm* to describe a flat calm however the etymology on 'malli' is obscure) [cf. Fær. *platta logn*: flat calm; E.dial. *plat*]

pleep (plip) (n) the cry of a bird; (v) to cry, as a bird and by extension to whimper (also **pleepsin**). [N. *plipa*: to peep; chirp; Fær. *pli*: the cry of a young gull]

pleepsit (adj) constantly complaining. [see above]

plenish (v) to supply, stock (e.g. house or farm) with furnishings, implements, etc. [Sc. *plenish*, O.F. *plenir*, from L. *plenus*: full]

plenishin (n) the internal fittings and furnishings of a house. [see above]

pling (see **plink**)

plink *plingk* (n) the act of making music on a stringed instrument. *Gie wis a plink apo dee fiddle afore we gang hame*; (v) universal usage – imitative of a quick, sharp sound (generally musical), as of a string being plucked or a piano played; additional meaning in Shetland – to twinkle. *See du de peerie stars plinkin idda mirk*. [imit. of *plunk* & *blink*; cf. N.dial. *blik*: a glance; a gleam]

plivver (n) plover (sub-family *Charadriidae*) i.e. lapwing; dotterel; ringed plover; (also **saandiloo**). [F. *pluvier*, from L. *pluvia*: rain (from the bird's restless behaviour before rain)]

plivver's page (n) dunlin (*Calidris alpina*). [E. *plover's page*: so named for its likeness to the plover]

ploo (plu) (n) a plough; (v) to plough. [O.N. *plógr*: a plough]

plook (n) a pimple. [Sc. *plouk, plook*: a small lump or knob; a pimple; Gael. *pluc*]

ploop (v) the sound made by a flame or boiling liquid. [E. *plop*]

plootch(in) (v) paddle; splash in water; (also see **pootle**). [imitative sound but see **platsh**]

plooter (v) potter aimlessly about or act idly; dabble in liquid esp. wading messily through wet ground; (also see **platch**, **slester**, **swittle**). [O.Sc. *plowter, plouter*, in same meaning – poss. imit. cf. Du. *ploeteren*: to dabble in water]

plot (v) to immerse the carcase of a pig in boiling water to facilitate the removal of bristle. [O.Sc. *plot*: to remove fleece or hair by scalding]

plöt (n) a whining noise; a complaint; (v) to whine; moan. [Sw.dial. *plutas* (from *plut*): a hanging lip; also poss. N. *plyta*: a small flute]

plucker (plukker) (n) sea scorpion (*Myoxocephalus scorpius*). [O.Sc. *plucker*: the angler fish (*Lophius piscatorius*); also sea scorpion]

plukk (v) to pull. *A'll gie dee car a pluck back apo de rodd*; to pull wool off a sheep (see **roo**); to pick, as flowers. *De bairns plukked de wild flooers abune de banks*. [O.N. *plukka*: to pluck; to pull]

plump (n) a heavy downpour of rain; to fall into water. *He's plumpit in de burn*. [E. *plump* – but with additional meaning in Sc. and Sh. to rain suddenly and heavily]

plunky (n) a prank; trick. [O.Sc. *plunk*: a truant]

poase (n) a hoard. [O.Sc. *pose, pois* – (of funds) money, treasure in safe keeping; cf. L. *depositum*]

pobie (n) a high hill; a tabu word used by haaf fishermen to denote high points on land – North Isles haaf fishermen referred to *De Pobis* which were hills on Unst (Saxa Vord and Herma Ness) – rowing out until these landmarks disappeared below the horizon. [N. & Sw. *pappe, pap*: both words used as placenames for heights in Norway]

pock (pok) (n) a net for catching fish, comprising of a bag attached to a long handle. [O.N. *poki*: a bag; a poke]

pocky (poki) (n) a paper bag, such as is used by shops. *Gie's a pocky a sweeties*; a pouch; a swelling. [O.N. *poki*: a bag; a poke]

pone (poan, pon) (n) first layer removed from moor when cutting peats; thin slice of turf used as initial covering before thatching a roof (now obsolete); (v) to crop closely. [N. *panna*: roof tile; L. *ponere*: to place]

pong (pung) (n) testicle (originally a purse). [O.N. *pungr*: a purse]

poo (n) the act of pulling; (v) to pull. [Sc.]

pooch (n) a pocket. [E. *pouch*]

pooer (n) a large quantity; strength. [Sc. form and usage of E. *power*]

pook (puk, pukk) (v) to kick or throw; to push with the foot; to hit. *A'll gie dee a pookin*. [N. & Fær. *buka*: to drub; beat; O.Sc. *pook, pouk*: to pluck; pull]

poorie (purri) (n) a cat, esp. a call or pet name. [N. *purre*: a cat (call-name)]

pooshin (pusjin) (n) a detestable object or person; poison. [O.Sc. *pousion*; also cf. N. *pysja*: an insignificant thing; N. *pøsel*: a little, ill-tempered creature]

poosie (posi, pusi) (n) a swamp; bog; quagmire. *Poosie aet dee* (May you fall in a bog and be swallowed up) – said in frustration to argumentative or troublesome person. [Sw. *pus*, N. *pus*: a pool; puddle]

poosk (pusk) (v) to poke about, as in searching for something (also **proag**). [N. *puska*: to fidget with; to pluck at]

pooskered (adj) physically exhausted. [O.Sc. *poust, pawste*: strength; rigour; power; thus *poustourless*: powerless; (O.Sc. *lege-pouste*, L. *ligia potestas*: 'free power' from which O.E. *liege*, 'free', remains)]

P

pooster (n) vigour; virility. [of same deriv. as above]

pootle (pottle, plooter) (v) to make little progress (at work); to work in an idle manner; to dabble in water; (also see **plootch**). [Fær. *putla, putl*: to trifle at work]

possack (n) an unappetising morsel; a 'dog's breakfast'. [cf. N. *puskutt*: dishevelled]

pow (n) the head. [O.Sc. *pow*: head of a human or animal; *poll* – hence *poll-ax, pole-ax*]

pöl (pödl (Westside)) (n) a pool; a land-locked bay. [O.N. *pollr*: a small, roundish creek or bay; Icel. *pollr*: a pool; swamp]

pör (n) a physically incapable person. *Shö's joost a pör* (the word may be accompanied by an adjective, e.g. *a fanted pör; a skinny pör*); (adj) poor. *A pör bein; a pör craitur*. [E. *poor*]

pör aamos (adj) feeble; frail; to be pitied. *A pör aamos body* – someone in need of charity; (also see **aamos**). [poor + O.N. *almusa*: alms (see **aamos**); M.E. *almus*: money given in charity]

pörta (purtnin) (n) poverty; an insufficient quantity of any kind of food. [N. *partningr*: a divided quantity; a part]

pram (v) to press down; squeeze together. [Du. *prammen*: to press; squeeze; N. *prempa*: to stuff; cram]

pramm (n) a dish of uncooked oatmeal mixed with milk or cream. [cf. Ork. *brammo*: gruel made of oatmeal and water; O.N. *barmr*; D. *bærm* and hence N. *brim, prim*: sediment; dregs; soft cheese made of whey]

preen (prin) (n) a pin; (v) to attach with a pin. [O.N. *prjónn*]

preeve (v) to taste. [O.Sc. *preve*: to approve; sanction; E. *prove*: test]

press (n) a cupboard; shelved closet or recess. [Sc. *press*: a cupboard, usually built into a recess; in but-and-ben crofts the but-end press generally served as a pantry]

pretty dancers (n) the aurora borealis (also **mirrie dancers**). [imitative of the colourful display and movement of the aurora]

prettikin (n) a prank; an act of mischief. [O.N. *prettr*: a trick]

prig (v) to implore or plead. [orig. obs. cf. O.Sc. *prig*: to haggle; *prigpenny*: a haggler; hard bargainer]

prink (v) to preen; to groom with vanity. [O.Sc. *prink*, E. *prank*: to show off; Du. *pronk*: show; finery (the latter being the most probable influence on the Sh. form of the word)]

proag (progj, prodj) (n) a poke or jab; (v) to poke around, as in search of something; also **poosk** to thrust, jab, or dig in the ribs; to make a hole in a piece of canvas, leather or the like. [O.Sc. *prog, progue*: to prick; prod]

proil (proll) (n) a collection of objects. *Dir a lokk a proil i yun press*. [Du. *prul*: trash; rubbish; junk – but with some influence from E. *prowl* (M.E. *proll*): to hunt about]

proint (prointi, prointer) (n) a sharp, protruding point; a jag. [cf. comb. of E. *prong* and *point*]

prood (adj) proud (as E. meanings); exposed; standing out from surrounding surface. [O.N. *prúdr*, E. *proud*, D. *prud*: fine; stately; magnificent – with additional meaning of 'standing proud', as a nail not fully driven in]

prummek (n) a teat; nipple; (in plural) a woman's breasts. [cf. properly a bud – O.N. *brum*: leaf-bud]

prunk (adj) smart; showy and having aplomb; to sit or be aligned upright. *He's sittin prunk apo de stab*. [N. *prunka*, D. *prunke*: to make a display of]

prut (proot) (n) a breaking of wind; (v) to break wind; to fart. [D. *prut*, Sw. *prutt*]

puckle (n) a single grain of seed; a small quantity; (see **haily-puckle**). [O.Sc. *pickle, puckle*: a grain of seed; a small amount; proverb: *Mony a puckle maks a muckle*]

puddins 1) (n) sausages made from sheep's entrails, inc. *mealy puddins* (containing oatmeal and suet); *black puddins* (blood puddings); 2) exclamation of annoyance – *Oh puddins!* or directed at an individual – *Puddins fur dee!* [Sc.]

pug (pog) (n) a small person; a boy. [N. *pøk*: a little boy; a bag]

puggie (n) stomach; belly. *Is dee puggie sore?* [O.N. *poki*: a bag; Sc. *poke*: a bag or small sack]

pulter (adj) very rough and agitated (of the sea). [N. *poltra*: to bubble up; well up]

pultrous (adj) (of a person) restless; unruly; wild and lustful. [L.Sc. *pultrous*]

pund (n) pound; enclosure for animals. (Shetland Old County Act: *That every scattald have a sufficient pund, under pain of ten pounds Scots*); Punds, Da Punds – common placename associated with local pound; (v) to impound stray animal(s). [O.E. *pund*: enclosure]

purl (v) 1) to poke; stir; esp. poke the fire. [N. *pura*: to poke; prod]; 2) to dig up small potatoes. *I tink I'll geng an purl wiz twartree peerie tatties for wir denner*. [D. dial. (Jutland) *purl*: collect]

purt (n) a guttery mess; a stagnant pool; metaphorically anything messy. [O.N. *pyttr*: a pool]

putt (v) to push; nudge. *Gie de door a putt*. [O.Sc. *put(t)*: to push; drive]

pyaa (pja) (n) outward indication of life. [N. *pæsa*: to pant; to breathe hard; Sw.dial. *päsa, pysa*; also Fær. *pøsa*: to exhaust]

pyaag (pjag) (v) to work with considerable effort, to the point of exhaustion. [see above]

pyaagit (pjaget) (adj) extremely exhausted. [see **pyaa**]

pyilk (pilk) (v) to extricate with a pointed instrument, as a whelk from its shell with the tip of a knife. [E.dial. & O.Sc. *pilk*: to pick; pluck; scrape]

pyukkleen (puckelin) (n) a small gift. [see **puckle**]

Q

Note: The Norn alphabet did not include the letter 'Q' and therefore **quaarl**, **quaig** and **quigga** might more correctly be spelled with a 'K' and listed accordingly except that modern-day spelling has dictated otherwise.

quam (hwamm) (n) a dale, esp. in placenames, e.g. Quam, Sandwick. [O.N. *hvammr*: a small dale]

quaarl (hwarl) (n) the crown of the head where hair grows in a circular pattern. [O.N. *hvirfill*: a circle; ring; crown of the head]

quaig (quey) (n) a heifer; a young cow before it has had a calf. [O.N. *kvíga*; Sc. *quey*]

queer fellow (de) (n) someone considered to be an opponent or potential opposition; euphemism for the devil; euphemism for death, esp. prior to mid-20th cent. when a person's death was only ever alluded to in remarks such as *he's awa*; *shö's no leevin*; *de queer fellow taen dem*. (*Hae's du been awaar o ony o de queer fellow?* An indirect question given by a Braewick crofter to persons who had been walking in the scattald and might have seen any dead sheep. If the answer was yes, the man would spit, *toeff*, *toeff*, a couple of times to **sain** his flock.)

quet (v) (S.Mainland) to stop; to cease from. *Quet dee shargin*. [E. *quit*]

quide (adj) (Yell) quiet; (v) to quiet; quieten. [Sh. variant on E. *quiet*]

quigga (kwigga) (n) couch grass (*Elymus repens*). [N. *kvika*; Sw. *qvicka*, *qvickrot*]

quoy (n) piece of enclosed and cultivated common land; used in placenames, e.g. Da Quoys, Quoyness. [O.Sc. *qui*, O.N. *kví*: a pen; fold; enclosure for animals]

Q

R

raab (rab) (v) to tumble, as a fall of stones or rocks in a wall. [N. *rap*: a slipping; a landslip]

raad (n) economy; avoidance of waste; (v) to economise; (also see **redd**). [N. & Sw. *rada*: to place in rows; to arrange; put in order]

raag (rag) (n) 1) disreputable person. [Sc. *rag*: a worthless, beggarly person; someone resembling a rag – '*rag-tag gipsy*', cf. N. *ragr*: timid; spiritless]; 2) light drizzle. [Sw.dial. *raag*: (to) drizzle; Icel. *hragla*: drizzle]; (v) to range or rove around in a generally aimless way. [Sw.dial. *rakkel*: a vagrant]

raamished (adj) fretful or waspish through lack of sleep (also **ramist**). [N. *romsen*: out of sorts due to lack of sleep – however, influenced by O.Sc. *rammished*: raging; crazy]

raan (ran) (n) the roe of a fish. [O.N. *hrogn*: roe; spawn; O.Sc. *roun*; Sc. *rawn*]

raase (v) to ransack or rob. [Sc. *ras*, also E. *raze*: to destroy]

raase (ras) (v) said of animals grazing the grass to the bare ground – *De sheep is raased de girse*. [N. *rasa*: to scrub; scrape; sweep; cleanse]

raem (n) cream; (v) to bubble over emotionally with effervescent chatter. [O.Sc. *reyme*, L.Sc. *ream*: cream; (v) to teem]

raem calm (adj) extremely calm, with the surface of the sea as smooth as cream. [see above]

raep 1) (n) to drip water. *De water wis raepin oot a him*. [O.Sc. *rap*: to fall, as a shower, with a sharp, tapping sound]

raep (rep) 2) (n) a clothes-line. [O.N. *reip*, O.Sc. *raip*: rope]; (v) to sew together roughly or poorly. [O.N. *rifa*: to sew (loosely)]

raeve (v) tore; (pt of) **raive** to tear. *He raeve his sark* (He tore his shirt); (also **raive, reeve, rive**). [O.N. *rifa*: to tear; rend; N. *rive*]

rafter (n) a tall person. [figurative of E. *rafter*]

rag (n) a poor, under-nourished person; said of a lean or hungry animal. [O.N. *hrak-*: something poor and wretched, cf. Sc. *rag*: indicative of a person in a ragged state]

raggie-willie (n) ragged robin (*Lychnis flos-cuculi*) owing to ragged edged petals. [Sc. *ragged-robin*: campion]

rag-nail (n) a torn or split fingernail; small part of nail grown into the flesh. [Sc.]

raik (rakk) (v) to aimlessly wander about (also **raag**). [N. & Sw. *rakka*: to wander; Sw.dial. *rakkel*: a vagrant]

rain (ren) (v) to glare (originally to let one's eyes rove). [Fær. *rena* (v, id); *rena eyguni*]

rain-gös (n) red-throated diver (*Gavia stellata*). [the name arises out of the bird's various calls which are said to foretell the weather: 'we're a' weet, we're a' weet, waur wadder, waur wadder' or at other times, 'dreadful drought, oh, oh, dreadful drought'. (Jessie Saxby, *Shetland Traditional Lore*)

raise (v) to stand freshly-cut peats against one another to facilitate their drying; (pt of) rise. *I raise oot a me bed*. [from O.N. *reisa*, E. *raise*: to lift up]

raised (adj) highly strung with a hint of mental instability. [O.Sc. *raise*: to infuriate; enrage; drive into a state of frenzied excitement]

raisins (n) small piles of peats set up to dry. [see **raise**]

raive (v) to tear (also see **raeve, reeve, rive**). [O.N. *rifa*: to tear; rend; N. *rive*]

rakki (n) a parrel or ring securing the sailyard to the mast, and moving up and down with the hoisting and lowering of the sail (also fishermen's tabu term for a dog). [N. *rakki*]

raldi (n) noise; clamour; a **raldihus** being a noisy house full of gaiety. [N. *ralla*: to gad about; to talk volubly; Sw.dial. *ralla*: to jump about; chatter]

rammi (n) a quarrel or brawl. [cf. *rami*: seamen's tabu word for cat, lit. 'that which has claws or paws'; N. & Sw.dial. *ram, ramm*: a paw; claw]

ramist (adj) peevish; fretful; (**raumished** (Yell)). [O.Sc. *rammished*: raging; crazy]

ramp (v) to boil vigorously; also said of one who is hot-tempered – *He wis fair rampin*. [from E. *ramp*, in the sense of raising the tempo, cf. '*ramp up prices*']

ramse (ramsk) (adj) having a harsh, bitter or unpleasant taste. [O.N. *rammr*: strong; rancid; harsh; bitter to taste]

ram-stam (adj) careless; headstrong. [O.Sc. *ram-*: a short burst of speed + *-stam*: to blunder on; stagger]

rang (wrang) (adj) wrong. [O.N. *rangr*: crooked; wrong; incorrect; L.Sc. *wrang*]

ranksman (n) one of two boats, generally sixerns, which fished in pairs at sea, for companionship or mutual aid. [O.Sh. *rank*: a bank in the sea; fishing ground ('Da Rank', Foula); N. *rante*: rant; ridge]

ransel (v) originally the official search of a house for stolen property by a **ranselman**, now a search for something lost; to rummage. [O.N. *rannsaka*: to ransack; to search]

ranselman (n) a local constable appointed under the old 'Country Acts' (17th cent.) with extensive powers to spy on his neighbours and enter any premises to search for stolen goods and apprehend the thief. He was also empowered to keep order in his local parish. Ranselmen were active in Shetland up to the mid-19th century. (The last recorded case of the appointment of ranselmen was at Fair Isle, where two were sworn in as late as 1869 following a series of petty thefts. (Nicolson, James R., *Shetland*, p.180)). [O.N. *rannsaka*: to ransack; to search]

rant (n) a dance; (v) to make merry in a noisy, boisterous way. [O.Sc. (n) *rant*: a spree; a merry-making; Ger. (v) *ranzen*: to frolic; spring about]

rask (n) luxuriant growth; (v) to group rapidly, esp. of corn. *De coarn is raskit*. [O.N. *roskvask*: to grow up; to ripen; Sw.dial. *raska*: to hurry on]

reck (rekk) (n) the span of a person's reach; (v) to reach. [O.N. *rekka*, *rekkja*: to reach; to stretch out]

redd (n) progress. *Dey'll be no muckle redd wi da tattie howe fae yun döless trooker*; (v) (commonly) **redd up** to tidy; to disentangle; to comb, as hair (see **redder**). To *redd up kin* – to sort out one's genealogy; establish a family tree. [O.Sc. *redd up*; N. & Sw. *rada*: to place in rows; to arrange; put in order]

redd (n) the scrape in a stream/river bed where a fish lays its eggs. [O.Sc. *raid*: the spawn of fish]

redder (n) a comb. [Sc. *red-kaim*]

redder (adv) rather. [variant on E. *rather*; Sc. *reder*]

reddins (reedins) (n) the fat (tripe) from sheep's intestines used for making sausages and puddings. [from O.Sc. *reid*: the stomach of an animal – hence *reddins*: fat obtained from same (see **reed**)]

reddin-straik (n) the final blow in a fight. [O.Sc. *reddings*: the act of separating or the separation of combatants + *straik*: stroke]

reddin up (n) spring-cleaning; any kind of tidying. *Geng an redd up de byre*. [O.Sc. *redd up*]

redwaar codlin (n) a cod which is reddish in colour through feeding among **waar**.

ree (ri) (n) a period of stormy weather; windy weather; (also see **Beltane rees**). [O.N. *hríd*: a spell of bad weather; N.dial. *rid*, *ri*: bad weather]

reeb (n) a stripe or streaky mark in cloth; **reebie** (adj) streaked; (also **ribek**, **reebie**, **reebit**). [N.dial. *rip*: a streak; stripe; Sw. *ripa*: a streak; line; groove; O.Sc. *reeb*: a narrow strip; a ribbon of land, wood, cloth, etc.]

reebald (n) a reprobate; a good-for-nothing rascal. [O.Sc. *reebald*, *reebelt*: wanton rascal; O.F. *ribaut* – hence E. *ribald*: licentious; foul-mouthed or coarse]

reebin(s) (n) the uppermost plank(s) in the side of a boat, also referred to as the **sheerstrake**. [N.dial. *rip*: a streak; stripe]

reed (redd) (n) the fourth stomach of a ruminant, the abomasum from which tripe is obtained. [O.Sc. *reid*: the stomach of an animal]

reein (n) the squeal of a pig; (v) to squeal like a pig. [O.Sc. *reen*: to squeal, esp. a pig; N.dial. *rina*, O.N. *hrina*: to squeal like a pig]

reek (n) smoke; (v) to smoke; in phrases: *to get one's kail through the reek* (to receive a scolding); *a reekin hoose* (a house which is inhabited). [O.N. *reykr*, Sc. *reek*, O.E. *rēk*, Du. *rook*: smoke]

reeky (adj) smoky. *De norderly is a reeky ert in wir shimley* (The northerly is a smoky direction in our chimney – the one that causes the chimney to back-draw). [see above]

reel (n) a commotion; a dance performed by 3 or 4 couples with set piece movements; the music to which a reel is danced. (In Shetland and Orkney dancers are said to be 'dancing' when they set to each other and to be 'running the reel' or 'reeling' when they perform the travelling figure. (DOST) [Sc. *reel*, Gael. *righil*: a lively dance, esp. Highland or Irish; a tune for such a dance, usually 4/4 time, sometimes 6/8]

reel (rill) (n) strong, dry wind. At the sign of a storm brewing one might say *He'll be comin wi a reel/rill*. [deriv. of **ree**, O.N. *hríd*: a spell of bad weather; N.dial. *rid*, *ri*: bad weather]

reenk (reenkie) (n) a ploy; a jaunt; (also **rink**). [cf. Sw.dial. *rinka*: to rock; L.Sc. *rink*: to gad about]

reesel (risl) (n) a vigorous shake or jolt; (v) to make an unsystematic and noisy search; to rummage; to shake vigorously. [cf. N. *rysja*: a shivering; *risl*: a sprinkling; *risla*: to sprinkle]

reest (n) a wooden framework – *de mutton reest* – on which meat was reestit; (v) to cure meat (usually mutton) by smoke-drying. [Sc. *reest*, *reist*, *reast*: to dry or cure with smoke]

reestit (adj) smoke-cured, e.g. *reestit mutton*. [see above]

reeve (v) to haul violently; deriv. of **raeve**, **raive**, **rive**. [O.Sc. *reeve*, *reave*: to grab; snatch impetuously; to plough up; E. *rive*: to wrench something open; O.N. *rífa*: to tear; rend; N. *rive*]

reffel (n) a tangle; (v) to tangle. [O.Sc. *ravel*: to tangle; fray out; Du. *ravelen*]

reffeled (adj) tangled. *A reffeled hesp* (a tangled skein). [see above]

regenwistie (-vista, -wista) (n) a lot of wind or wind-driven rain; a place greatly exposed to wind or rain. (N.Yell) [O.N. *regn*: rain; cf. O.N. *rekandi*: driving]

reksed (n) stiffness in muscles. *A'm joost reksed wi yun wark*. [N. *riksa*: to creak]

rem (n) ramble on, in speaking; to talk nonsense. [O.N. *remja*: to roar; to wail; N. *remja*: to emit loud and long-drawn cries; to bleat]

rensh (v) to rinse. [O.Sc. *reenge*, *rench*; E. *rinse*; E.dial. *rench*; F. *rincer*]

rest (v) to cover a fire with ashes to impede combustion yet keep the coals 'alive' for an extended period (also **smoor** or **bank**). [Sc., E. *rest*: in sense of inactive]

restit (adj) smoored, as a rested fire in which ash has been piled up over burning coals. [see above]

restin-shair (n) a settle or long wooden seat with back and arms. [O.Sc. *resting-chair*, *-chayre*]

retta-daek (retta-gord) (n) a projecting wall or fence at a crö to guide sheep in. [O.N. *rettargardr*: a fence surrounding an enclosure – the second part of the word being superseded in *retta-daek* by L.Sc. *dike*: a wall; fence]

rex (raex, rekk) (v) to stretch; to reach. *Rex me doon yun caird fae da brace*. [N. *rekkja*: to stretch out; D. *række*: to stretch; to hand over]

rexter (n) a driving; a chasing; a long and difficult undertaking. [O.N. *rekstr*: a driving; N. *rekster*: a walk; roaming about; a path; road, esp. for cattle]

richt (adj) right (also **rycht**). [Sc.]

rick (rikk) (v) to catch a fish by an upward jerk of the line; a sharp, upward jerk with a line and hook; to become caught (snagged) on something. *Dunna rikk apo de toarny wire*. [O.N. *rykkr*: a quick pull]

ricker (rikker) (n) an improvised gaff for landing fish. [N. *rykkjar*: a kind of fish hook]

ride (v) to be in heat, as a cow. [O.Sc. *ride*: to mount, as to copulate]

riddlie(s) (ridli, rolligrot) (n) pebble(s) on the beach (esp. Westside). [D. *rullesten*, N. *rullen*: roundish pebble + *grøt*: stone]

rift (n) a belch; (v) to belch; (see **brunt rift**). [L.Sc. *rift*; also cf. O.N. *repta*, *rypta*: to belch]

R

rig (n) 1) a plot of land; field; 2) backbone (**riggie**, **riggibenn**) or spine of person or animal. [O.N. *hryggr*: a ridge – in the sense of land cultivated in ridges]

rig (**rig up**) (v) set to rights; tidy. *Geng an rig yun brokken grind. Du'll hae ta get dis hoose riggit afore dey come.* [cf. E. *rig* (in nautical useage): adjust a ship's rigging]

rig-aboot (n) an antiquated system of alloting plots of land or **rigs** (see above) on a rota-system to tenants so that no crofter should be disadvantaged by inferior land; also known as **runrig** or **rigga-rendal**. [O.Sc. *runrig*; Gael. *roinn-ruith*]

riggament (n) dress; unstylish or odd dress. [cf. E. *rig*: clothing]

riggamifixin (adj) makeshift. [see **rig**]

rigget (n) said of an animal having a contrasting stripe of colour on its back, esp. a white stripe (a cow of this coloration would commonly be called 'Rigga'). [O.N. *hryggjóttr*; Fær. *ryggjutur*; L.Sc. *riggit*]

riggi (n) raised stitch in knitting; garter stitch. [O.N. *hryggr*]

riggie (**riggibenn**) (n) the spine or backbone. [O.N. *hryggr*]

riggin (n) the roof-ridge of a house. [O.N. *hryggr*; O.Sc. *riggin*]

rig-röni (n) a heap of stones gathered from cultivated ground (also see **rönnie**). [O.N. *hryggr*: a ridge + O.N. *hraun*: stone-heap; stony ground]

rikkel (**rinkel**) (n) an emaciated animal or person; used in phrase *a rikkel (rinkel) o banes*. [cf. Sw.dial. *rikkel*, *rukkel*: something loosely and badly put together; a very lean person; N. *rangl*: a skeleton; lean body; E.dial. *rickle*: in same sense as the Sh. word]

rimska (n) a coltish or lecherous mood. [deriv. of O.N. *rimma*: noisy onset; Icel. *rymja*: (in sense of) to make a noise]

rin (v) to run; said of an animal pulling at its tether – *rinning at de stake*. [Sc. *rin*]

rin (**rinn**) (v) to collapse or slide, as a bank of earth or a wall; a landslip. [orig. O.N. *hrynja*: to fall; now Sc. *rin*, *run*]

ringlit (**ringet**) (adj) horizontally striped, as *a ringlit cott* (a striped skirt). [N. *ringutt*: having circular or cross stripes of a certain colour]

rink (v) to work energetically. *He wis rinkin awa at de fiddle*; (related to **reenk**). [cf. Sw.dial. *rinka*: to rock; L.Sc. *rink*: to gad about]

rinklabens (n) a wretched, bony animal (also **harlibens**). [cf. N. *rangl*: a skeleton; thin body; Sw.dial. *rinka*: a feeble, emaciated animal]

rinkel (n) a tinkling noise; (v) to tinkle, as to rattle coins in a pocket. [N. *ringla*]

rinks (v) 1) to rattle, as a poker in the fire. *Rinks up de fire and gie wiz some haet, boy*. [O.Sc. *rink*: to rattle]; 2) to be occupied in high-jinks. *De bairns wiz rinksin aboot.* [O.Sc. *rink*: prowl about restlessly]

rint (**rintel**) (n) a piece of ragged clothing. [prob. deriv. **rant**, Sw.dial. *rannt*: a rag; a ragged person]

rinty-pells (n) rags; tatters; ragged clothes. [see above + **pells**: ragged clothes]

rip (n) a handful of cornstalks. [N. *ripe*: a cluster of seed; *ripa*: to strip off a cluster of seed; Fær. *ripa*: to strip ears of corn from the stalk; O.Sc. *rip*: a handful of unthrashed corn – poss. of *reap*]

rip (n) a disreputable person. [Sc. *rip*: a disreputable person; a reprobate]

rip (v) to cut along the top of a peat-bank preparatory to the removal of turf when **flaein**. [E. *rip*: to slash or tear open]

rip (v) to walk quickly; to knit or sew hurriedly – usually in a slovenly manner. *Shö joust ripped at yun gansey ta get it by wi*. [Icel. *hripa*: to do hurried work; cf. O.N. *rifa*: to sew (loosely)]

ripe (n) coarsely executed work; (v) to clear ashes in a fire-place with a poker (similar to **rinks**); to employ a pipe-cleaner on the stem of a pipe; to dig up potatoes. *Da whole toon's oot ripen d tatties*. [Sc. *ripe*: to ransack; N. *rippa*: to hasten; Icel. *hripa*: to do hurried work]

rippek (n) kittiwake (*Rissa tridactyla*) (also see **weeg**). [Fær. *ryta*: three-toed gull; O.N. *rjúpa* or *ripa*, Sw. *ripa*: ptarmigan]

ripper (n) an implement used for cutting peat turfs, as in **rip**. [see above]

risk (v) to cut grass with a sickle. [O.N. *ryskja*: to pull; N. *ryskja*: to tear off grass]

risp (n) a file or rasp; the sound of a rasp. [O.N. *rispa*: scratch]

rissenin (**risn**, **risen**) (adj) shimmering. [N. *risna*: to make one shudder or shake violently]

rissie (**riss**, **rissi**) (n) a ridge. [N. *ris*: a rising; elevation; ridge]

rit (**ritt**) (n) a sheep's earmark consisting of a vertical slit. [N. *rit*: a line; *rita*: a line; streak; D.dial. *ritte*: a cut]

rive (v) to tear; tear at; work vigorously. *See du him rivin amang da tatties*; (also see **raeve**, **raive**, **reeve**). [Sc. & E. *rive*: to wrench something open or tear it apart; plough up; tug; tear or split]

rivin a de dim (n) dawn (lit. 'the tearing apart of darkness') (see **dimriv**). In some parts of Shetland the pronunciation would more accurately be rendered as *raivin* **a de dim**). [N. & Fær. *riva*: to tear; (of weather) to clear up + O.N. *dim(m)*: (slight) darkness]

rivlin (n) a shoe made of untanned animal hide and moulded to the shape of the foot while still pliant, having the hair outermost. [O.N. *hriflingr*; O.Sc. *rivlin*]

rivvick (**rivek**, **riva**) (n) a deep cleft or fissure. [O.N. *rifa*: a rift; cleft; fissure]

ro (n) a carcase – commonly 'rotten ro'. [O.N. *hræ*: a carcase]

roan (**rander**) (v) to rob, esp. a bird's nest; plunder. [N. & Sw.dial. *rana*, D. *rane*: to rob; plunder; O.N. *ræna*]

robbie cuddie (n) wren (*Troglodytes troglodytes*) subs. *Zetlandicus*.

robbi rutl (**robbi roitl**) (n) diarrhoea (lit. 'bubbling liquid noise') (also see **rutl**). [O.N. *rófa* (*roven*): a tail; the stump of a tail + N. *rutla*: to rattle; to make a noise on shifting anything]

roilt (**rolk**) (n) a large object or person [N. *rulk*, Fær. *rulkur*: a bulky, unshapely thing; a bundle]

ron (roan, rone) (v) of an animal, esp. a sow or bitch, seeking a mate. *De bikk is ronin* (The bitch is seeking). [D. *ronne*: of a ram after sheep; Sw.dial. *rana*: to be in heat]

roo (ru) (v) to pluck the wool off a sheep, usually in summer (the common method of obtaining wool from pure-breed Shetland sheep until late 20th century when improved husbandry and the gradual introduction of cross-breeding ensured continuous growth of fleece, making shearing necessary in most cases); a pile or heap of something. *A roo a stanes*; (also see **roog**). [N. *rua*: to pluck the loose wool off sheep]

rooder (n) barnacle (*Cirripedia*). [O.N. *hrúdr*: crust; scab; a kind of shellfish (*Cirripedalia sessilia*)]

roodery skerry (ruderie-) (n) a rock covered with barnacles. [O.N. *hrúdr*: crust; scab + *sker*: a rocky island; a reef]

roog (rug, roo) (n) a heap or pile; a large clumsy person; (v) to gather in heaps. [O.N. *hrúga*: to heap; pile up]

rook 1) (n) a smoke; (v) to smoke, as a pipe. [N. *røyk*: smoke; Du. *rooken*: (to) smoke]; 2) (v) to cheat. [E. *rook* (slang): a cheat; a swindler; esp. a card sharp]; 3) (n) a poor emaciated creature. *De pony hed come t be a pör rook o a craitur*. [der. of N.dial. *ruka*: a heap, as *a ruk of banes*]

room (n) space between the thwarts in a boat. [O.N. *rúm*: compartment of a boat or ship] J. Spence, *Folklore*, states: 'The boat was divided into six compartments – fore-head, fore-room, mid-room, oost room, shott, hunnik or kannie.'

rooscadd (ruskad) (n) food (bread) burned black on the outside and uncooked in the middle. [O.N. *hrár*: raw + L.Sc. *scad*, *scaude*; E. *scald*]

roose 1) (n) a big, blazing fire. [E. *roast*: to be excessively hot]

roose 2) (v) to make haste. *Roose dee, boy!* [O.N. *ræsa*: to set going; N. *rus*: onrush; hurried work]

roosk (rusk) (n) a stout, strong person; a big, strapping man; a luxuriant growth of hair. [O.N. *roskr*: full grown; mature; cognate with *riska*, *riskva*: to grow; ripen]

roost (rust) (n) a strong tidal current, e.g. Sumburgh Roost. [O.N. *rost*: whirlpool; strong current]

rooster (n) a strongly blazing fire. [cf. E. *roaster*: excessively hot day]

rooth (ruth) (n) that part of the gunwale on which the oar rests in rowing, generally reinforced with a clamp of hard wood or iron to protect against wear from friction caused by the oar. [N. *ro*: a rowlock; O.N. *ródr*: a rowing]

rose (n) an inflammatory disease (*erysipelas*), marked by a bright redness of the skin. [cf. E. *rose*: erysipelas]

roset (n) hard resin (obtained by mixing turpentine with dead pine wood), as used on the bow of a fiddle. [E. *rosin*]

rost (rustju) (n) an unpleasant burning sensation, as may be caused by midges; disorder; confusion; great haste. *He wis in an erse rost ta catch de bus*. [cf. Icel. *rú og stú*: disorder; confusion; hubbub]

rotchie (n) little auk (*Plautus alle*). [cf. Du. *rotje*: petrel]

roup (n) an auction sale; (v) to sell by auction. [Sc. *roup*: a sale by public auction; of (v) *rouping*: the act of crying or cawing]

rout (n) a shout; (v) to shout. [Sc. *rout*: to roar; bellow; O.N. *rauta*]

rovek (n) cleft between the buttocks. [O.N. *rauf*: a hole; opening; anus]

rowe (v) to roll (also **rowl**). [O.Sc. *rowe*, *rowl*: roll]

rower (n) a roll of combed and carded sheep's wool ready for spinning. [E. *rolag*, Gael. *ròlag*, dimin. of *rola*: a roll]

rowl (v) to roll. [see **rowe**]

rowt (rocht) (n) (pt of) work (also **wrowt**, **wrocht**, **wrouht**). [E. *wrought*]

röd (n) empty talk; (v) to talk on and on in a babbling manner. [O.N. *ræda*: to speak, with N. *rjoda*: (in the sense of) to twaddle; cf. O.N. *hrjóda*: to emit coarse sounds; to snore]

röd (röid) (v) to drizzle. [Icel. *hrjóta*: to drizzle; Fær. *rota*: rainy weather]

röf (n) a roof; (v) to put on a roof. [E. *roof*]

röl (n) a young horse or Shetland pony (see also **staig**); *A pellet röl* – a pony that is losing its coat, leaving hair hanging in **pells**. [O.N. *hrøyfi*: the fleece of a sheep; N. *ruvel*: a rough-haired, shaggy animal; N. *røyvlen*: untidy; disarranged]

rönnie (røni) (n) a heap of stones; a prominent rock on a hillside; (also **rig-röni**). [O.N. *hraun*: stone-heap; stony ground; Fær. *reyn*: stony ground; stony height. Note: Ronas Hill could possibly derive its name from this meaning though more probably from O.N. *raud*, meaning red, owing to the red granite that forms much of its landscape]

rös (v) to commend highly. *He hes a greht rös o dee* (He praises you highly). [O.N. *hrósa*: to praise; to boast]

röt (n) a root; (v) to poke about in search of something. [O.N. *róta*: to turn upside down; to stir up; to disturb; N. & Sw. *rota*, D. *rode*: to rummage, in the sense of rooting up (earth)]

röv (n) a washer to which a nail, or **sem**, is fixed, thus making a rivet – hence **sem an röv** – used to fasten planks of a boat. [O.N. *ró*, O.Sc. *roove*, *ruve* (v): to rivet; clinch]

ruckly (rukklie) (adj) wrinkled, as corrugated iron. [O.N. *hrukka*: a ruck; wrinkle; N. *rukla*: a raised rib; a wrinkle; E. *ruckle*: a crease]

rudge (rug) (v) to gather up loose stones from a piece of arable land. [O.N. *hrúga*: to heap; pile up]

rug (rogg, rukk) (v) to tug with intermittant jerks. [O.N. *rykkr*: a jerk; a quick pull]

rugg (ruk) (n) strong tide (also see **affrugg**). [O.N. *reka*: drift; cf. Fær. *rák*: set of current]

rukkel (n) an untidy heap, as a collapsed dry-stone wall. [Icel. *hrúka*, N. *ruka*: a pile; Sw.dial. *rukkel*: something badly erected]

rukkli (adj) rough. [see above]

rummel (n) a rumble; noise. [N. *ruml*]

rummel (ruml) (v) to collapse, as loose stones. [N. *rumla*: to rumble; clatter]

rummelation (rummlieation) (adj) in a state of tumbled-down untidiness. *Yun daek is in a rummelation*. [see above]

R

rumse (rumsel, rums) (v) to rummage. [E. *rummage*, N. *rumska*: to shake]

run (adj) 1) curdled, as of milk. [Sc. *run*: coagulate]; 2) collapsed, as *a run waa* – a collapsed stone wall. [of E. *run*: to unravel]

runch (n) a spanner or wrench. [Sc. variant of E. *wrench*]

rung (rong) (n) a whack with a stick (also **runk**). [Sw. *runga*, D. *runge*: to ring; to resound; O.N. *hrang*: a noise; din]

runk (n) to ring or resonate, as a fiddle being played. *Bertie gied wis a runk apo d fiddle afore we left*. [see above]

runk (n) a break in bad weather; (v) to ease, weather-wise. [O.N. *rakna*: to recover after a swoon, also to pass off]

runk (n) a big person or animal. [O.N. *hrúnki*: something large]

runnick (n) an open drain or gutter which carries manure from a **byre** to a **midden** (also see **oiler**). [cf. O.N. *renna*: a run; a course; N. *renna*: a ditch; Fær. *runa*: the ordure from a byre-gutter]

runrig (n) an antiquated system of alloting plots of land or **rigs** (see above) on a rota-system to tenants so that no crofter should be disadvantaged (also see **rigga-aboot**). [Sc. *runrig (rundale)*: a form of land tenure]

runshick (runshie) (n) wild radish (*Raphanus raphanistrum*) or charlock (*Sinapis arvensis*); weeds with yellow flowers commonly found in cornfields. [Sc. & E. *runch*; O.Sc. *ruinch*, *ruincheoch* – orig. obs.]

runt (n) the stem of a cabbage – *a kail runt* (see **kale**). [Sc. *runt*: dried up; decayed stock; O.Sc. *runt*: a tree-stump]

rushie (n) coarse; rough-fibred; *rushie bag* (hessian bag). [cf. Sw. *ruskig*: of weather, drizzly; in sense of tousled, with bristling hair]

russa (n) a mare. [O.N. *hryssa*]

russie (n) a horse; stallion. [O.N. *hross*: horse]

rutl (rottel) (v) bubble; rattle, as a kettle boiling; (also see **robbi rutl**). [N. *rutla*: to rattle; to make a noise on shifting anything]

rycht (adj) right (also **richt**). [Sc. *richt*, of E. *right*]

S

saa (v) saw; (pt of) see; to sow seed. [Sc. variant of E. *saw* & *sow*]

saand (sand) (n) sand – both long and short *a* are used, esp. in placenames, e.g. Sandness, Sandwick. [O.N. *sandr*: sand]

saandiloo (sandilu) (n) ringed plover (*Charadrius hiaticula*) (also **plivver**). [O.N. *ló*, N. *lo*: golden plover; Icel. *sandló*: ringed plover]

saandy eel (n) the sandeel or launce (*Ammodytes tobianus* or *Ammodytes lancea*) also known as **geddek or giddek**; any of several eel-like fish that bury themselves in wet sand at ebb-tide. [E. *sandeel*]

saat (saut, salt (with short *a*, not as E. *solt*)) (n) salt; in placenames, e.g. Saltness (Westside), where sea-water was boiled to extract salt. [Sc. *saut*; O.N. *saltr*; E. *salt*; O.E. *sealt*; L. *sāl*]

saatbrack (n) the spray and foam from breaking waves. *As saat as brack*; (lit. 'salt-break').

saat cuddie (n) originally a straw container for holding salt, hung beside the fire, now a custom-made lidded box. [Sc. *saut-box*]

sab (sabb) (v) to soak; saturate; (pp) **sabbet** *I got sabbet comin fae de banks*; (n, adj) **sabbin** *Me claes is joost sabbin*. [N. *sabba*: (in sense of) to spill water; *sabben*: heavy and rainy (of the air); muddy (of the roads)]

sae 1) (adv. conj. or interj.) so. [Sc. form of E. *so*]

sae 2) (n) a wooden tub with two lugs for lifting or to pass a pole through for transport by two persons, used for carrying water or washing. [O.Sc. *say*: bucket; M.E. *soe*: tub; O.N. *sár*: a cask]

saed (n) a full-grown saithe – commonly coley or coalfish (*Gadus virens*). [O.N. *seithr*]

saed fool (n) lesser black-backed gull (*Larus fuscus*) (lit. 'saithe fowl'). [see above]

saek (see **sic**)

sail (v) to move slowly; to creep along. [not in E. sense of 'effortless progress', cf. N. *sila*: to move slowly; Sw.dial. *sila*: to trickle gentle]

sailor's hope (n) scurvy grass (*Cochlearia officinalis*). [so named for the high vitamin C content in the edible leaves which can be added to salads]

sain (v) to bless. [O.E. *segnian*: to confer a blessing; to sign (with the cross); O.Sc. *sane*, Sc. *sain*: to make the sign of the cross; L. *signum*: a sign]

sair (ser) (v) to suffice. [Sc. *ser*, *sair*: to serve; to be sufficient]; (adj) painful; sore; severe; (of weather) severe, stormy. *Wir hed a sair spell o wadder*; (of anything distressful) *He's sair pitten aboot*. [cf. O.N. *sárr*: sore – which in Sh. ought to give *sor*, corresponding to E. *sore*, however **sair, sare** suggests O.N. *sjúkr ok sárr*: sick and wounded (Jakobsen); Sc. *sair*]

sal (sall) (v) shall, frequently contracted to *I'se* (I shall) (also see **sanna**). [E. *shall*]

salist sa–*list* (v) to pause for a moment. *Du can surely salist a peerie start; dir nae hurry*. [cf. N. *sala*: to move lazily and slowly; also *søle*: a slow, dilatory person]

sally (v) to dawdle along. *Shö wis sallyin up de brae*. [poss. a reversal of E. *sally*: a rushing forth, or confusion with *dally*: to waste time; to dawdle; also cf. **salist** (see above)]

sam (n) same. In phrases: **dat sam** just so; **wi dat sam** in that very moment. [E. *same*]

sammas (conj) as if; same as if. *De bairn wis gowlin sammas shö wis hurt*.

sang (n) song. [Sc.]

sanna (v) shall not (see **sal**). [E. *shall-not*]

santet (*san*-tet) (v) made to disappear in a mysterious fashion. [Sc. *saunt*; E. *saint, sainted*]

Santie's bird (n) any bird seen in close proximity to a house during the weeks leading up to Christmas is often referred to by parents as 'Santie's Bird' – the bird supposedly having been sent by Santa Claus to eavesdrop and spy on potentially naughty children with a view to deciding whether or not they deserve presents. [Sh. folklore]

sap (n) small quantity of liquid. [Sc. *sap, saup*; E. *sip*]

saps (n) bread soaked in milk. [O.Sc. *saps*: bread soaked or boiled in milk, ale, gravy, etc.]

sara-blind (n) long-legged spider often seen in peat-hill. [cf. Sw.dial. *saren*: the devil]

sara-slöb (n) lion's-mane or giant jellyfish (*Cyanea capillata*). [Sw.dial. *saren*: the devil + N. *slip*; O.N. *sleipa*]

sark (n) a shirt. [O.N. *serkr*; O.Sc. *sark*]

sary (adj) touchy. [O.Sc. *sary*: sorry – of *sair*: sore]

sassermaet (saucermeat) (n) minced meat, generally beef, to which seasoning and spices are added (a Shetland speciality). [N. *sakesmat*: intestines minced for meat sausage; O.N. *saxa*: to hack; cut]

scad (skad) (n) a hurry. *He's aye in a scad*. [cf. O.N. *skot*: a shooting; a shot; N. *skot*: great speed; N. *skota*: to rush heedlessly and noisily]; (v) to scald. [Sc. *scaud*; E. *scald*]

scaddiman's heid; scabbiman's heid (Lerwick) (n) edible sea-urchin or the shell thereof (*Echinus esculentus*) (also **julter, yulter**). [L.Sc. *scaudman's head* = scalded man's head]

scaff (v) to eat up. [E. (slang) *scoff*: to eat food greedily; O.Sc. *scaff*: to scrounge]

scaffie (n) a street cleaner. [O.Sc. *scaffie*, of E. *scavenger*: a street sweeper]

scam (n) a mark; stain or blotch. [O.Sc. *scaum*: a singe or blemish; E.dial. *scam*: to stain; discolour, cf. O.N. *skafa*: a small cloud – in the Sh. sense of *Der no a scam apo de lift*; N. *skjemma*: to spoil]

scarf (see **skarf**)

scart (v) to scratch. [O.Sc. *scart, scrat*: scratch; M.E. *scratte*]

scat (skatt) (n) land tax formerly paid to the crown for arable lands in Shetland. [O.N. *skattr*: to impose tax; N. *skatta*: to pay taxes]

scattald (skattald) (n) the common grazing allocated to crofters in Orkney and Shetland; hill pasture (the term originally included all land within a **toun**, including arable). [The word does not appear in O.N. or N. but appears to be derive from **skatt** (see above), denoting *land which is taxed for its use*]

sclate (n) slate – used as roofing tile or a writing slate. [O.Sc. *sclater*; O.F. *escalate*; E. *slate*]

sclater (n) a woodlouse (*Oniscus asellus*), so named because it is commonly found under slate roof tiles (also **slater**). [Sc.dial. *slater*, also Aust. & N.Z.]

sclates (n) flat pieces of wood fixed to the shank of an oar to prevent its being chafed on the rooth during rowing. [so named for its similarity to a slate (see **sclate**)]

sclaterscrae (n) a term of abuse to describe a self-important person who talks volubly about topics he or she knows little about. The term is somewhat obscurely derived from an earlier 19th cent. meaning when *sklattiskre* or *skrattiske* denoted a dunlin (*Calidris alpina*) (see **ebb-sleeper**). [N. *skrata*: to cackle; chatter + O.N. *skreid*: a swarm; flock] Thomas Edmondston, *Glossary of the Shetland and Orkney Dialect* (1866), has 'sclatyscrae, a person so very contemptible as only to be likened to a "slater", a slimy worm found under the ebb-stones', however, Jakobsen believes this use of the word is not confirmed and may be due to a misunderstanding.

scoarn (v) to mimic. [Sc. *scorn*, with the additional meaning of mocking mimicry]

scobbins (skobbin, skovin) (n) porridge or cereal sticking to the bottom of the pan during cooking and partly burned; the scrapings from a pan. [N. *skova*, Sw. *skofva*, Icel. *skófir*: scrapings, esp. crustation in the bottom of a vessel]

scooder (skolder) (v) to singe; to scorch. [D. *skolde*; N. *skaalda*; Icel. *skálda*]

scoom (skum) (n) foam; froth; (v) to sweep away; to skim; to drive out. [N.dial. *skum*, Fær. *skúm*: scum; Fær. *skúma*: to skim]

scoomer (skumer) (v) implement for skimming a fish kettle. [see above]

scoomfish (v) to choke or suffocate from smoke or heat. [Sc. *scomfish*: to stifle; disgust; E. *discomfit*; cf. O.Sc. *scumfish*, *scoomfyt*: to suffocate]

scoor (n) a wash; diarrhoea; (v) to wash; scrub; purge. [E. *scour*, with both meanings]

scoot (n) bird excrement; (v) to squirt; to excrete in a thin stream, as of birds (see **scooty-alan**). [Sc. *scoot*: to squirt]

scooty-alan (skuti-alen, scootie aalin) (n) arctic skua (*Stercorarius parasiticus*). [The bird derives its name from the habit of diving on other birds, squirting stinking fluid on them to deprive them of their food which it then takes to its own young. Sc. *scoot*: to squirt; **alan** is poss. an older D. & Sw.dial. synonym for the same action – *adel*: urine; liquid manure]; (also see **alamootie**).

scord (skord) (n) a cleft in the skyline of a hill; common placename, e.g. Scordaback, Byre o Scord. [O.N. *skard*: a notch; a defile]

scordet (adj) scored; cracked by exposure to weather, as in chapped hands. [of same deriv. as **scord**]

scowe (n) a barrel stave. [O.Sc. *scow*: a strip of wood; a lath; Du. *schoof*]

scowed (adj) bent; curved; warped. *Yun plank is scowed.* [see above]

scöl (skül, skule) (n) school. [Sc. *scule*, *skule*; E. *school*]

scöl-bairns (skül-, skule-) (n) pupils. [E. *school* + O.Sc. *barne*, *bairn*, O.N. *barn*: child]

scöl-wark (skül-, skule-) (n) studies. [E. *school-work*]

scöp (n) a scoop for bailing out a boat; (v) to scoop. *Scöp up yun coarn sidds*; (also see **owskerri**). [E. *scoop*]

scran (n) odds and ends of rubbish; a contemptious term for meagre or unsubstantial things; (v) to gather such objects. [Sc. *scran*: odds and ends of food, provisions; *bad scran to you* – bad luck to you (Irish saying)]

scratcher (n) (slang) a bed. [Sc. originally a doss house term for a bed, presumably owing to the liklihood of finding lice or fleas]

screecham (skreekum) (n) (slang) whisky. [O.Sc. *screich* (slang): whisky; cf. Sc. *skeechan*: a type of beer; Gael. *caochan*: fermented liquor]

screed (n) a swarm. *A screed o midges*; a large quantity or crowd of anything; (v) to teem; to swarm. *De krang wiz skreedin wi maeds* (The carcase was swarming with maggots); (also see **scry**, **skrid**). [O.N. *skreid*: a creeping; a motion forward; advancing flock; crowd]

screedin (skredin) (adj) swarming. [see above]

scribe (n) handwritten word or line of writing. *Du better send a scribe tae aald daa noo he's poorly.* [E. *scribe*: a writer; a pointed instrument to mark lines on wood or metal; to write; L. *scribere*: to write]

scriech (n) a screech; (v) to screech. [E. *screech*]

scrime (skrim, skrime) (v) to peer; to see something with difficulty. [N. *skrima*: to appear faintly; to have weak eyesight; Fær. *skríma*: to see faintly]

scrit (skritl, skrit) (n) a scraping noise, e.g. the sound of a pen writing; a rent or tear. *Shö's aye in a scrit t finish de hoosewark*; (v) to strike a match; to write. [N. *skrikka*: to emit a scraping sound]

scry (skre) (n) a swarm (also **screed**, **skrid**). [O.N. *skreid*: a creeping; a motion forward; advancing flock; crowd]

scud (n) a blow given with the open hand. *He gied me a scud*; (v) to beat (smack) with the open hand. [Sc.]

scudder (n) a quick, passing shower; a squall. [L.Sc. *scouther*: a slight flying shower; O.N. *skotra*: a heavy, passing squall]

scunge (v) to chase away; to clear out; (also see **skunge**). [N. *skunza*: to push; to set in motion; Sc. *scunge* (n): to scrounge; prowl about in search of food, as a dog, and by extension the act of removing a 'scunger']

scunner (n) repugnance; aversion. *Wir dug took a scunner tae de maet*; an objectionable person. *He's a scunner*; (v) to be sickened by. *De sicht o yun fair scunners me.* [Sc. *scunner*, with same meanings; cf. M.E. *scurn*: to shrink]

scutter (n) a messy job. *Yun's a right scutter du's made dere*; (v) to do work in an inept, slovenly way, thus making a mess of it (also see **slutter**). [O.Sc. *scutter* – variant on *skitter*: to slither or slip; M.E. *skite*]

sea (n) besides meaning the ocean, also wave(s). *Dir a heavy sea runnin ida soond*. [O.N. *sjór*: sea; waves]

sea craa (n) razorbill (*Alca torda*). [poss. named for its call]

sea-feirdy (sea-ferdi) (adj) seaworthy. [-*feirdy*, cf. L.Sc. *feirdy*: quick; active; O.N. *ferðugr*: ready; prepared]

sea-flech (n) the sand hopper (*Talitrus saltator*). [E. *sea* + O.Sc. *fleche*, O.E. *flēah*: flea]

see (v) to take note of; observe. *See du him!*; to be attentive to. *A'll hae ta see till de hens*. [O.N. *sjá*: see; *sjá til*: to look at; to listen to]

seek (v) to be on heat, as a bitch in search of a mate. *I'll hae t lock up wir dug while yun bick is seekin*; to seek up to; to draw close to. *De peerie ting will aye seek up tae dee while du hes a pockie o sweeties*; *seek tae* – to strive for. [Sc.]

seem (v) heed; pay attention – commonly used in a negative form. *Never seem him an he'll gie up wi yun haverin*. [cf. E. *besee*: to look at; O.E. *besēon*]

seemly (adj) comely; of pleasing appearance. *Yun claes is no seemly*. [archaic Sc., O.N. *sœmaligr*: fitting]

seevin (n) seven. [*seeven* – Sc. form of E. *seven*]

seggie-flooer (seg, sig, siggie) (n) the yellow iris (*Iris pseudacorus*). [O.N. *seggr*, O.Sc. *seg*: sedge + Sc. *flooer*: flower]

seich (n) a sigh; (v) to sigh. [O.Sc. *sich, sych*]

sekk (n) a sack. [O.N. *sekkr*: a sack]

selkie (sylkie) (n) a seal. [Sc. *silkie, silky, selkie*; O.Sc. *selich*; O.E. *seolh*]

sem (seam) (n) a type of nail used in boat-building (see **röv**). [O.N. *saumr*: nails]

send (n) a kick. *A'll gie dee a send wi de tae a me böt*; also in exp. *Dir some send apon him de day* (He's making some speed, haste). [cf. N. *senda*: (to send) in sense of *throw out*]

set (n) a seed potato; a fishing line or net (the article itself, as opposed to E.); (v) the laying of either; (v) to plant – potatoes, kale, etc.; raise peats against one another for drying (see also **lay in**); be of use to; serve. *Hit wid set dee better ta listen*; plant a row (of potatoes, etc.). *Set de geng*; used in phrases: **set aff** depart; **set aff** to finish planting. *A'll joost set aff dis geng afore twal time*; **set aff** to measure off a plot of land; **set at** to sit and relax; **set by** to place aside; reserve. *Set by dee makkin*; *Set by some tatties fur me*; **set de kröl** arch the back; **set de sleb** protrude lower lip; pout; **set doon** be seated; **set fae** to place away from. *Set dee cup fae dee*; **set in** to be seated, usually at a table; **set in** move shorewards, as a tide or shoal of fish. *De silleks set in de streen*; **set on** to keep a young animal over winter with a view to adding it to the flock; to work hard; [O.N. *setja saman*]; **set on** to strive; press on; **set on** ignite. *Set on a fire*; **set owre** to ferry across; **set til** start a fight; **set tö** close. *Set tö de door*; **set up** to improve one's station in life; to develop, as a shower of rain. *I tink he's settin up a shooer owre by*; to provoke; incite; to encourage. *I keen du wis set up tae say yun*; **set up** put forward. *Dunna set up dee cheek ta me*; **set up** rearrange peats in a fire. *Boy, set up de fire* [O.N. *setja* – note: E. *settan* is cognative with the O.N. however there are subtle differences in meaning as represented in most of the above]

setter (n) an area of pastureland; common suffix in croft and district names, e.g. Aithsetter, Mursetter. [O.N. *sætr*, N. *sæter*: mountain pasture; dairy land]

Setterday (n) Saturday. [*Seterday* – Sc. form of E. *Saturday*]

setnin (n) a weaned lamb that has been added to a flock of breeding ewes. [of O.N. *setja*]

sha (shaa) (v) show. *Sha me yun du's workin wi*; (pt) **shew**; (pp) **shaan**. [Shet. variant on Sc. *shaw*; E. *show*]

shaald (adj) shallow. [O.Sc. *schald*; O.E. *sceald*]

shaav (shaave) (v) to gnaw. *De coo is fairly shaavin at de neeps*; to hack. [cf. N. *kjava*, (*kjafsa*): to move the jaws; wrangle; Sc. *chaw*]

shackleben (shacklebane) (n) the wrist (*Carpus*). [O.Sc. *schakilbane*: wrist]

shaef (n) a sheaf; (pl) **shaeves**. [O.Sc. *shaif*; E. *sheaf*]

shaela (sjela) (n) hoar frost or cold dew; wool of dark bluish/grey with whitish points; (adj) of anything dark grey with a lighter tinge on top – *a shaela gimmer*. [O.N. *héla*, N. *hela*: hoar frost – hence wool of this colour]

shair (n) chair. [Sh. form of E. *chair* (*sh* substitute for *ch*)]

shakk (n) wheatear (*Oenanthe oenanthe*). [see **sten-shakker**]

shakkins o da böddie (n) last remnant contents of a basket; also applied to last child in a large family; (see **böddie**). [Sc. *shak*: shake + cf. Icel. *byda*: wooden tub; Fær. *bydi*: milk pail]

shalder (sjalder) (n) oyster catcher (*Haematopus ostralegus*) deriv. of 'scolder' – imitative of its alarm call. [Fær. *tjaldur*; O.N. *tjaldr*]

shalmillens (shaelmillins) (n) smithereens, as crushed shells (also see **millin**). [Sc. *shale*: shell + **millin** N. *myl*: a particle]

sham (sjamm) (v) to distort the face; scowl; grimace. [O.N. *kjamma*: to move the jaws; E.dial *cham*: to chew; gnaw – hence *champ*: to ruminate]

shams (sjams) (v) to make a loud smacking noise when eating. [O.N. *kjamsa*: to chew – poss. champ audibly; Icel. *kjamsa*: to move the jaws]

shance (n, v) chance. [Sh. *sh-* substitute for E. *ch-*]

shanty (shantie) (n) a chamber pot. [O.Sc. *shantie, chanty*]

shap (v) to chop; to mash, as potatoes. [Sc. form of E. *chop*]

shappin-can (n) a quart container. [Sc. *shopin, shoppin*: an old Scots measure containing about one English quart; O.Sc. *schoppin*]

shappin-tree (sjapin-tree) (n) potato masher. [O.Sc. *shappin-stick, shappin-tree*]

shappit (adj) mashed, as *shappit tatties*; (v) hit, as *I shappit me toom*. [O.Sc. *chapped-*]

share (v) to cut corn; (pt) **shör**; (pp) **shoarn**. [O.N. *sjera*: to cut; E. *shear*]

sharg (sjarg, snjarg) (n) a nagging person; (v) to nag; to fault-find; to argue unyieldingly. [Sw.dial. *sarg* (*sjarg*): a grumbling and scolding; *sarger*: a person always scolding]

sharl-pin (sharl, sjarl-pin) (n) the pin of a wooden door hinge. [O.N. *hjarri*: a hinge; door-hinge]

sharn (n) cow dung; excrement. [O.Sc. *scharn, sharn*]

sharny (adj) something soiled by **sharn**. [see above]

S

67

sharp (adj) sour, as milk. [of E. *sharp*: (in sense of affecting the senses) pungent; tart, etc.]

shask (sjask) (n) 1) haze; mist; drizzly rain; (also **ask**). [O.N. cf. *hoss*: greyish; *aska*: ashes; E. *haze*]; 2) slavery; drudgery (see **disjaskit**). [dimin. of O.N. *dasast*: to become weary, exhausted; also cf. O.Sc. *daisket*: exhausted; *jaskit*: jaded; worn out]

shaste (v) to chase. *Whitna dug's yun shastin de kye?* [O.Sc. *shase*; Sh. *sh*- substitute for E. *ch*-]

sheave (n) a slice of bread or cake. [Sc. *shive*; O.Sc. *shefe*; M.E. *sheive*]

sheekbenn (n) cheekbone. [Sc. *sheekbane*; Sh. *sh*-substitute for E. *ch*-]

sheek-for-showe (adv) cheek by jowl. [*sheek* = Sc. form of E. *cheek* + O.Sc. *chow, choll*: cheek or jowl]

sheeks (n) cheeks; a chatterbox; (v) to prattle incessantly. *He's aye sheeksin an shargin. Hadd dee sheeks!* (lit. 'shut your mouth' – refrain from talking). [Sc. *sheek*: cheek; the side of the face, with extension of meaning in Shetland to voluable talk]

sheeksfoo (n) mouthful (lit. 'cheeks-full').

sheeksy (sheeksie) (adj) excessively talkative. [see **sheeks**]

sheeks-rivin (-raivin) (n) jestful expression to describe a meeting or discussion; a talk-fest. *Der bön sheeks-raivin dis past twartree oors.* [**sheeks** (see above) + Sc. & E. *rive*: to wrench something open or tear it apart; plough up; tug; tear or split]

sheeld (n) fellow (also **sheelder**). [of Sc. *chield*: child; with ext. in meaning to a lad, fellow – similar to Sh. usage of the feminine **lass**]

sheen (v) to shine. [Sc. *sheen*; O.Sc. *schene*]

sheenge (v) to change. [S. *sh*- substitute for E. *ch*-]

sheep's gaet (n) path made by sheep travelling in single file. [E. *sheep* + O.N. *gata*: a road; a path; Sc. *gate, gait*]

sheephadd (n) a sheep-proof walled enclosure. [*sheep* + O.N. *hald*: hold; grip; Sc. *hald, hauld*: a hold]

sheerlin (v) to sing gaily, esp. of birds. [Sc. *chirl*: a low, warbling sound (imitative of birds)]

sheet (n) in expression *ta gie sheet* – to let rip; drive at full speed; also *gie him sheet* – hammer, beat or scold someone. [of E. *sheet*: the corner rope that controls movement of a sail; Sc. *sheet*: to let rip; flee; run for it]

sheltie (n) Shetland pony. [dimin. of *Shetland*; O.N. *hjalti*]

shenge (shange) (v) change. [Sh. *sh*- substitute for E. *ch*-]

Shetland (n) the name of the group of islands lying north east of Orkney; prefix for a number of animals and articles of Shetland origin: **Shetland pony (sheltie)** small, hardy pony with a thick, shaggy coat, popular as a child's pet throughout the world; **Shetland shawl** fine, handknitted lace-work shawls made from Shetland wool in 1-ply 'cobweb' yarn (esp. in Unst), lace 'hap' yarn, or 2-ply worsted yarn; **Shetland sheep** a diminutive breed of sheep, producing wool in a variety of natural colours including black, **moorit**, grey and white; **Shetland sheep-dog** (referred to by Kennel Clubs as **Shetland Collie**) a diminutive type of Scotch Collie universally bred as a pet or show dog – not suitable for sheep work; **Shetland wool** the fine-micron wool produced by Shetland sheep and worsted spun for the production of **Fair Isle** garments and fine shawls. [O.N. *Hjaltland* – see entry under that name]

Shetlandic (n) the traditional speech or dialect of the Shetland Isles; the substance of this dictionary.

shew (v) 1) (pt of) show. *He shew de new dug he'd bowt*; (also **shaaed**). [E. *show*]; 2) to sew. [O.Sc. *schew*: to sew]

shickenwirt (n) chickweed (*Stellaria media*). [Sh. *sh*-substitute for *ch*- + O.Sc. *wort*: a root]

shift (n) a change of clothing; (v) to move quickly. [E. *shift*, but in these senses now only colloq. or dial]

shiggle (n) a shake; (v) to shake. [Sh. variant on Sc. *jeegle*; E. *jiggle*]

shiggly (adj) shaky. [see above]

shill (v) to bite; to remove flesh from a shellfish with a knife; to hollow out. *De bairns wir shillin neeps for Halloween lanterns.* [O.Sc. *schele*: to husk; shell, as peas; also cf. *shuil*: to shovel]

shilpet (adj) sour. [O.Sc. *shilpit*: thin; puny; wishy washy; sour; tart]

shimley (n) chimney. [Sh. *sh*- substitute for E. *ch*-]

shimley-neuk (n) chimney corner; ingle-nook. [see above]

shimley-sheek (n) chimney-cheek; inside wall of chimney. [see above]

shin (n) the chin. [Sh. *sh*- substitute for E. *ch*-]

shiv (n) a shove; (v) to shove. [E. *shove*]

shivvel (n) a shovel; (v) to shovel. [E. *shovel*]

shoard (n) a prop; (v) to prop up a beached boat; to support. [N *skorda*, O.N. *skorda*: to keep in equilibrium, esp. to put stays under the sides of a boat in conj. with E. *shore*: (n) a prop; (v) to prop]

shock (v) to choke. [Sh. *sh*- substitute for E. *ch*-]

shokkin (adj) thirsty. *A'm shokkin; shokkin wi trist.* [Sc. *chock* – variant of E. *choke*]

shocks (n) the jaws. [O.Sc. *chouk, chokkeis*: the jaw; N. *kjoke*: the cheek; N.dial. *kók*: jaws]

sholgirse (sholgry girse) (n) yarrow (*Achillea millefolium*). [cf. O.N. *hjól*, N. *hjul*: a wheel – from the wheel-like shape of the flower + *girse*: grass]

sholmark (n) a sheep's earmark described as a slit which divides the ear into two lobes, or a crescent bite out of the end. [deriv. of O.N. *hjálmr*: a helmet – and thus **sholmit** an animal having the appearance of wearing a helmet which conceals the ears (see below)]

sholmet (sholmit) (adj) of a cow or sheep with a white face. [N. *hjelm*, O.N. *hjálmr*: a helmet; Icel. *hjálmóttr*]

shoo (sju) (v) to propel a boat stern foremost by rowing backwards. [cf. O.N. *skjóta*: to shove; Fær. *skjóta*: to back with the oars]

shooder (n) shoulder. [E. *shoulder*; O.E. *sculdor*]

shooie (sjui) (n) arctic skua (*Stercorarius parasiticus*). [cf. Icel. *kjói*; Fær. *kjógvi*]

shoopilti (n) a water nixie; water sprite; (lit. 'water boy'). [O.N. *sjor*: sea + *piltr*: a boy]

shoormal (shoormil) (n) high tide mark; the turning point of waves breaking on a beach. [O.N. *sjóvar*: of the sea + *mál*: measure; limit]

shorebod (n) breaking sea. [O.N. *sjóvar*: of the sea + *bodi*: a sunken rock or the sea breaking on a sunken rock; eddying, bubbling motion of the sea]

shott (shot) (n) the sternmost compartment of a sixern, used for holding the catch. [O.N. *skutr*; N. *skot*. J. Spence, *Folklore*, states: 'The boat was divided into six compartments – fore-head, fore-room, mid-room, oost room, shott, hunnik or kannie.']

show (n) the leaves of a potato plant. [Sc. *shaw*, variant of E. *show*, O.E. *shive*: a slice & *sheave*]

showe (n) a piece broken out of something, e.g. a broken bowl. *Dir a showe oot a de side o 'im*; (v) to chew; to argue. [Sh. *sh-* substitute for E. *ch-*]

shö (pron) she; also used impersonally in reference to objects, esp. boats. *Shö can fairly go ta windward*. [Sh. pronunciation of E. *she*]

shöl (shuul) (v) to shovel out. *Du can shöl oot yun trailer*; to walk in a shuffling manner. *He aye shöls alang in yun smucks*. [O.Sc. *shule*, *shuil*: to shovel; *shuil-fit*: one who has flat shovelling feet – hence to *shuil*]

shölibrod (skolabrod) (n) an old dilapidated article. *A aald shölibord o a boat* (An old, unseaworthy boat). [O.N. *skál*: a fragment; N. *skaalbrot*: a small, old bowl, (properly) a piece of a bowl]

shön (sjonn, **shun)** (n) 1) a small loch; used in placenames, e.g. Da Loomishuns. [N.dial. *tjørn*; O.N. *sjór*; E. *tarn*: a pool or small lake]; 2) (pl. of shoe) shoes. [Sc. *shoon*]; (adv) soon. [Sh. variant on E. *soon*]

shud (sjöd, **sjodd)** (n) shuffling sound; distant sound of the sea near the shore. [N. *sod*: partly a seething, boiling, partly a soughing, roaring, murmering]

shug (sjogg) (n) 1) light drizzle. [Icel. *saggi*: dampness; N. *søgg*: damp; moist; wet; O.N. *sægr*: rain]; 2) thick, luxuriant grass. [O.N. *pjukkr*: thick; dense]

shuggy (sjoggie) (adj) drizzly weather. [see above]

shurg (sjorg) (n) wet gravelly soil. [O.N. *saurr*: mud; dirt; N. *saur*: dirt (partly used of) gravel; N. *saura* (v): is used in sense of 'to fill with gravel']

shurl (sjorl) (n) corn bunting (*Emberiza calandra*) (also **trussie laverek**, **docken sparrow**). [cf. O.N. *hjarra*: to creak; grate – imit. of corn bunting's song which is a monotonous jingling, grating sound]

shut (v) the act of casting line(s) or net(s) overboard in fishing. [Sc. *shuit*; E. *shoot*: as to 'shoot a net']

sib (n) relatives; (adj) related by blood; (also see **freend**). [E. *sib* (n): a blood relation]

SIC (abbrev) Shetland Islands Council.

sic (saek) (adj) such (also **siccan** and **sicna**). *For sicna onkerry*. [Sc. *sic* (*siccan*) also *siclike*: suchlike]

sic an sic such and such; so and so. [see above]

siccar (adj) obstinate; firmly sure. *Du'll no change his mind*, *he's siccar*; (of the weather) inclement; harsh. *Dat's a siccar caald du's gotten*. [Sc. *siccar*, *sicker*: sure; certain; firm]

sicht (sycht) (n) sight. [*sicht*, Sc. variant of E. *sight*]

siclaek (adj) used in regard to health – so so, not so bad, much of a muchness; one thing and another of similar articles. *Cups an plates an siclaek*. [O.Sc. *siclike*]

sid (adj) a small quantity. *A sid a tae*. [O.N. *sáð*: a small portion; a trifle; N. *mjølsaad*: a trifle of meal]

sidd (n) a sheep's earmark. [cf. Icel. *sið*: a wedge]

siddy (adj) of badly winnowed meal which still contains **sids**. [see below]

sidelins (adv) sideways. [O.Sc. *sideling*: at the side of; from the side]

sidewyes (adv) sideways.

sidey-for-sidey (adv) side by side.

sids (n) the inner husks of oats, separated during winnowing. [L. Sc]

sigg 1) (interj) used to urge a dog to the chase. *Sigg him!*; (v) to urge a dog to attack. *He's aye siggin de dug ontae de cat*. [O.N. *siga*: to incite a dog; E. *seek*]; 2) (n) a patch of hard skin; a callous. [O.N. *sigg*: callosity; Icel. *sigg*, id., N.dial. *sigg*: pig skin; bacon-rind]; 3) (v) to press together; to tighten. *Yun jam-jar lid's sigget on*. [cf. N. *sigra*: in sense of to collapse; O.N. *siga*: to sink down; *siga saman*: to close]; 4) (n) heavy swell. *Dir a sigg idda sea*. [O.N. *sig*: a sinking; gliding]

siggie (siggi, **sig)** (n) the yellow iris (*Iris pseudacorus*) (also **seg**, **seggy-flooer**). [O.N. *seggr*, O.Sc. *seg*: sedge]

signify (v) to be of consequence. *I doot hit signifies* (I suspect it matters). [E. *signify*, with extension in meaning]

sile (n) short iron or wooden bar fitted to a socket across the eye of an upper millstone and which engages the mill-wheel to cause the stone to turn. When the stone goes too fast it sometimes comes off the sile, putting the grinding process out of action. Hence the expression applied to an out-of-sorts person – *aff o dee sile*. [N.dial. *sigle*; Sw.dial. *segel*, *sil*]

sill (n) the milt of a male fish. [O.N. *sil*, Icel. *sili*: fry, esp. of salmon]

sillek (sillock) (n) a coalfish (*Pollachius virens*) in its first year (also see **piltek**). [O.N. *silungr*: a kind of small salmon; N. *svilung*: young salmon]

silly (adj) feeble; sickly. [Sc. (obs.) *silly*: pitiable; feeble]

simmens (simmonds, **simmen)** (n) straw ropes; heather-floss used to hold down roof thatching or cornstack. [O.N. *sima*: a straw rope; O.Sc. *siming*]

simmer blink (n) a short glint of sunshine. [O.Sc. *simmer*: summer]

simmer dim (simmer höm) (n) the twilight of a Shetland summer evening; the time between sunset and sunrise in midsummer, when it is never quite dark; (also see **hömin**). '*Whaar da grit grey sea lies skulkin ida dim*, *saft Simmer-höm*' (John Peterson, *Shetlan.*) [Sc. *simmer*]

simmermal (simmermil) (n) 3rd April, traditionally regarded as the first day of summer and reckoned to have the weather-pattern for summer; (originally the date was 14th April and marked the beginning of the summer half of the year. The choice of 3rd rather than 1st April, may be connected to the **borrowin-days**). [N. *sommarmal*; Fær. *summarmáli*; O.Sc. *simmer*: summer + O.N. *mál*: a goal; limit]

simmermal dance (n) the shimmering effect of light on a hot summer's day. [for *simmermal* (see above)]

simmer mirr (n) the movement of air caused by heat which blurs the view or creates a mirage. [Sc. *simmer* + N. *mirra*: to tingle; prick; itch]

simmit (simmet) (n) undergarment or vest usually made of wool or flannel. [O.Sc. *semat*: a Roman vest; E. *samite*: heavy silk fabric used for clothing in medieval times]

sin (conj) since. [O.Sc. *sen*, Sc. *sin* (shortened from *sithen*): since]

S

sin syne (prep) from the time that; since (also **fae syne** (see **syne**)). [Sc. *syne*: then; next; afterwards; later; ago; *lang syne*: long since]

sinder (v) to sunder; separate; disperse. [Fær. *syndrast*; L.Sc. *sinder*)

sindry (adv) asunder (also **asundry**). [O.Sc. *sindry*; M.E. *sundar*; O.E. *sundrum*, *syndrig*]

sink (v) to destroy; bring to ruin; (lit. to descend into Hell); used as a curse – (*God*) *sink dee!* [Sc.]

sinknation (n) spate of curses, in the manner of *damnation*. [see above]

sinnen (n) sinew. [L.Sc. *sinnon*; O.Sc. *senown*]

sinni (n) a small kiln, usually at the end of a barn. [*sinni* = *sonn*, *soin*, cf. Gael. *sorn*: a kiln]

sinni girse (**sinna-girs**) (n) long, tough grass growing among rocks on the sea-shore. [O.N. *sina*: old withered grass which has stood through the winter]

sint (n) a very small quantity. [L.Sc]

sipe (n) a very small quantity of liquid. [Sc.dial. *sipe*: to soak through; to seep or ooze; O.E. *sipian*, Fær. *soppur*: a wisp of hay (prob. not related)]

sirpin (adj) soaking wet, esp. of food – thin batter; soft watery dough, etc. [N. *sørpe*: slush; wet mass; *surputt*: muddy]

sistie moose (n) wren (*Troglodytes troglodytes*) subs. *Zetlandicus*. The mouse's relative. [Fær. *musabrodir*: the mouse's brother]

sit (v) in exp. which differ from E. and are related to [O.N. *sitja*: (in sense of) 'to stay' rather than 'be seated']: *A'm no gyaan ta sit lang*, could be said by someone already seated and means 'I'm not going to stay long'; *He's sitten in Houll fur fifteen year noo* (He has stayed in Houll…); *Ir you joost gyaan ta sit oot de fire?* (Are you going to stay still and let the fire go out?)

sitten (adj) said of a fertile egg that is partly incubated and has an embryo chicken in it. [O.N. *sitja* (see above)]

sitter (n) disappointment; an unexpected setback. *He got a richt sitter whan shö telt him de news.* [Sc. (slang) *sitter*: an easy dupe; 'a sitting duck']

sixern (**sixareen**, **sekserin**) (n) a Norwegian designed, broad-beamed, six-oared clinker-built boat with raked stem and stern and having a dipping lug sail, predominantly used as a fishing boat, esp. the **haaf** or deep-sea fishing of 18th and 19th centuries; (compare **yoal**). [O.N. *sexæringr*: six + *ár*: oar; Icel. and Fær. *sexæringur*]

sjöl (**söl**) (n) a sheep's earmark; a cleft. [cf. O.N. *súla*: cleft implement; Icel. *sýling*: angular incision; Fær. *sýldur*: (of an animal's earmark) marked with an incision in the top of the ear]

skaap (**skab**) (n) a bed of mussels; rocky ground covered with a stratum of shellfish; sea floor. [L.Sc. *scaup*: bank of shelfish in the sea; O.Sc. *scalp*, N. *skabb*: stony place]

skaar (**skar**) (n) a small quantity. *Du'll tak a skaar o tae afore du gengs.* [N., Fær., Icel. *skar*: snuff of a candle; O.N. *skard*: a shard]

skae (**ske**) (v) to happen; come to pass. *I'll no shenge me mind whitever may skae.* [D. & Sw. *ske*, N. *skje*: to happen]

S

skaer (**sker**) (v) to scarf-joint two pieces of wood together, as planks of a boat; (n) a joint made in this way. [N. *skar*: a scarfing joint; O.N. *skor*: edge; joining of boards, so that the lower edge of each overlaps the upper edge of that below]

skaer taft (n) a rower's seat; bench; thwart or **taft**. [O.Sc. *thoft*, L.Sc. *thaft*: a thwart]

skail (v) to disperse; scatter. *De kirk fok wis wint ta skail afore de choir wir dön.* [Sc. *skail*, M.E. *scail*, O.Irish *scáilim*: to scatter]

skairet *sky-rit* (adj) brightly coloured. *Dat's a skairet blouse du's wearin.* [O.Sc. *sykrit*: completely mad, thus in Shetland sense poss. 'scary']

skale (**skell**) (v) a crash or cracking sound. *Dey wir naethin bit de skale a de lemm.* [O.N. *skellr*: a cracking blow; a smack]

skalva (n) large flakes of falling snow. [O.N. *skalvi*: snowdrift, with additional deriv. of N. *skaf*: something scraped off; thin snowfall]

skam (n) a mark; scratch. *Dir no a skam apo dat dresser.* [cf. O.N. (v) *skemma*: to scratch; injure]

skarf (**scarf**) (n) shag (*Phalacrocorax aristotelis*), also cormorant (*Phalacrocorax carbo*); (also see **brongi** (**brongiskarf**), **loren**). [O.N. *skarfr*, O.Sc. *scart*: scarf – cf. the Sh. exp. *Ta baet de scarf* – to beat one's hands cross-wise around the shoulders to keep warm; with the bird's name possibly originating from a comparison to the manner in which it folds its wings (see **barflog**)]

skat rooth (**skotnaruth**, **-routh**) (n) a method of rowing a boat whereby one man on the for'ard seat and one on the mid seat each ply a single oar. [O.N. *skotta*: to back a boat, stern foremost, though in Shet. a form of punting with oars; N. *skota*: to propel a boat, stem or stern foremost, by punting + O.N. *rodr*: the act of rowing]

skave (**skev**) (adj) crooked; squint. [O.N. *skeifr*: oblique; askew]

skavel (**skevl**) (v) to set askew (also see **skevelled**). [N. *skjevla*: to push something so that it goes askew; to pull out of its right position]

skeb (see **skepp**)

skebbek (n) an old, worn-out shoe; (adj) crooked and clumsy; twisted, esp. of the foot. [N. *skevra*: to distort; make askew]

skeek (v) to manage or use economically. [of Sc. *skeeg*: the smallest portion of anything; the least drop]

skenkhoch (n) a ham joint. [cf. N. *skinka*: ham; loin; L.Sc. *skink*: shin of beef]

skepp (n) a big straw basket, or **keshie**, used for holding corn-straw in a barn. [O.N. *skeppa*: a bushel; measure; Sc. *skep*: large round basket of wickerwork or straw]

skeet (v) to skim across the surface of water. *See du, dir skeetin stanes apo de loch*; to squirt. [*skeet*, Sc. form of E. *skate*, with additional meaning in O.N. *skjóta*, N. *skyte*: to shoot]

skeetik (**skitek**) (n) cuttlefish (*Sepia officinalis*). [doubtless from its ability to **skeet**, or squirt fluid (see above)]

skeetitrumps (n) wild angelica (*Angelica sylvestris*) (also **spoots**, **spootitrumps**). [N. *skvetta*: a squirt + E. *trump*: trumpet, so named because children used the hollow stalk of the plant as a *swettek*: (or) squirt]

skekler (skudler, skodler) (n) a guizer; manager of a feast; master of ceremonies; the leader of a band of guizers. The leader of such a band of masked persons was distinguished by a tall conical straw-hat, interwoven with coloured ribbons. Such hats were still being used by guizers in North Yell and Walls (and probably elsewhere) as late as 1960; (v) **skekl** to dress in disguise. [N. *skotrar*: one who takes part in a masked procession, performing dances, scenes, etc., at a wedding feast]

skelf (n) a shelf; a ledge of rock; a splinter. [O.Sc. *skelf*: shelf; Sc. & E. *skelf*: splinter; O.N. *skjalf*: bench; seat]

skelk (skeelk) (n) a loud, mocking laugh; (v) to laugh loudly. [O.N. *skelkja*: to mock one; *skellihlátr*: roaring laughter]

skelp (n) a slap with the open hand; (v) to spank; hit with the open hand. *Du soodna skelp bairns*; to move rapidly. *He's aye skelpin doon de brae on yon bike.* [Sc. & N.E. *skelp*: to slap; to move along briskly; Gael. *sgealp*: a slap with the open hand]

skelp (n) a slab or slice. *Tak a skelp aff a de cheese.* [L.Sc. *skelp* – variant of *skelb* in same meaning]

sken joop (n) an oilskin coat, esp. as worn by fishermen (see also **smooky**). [E. *skin* + O.Sc. *joup, jawp, jupe*: a kind of jacket worn by men, a tunic]

skeo (n) a small, dry-stone building designed to admit air and used for drying or curing fish, mutton, etc.; a term now used to describe a poorly built house; (see **vivda**). [N. *skjaa*: drying house; Ice. *skja*: a shelter; O.N. *skjar*: a window-opening]

skeptin (n) razor shell (*Solenidae*). [O.N. *skapt*: a handle; shaft – hence **skeptin** owing to its shape]

skerpin (n) wind-dried coalfish. [O.N. *skerpa*: to make sharp, hard and dry; cf. N. *skerpefisk*: wind-dried fish]

skerry (skerri) (n) a rock or small islet in the sea, esp. one which is only exposed at low tide. Out Skerries – low-lying islands NE of Whalsay. [O.N. *sker*: a rocky island; a reef]

skevelled (skiveld) (adj) out of alignment; misshapen. [N. *skjevla*: to push something so that it goes askew; to pull out of its right position]

skew-wheef (adv) squint; crooked. [colloq. Sc. *skew-whiff*: crooked; awry]

skilderin (skilders) (n) splinters; flakes of broken enamel or similar. [deriv. O.N. *skilja*: to part; break in pieces]

skile (skäil) (v) to peep or peer out from under a cap or eye-shield; to look sideways. [of O.Sc. *skellie*: squint-eyed; D. *skele*]

skilin brod (n) the board which covered the opening in a thatched roof (a louvre) to allow smoke to escape (archaic). [see above]

skirl (v) laugh shrilly. [N. *skryla*: to wail; *skrella*: to shriek with laughter; Sc. *skirl*: to shriek or sing shrilly; to make the sound of the bagpipes]

skit (skitt) (n) excrement. *Du's spaekin skitt.* [O.N. *skitr*: dirt; excrement; N. *skita*: diarrhoea; O.Sc. *skitter*]

skitter (n) diarrhoea. [see above]

skitter ida slap (n) the last load of corn to be brought home at harvest-time; the messy dregs of the harvest no one particularly wanted. [O.Sc. dr. of *skitter* (see above)]

skitteroolet (n) a disparaging description of an impudent youth or person held in low regard; a brat. [O.N. *skitr*: dirt; excrement + cf. N. *ulæta*: cry; unpleasant sound – hence a whimperer; Icel. & Fær. *ólæti*: bad manners; rude behaviour; noise]

skjaag (stjag) (n) a pen for geese; (v) to put geese in a pen. [O.Sw. *stighia*, Sw.dial. *steg*: a pen; sty; enclosure]

sklent (n) a long tear; (v) to tear; lacerate; rip, as a piece of cloth. [Sc. *sclent, sklent*: a cut made by shears off line; a slanting cut, of E. *slant*]

skoag (n) a fishing line, esp. the snell and hook section which frequently has a short iron rod attached to it. [N.dial. *skak*: the swingle-tree or tracebar of a cart or carriage (from similarity of structure)]

skoilt (n) a broken fragment. [deriv. of **skell**: fragments of a hard object broken by a fall; O.N. *skellr*: a cracking blow; a smack]

skoit (n) a purposeful look; (v) to look inquiringly; peer inquisitively. [cf. O.N. *skoða*: to view; D. *skotte*: to peep; look furtively; N.dial. *skyttra*]

skol (skoll) (n) oblong wooden box to keep fishing lines in. [O.N. *skál*: a bowl]

skooie (n) great skua (*Stercorarius skua*). [Fær. *skúúir, skúvur*; O.N. *skúfr* (the origin of Latin *skua*)]

skoolm (skulm) (v) to scowl. [N. *skulma*: to scowl]

skordi (skurdi) (n) earwig (*Forficula auricularia*) (also see **spurrytail, forkietail**). [O.N. *skard*: a notch – due to forked tail]

skorie (n) young gull (*Laridae*) or any species of gull still in its juvenile speckled grey/brown plumage. The name applies until the plumage turns white, when a gull is commonly called a **maa** – however, in Lerwick all gulls tend to be called **skories**. [O.N. *skári*, N. *skaare*: a young gull]

skovins (n) see **scobbins**

sköfsin (sköfl, sköfel) (v) to walk clumsily; to shuffle. [Sw.dial. *skyffla*: to walk quickly but unsteadily]

skreebie (adj) cowardly; timorous; fearful. [O.Sc. *screebie*, E. *scurvy*: (in the meaning of) shabby; vile; contemptible]

skrid (skride) (n) a flock or crowd in motion; a number of creeping things; note: the anglicised long *i* pronunciation (*skride*) refers rather to a large quantity. *A skride o bairns*; *A skride o peerie tatties*; (v) to teem; to swarm. *De krang wiz skreedin wi maeds* (the carcase was swarming with maggots); (also **screed, scry**). [O.N. *skridr*: a creeping, gliding motion; an onward moving crowd or flock]

skrieve (v) to write (also **scrit**). [Sc. *scrive, scrieve*: to write, esp. with swift fluency]

skrit (skritt) (v) to hurry. *Shö's aye in a skrit ta finish de hoosework*; (also see **stritt**). [cf. N. *strita seg*: to exert or brace oneself; Sw.dial. *stritta*: to hop; go in skips and jumps]

skrivlin (skrövlin) (n) a small stack of corn, usually one of several temporary stacks in the field, from which the final **skroo** will be built; (v) **skrivl** to build sheaves (**stooks**) of corn into a **skrivlin**. [O.N. *skrúf*: a stack; corn-stack]

skroil (n) fragments. [N. *skrella*: to break a hard object, esp. earthenware; (**skroil** and **skoit** are associated words)]

S

skroo (skru) (n) a stack of corn, esp. the large, final harvest stack (also see **skrivlin**); (v) to build a corn stack. *A'm been skrooin de aets.* [O.N. *skrúf*: a corn-stack; O.N. *skryfa* (v): to stack the corn]

skrolti (n) a glutton. [D. (colloq) '*skrutte i sig*': to stuff oneself; D. *skrut*: stomach]

skrotti (scriota) (n) lichen (*Parmelia saxatilis*) and (*Lichen parietinus*) used for making dye; the brownish yellow or reddish orange colour extracted from lichen. [Sc. *crotal*, *crottle*, Gael. *crotal*, O.Sc. *skrottie*: lichens used for extracting dye]

skrovvel (skrovl) (v) to scratch, as a dog at a door trying to get in or out; to grope. [Icel. *skráfa*, N. *skraava*: to creak; crackle; rustle]

skröf (n) the surface layer of something, esp. the sea. [Fær. *skruva*: scab on a sore; N. *skurva*, D. *skurv*: scurf; N. *skraama*, *skruma*: crust – all are cognate words]

skröfl (v) to kick among earth. [O.N. *skryfa*]

skröl (scroll) (n) a harsh, screeching sound; a roar; a mournful bellow such as is commonly made by a bull or cow. [N. *skrolla*: to shout; roar; make a noise; also cf. N. *skrella*: to crack; crash]

skruffel (skrovl) (n) a rustling sound; (v) to rustle or scratch; to scrape, esp. an animal; (also see **skröfl**, **skrovvel**). [O.N. *skryfa*]

skrug (skrog) (v) to take shelter against bad weather, though not necessarily to crouch in doing so (see **crug**, **skyug**). [cf. D. *skrugge*, *skrukka*: to crouch; O.N. (Icel) *kroka*: to bend oneself; to huddle oneself up (against bad weather); Fær. *kroka*: to take shelter from rain and bad weather]

skruttle (v) to boil vigorously, as a kettle. [cf. Sw.dial. *skratta*: to produce a cracking sound; N. *skratla*: to crackle; rustle; rumble]

skubb (skobb) (n) light, misty drizzle; drifting clouds. [cognate of Fær. *skubbutur*: muddy; of a dull mixed colour; greyish]

skudd (skod(d)) (n) lumps of foam on the surface of the sea; a drifting mass being driven in to the shore by waves. [O.N. *scot*: something driven or floating along]

skuddimöld (n) loose, dry peaty soil. [cf. N. *skota*: to shovel; to scrape; O.N. *skota*: to shove]

skult (skolt) (n) the skull. [N. *skolt*: the forehead; skull; cranium]

skunge (skonzj) (v) to thrust; push; drive out or away. *Du'll hae t skunge yun hens oot o de coarn afore dey akker hit.* [N. *skunza*: to push; set in motion; Sc. *scunge* (n): to scrounge; prowl about in search of food, as a dog, and by extension the act of removing a 'scunger']

skurm (skorm) (n) an outer shell, esp. an egg-shell. '*A trowie bukkie's marlet skurm*' (A snail shell's mottled surface) – (James Stout Angus, *Da Kittiewake*). [N. *skurm*, *skurn*: a hard shell (nut or egg-shell)]

skurt (n) bosom; the encompassance of one's folded arms. [D. *skjød*: lap; bosom; with 'r' inclusion from E. *skirt*; N. *skjört*]

skurtfoo (n) an armful. [*skurt* (see above) + Sc. *fou*: full]

skutamillaskrua (skottamilliskrua) (n) the game of hide-and-seek when played among corn stacks. [Icel. *skotta*: to run to and fro + *milla* = O.N. *millim*, *millum*: between + *skroo* = O.N. *skrúf*: a corn-stack]

skyefset (adj) askew. [O.N. *skeifr*: oblique; askew; poss. of *skev-fitted*: having a crooked foot (Jakobsen)]

skyimp (skimp) (n) ironical praise; (v) to praise in an ironical way. *I keen du's only skyimpin, A'm no a föl.* [Icel. *skimpa*: to mock; scorn]

skyinbow (skin-bowe) (n) Shetland reel tune played on the fiddle. [a *skin-bowe* was a buoy, made of calf or sheep skin, commonly used in Shetland before glass and wooden floats were imported, thus *skyinbow* was a simile used to differentiate the distinctive Shetland reel tunes from the Scottish ones – comparable to calling something *homespun*]

skyoamit (skjomet, skumet) (adj) sickly looking (having a greyish or yellowish colour). [N. *skum*, *skumen*: gloomy; dingy; Fær. *skúmutur*: having a dirty-greyish (yellowish grey) colour]

skyug (skugg) (v) to take shelter in the lee of a wall or bank. [cf. O.N. *skugga*: to shade (in the sense of to give shelter from a shower of rain); D. *skrugge*, *skrukka*: to crouch]

skyumpik (skjumpek, skjumpi, skyumple) (n) edge peat, the first cut from the outside of the bank, usually spoiled by frost and thrown down in the greff. [D.dial. *skumpe*: flat turf, cut from the greensward; loose turfs cut from the top-layer of peat bog; Sw.dial. *skimmpa*: to cut carelessly large pieces of something]

slacky (slakki) (n) a low-lying hollow; a valley among hills. [Icel. *slakki*: a depression; N. *slakkje*: a small depression]

slag (v) to stretch out of shape, as a garment. [O.N. *slakr*: slack; N. *slakna*: to become slack]

slagget (adj) loose; slack; shapeless. *Dee gansie is aa slagget.* [see above]

slap (n) a gap or opening in a wall, usually drystone; a breach; (v) to breach a wall. [O.Sc. *slop*: a gap; opening]

slashy (adj) relatively heavy rain. *Wir hed siccan a day o slashy shooers.* [Sc. similar to **blashy**, partly imit. of heavy rain 'slashing']

slater (n) the wood-louse (*Oniscus asellus*) so named because it is commonly found under slate roof tiles (also **sclater**). [Sc.dial. *slater*; Aust. & N.Z.]

slaver (slever) (n) saliva; (v) foolish talk; to salivate. *De shokkit coo wis slaverin.* [N. *slevja*: to slaver; to splash with mud]

sleb (n) the underlip; (v) to protrude the lower lip; to pout. *Du needna set de sleb* (You needn't pout). [Sw.dial. *slip*: lower lip]

slefset (adv) slovenly. *A slefset craitir.* [N. & Sw. *slafsutt*: careless; one that slops liquid]

sleekit (adj) sly. [O.Sc. *slekit*: smooth, of words – plausible; flattering]

sleeky (n) conger eel (*Conger conger*). [O.Sc. *sleekie*, imitative of smooth and slimy]

slepse (sleps) (v) to eat greedily; to shovel food into the mouth; '*A'll sleps laek a grice ita curry and rice fae a pannikin i me lap*' (Robert W. Tait, *Farewell ta Yell*); to kiss excessively. [O.N. *lepja*: to lap; N. *slabba*: to smack; lick; suck continually; to spill liquid; also poss. O.N. *slefa*: to dribble; slaver]

slester (n) a sloppy, sludgy mess. *De neep rig is aa in a slester wi de wind an rain*; (v) to work messily in mud or liquid; to make messy. *Slestered wi gutter* (Covered in mud). [of E. *slush*, *slosh* & N. *sluska*: to splash]

slicht (slycht) (adj) calm; smooth, as unruffled waters; at the same level. *He cut de post aff slicht wi de aert.* [O.Sc. *slicht*, (E. *slight*), O.N. *slétta*: a level playing field]

slidder (v) to slide; slither; slip. [L.Sc. *slidder*; N. *slidra*]

slip (v) to let go; **slip de ram** release the ram into a flock for mating; **slip me aff** let me go – *Slip me aff at de Toon Hall*; **slip (oot)** release; let out of confinement – *Did du slip de kye?*; (pp, adj) **slippit** of an animal released from its tether. [Sc. & E. *slip*; O.Sc. *slippon*]

slöb (n) jellyfish (*Aurelia aurita*) (also see **sara-slöb**). [N. *slip*; O.N. *sleipa*]

slöbi (n) a big, overhanging lip; big, protruding mouth. [Sw.dial. *slip*: lower lip; N. *slapa*: to hang loosely down]

slochin (n) a slough; a heavy coating. *He gie'd de rigs a right slochin a muck.* [Sc. *slocken*: drench, soak, etc.]

slokk (slock) (v) to slake or quench a thirst; to extinguish a fire or a light; (adj) **slokket** extinguished. *De fire is slokket* (The fire has gone out). [O.N. *slokinn*, (pp of) *sløkva*: to be extinguished; cf. Du. *slok*: a drink; *slokkin*: to gulp; Sc. *slocken*]

slokkenin (n) a thirst-quenching drink. [see above]

sloo (slu) 1) (n) a slovenly, lazy person; *midden sloo* – a derogatory term for a such a person; (v) to loiter idly. [D. *slu*, N. *slu*, *slug*, Sw. *slug*: sly, wily; O.N. *slægr*, in a cognative way]; 2) (n) layers of manure or other material (a sloo of muck then a sloo of waar, as manure on a midden); muck spread on a field. *Dir a sloo a muck on de rigs.* [O.N. *slæða*: to trail or spread manure]

sloob (slobb) (n) gelatinous, slimy mass. [Icel. *slubb*: offal from fish; N. *slubb*: mire; muddy mass; Fær. *slupur*: glutinous; slimy matter]

sloomit (adj) artful; cunning; underhand. [Sw.dial. *slug*: sly; wily]

slott (slot) (n) a Shetland dish – diced fish liver, roe, flour (oatmeal) and seasoning mixed into dumplings and boiled. When cool, the dumplings are sliced and pan-fried in butter and served hot (Margaret Stout). [N. *klot*: a lump; round cake, esp. flour-dumplings]

slud (slod) (n) an abatement between showers; a lull in rough weather. [N., Icel. & Fær. *slot*: cessation; lull in storm or rough weather]

slug (n) an overall worn by women; a loose, upper garment. [cf. Sw. *sloka*: to hang limp; to flap]

slundy (slondi, sloindie) (n) a throng; a crowd of idlers; a spate of abuse. [cf. Sw.dial. *slunt*: an idler; a vagrant; N. *sludd*: a mob; (Sw. *slödder*); N. *slod*: a flock]

slunk (v) to flop down limply; to slink or creep about furtively. [N.dial. *slunk* (n): a sluggard; *slunka* (v): to go in a sluggish manner]

slurd (slord) (n) fine, misty rain; drizzle. [deriv. of *slodder* (*sluder*): sleety rain; N. *slutr*, Icel. *slytr*: sleet; sleety rain; N. *slett*: a sprinkle; splash]

slushit (slosset) (adj) slovenly; shabby. [N. & Sw. *slusk*: slovenliness; shabbiness]

slutter (slotter) (n) a mess – the result of slovenly work. *Dunna slutter de soup doon dee claes*; a miry mass; spilt liquid; (also see **scutter**). [N. *slutr*: slush; impure mixed liquid]

sly (n) algae bloom; green slime on stagnant water. [N. *sli*, O.N. *slý*: conferva and other slimy, green algae; L.Sc. *sloum*]

smaa (smaal) (adj) narrow; slim. *Gie me de smaalest bit du haes.* [Sc. *sma'*, O.N. *smalr*: small; narrow]

smaa drink (n) weak liquor. *He tinks he's nae smaa drink* – of one who has a high opinion of himself. [E. 'small beer'; Sc.]

smatshet (n) a mischievious child; a rascal. [O.Sc. *smatchart*, *smatcher*: a small insignificant person; mischievious child; rogue; cf. O.N. *smár*: small; little (obs. Sh. *smutt*: small; far too small or short)]

smeeg (smig) (n) a mocking smile; a smirk; (v) to smirk. [D.dial. *smige*, N.dial. *smikja*: to ingratiate oneself; Sw. *smeka*: to flatter; caress]

smirl (n) merlin (*Falco columbarius*); in placenames Smirla Burn, Smirla Water. [Icel. *smyrill*; Fær. *smyril*]

smissleen (smirslin) (n) applied to several species of sand-burrowing bivalve shells, particularly the blunt gaper (*Mya truncata*). [Icel. & Fær. *smyrslingur* (poss. due to its white shell)]

smit (smitt) (n) infectious disease. *He's gotten a smitt*; (v) to infect with disease. *Du'll smitt me wi yun feerie.* [N., Fær. & Sw. *smitta*; D. *smitte*; E. *smite* (n) *smitten*]

***smokk (smukki)** (n) a sleeveless or short-sleeved pinafore; a smock. [cf. O.N. *smokkr*: woman's plastron]

***smook (smuk)** (v) to put on or slip into something. [cf. N. *smock*, *smukk*, Sw.dial. *smock*: a covering; a finger-stall]

***smooky (smuggi)** (n) a oilskin smock, as worn by fishermen (see also **sken joop**). [cf. O.N. *smøygja*: to slip on or off]

* The etymology of these words is somewhat confused owing to inconsistencies in spelling; essentially they are closely interconnected; also see **smucks**.

smoor (smoar) (also see **smore**) (n) smoke; (v) to douse a fire or light; to smother; (also see **rest**). [O.E. *smorian*]

smoorikin (n) a kiss (presumably a smothering, passionate one). [see **smoor**]

smoosh (v) gently stew; simmer; also said of over-boiled potatoes: *De tatties ir geen in smoosh.* [Sh. slang]

smoot (smut, smutt) (v) to slink; to move furtively; to hide. *Smoot yun sweetie in dee pooch.* [N. *smyta*: to hide away furtively]

smora (n) clover; **red smora** red clover (*Trifolium pratense*); **white smora** white clover (*Trifolium repens*). [N. *smæra*: clover; N.dial. *smære*: clover]

smore (v) to drown; to smother or suffocate. [O.E. *smorian*]

***smucks** (n) slippers of any kind, esp. carpet slippers; originally clumsily-made, thick, woollen boots or shoes. [N. & Icel. *smokka*, see *words above]

smuksin (adj) *smuksin aboot* – shuffling about in clumsy footwear. [see above]

smush (n) fine drizzle. [L.Sc. *smush*]

sna fool (snaw-ful) (n) snow bunting (*Plectrohenax nivalis*) (lit. 'snow-fowl'). [O.N. *snjófugl*; Fær. *snjófuglar*; D.dial. *snefugl*; O.Sc. *snowfleck*]

snaa (snaw) (n) snow; (v) to be snowed in. *Dis moorie caavie will laekly snaa de byre door.* [O.Sc. *snaw*; E. *snow*]

S

snaar (snar) (n) the turn of the tide; a tide rip; kink in a rope; in placenames, e.g. Snarravoe, Unst. [N. *snar*: a twist; kink; O.N. *snara*: to turn; to twist]

snapper (v) to stumble; trip. [O.Sc. *snapper*: to stumble, esp. of a horse; M.E. *snapir*]

sneck 1) (n) a door-latch; (v) to fasten a latch. [Sc. *sneck*: a latch]; 2) (n) a notch. [L.Sc. *sneck*; O.N. *snikka*]; 3) (n) inshore fishing grounds (originally **skor**). [cf. O.Sc. equiv. of O.N. *skor*: a fishing-ground close to the shore – properly a score; furrow; (a codlin score)]

snee (sni) (v) to cut. *Snee aff a bit a cheese*. [O.N. *sniða*: to cut]

sneeb (v) to snow gently. [cf. L.Sc. *sneet* – comb. of snow and sleet]

sneester (n) a private chuckle; (v) to laugh quietly; snigger. [prob. of both L.Sc. *snitter*: suppressed laughter, and *sneeter*: snigger; giggle]

sneet (snit) (v) to blow one's nose. [O.N. & N. *snyta*, to blow one's nose; to snuff a candle]

sneet-cloot (n) handkerchief. [*sneet* (as above) + *cloot* (Sc. *cloot*: a cloth)]

snib (n) a small bolt or catch for window or door; (v) to fasten with a snib. [Sc. *snib*, cf. L., Gr. *snibbe*: beak]

snibb (v) to cut close; to cut right off; to cut hair very short. [cf. N. *snubba*: to snip off; O.Sc. *snib*: restrain; rebuke]

snick (v) to switch on or off, esp. a light switch. [Sc. *sneck*]

snippek (snippik) (n) snipe (*Gallinago gallinago*). [N. *snipa*, D. *sneppe*, Sw. *snäppa*: snipe]

snipper (snipr) (v) to pucker; to wrinkle. [O.N. *snerkja*: to wrinkle up; N. *snypra*: to wrinkle; pucker; Sw.dial. *snörp*: something contracted, drawn together]

snippet (adj) brusque; snappish. *Shö wiz braaly snippet wi me*; (also see **klipet**, **nippet**). [cf. N. *snypsen*: snappish; surly]

snitter (n) 1) a biting cold wind. [Fær. *snertur*: bad weather, with cold; D. *kuldesnert*: sting of cold]; 2) bad mood; bad temper; a twist or knot in thread; (adj) **snitteret**. [cf. N. *snerten* (adj): easily offended]

snog (n) food in general. *A'll hae t mak wis some snog*; (originally **snoggjet** a thick cake or bannock, formerly one baked in ashes).

snoilt (snölt) (n) furrowed knot between eyebrows; *To set a snoilt* (to make an angry face). [Sw.dial. *knollt*: a lump; N. *knultra*: knot; unevenness]

snoiltit (adj) close cropped, as a cow's horns or very short hair. [N.dial. *snollette*, D.dial. *snoldet*, *snollet*: close-cropped; wearing one's hair or cap close]

snore (v) to sniff; snuffle, as with a cold. *Du's snorin in a caald*. [cf. O.N. *snor*: mucus of the nose; *snoðra*, *snuðra*: to sniff]

snorie-ben (n) a child's toy, consisting of a short piece of wood or bone suspended on a string, which when spun makes a 'snorie' noise. [cf. O.N. *snara*: to turn quickly – but prob. also assoc. with E. *snore* + Sc. *bane*: bone]

snöd (n) the spiralled twist in rope strands; a twist in temperament. *Du's pittin him in a rycht snöd noo*; (v) to twist a rope. [O.N. *snúdr*: a twist; loop at the end of a line or rope; Fær. *snúdur*: a twisting; tangle]

snöl (n) a simpleton; a stupid, listless and lazy person. [cf. D. *snøvle*, N. *snulla*: to snuffle, however cf. O.Sc. *snool*: a snail]

snug (snugg) (v) to make tidy. *Snugg up yun claes*. [Sw. *snygga* (from *snygg*) (adj): clean and neat; tidy]

snug-ooed (adj) short-haired; close-cropped wool. [O.N. *snoggr*: curtailed; short-haired; smooth]

snug-shordet (adj) comfortably seated (see **shoard**). [*snug* + *shordet* = **shoard**: support; O.N. *skorda*: to keep in equilibrium, esp. to put stays under the sides of a boat]

snuids (n) gut on end of fishing line to which hook is fastened. [Sc. *snood*]

snurdipin (n) a rope fastener for a door (a rope is attached centrally on the outside of the door to form a loop through which a stick is passed. The device is then twisted to shorten the loop until the stick jams across the door-posts to secure the door). [the root meaning of this word is found in N. *snurla*: to twist (see below)]

snurl (n) a kink in a line or length of yarn; a frown or wrinkled brow (see **snurdipin**); (v) to twist; to tangle, kink or knot, as rope or yarn. [N. *snurla*: to twist; *snurle*, *snurla*, *snurull*: tangle; L.Sc. *snurl*: to wrinkle]

snurt (snort) (n) mucus; rheum from the nose; the burnt end of a wick. [O.N. *snor*: rheum]

snush (snus) (n) a sniff or snort; (v) to sniff or snort. [N. *snusa*, D. *snuse*: to sniff; scent; also to take snuff]

snyirk (snirk) (n) a creaking sound; (v) to creak. *De door a de aald hoose snyirkit an gluffed me*. [N. *knerka*, D. *knirke*: creak]

snyivveries (snivri(s)) (n) wooden toggle fasteners on a garment. [O.N. *knyfri*, *knypri*: knot; lump; N. *knuvr*, *knuvre*: snout-ring; pin for fastening door-latch]

snyösk (snosk) (v) to sniff or snort in an irascible manner. [N. *snaska*: to sniff]

so (so so) (adv, interj) conveying various meanings according to voice inflection: *So so* – reassurance and comfort (said gently, and perhaps accompanied by a pat on the head); *So!* – enough said (stated emphatically); *So so, blissins be wi dee* – end of conversation, farewell; *So so* – resignation or acceptance (with, or without a stifled sigh). [Sc.]

soag (sog) (n) in a semi-comatose state; half-asleep; sometimes said of whales *sogin alang* – making languid progress; (also see **sob**). [cf. O.N. *sofa*: to sleep; S.dial. *såka*, *soka*: to dawdle; of slow, lazy movement]

soaroo (n) the Devil; used as a mild curse with humorous overtones, expression of provocation or exasperation. [O.Sc. *sorra*, *soaroo*: the Devil. *The muckle sorra* – the one who brings sorrow (or more properly) the one who brings mischief]

sob (v) to sleep lightly; doze; (also see **soag**). [cf. O.N. *sofa*: to sleep; S.dial. *såka*, *soka*: to dawdle; of slow, lazy movement]

soch (n) the sound made by a variable wind blowing through trees or a drystone wall; a deep sigh; (v) to sigh deeply. [O.Sc. *souch*: a rushing sound; the sound of wind]

sock (n) any woollen garment in the process of being knitted. *Tak dee sock, lass* (Take up your knitting) – once a common parental instruction to a young girl when the family were gathered around the fire in the evening. [orig. E. *sock* – extended in Sh. to apply to all knitting]

soe (so) (n) half-boiled limpets chewed then spat (**sproaned**) on the sea to produce an oily matter on the surface designed to attract fish; (v) to spit or throw half-boiled/chewed limpets or other matter on the surface of the sea to attract fish; (also see **knock-soe**). [O.N. *sáð*: that which is sown (spread), as seed]

soge (n) overcome by weariness; (v) to administer a blow with the fist. *I'll soge dee*; to knock senseless; (related to **soag**; also see **sove**). [O.N. *svæfa*: to lull; *sæfa*: to kill; slaughter]

soitl (sotl) (v) to slurp, as pigs at a trough. [N. *susla*; *sutla* to splash; slop; to gurgle]

solan (solon gös) (n) gannet (*Sula bassana*). [O.N. *sūla*: gannet]

solemn (adj) extremely bad – usually of weather. [Sh. extension in meaning of E. *solemn*: sombre; gloomy or awe-inspiring]

songie (songi) (adj) a hermaphrodite – applied to animals; a non-prolific ram. [obs. Sh. **kwingi** – N. *kviast*: to pine; *vankvia*: an ill-thriven animal]

sonsie (adj) of women, comfortable-looking; good-natured; comely; buxom. [Sc. *sonse*, *sonsy*, *sonsie*, Gael. *sonas*: good fortune]

soo (n) a female pig. [Sc. form of E. *sow*]

sooans (sowans) (n) an oatmeal dish, also called **virpa**, originally made with fermented corn-husks, now with oatmeal which is fermented in water for 5-8 days then strained, and boiled gently like porridge until thick. The residue liquid is called **swats**. [Sc. *sowens*, of Gael. *sùghan*]

sood 1) should; (pt of) shall. [Sc. *sud*, variant on E. *should*]

sood 2) (adv, n) south; towards the direction of south; of southerly weather. *He's gyaan idda sood*; (also **sud**). [O.N. *suðr*; L.Sc. *sooth*]

sook (suk) (n) a drying wind. *Dir nae muckle sook de day* – a washer-woman's lament; (v) to dry in a favourable wind; *Sookit piltiks* (wind-dried coalfish); (also see **drocht**). [O.N. *súgr*: a sucking; Icel. *súgr*: a draught of wind; Sh. variant on Sc. *souk*]

sookies (n) lousewort (*Pedicularis sylvatica*). [so named because children sucked the flowers for the nectar]

sooky (adj) having a good drying quality (see **sook**).

sool (sul-board) (n) the plank in a Shetland boat which lies just above the water-line – above the **hassens** and below the **reebins**. [O.N. *sólbrod*, *sólbyrdi*: the gunwale of a vessel]

soolbrigdi (sulbrigdi) (n) basking shark (*Celorhinus maximus*) (also **brigdi**, **hobrigdi**). [O.N. *sól*: sun + cf. N. *bregða*: to alter; shift; move quickly; O.E. *bregdan*; (note: the shark's habit of basking on the surface of the sea does not seem to equate with the meaning of *bregða*, although when disturbed, the shark makes off with a sudden burst of speed)]

soolp (sulp) (n) soft, moist, decomposed mass; something saturated by moisture; (adj) **soolpin** saturated. *Dee feet is joost soolpin*. [N. *skvalpa*: a wet, splashing mass; *surp*: mire; mud]

soom (sweum) (v) to swim. [O.N. *symja*; L.Sc. *soum*, *soom*]

soomin (summin) an inundation; a great quantity. *A soomin o pilteks*. [N. *sum*: as a poetical name for the sea]

soond (n) a narrow strait between islands, e.g. Bluemull Sound; a narrow inlet or bay. [O.N. *sund*: a sound]

soor (adj) sour. *Soor plooms*. [O.N. *súrr*: sour]

soorik (surek) (n) sorrel (*Rumex acetosa*). [O.N. *súra*: sorrel; L.Sc. *sourock*]

soosed (v) simmered; cooked without boiling. [apparently an extension of Sc. *souse*: to immerse in water; steep]

sooter (n) fan mussel (*Pinna fragilis*). [etymology obs., possibly related to the shell being used in early days as a koli lamp and therefore 'the one that soots']

sooth-boat(s) (n) any of the ro-ro passenger ferries plying between Aberdeen and Lerwick (also **nort-boat**). [Sc.]

sooth-moother (n) other than native-born Shetlander; an immigrant or visitor to the islands. The expression dates from a period when all incomers to Shetland arrived by sea via the **south mouth** of Lerwick harbour and not because they speak with a 'sooth mooth'; (also **incomer**). [Sh. colloq. exp. of Sc. *sooth* (E. *south*) + *mooth* (E. *mouth*)]

sooth-spokken (v) speaking English or Scots as opposed to Shetlandic.

soss (sus) (n) a sloppy, wet mess. [N. *sus*: jelly; soft mass; *sussa*: to slop with wet things]

sot (adv) the emphatic correlative of *not*, meaning on the contrary, used to contradict a negative assertion. *Tis not! Tis sot!* [Sc. *sot*, *sut*]

soumin (n) a crofter's sum entitlement of livestock on the **scattald**. [Sc. *souming*: the determination of the numbers of *soums* that may be appropriated to common pasture; L. *summa*: sum; total]

sove (v) to administer a blow with the fist. *I'll sove dee*; to knock senseless; be overcome by weariness; (also **soge**). [O.N. *svæfa*: to lull; *sæfa*: to kill; slaughter]

sowder (n) solder; (v) to solder. *A'm gyaan ta sowder de hol in de kettle*. [E. *solder*]

sowdian (soudien) (n) a big, clumsy, corpulent person. [O.Sc. *soudan*, *sowdan*]

sowl (n) said of a person (*pör sowl*) to indicate pity (*de peerie sowl*). [E. *soul*: a person – *she's a kind soul*]

sörmoos (n) sign of life. [orig. obs.]

spaegie (spaigie) (n) stiffness or pain in back or legs caused by over-exertion (also see **creeks**, **hansper**). [N. *speika*: to walk stiffly]

spaek (v) to speak; hold a conversation. *Mind an spaek alang wir Jessie whin du's in Lerook* (Remember to visit for a chat...); (pt) **spak**; (pp) **spokken**. [Sc. & Sh. extension of E. *speak*]

spaekalation (n) a talking-point with the hint of scandal in it. [Sc. *speculation*: a spectacle; the subject of remark and gossip]

spang (spund, spond) (v) to run with long, bounding strides. [N. *spana*: to strain; to stretch out; *spøna*: to run fast]

sparrel (sparl) (n) the long intestine, esp. that of a cow; **sparls** a dish made of chopped meat (**sassermaet** or **sparrel-maet**) stuffed tightly into the scrubbed and salted intestine and hung to dry (three weeks to a month). [Fær., O.N. *sperðill*: the rectum; N. *speril*, *sperel*: tail; a thin or slight figure]

speer (v) to spurt or squirt. [N.dial. *spira*, O.N. *spíra*: a stalk or shoot]

speet (n) a heavy shower of rain; also **thunder-speet** heavy rain accompanied by thunder; (also see **Lammas-speet**). [the opposite of Sc. *spit*, which is to rain in scattered drops]

spell (n) a wood-shaving (also **spellick**). [N. s*pel*, *spela*: a flat splinter; Sw.dial. *spel*: shaving]

spend (v) to wean. [Sc. *spane*, *spean*: to wean; M.L.Ger. *spanen*; O.F. *espanir*]

spendin brash (n) slight ailment which causes crying in a child, related to weaning and frequently not defined. *Hit's just a brash.* [Sc. *spean*: to wean + *brash*: an attack or illness]

spent (n) of a fish in poor condition. [Sc. *spent*: used up; exhausted (a spent fish being one exhausted after spawning)]

spikk (spik) (n) fat; whale blubber. [O.N. *spik*: blubber]

spilt (adj) leprous. [cf. O.Sc. *spilt*, of damaged goods; cf. E. *spoilt*]

spjaal (spjaalg, spjel, spjelgit) (v) to splay; thrust out arms and legs; to lie stretched out; gone out of shape. *Me gansie is spjaalgit.* [N. *spjelka*: to make awkward movements with the arms; the word is also related to N. *spela*, Fær. *spæla*: to play, as children or kittens sprawling and kicking]

spjetak (n) a fool. [deriv. of N. & D. *spektakel*, Fær. *spektakkul*: prop. sight, and hence a spectacle]

spleet new (adj) brand new. [Sc. *split-new*: brand new, as new as freshly split wood; Du. *splinter-nieuw*]

splore (n) hubbub; commotion; agitation. [Sc. *splore*: an escapade; a row, a scrape – poss. a word coined by Burns]

spo (v) to foretell; predict. [O.N. *spá*: to forbode; Sc. *spae*: to foretell; divine]

sponget (adj) black with white spots (or converse). [O.N. *spong*: a spangle]

spoilkin (spjolkin) (n) piltocks or sillocks, slit open and roasted with the livers inside them. [O.N. *spila*: to stretch out (to split or cleave). Fish were split and a wooden skewer or *spjolk* inserted before hanging in the open to dry]

spooie (spui) (n) curlew (*Numenius arquata*) (also **whaap**). [O.N. *spói*: curlew (imitative of the bird's call); obs. E. (Norfolk) *spowe*]

spoot 1) (n) the razor shell (*Solenidae*); a quick movement; a sudden dash. *He made a spoot fur de barn afore de rain cam*; (v) to squirt. [O.Sc. *spoutt*, so named for its ability to jet liquid as a means of propulsion or when disturbed]

spoot 2) (n) a spring or waterfall. [of E. *spout*]

spoots (spootitrumps) (n) wild angelica (*Angelica sylvestris*) (also **skeetitrumps**). [N. *skvetta*: a squirt + E. *trump*: trumpet, so named because children used the hollow stalk of the plant as a *swettek*: (or) squirt]

spölli (spullie) (v) to throw around; break up; lay to waste; create a commotion. [O.Sc. *spulze*: to plunder; O.F. *espuille*: spoil; *espoillier*: to plunder]

spön (spunnin) (n) a spoon. [O.N. *spónninn*]

spör (v) to ask; consult; enquire; to propose marriage; **spörin bottle** a bottle of whisky presented to a girl's father when seeking her hand in marriage. [O.N. *spyrja*: to find out; to ask advice; Sc. *spier*, *speer*]

sprech (n) a shrill cry; (v) to cry, esp. a child's shrill cry of distress. [O.Sc. *spraich*: a yell; a shriek]

spret (v) to burst or rip open; tear asunder. [O.N. *spretta*: to rip up; to tear apart]

sprickle (sprikl, sprikkel) (v) to wriggle; flap about, as a fish on a line. [Icel. *sprikla*: to lay about one; to make quick, violent movements]

spricklet (spreklet) (adj) speckled; spotted. [N. *spriklutt*, *spreklutt*; L.Sc. & E.dial. *spreckled*]

spring 1) (n) a lively tune – one which will *pit a spring i dee step*. [O.N. *springa*: to run; leap; E. *spring*: leap]

spring 2) (v) to burst. [O.N. *sprengja*: to cause to burst]

sprit (n) a dash; (v) to sprint; run fast. [O.N. *spretta*: bound; leap; rush; Sw. *spritta*: to jump; leap; spring]

sproan (spron) (v) to spray; to eject liquid. [N. *spræn*: a jet of liquid]

spronins (n) bird excrement. [see above]

sproot (v) to sprout, as seeds; to spit. [N. *spruta*, D. *sprude*: spurt; gush]

spunder (spund) (v) to rush or race. [N. *spøna*: to set off; make haste; to run fast]

spune (spön, spunnin) (n) a spoon; the jugular notch of the sternum. *'He measured fower an twinty k-nuckles fae de spune o his breest tae de k-not o his trapple.'* – Sh. dialect version of Lawrence Tulloch's description of a Kalathumpian in his folk tale *The Trow's Boat*. (*The Foy and other Folk Tales*; The Shetland Times Ltd, 2006.) [O.N. *spónninn*: a chip; a spoon]

spunk (n) a spark. [O.Sc. *sponk*: a spark; minute particle; a flicker; cf. Gael. *spong*: tinder]

spurrytail (n) an earwig (*Forficula auricularia*) (also see **forkietail**, **skordi**). [spurry = spord, O.N. *spordr*: tail, esp. of a fish; pointed end]

spyolk (spjolk) (n) a splint; (v) to support a broken limb with a splint. [O.N. *spjelka*: to stretch out with splints]

squad (n) group of guizers or entertainers participating or performing at an **Up-Helly-A'** festival. [E. *squad*: a group of players]

staag (stag) (v) to walk stiffly and with apparent difficulty. [O.N. *staka*: to stagger; stumble]

stab (stabb) (n) a fencing post; a block of wood used as a seat; a whale vertebrae used for the same purpose. [O.N. *stabbi*: a block; stub of a tree]

stack (stakk) (n) 1) a pillar-like eroded remnant of coastal cliff free-standing in the sea (there are hundreds scattered round the Shetland coastline), e.g. The Drongs (Hillswick); Out Stack (Oosta) – the most northerly point of Britain, lying nearly 1km north-west of Muckle Flugga. [Fær. *stakkur*: stack; high rock in the sea]; 2) a peat-stack; (v) to pile up or build a peat-stack. [O.N. *stakkr*: a stack or pile]

stack-steid (stakk-steed) (n) the foundation of a peat-stack, the skilled laying of which will ensure the peats remain secure throughout winter's gales. [**stack** (see above) + **steid** O.N. *stedja*: to cause to stand still; to put into a firm, immovable position]

S

staig (n) a young horse. [Sc. *staig*, *stag*: a colt or stallion; O.Sc. *staig*: a young horse (1-3 yrs) of either sex, not yet broken to work]

stammerin (stamron) (n) the transom knee which binds the sides and stems together in the bow and stern of a boat. The stern stammerin is used as a seat for the helmsman. [O.N. *stafn*: stem; stern + *rong*: knee-timber; Fær. *rong*: a seat in the stem or stern of a boat]

stang (n) a twinge of pain; a sting; (v) to sting. [O.N. *stanga*: to prick; sting; L.Sc. *stang*]

stank (n) a water-filled ditch. [O.Sc. *stank*: a ditch; a pool; O.F. *estanc*: a pond]

stap (stapp) (n) a Shetland dish comprising fish livers and the soft parts of fish heads, esp. haddock, chopped together, mixed with salt and pepper and boiled, then served hot in a pie-dish with a little butter; broken or crushed mass. *Hit's aa in stapp*; (v) to stuff or cram. *He stappit de oo inna de sekk*. [O.N. *stappi*: a pounded up mass; Icel. *stappa*: minced meat or fish with potatoes; O.Sc. *stappit-heads*: boiled haddock head stuffed with a mixture of oatmeal, onions and seasoning; orig. *stap* or *stappit* referred to any dish involving stuffing forcemeat into fish-heads or similar]

stapple (staapil) (n) a pipe-stem, esp. clay pipe. [Sc. *stapple*, *stopple*]

stari (n) a starling (*Sturnus vulgaris*) (also **stirlin**). [O.E. *stearn*, of L. *sturnus-*]

starn (n) a star; a white blaze on an animal's forehead. *De starnet yowe*. [O.N. *stjarna*: star; O.Sc. *stern*, *starne*: star; *starnie*: starry]

start (n) a short space of time; **peerie-start** a shorter time-span; a moment. [L.Sc. *start*]

starty (adj) irritable; excitable. [Sc. *startle*: to surprise or frighten suddenly; *startly*: apt to start]

starvin (adj) suffering from cold; freezing. [Sc. *sterving*, *stairving*: close to dying of hunger or cold; Sc. variant on E. *starving*]

stave (n) curved side-section of a barrel; used in fig. exp. *Ta geng in staves* (To fall to pieces). [O.N. *stafr*: stave of a bucket or barrel; N. *stav*; Fær. *stavur*; E. & Sc. *stave*]

steek (v) to shut – eyes, door, fist, etc. [O.Sc. *steke*: to block; obstruct; shut]

steekit (adj) extremely dense, as fog; also **steekit stimna** very thick smoke or mist. [O.Sc. *steke*: to block; obstruct; **stimna** = *stomna*; N. *stabbande myrk*: pitch-dark from *stabbe*: stub; block; trunk]

steepel (steeple) (n) a quantity of fish stacked crosswise to dry. [O.N. *stopull*: pillar; steeple; tower; O.Sc. *steple*: to pile up in a stack; Du. *stapel*: a heap; *stapelvisch*: half-fried fish]

steer (n) a bustle; stir; commotion. *Dey wir in a rycht steer owre d flittin* (also **upsteer**). [O.Sc. *stere*: to stir; move]

steid (steed) (n) a foundation; a compact shoal of fish. [O.N. *stedja*: to cause to stand still; to put into a firm, immovable position]

sten (steen, ston) (n) stone. [O.N. *steinn*; L.Sc. *stane*]

stenbiter (n) Atlantic wolf-fish – also known as Atlantic catfish (*Anarhichas lupus*) (lit. 'stone biter'). [N. *steinbit*, Fær. *steinbitur*, so named for their large and powerful jaws]

stend (v) to walk with lengthened strides and in a determined manner. [O.Sc. *stend*: a leap; bound; poss. of 'extend' – to lengthen one's stride]

stengle (stengl) (v) to close a gap by means of a temporary barrier. [N. *stengla*: to support with a spar; shore up; close; bar]

stengle (stengl) (v) to stumble; walk in a jerky motion. [N. *stangla (stingla)*]

stenkle (stenkal) (n) wheatear (*Oenanthe oenanthe*). [see below]

stenloopen (stenlupen) (n) blood-blister – a common injury when building stone walls; (adj) bruised by fingers or toes being crushed by a stone. [D. *stenløben*: become hard and lumpy (esp. of gunpowder)]

sten pikker (n) turnstone (*Arenaria interpres*). [onom. *stone – picker*]

sten-shakker (n) wheatear (*Oenanthe oenanthe*) (see also **stenkle**, **stinkle**). [O.Sc. *sten-shakker*, *stane-chacker*, so named for its call sounding like two stones being knocked together]

stent (v) to stretch. [O.Sc. see **stend**]

steuch (n) a cloud of dust. [cf. L.Sc. *stech*, *steigh*, *stoicht*: foul smoke; obnoxious atmosphere]

stiggy (stiggie) (n) a stile, commonly formed by steps in a drystone wall, for climbing over; a steep path. *He's gyaan up de stiggie*. [O.N. *stigi*, N. *stige*: a ladder; steps]

stigg (n) loathing; disgust. [N. *stygg*: aversion; dislike]

stiggisom (adj) disgusting. *Dat maet is stiggisom*; (also see **stuggit**). [see above]

stikk (n) an article of clothing; esp. when used in negative sense. *He hedna a stikk apon him*. [O.N. *stykki*: a piece; a piece of cloth]

still an on (adv) nevertheless. *Still an on du'll hae t go*; none-the-less. [colloq. exp]

stime (v) to peer shortsightedly. [Sc. *styme*, *stime*: to peer; Sw.dial. *stimma*: steam; fog]

stimin (adj) intoxicated. [of Sc. *styme*, with extended meaning of 'blind drunk']

stimna (stomna) (n) 1) stamina; strength. [O.N. *stofn*: foundation; N. *stomn*: stem; trunk; strength]; 2) thick fog (also **stumba**)). [Sw.dial. *stimba*: steam; N. *stum (myrk)*: pitch-dark; Fær. *stumt*: very dense (dark; misty)]

stinkle (stenkel) (n) wheatear (*Oenanthe oenanthe*) or stonechat (*Saxicola torquata*) (also see **sten-shakker**). [O.Sc. *sten-shakker*, *stane-chacker* – so named for its call sounding like two stones being knocked together]

stirlin (n) starling (*Sturnus vulgaris*) (also **starn**). [O.E. *stearn*, of L. *sturnus-*]

stirn (v) to shiver (stiffen) with cold. [O.N., Fær., Icel., *stirðna*: to become stiff (with cold)]

stivven (stivn) (v) to stiffen; become rigid. *Stivvenin wi caald*. [N. *stivna*, D. *stivne*: to grow stiff]

stivle (v) to thrive; fill out; strengthen. [N. *stivleg*: substantial; having good qualities]

stoal (stol, stoil) (n) an old story, saga or legend. [orig. obs.]

stock (n) heart of a cabbage; the whole cabbage; kale-stock. [Sc. *stock*: the hard trunk or stem of a herbaceous plant, esp. cabbage; the whole plant]

stock-dyook (-deuk) (n) mallard (*Anas platyrhynchos*). [A number of birds have the prefix *stock* in provincial English and Scots, e.g. *stocknit* (sheldrake); *stock duck* (mallard); *stock hawk* (peregrine falcon); *stock owl* (eagle owl); *stock whaap* (curlew); however the etymology of the word usage is uncertain. cf. – '"stock" is applied to any creature, or thing, which is the largest of its congeners, e.g. "Stock-holm", the largest of a group of islands, has given that word as the name of Sweden's capital' – Jessie Saxby, *Shetland Traditional Lore*; N. *stokkand*; Fær. *stokkont*: mallard]

stock haak (hawk) (n) peregrine (*Falco peregrinus*). [see above]

stock-whaap (n) curlew (*Numenius arquata*). [see above]

stoit (n) a fit of stubbornness; obstinacy. [N. *støyt*: a bump; collision; shock]

stoiter (stotj) (v) to walk with feeble, faltering steps; to stumble. [N. *stota*: to walk with short, stumbling steps]

ston (sten, steen) (n) a stone. [O.N. *steinn*; L.Sc. *stane*]

stoo (n) a sheep's ear-mark, where the tip of the ear is snipped off in a backward cut; (v) to cut or crop. [O.N. *stýfa*: to cut off; curtail]

stook (n) a number of sheaves of corn, between 6 and 12, set up to dry in a line of pairs together in a harvest field; (v) to set up sheaves. *He's geen t stook coarn*. [O.Sc. *stouk*]

stookie (n) a dull, slow-witted person. *Dunna staand dere laek a stookie*. [Sc.]

stoop (stoup) (n) a post; the leg of a bench. [O.Sc. *stoup*]

stoor 1) (v) to stare in a downcast manner. [O.N. *stúra*: to be sad; to fret; N. *stura*: to be downcast, thoughtful and quiet]

stoor 2) (n) dust; (v) to move at speed. *Shö wis gyaan stoorin aboot*. [Sc. *stour*: battle; assault; turmoil; dust]

stoor (stur) 3) (adj) large; big. *A stoor a wind*; also in placenames, e.g. Papa Stour (Large Priest Isle). [O.N. *stórr*: big; large]

story-wirm (n) the grub of the crane-fly or daddy-long-legs. [L.Sc. *story-*, *torie-worm*, of Gael. *toran*: 'the borer', with Sc. *-ie* diminutive ending]

stot (n) a young castrated ox; a steer; (also **strick**). [O.Sc. *stot*: a steer; O.N. *stútr*: an ox; bull; N. *stut*]

stot (v) to bounce or rebound. *De hail wis stottin aff a de rodd*; to stagger; walk unsteadily, as one intoxicated. [cf. O.N. *stauta*, D. *støde*, Ger. *stossen*: to push; thrust; butt; O.Sc. *stot*: bounce; rebound]

stowen dunt (adjectival phrase) *a stowen dunt* – an unforeseen and sudden encounter. [Sc. *stoun* (astound): to stun + *dunt* – O.N. *dyntr*: a din; heavy fall; push; N.dial. *dunt*: a blow; bump]

stöd (v) (pt of) stand (Sh. **staand**). [E. *stood*]

stöels (stol) (n) the cut end of a sheaf of corn (the root end). [N. *styl*, (*støle*, *stjøl*): stalk; the lower end of a straw]

stöl (n) a stool. [O.N. *stóll*: a stool; chair]

stör (n) a small Dutch coin (*stiver*), the most common currency in Shetland during 17th and 18th centuries, eventually devalued to be practically worthless. *Yun's no de wirt o a stör* (That's not worth a penny). [Du. *stuiver*: a coin equiv. to one-twentieth of a guilder; E. & Sc. *stiver*: a very small coin; the smallest possible amount]

strae (n) straw. [Sc. variant on E. *straw*]

straen (adj) made of straw. [L.Sc. *straen*, *straen-thacket*: straw-thatched]

straff (n) predicament; dilemma; state of agitation. [cf. N. *straff*: punishment; Du. *straf*: trial; anxiety; Ger. *strafe*]

stramash (n) hurly-burly; disturbance; turmoil. [Sc. *stramash*: disturbance; tumult – orig. doubtful – cf. O.F. *escarmoch*; E. *skirmish*]

stramp (n) tramp; (v) to walk firmly. [Sc. *stramp*: to tread; stamp; trample]

strange (v, adj) to be amazed. *We wir stranged at d yarns he telt wis*; wonder; surprise. *I stranged at aa he said*. [Sc. form of E. *strange*]

stravaig (v) to roam; to wander about idly or without purpose. *He stravaigit fae de path and wis forlegen*. [Sc. *stravaig*]

streek (v) to lay out a corpse for burial. [Sc. *streek*: to stretch; lay out for burial]

street (de) (da street) Commercial Street, Lerwick – commonly referred to simply as 'de street'. *Dir datn uncan fok alang de street dis days*.

strem (n) spring tide. [O.Sc. *strayme*: stream, also tide]

stret (adj) stretched, as in tight clothing. [E. *stretched*]

strick (n) a young bullock; a stirk or steer; (v) to strike; (also **stot**). [E. *stirk*: a yearling ox or cow; O.E. *stirc*: calf]

stridey-legs (adv) astride, as seated on a horse or pony. [Sc. *stride-legs*: astride]

striffen (n) membrane covering intestinal fat of an animal. [L.Sc. *striffen*: a thin membrane; Gael. *streabhan*]

string (n) a strong sea current, as evidenced by streams or 'strings' of foam on the surface of the water. [O.N. *strengr*: longitudinal strip; a stream]

strinklin (n) a thin coating; a sprinkling. [Sc. *strinkling*: sprinkling; O.Sc. *strinkle*: to over-spread]

strip (v) to draw out the last drops of milk from a cow's udder, usually by means of thumb and index finger only, thus ensuring the cow's milk production will be maintained for as long as possible. [D. & Sw.dial. *strippe*, *strippa*: to milk out]

stripe (n) a burn or streamlet. [O.Sc. *stryp*: a small stream; a rivulet]

stritt (n) a brisk pace; strut; (v) to walk briskly; to strut. *Shö wiz gyaan strittin aboot*; (also see **skrit**). [cf. N. *strita seg*: to exert or brace oneself; Sw.dial. *stritta*: to hop; go in skips and jumps]

strodie (strodi) (n) a laneway between two walls; a grassy strip between two cultivated pieces of ground; (see **gorstie**). [O.N. *stræti*: a road; fence]

stroint (stront) (n) a pipe; a spout; a tube; a narrow-fitting garment; (adj) pinched. [N.dial. *strunt*: spout; funnel]

stroint-pipe (n) the mouth of a drain; an effluent pipe. [see above]

strood (strud) (n) a suit of clothes; (v) to outfit with clothes or kit of any sort. [O.N. *skrúd*: festal dress]

stroods (n) the set of ropes from a ship's masthead to its gunwales which give lateral support to the mast – the shrouds. [previously, a complete set of anything – sails, shrouds, equipment or gear of any sort; O.N. *skrúd*: tackle; gear; furnishings; E. *shrouds*]

S

stroop (n) the spout of a kettle or teapot. [Sc. *stroup*]

stroopie (n) colloq. expression for a teapot and by association, a cup of tea. *Du'll tak a stroopie afore du gengs.* [see **stroop**]

strops (n) trouser braces. [Sc. *strop*: a strip of leather]

strödiment (strodda-) (n) mood of agitation or high excitement. [Sw.dial. *stritta*: to rush out suddenly; to spout; spurt]

strug (strogg) (n) laborious work. [O.N. *strjúka*: a stroke]

strynd (strind) (n) inherited characteristics. [L.Sc. *strynd*, *streind*, *stryne*: a particular cast or disposition]

stu (v) (of a mare) to be in heat. *De mare is stuin.* [N. *stoda*: of a horse running with the mares; Sw.dial. *stoa*: (of a mare) to be in heat]

studge (n) a short, stout person; (v) to walk heavily, esp. when weighed down with a load; trudge. [L.Sc. *stodge*: to walk laboriously; plod; trudge]

stuggit (adj) replete; stuffed full; (also see **stiggisom**). [originally there were overtones of disgust – *he stuggit at it* (he felt disgusted at eating it); Icel. *stugga vid*: disgusted with]

stumba (n) thick mist. *Steekit stumba* – a thick fog through which it is impossible to see; (also **stimna**, **stomna**). [Sw.dial. *stimba*: steam; N. *stum(myrk)*: pitch-dark; Fær. *stumt*: very dense (dark; misty)]

stumse (stums) (v) to be speechless from surprise or consternation. *I wis fairly stumsted be dat.* [N. *stumsa*: to be unable to find words]

stunk (stonk) (n) a pant; (v) to pant from exertion. [N. *stanka*, *staanka*: to groan; pant; sigh deeply, as in great exhaustion]

sturdy (n) a sheep's disease brought on by the larvae of a tapeworm which causes a watery tumour to form on the brain causing staggering, giddiness and eventual collapse. [Sc. *sturdy*, O. Fr. *estourdi*: stunned; dazed]

sturken (storkn) (v) to become thick; coagulate. [O.N. *storkna*: to coagulate]

stylk (stilk, stijlk) (n) a straw; a stalk of oats. [N. *stilk*; O.N. *stilkr*]

styooch (n) dust; spray off the sea; turmoil. *Dis reddin up maks sic a styooch* (This spring-cleaning makes such a dust); (v) to give off smoke; to work busily. [O.Sc. *stew*: dust; vapour]

sudd (sudderd) (n) the compass point of south; (adj) lying towards the south. *De wind is sudderdly de day*; (also **sood**). [O.N. *sudr*]

sukkalegs (sokkaleggs) (n) sock-gaiters that have no feet. [Fær. *sokka-leggald*: stocking-leg]

sukkamire (n) a swamp. [O.N. *sokkva*: to sink + E. *mire*]

sulbrigdi (n) basking shark (*Cetorhinus maximus*) (also **brigdi**, **hobrigdi**). [cf. N. *bregda*: to alter; shift; move quickly; O.E. *bregdan*; (note: the shark's habit of basking on the surface of the sea does not seem to equate with the meaning of *bregda*)]

sungaets (singaets) (adv) left to right; clockwise, as the path of the sun – associated with superstitious ritual behaviour; (opposite to **widdergaets**). [O.Sc. *sonegatis*, *sungates*]

sutshkin (sutchkin) (n) a sibling – brother or sister of same parents. [O.N. *systkin*; N.dial. *sys(t)kin*; D. *søskende*]

swaabie (swabek) (n) great black-backed gull (*Larus marinus*). [orig. *swartbak* – O.N. *svart-bakr*: black-backed gull]

swaander (n) a stagger; (v) to stagger. *He geid a swaander dan drappit doon.* [orig. obs. cf. E. *swagger* (and *wander*)]

swaar (n) 1) a swathe of corn or grass cut by a scythe. [E. *sward*]; 2) the darkest time of night; *De swaar o de dim* – the darkest part of the short summer night. [N. *sval*: dusky; dark; dim]

swaara (swara) (n) thick, soft woollen yarn used for knitting underclothes; the garments themselves; (adj) made of above yarn – *swaara draaers.* [O.N. *svarr*: heavy]

swaarlik (swarlek) (n) a muddy hole, frequently a smelly one. [N. *svervel*: a whirlpool]

swab (swabb) (n) a wet cloth (see **cloot**).

swack (adj) able; industrious; full of energy. [Icel. *skvak*: movement; shaking]

swally (v) to swallow. *Showe yun afore du swallies it.* [Sh. variant on E. *swallow*]

swapp (n) a blow; a gust; (v) to strike a sudden blow; to fling; cast, as a fishing line; to gust, as wind. [O.Sc. *swapp*: to leap suddenly, violently; M.E. *swap*: to strike]

swarf (n) a swoon; a fainting turn. [O.Sc. *swarff*: swoon]

swarfish (n) butterfish (*Pholis gunnellus*), a small, eel-like fish with characteristic black spots along its back, found in shallow tidal waters of the N. Atlantic. [N. *svalfisk*: a tiny fish near the shore, also *tangsprell*; other common names – **brunklet**, rock-eel, gunnel]

swart (adj) black. [O.N. *svartr*: black]

swartback (n) great black-backed gull (*Larus marinus*) (also **swaabie**). [O.N. *svart-bakr*]

swash (n) a considerable quantity of drink. *I doot he's hed a rycht swash afore he's dat paloovious*; the sound of water splashing. [Sc. *swash*: a wash of liquid; the sound of splashing liquid]

swats (n) the fermented liquid in which oatmeal has been steeped for making **sooans**, used as a refreshing drink. [O.Sc. *swaittis*, O.E. *swatan*: beer]

swee (n) a large dram such as might cause a stinging sensation in the mouth. *A swee i dee mooth*; (v) to sting, as from a burn; to singe; to hiss, as spilled water under a heating pot. [N. *svi*: to burn; *svie*: a tingling pain; O.N. *svída*: to scorch; Sc. *sweal*]

sweel (n) a swivel, esp. an anti-kink device on a tether (see **swill**); (v) to swing around; to swivel. [O.Sc. *swele*: swivel]

sweem (v) swim; (pt) **swöm**. [E. *swim*]

sweerie (n) a container or frame for holding yarn-bobbins; (adj) lazy. *He aye wis a sweerie so and so.* [O.Sc. *swere*: lazy – hence a **sweerie** being a box to make craftwork easier, cf. *lazy-susan*: a revolving tray to give easy access to dishes on a table]

sweerie (swirrie) acronymic slang for Scottish Women's Rural Institute (SWRI).

sweerie-geng (n) the first row of knitting after casting on, supposedly the most difficult to accomplish. [Ger. *schwer*: heavy; difficult]

sweet (adj) of fresh milk. [Sc. usage of E. *sweet* – i.e. not sour]

sweetra (n) laziness. [O.Sc. *swere*: lazy]

S

sweevel (n) whirlwind; gust of wind swirling round a corner. *A sweevel a wind at de byre gaevil*; (v) to swing about. [O.N. *sveifla*: a swinging round; pron. influenced by E. *swivel*]

swettek (swittek) (n) a squirt; a hollow stalk (commonly wild angelica) used to squirt liquid (see **skeetik** and **skeetitrumps**); wild angelica (*Angelica sylvestris*). [N. *skvetta*: a squirt]

swick (n) a cheat; a swindler; (v) to cheat. [O.Sc. *swik*: deceit; O.E. *swika*]

swidder (n) in a state of indecision; (v) to be undecided; to vacillate. [Sc. *swither*]

swill (sweel) (n) a swivel on a tether; a wash; (v) to wash or rinse; to wash down. *Yun reestit mutton needs a swill o tae t tak de saat fae me mooth*. [O.Sc. (n) *swele*: swivel; Sc. (v) *swill*: to rinse; O.E. *swilian*: to wash]

swinkle (swinkl, swinkel) (n) splashing sound, as water being gently agitated in a container; (v) to splash gently. *A'm drukken too much an me guts is swinklin*; (compare **swittle**). [N. *skvinkla*: to splash; D. *svinke*: to move this way and that]

swinklan (adj) full of drink; drunk. [of **swinkle** (see above)]

swine-moothed (adj) having a projecting upper jaw, (compare **hoe-moothed**). [O.N. *svin*: swine + Sc. *mooth*: mouth]

swird (green swird) (n) a piece of grassy ground. [O.N. *svordr*; E. *sward*]

swirten (v) to flatten, as wind flattening corn. [cf. N. *svarda*: (in sense of) to stretch out on the sward, or grassland]

swittle (switl, swittel) (n) anything watery, as thin soup or weak tea. *Dir still a coarn o swittle ida pot* (There's still a little weak tea in the pot); (v) water being agitated in an open situation as the action of ducks or children dabbling in shallow water (compare **swinkle**). [N. *skvitla*: to sprinkle; splash]

swöm (v) (pt of) swim (Sh. **sweem**). [E. *swam*]

sye (n) a scythe. [E. *scythe*; O.N. *sigthr*]

sye (v) to strain liquid through a sieve. [Sc. *sye*: to strain; O.E. *sīon*, *sēon*: to strain]

sye-sten (n) a whet-stone for sharpening scythes. [E. *scythe-stone*]

syer (n) a sieve, esp. a milk-sieve. [see above]

syer-cloot (n) a piece of muslin laid inside a sieve to catch finer particles when straining milk. [Sc. *sye*: to strain + *cloot*: a cloth]

sygonical (adj) (N.Yell) colossal; enormous; awesome. [a mid-20th cent. Sh. example of the now common trend to invent composite words such as *humungous*, *gianormous* – cf. deriv. of E. *cyclonical*]

sylkie (selkie) (n) a grey seal (*Halichoerus grypus*) or harbour seal (*Phoca vitulina*) (also **haaf fish**). [Sc. *silkie*, *silky*, *selkie*; O.Sc. *selich*; O.E. *seolh*]

synd (n) a rinsing; (v) to rinse an article after washing it. [M.E. *sind*: to rinse (poss. of O.N. *synda*: to swim)]

syne (adv) since; later; *fae syne* (from that time); *lang syne* (long since). [Sc. *syne*]

S

T

ta (t) (prep) to. *A'm gaan ta de shop t fetch de errands*; (also **tae, til**). [Sc. *tae* – form of E. *to*]

taand (tand, taund) (n) a glowing coal; a small piece of burning peat; a fire-brand; *a lowin taand* (a glowing peat). [O.N. *tandri*: poet. of fire; *tandraudr*: fiery; red]

taas (n) 1) narrow strips of light. *Da hidmost taas o da day* (The last glimmers of sunlight – frequently seen in fan-shaped strips behind cloud); 2) a strap, cut into strips at the end, used for corporal punishment. [Sc. *taws, tawse*: a leather strap]; 3) fine roots of a plant; (pl) **tæger** (see **taegirse**). [O.N. *tág*, N. *taag*: root fibre]

taat (tott) (n) thick worsted yarn as used for tatting rugs; *a taatit heid* (a matted head of hair); lumps of matted hair. [O.N. *páttr*: tuft; part; a single strand of rope; cf. E. *tat (tatting)* the art of making knotted rugs]

taatit (adj) something made from **taat**. [see above]

taatie (n) a potato. [Sc. *tattie (pitawtie)*]

taatie-boky (n) a scarecrow; thick discharge from the nose. [Sc.]

taatie-craa (n) a child's toy made out of a potato into which gull feathers are stuck. When thrown in the air it spins and makes a whirring noise. [Sc. *tattie*: potato + *craa*: crow]

taatie-möld (n) potato ground. [Sc. *tattie*: potato + *möld*: (earth mould); O.N. *mold*: mould]

taav (v) to temporarily caulk a ship's timbers; to pack solidly. [N. *tav*: (collectively) fibres; rags; *tave*: a patch; a small unravelled piece]

taavrins (n) roots of plants; rags. [N. *tav*: (collect) fibres; rags]

tabnab (n) a sweet snack; any sweet titbit to accompany a cup of tea. [originally British Merchant Navy slang for a small item of food offered at break times, esp. morning break]

tack (n) a tenure; all that land pertaining to one lease. [Sc. *tack*]

tae (n) tea; toe; (adj) the one, as in *de tae side or de tidder* (the one side or the other); (prep) to. [O.Sc. *ta*, Sc. *tae*: to; the one; toe]

taeg (n) a strip of land; commonly the second part of placenames referring to strips of land, e.g. Tuntegs. [O.N. *teigr*: measured strip of land]

taegirse (tæger) (n) wild (creeping) thyme (*Thymus praecox*). [cf. O.N. *tág*, N. *taag*: root fibre – owing to creeping fibrous stems of the plant referred to in plural as *tæger* (see **taas**)]

taek (tekk) (n) straw, heather or turf, used as protective covering of thatch on houses and corn-stacks; (v) to thatch a roof. [O.N. *pekja*, L.Sc. *thek, theek*, Sc. *thack*: thatch]

taek-gaet (n) the part of a house wall-head where a thatcher stood while working. [Sc. *thack-gait*]

taekit (adj) thatched. [L.Sc. *thekit*: thatched]

taen (ten) (v) taken; (pt of) **tak**; (also **tön**). [(pt of) Sc. *tak* – *tain, tane*]

taen up (v) arrested. *He wiz taen up fur drink drivin*. [Sc. equiv. *lifted*]

taer (n) a teardrop. *Yun reek hes broucht taers t me een*. [E. *tear*]

taft (n) an oarsman's seat in a boat; a thwart; (each seat has its designation) *eft taft* – bench nearest the stern; *fore-taft* – bench nearest the bow; *mid-taft* – bench in centre of boat; *skaer-taft* – one next to eft-taft. [O.Sc. *thoft*, L.Sc. *thaft*, O.E. *pofte*, O.N. *popta*: thwart]

tag-set (v) to worry at, as a dog harassing sheep. [obs. cf. Sc. *tague*: tongue, as in 'tongue-lash' or harass]

taing (teng) (n) a flat tongue of land projecting into the sea. [O.N. *tangi*: long, low, narrow tongue of land]

tak (v) to take; to assume; (pt) **taen**; (n) a taking up; a catch of fish. *Yun's a fine tak du hes, boy*. Phrases: **tak aboot** to secure a crop against bad weather; to wrap up before venturing forth; **tak at** go ahead; **tak baand** moderate (one's behaviour); said to riotious children or individual – *Will du tak baand* (an order, not a question); [O.N. *band*: (in sense of) tie up and therefore bring under control]; **tak efter** resemble; **tak ill wi** take badly with; take offence; **tak in for** speak well of; **tak on** take the consequences; to lament; to revel – *Dey wir takkin on an haen a fun*; to work very hard; **taen til** (adj) noted; **tak up** look after; **tak up ita, tak up itil** (also **tak up anunder**) to show an interest – *I heard yun spaekalation but I nivir took up anunder it*; **tak weel wi** to show friendliness; (in negative form) **nae tak** the fish are not biting – *Dir nae tak apo de fish de night*; **tak wye** set off – *When did he tak wye for Bressa?* [O.N. *taka*: take; *takka etter*: take after; *taka til*: to take to; to begin]

tale (tell) (n) a saying; a remark. *Hit's come tae my tale* (It has happened as I said it would). [an O.N. expression rendered into E.]

Tammasmas (n) St Thomas's Day. [The winter solstice (21st December), so chosen to commemorate St Thomas because he was the disciple who remained in the 'night of unbelief and doubt' for the longest time]

tammy noddie (n) a child's name for sleep – equiv. of Sandman or Wee Willie Winkie. [L.Sc. *Tammie Noddie*: a story which can only be told if the listener agrees not to speak in the middle of it; a spell which is usually broken by affirmation to the question 'Will ye no?']

tammy norie (tammi-nori) (n) the puffin (*Fratercula artica*) (also **norie**). [cf. onomat. owing to the call being a purring sound cf. N. *knurra*, D. *knurre*: to produce a sound; to grumble; murmur]

tamto (n) heyday. [orig. obs. cf. L.Sc. *taptoo*: a state of excitement; eagerness; desire]

tane (pron) the one. [Sc. *tane (the tane)*: that one; the one]

tang (n) coarse seaweed, esp. (*Fucus*), which grows above the low-water mark, as opposed to **waar** which grows in deeper water. [O.N. *pang*; N. & Fær. *pang*, D. *tang*: seaweed]

tang-bowes (n) the gas-filled balls on the stalk of tang (*Pneumatocysts*) (lit. 'tang-buoys'). [see **tang**]

tangel (n) the stalk of kelp; *a waari tangel*. [see **tang**]

tang-fish (n) common, or harbour seal (*Phoca vitulina*). [see **tang**]

tangie (n) Shetland's version of the legendary kelpie or sea-horse, (compare **nyuggel**). [see **tang**]

tang-sparrow (-sporrow) (n) rock pipit (*Anthus spinoletta*) (also **banks-sparrow**) – so named for its shore-line habitat, as opposed to **hill-sparrow** the meadow pipit (lit. 'tang-sparrow'). [see **tang**]

tang-whaap (n) whimbrel (*Numenius phaeopus*) so named for its frequenting of tidal regions where it occasionally feeds on burrowing crabs it finds amongst the **tang** [see **tang** + Sc. *whaup*: a (little) curlew] It can be argued that the curlew **whaap** or **spooie** (*Numenius arquata*) is properly the **tang-whaap** as this species is more commonly found feeding in the ebb rather than the whimbrel which favours its moorland breeding grounds. In Faroe <u>curlew</u> = *tangspogvi* while <u>whimbrel</u> = *spogvi*.

tant (adj) (of a roof) very steep. [O.N. *þandr* – of (v) *þenja*: to stretch; extend]

tantle (v) to anger and upset. [L.Sc. *tanter*: to argue; to rage; N.dial. *tandra*, *tantra*: to scold; pick a quarrel; cf. E. *tantrum*]

tanyik (tantjek) (n) a tooth. [O.N. *tannu*: tooth]

tapster (n) top dog; the boss; (lit. 'topster' – one who tops all).

tap-swaar (adj) top-heavy. [L.Sc. *tap*: top + O.N. *svarr*: heavy]

tarrow (v) to reject or refuse, esp. food; to be fussy over food. [O.Sc. *tarow*: to be reluctant]

tari (tarry) (n) seaweed. [O.N. *þari*: seaweed]

tarry krook (taricrook, tarigrep) (n) a two-pronged rake used to gather seaweed for manure. [O.N. *þari*: seaweed – hence N. *taregreip*: implement (fork) for gathering seaweed used for manure]

tash (n) a disgrace; a character blemish. [Sc. (v) *tash*: to disarray; to soil or stain; Fr. *tacher*]

taupie (N. Yell) (n) a long, baggy coat. [Sc. *taupie* (n): a clumsy, careless person, esp. a young woman; (adj) awkward; slovenly]

teached (pt of teach) taught. *Shö teached me ida skule*; (also see **towt** and **laerned**). [Sh. variant on E. *taught*]

tedder (n) a rope for fastening an animal to a stake; a tether. [L.Sc. *tedder*; E. *tether*; O.N. *tjódr*; M.Du. *tudder*]

teddisome (tedisome) (adj) boring; tiresome. [E. *tedious*]

tee (n) thigh; leg of mutton. [O.N. *thjō*: thigh; O.E. *thēoh*]

teesh an exclamation of disgust. *Teesh! Teesh! Dunna dö yun*; (also see **fyach**). [imit. of various words intended to express disgust esp. to a child; L.Sc. *feech*]

teet (v) to steal a glance; a quick peep; (n) a surreptitious peep. [O.E. *tōtian*: to peep; cf. Sw. *titta*: to peep]

teeth (n) tooth. *I got wan teeth oot yesterday*. [Sh. idiomatic reversal of the E. plural]

teetik (titek) (n) meadow pipit (*Anthus pratensis*) (also **hill-sparrow**). [N. *tita*: a small bird; (titmouse; sparrow); Sc. *titlark*]

tell (v) to repeat; say by heart; recite. *De bairns aye tell a prayer afore dey geng t bed*; in expressions: **tell aff** to count – *Tell aff every een*; **tell apo** show effect on – *Yun feerie is tellin apo dee*. [O.Sc. *tell*, in this usage; O.N. *telja*: to tell; relate; repeat gossip]

telt (v) told. *I telt her no ta come*. [Sc. *tel*, *tald*]

tengs (teings) (n) tongs; fire-tongs. [O.Sc. *taingeis*: tongs]

tentily (adv) cautiously. [L.Sc. *tentifly*: tentatively]

terrible (adj) exceedingly; extremely. *He's a terrible fine man*; *shö's a terrible boannie lass*; (also see **awful**). [L.Sc. *terrible* & *awful*, in same meanings]

thoosan taes (n) a centipede. [Sc. lit. 'thousand toes' and consequently a gross exaggeration as the most common centipede in Britain is the brown centipede (*Lithobius forficatus*) with 15 pairs of legs. Of other species the garden centipede (*Geophilus*) has the most with 40-80 pairs of relatively short legs – no taes]

Thule (n) Shetland (also **Ultima Thule**). [L. *Thūlē*; Gr. *Thoulē*; the Greek explorer, Pytheas, stated '*Thule is a six day's sail north of Britain, and is near the frozen sea*'; the most northerly land, variously identified as Shetland, Iceland or Greenland]

tial (tyal) (n) a fastening or tie; anything used for tying (cord, string, ribbon, wire). [M.E. *tyall*; O.E. *tyzel* – later assimilated to *tie*]

tidder (pron) other. *De tane an de tidder* (The one and the other). [Sh. rendering of E. *th*]

tide-lumps (n) rough patches in the sea caused by tidal currents. [E. *rip*, *tide-rip*]

tief (n) thief; burglar. [E. *thief*; N. *tyv*]

Tiesday (n) Tuesday. [E. *Tuesday*]

tieve (v) to commit theft. [E. *thieve*]

tieves nacket (n) lapwing (*Vanellus vanellus*). [L.Sc. poss. onomat. of bird's call 'thevis nek']

tift (v) to throb. [cf. Sw.dial. *tuffsa*: to beat softly]

tig (tigg) (v) to beg. [O.N. *tiggja*: to receive; accept]

tigger (n) a begger; one who **tigs**. [see above]

til (prep, adv) to (also **t**, **ta**, **tae**). *Shö sent for de doctor til him*. [O.N. *til*]

tilfer (n) movable bottom board covering a boat's keelson. [O.N. *tilfar*: row of planks forming a loose deck in a vessel]

timmer (adj) tone deaf; having no ear for music; tuneless. [cf. L.Sc. *timmer*: bashful; timid]

ting (n) 1) a child. *De peerie ting*. [Sc. *thing*: said of a living creature in tolerant affection or kindly reproach]; 2) old district court or assize (Delting, Lunnasting, Nesting, Aithsting); central court, Tingwall (later moved to Scalloway under Earl Patrick); (also **law-ting**). [O.N. *ting*: a court; assembly, esp. for settling lawsuits]

tinn (v) of mist or clouds clearing. *He's tinnin idda wasterd* (It's clearing to the west). [cf. O.N. *þynna*: to make thin; E. *thin*]

tint (v, pt) lost; mislaid. *I canna fin me purse, A'm tint it*. [M.E. *tynt*: lost]

tinter (n) a minuscule quantity; the least hint or trace of colour. [N. *tint*: very small portion; trifle]

tip (tipp) (n) a small drop, usually of milk; (v) to extract a small quantity of milk from a cow, such as might serve to provide for a cupful in haste. [N. *tippa*: to drip; *tipla*: to press out drop by drop]

tipper (v) to walk on tiptoe or with a jaunty tread; to stand on an edge just able to balance. [Fær. *tepur* (adj): near the edge; L.Sc. *tipper*: to walk unsteadily or on tiptoe]

tird (n) state of agitation. *He aye gets in a tird afore gyaan ta de doctor*; (v) to bustle; get on quickly with work; to hurriedly pull on one's clothes. [L.Sc. *tirr*, *tirn*]

tirl (v) to whirl; twirl; turn head-over-heels. [O.Sc. *tirl*: to ripple]; (n) the wooden wheel fitted with paddles which is revolved horizontally by a mill stream under a Shetland mill to operate the grinding stone above by means of an interconnecting spindle. [Fær. *tyril*: a milk-whisk; Sw.dial. *tyril*: churn-staff]

tirn (adj) cross; bad-tempered; cantankerous. [N. *tirren*: cross; irascible; O.N. *tyrrinn*]

tirrick (n) Arctic tern or common tern (*Sterninae*) – imitative of the bird's alarm call. [L.Sc. *tirrock*, *tarrock*]

tirri-mirri (n) a noisy commotion; a state of agitation (also **kirr mirr**). [N. *terr*: hurried bustling about; hot haste + N. *mirra*: to tingle; prick; itch]

tirse (n) a state of irritation; short-tempered. [N.dial. *tersa*: to drive; force; exert, in sense of irritated excitement; cf. E. *terse*]

titt (v) to walk with short, quick steps. *Shö wiz gyaan tittin aboot*. [Fær. *tita*: walk quickly with short steps]

titter (v) to shake; tremble; shiver (also see **pipper**). [O.N. *titra*: shake; shiver]

tittie (n) a girl; a young woman. [N.dial. *titta*: girl; lass; young woman]

tiv (tivek) (n) a tuft of grass or similar; a remnant piece. [N. *teve*: a rag; scrap]

tivlik (tivla, tivl) (n) joint or vertebrae in the backbone (also **lith**). [N. *tavla*, *tovla*: dorsal vertebrae]

tize (v) to entice; coax. [L.Sc. *tice*, *tyce*; O.Sc. *tys*, *tyst*]

tjoik (n) cake (Whalsay). [O.N. *kaka*; E. *cake*]

tjordin (n) thunder. [D. *torden*: thunder]

toam (tome) (n) a fishing-line. [O.N. *taumr*: rope; rein; Fær. *teymur*: the lower end of a fishing-line or a short line to which a hook is fastened]

toarn (n) torn. *Dee breeks is toarn*; thorn; **toarny-ware** barbed wire. [E. *torn* & *thorn*]

tocht (n, v) thought (also **towt**). [L.Sc. *thocht*]

toeff (v) to spit; to imitate the sound of spitting. [imit]

toft (n) the site (or former site) of a house or buildings, commonly in placenames, e.g. Toft (mainland ferry terminal for Yell Sound crossing). [M.E. *toft*; Sc. *taft*, from O.N. *topt*, *tupt*, *toft*]

toilter (n) a short, thick-set person – commonly used as a nickname. [cf. N. *tult*, *tuldr*, *tultr*: a bundle]

toint (n) sulk; huff. [L.Sc. *toit*]

tome (n) a rope or (fishing) line. [O.N. *taumr*: rope; rein]

too (tu, tut) (v) to sound a horn; blow a trumpet; toot or hoot. *Ee tut an du's ut* (said to an old lady with an ear-trumpet in church). [N. & Sw.dial. *tuta*]

tooder (toosel) (v) to tousle; rumple; dishevel. [O.Sc. *towsill*]

tooderie (adj) tousled. [see above]

tooel (n) towel. [E. *towel*]

toog (tug) (n) a mound (also **mooratoog**). [O.N. *túfa*: a mound]

toom (tum) (n) the thumb. [O.E. *thūma*]

toon (tun, toun) (n) area of arable land leased from an estate for a **croft** and incorporating **infields**, **outruns** and **scattald**; any section of the aforementioned (also a **park**) – *I'm pitten de kye ida lower toon (park)*; strips of arable fields where crops are grown; a group of crofts in proximity to one another; a small community of houses; a town; Lerwick. *We'll maybe tak a run inta de toon de moarn*. [O.N. *tún*: fenced plot; home field; farm-yard; Sc. *toon*, *toun*: town, in latter meanings]

toonmals (n) tenants' permanent land-rights adjacent to their dwellings, as opposed to **runrigs**. [O.N. *tún*: fenced plot; home field; farm-yard + *male*: rent; tenancy; O.N. *mál*: agreement]

toorie (toorie-kep) (n) a knitted woollen cap (with or without a pom-pom). [Sc. *toorie*, *tourie*: the pom-pom on a cap or bonnet; *toorie-bonnet*: a cap with a toorie]

toosk (toosek, tusk) (n) tuft of hair; matted or tangled mass. [N. *tuksa*: tangled mass]

tooskit (tusset, tussen) (adj) dishevelled; tousled. [N. *tysen*: tousled; L.Sc. *touse*: to disarrange; crumple]

toot 1) an interjection indicative of harsh disagreement (also see **hoot**). [Sc. toot – imit. of a snort of disgust]

toot 2) (n) a dram; a swig of liquor. [Sc. *tot*: a dram]

toot 3) (n) a small child or animal. *Shö wiz a peerie toot*; a short spell of work. *Gie me a toot at it*. [O.N. *tuttr*: a dwarfish being]

torch (n) long piece of wood with inflammable material tied to one end, lighted and carried at Up-Helly-A' procession by **guizers**.

tottim (n) a spinning top. [L.Sc. *totum* (*tottum*, *totem*): a four-sided disc-top spun in a game of chance, each side was marked with a letter 'T' signifying L. *totum*: the whole lot]

towe (v) to thaw; to tow, as a boat; (n) a thaw; (also see **uppslag, uplowsin**). [E. *thaw*]

townet (tounet) (n) a knitted garment – originally the preparation of wool for worsted; carding and spinning. [N. *tonad*: wool to be made into worsted; O.N. *tó*: uncleaned wool or flax]

towt (tocht) (n, v) thought. [Sc. *tocht*; E. *thought*]

towt (pt of teach) taught (also see **laerned** and **teached**). [Sh. form of E. *taught*]

tows (n) fishing lines; boat halyards. [Du. *touw*: rope; string; cord; O.Sc. *tow*: a rope]

toyik (toyack) (n) a small straw basket. [N.dial. *taaje*, *taagje*: a basket; creel (one made from tree-roots); O.N. *tágr*: root]

tö (adv) too; likewise; in phrase **lay tö** close. *Lay tö yun door afore we freeze*. [Sh. variant of E. *to*]

töd (v) to talk incessantly. [O.N. *tauta*: to mutter; whimper]

tö-faa (n) a porch added on to an existing wall and having a lean-to roof. [Sc. *to-fal*; M.E. *tawfall*]

tölli (töllie) (n) brawl; fight; quarrel. [O.F. *touillier*: strive; stir up; dispute]

töls (n) implements for rope twisting (also **tömikins**). [O.N. *tól*: a tool]

töm (v) to pour, as rain; to empty. [L.Sc. *tume*: heavy fall of rain]; (adj) empty; hollow. *De neep wiz toom*. [O.N. *tæma* (v): to empty]

tömald (n) a heavy downpour of rain. [L.Sc. *tume*]

T

tömikins (tömi-keys) (n) implement used in rope-making for the purpose of twisting the strands, esp. twisting fishing lines and tethers. [O.N. *taumr*: rope]

tön (n) tune; (v) (pp of) take; (also **taen**); (in Burra and Scalloway – (pt) *He tön an oor ta dell de rig*; also (pp) *I wis tön aback at whit he said.*) [Sc.]

tö-name (n) a nickname. [L.Sc. *to-name*; M.E. *toname*: nickname; assumed name; alias]

tö-tak (n) a person of low reputation or poor character, known for their foolish or depraved behaviour. [Fær. *tiltak*: a person much spoken of – usually disparagingly; the subject of idle reports]

traa (traan) (n) a spasm (see **watertraa**); (v) to twist. [O.Sc. *thraw(e)*: to twist]; [E. *throe*: a pang; pain]

traan (adj) obstinate; crabbed; perverse. [O.Sc. *thra*, *thrawn*]

traawirt (adj) stubborn; obstinate. [O.Sc. *thrawirt*: obstinate]

trachle (n) tedious work. [L.Sc. *trachle*: struggle]

trachled (trachlit) (adj) harrassed; overworked. [Sc. *trachlit* – of Gael. *treachailte*: loosed; spent; tired]

track (n) a period of time; a settled or continuing spell of weather. [L.Sc. *track*]

traep (v) argue persistently. [O.N. *trár*: obstinate, cf. O.Sc. *thra*, *thrawn*]

traik (trek) (v) to walk about aimlessly. [L.Sc. *trodge*; E. *trudge*]

traivel (v) walk. [L.Sc. *travel* (in same sense)]

tralldom (n) trial; hardship. [N.dial. *trældom*: hard, tedious labour; E. *thralldom*: slavery]

trams (n) the shafts of a barrow or cart; by transference, long legs – not necessarily shapely. [L.Sc. *tram(s)*]

trang (n) intimacy; close friendship; said of a courting couple: *Dir trang*; (adj) distraught; over-worked; hardpressed. [O.N. *þrongr*: narrow; tight; constricted; difficult; N. *trong*: difficult; troublesome; L.Sc. *thrang*: crowded; stressed]

transe (n) passage connecting the but and ben-end of a cottage. [O.Sc. *trans*: an alleyway or passage; L.Sc. *transe*; F. *transe*]

trap (n) a ladder. [Sc.]

trapple (n) the windpipe. '*He measured fower an twinty k-nuckles fae his spune tae de k-not o his **trapple**.*' – Sh. dialect version of Lawrence Tulloch's description of a Kalathumpian in his folk tale *The Trow's Boat*. (*The Foy and other Folk Tales*; The Shetland Times Ltd, 2006.) [L.Sc. *thrapple*; O.Sc. *throppill*: throat; windpipe]

trath (interj) truth; in faith; used in exclamatory remarks, i.e. *Dat in trath!* [Sc. *troth*; M.E. *trewde*]

trave (n) twenty-four sheaves of corn (the corn harvest was once commonly counted in traves). *We got tree traves aff a de lower rig.* [cf. O.N. *þrefi*: a heap of two dozen sheaves; Icel. *threfi*; D. *trave*]

tread (v) to copulate, esp. birds. [Sc. *tread*: domestic cockerel; (of a male bird) to copulate]

treffs (trafs) (adj) frayed or tattered. [N. *trav*: frayed; ragged mass; tatters]

trefset (adj) ragged; tattered; untidy. [N. *trefsutt*: frayed at the edges]

tremsket (adj) untidy; ragged. [see above]

trentlet (adj) of a lanky person; (of clothes, esp. women's) tight, close-fitting, such as to give a slender figure. [cf. N. *trantle*: cleft stick, somewhat thicker than a hedge-stake; D. *trind*: cylindrical]

tresh (v) to thrash (thresh) esp. in separating grain from husks and straw; (pt) **trosh**. [Sc. *thresh*]

treshel-tree (n) the wooden sill of a doorway; threshold (note: **tree** indicates wooden as opposed to stone thresholds). [O.N. *tré*: wood + L.Sc. *thrashel*, E. *threshold*; deriv. from 'thresh (thrash)' in the older sense of to trample]

trift (n) work; worthwhile enterprise. *Ill trift biggs ill daeks*. [Sc. *thrift*: work; industry]

trig (adj) trim; neat; orderly; (v) to make tidy. [O.N. *tryggr*: faithful; secure; Sc. *trig*]

trinky (trenky, trinki) (n) narrow ravine, passage or trench. [N. *þronga* (adj): narrow]

trist (v) to squeeze with a twisting action; wring; press. [O.N. *þrysta*: to press; squeeze; force; compel]

trist (n) thirst; the craving for something, esp. drink; (adj) **tristy** suffering from thirst. [Sh. spelling of E. *thirst*]

triv (n) odds and ends, esp. worthless material. [N. *treve*, *trifsa*: small rag; tatter; Fær. *trevsi*]

trivvel (v) to grope; fumble. [O.N. *þrifla*: to feel one's way; grope]

tro (v) to throw; to be sick; throw up. [Sc. *thraw*]

troag (trog) (v) walk heavily; trudge. [N. *troka*: to stamp; tramp; L.Sc. *trodge*; E. *trudge*]

trointle (troitl) (v) to mutter; grumble (without necessarily addressing anyone in particular). *Whit's du trointlin aboot?* [of Fær. *trunter*: a protruding mouth, snout, thus F. *moue*: a grimace of discontent]

troke (v) to bargain; to barter; to have dealings with. *A'm haen nae troke wi yun.* [E. *truck*, L.Sc. *trock*, *troke*, F. *troque*: barter]

troo (tru) (v) to believe in something or someone. *Troo du dat!* (Believe that!). [O.N. *trúa*, L.Sc. *trow*, *troo*: to believe]

trooen (n) a trowel. [L.Sc. *truan*, *trooel*]

trooker (n) a rogue; a disreputable person. [L.Sc. *troaker*: a bargainer; dealer; pedlar (see **troke**) and by extension, a cheat; a rogue; a 'bad lot']

trooter (n) one who fishes for trout. [Sc. *trouter*]

troot(s) (n) trout (*Salmonidae*) – all species including salmon, brown trout, sea trout and rainbow trout, the 's' plural being peculiarly Shetlandic in manner of usage. *Wir bön at de troots* (We've been trout fishing). [E. & Sc. *trout*, (pl. rarely) *trouts*]

trot (n) throat. [Sh. spelling of E. *throat*]

trow (n) supernatural being from Scandinavian mythology (*troll*) passed into Shetland folklore. Trows are said to live underground in **trowie knowes** or **hadds**, coming forth at night to enact their betwitching powers and mischief on people and animals. Their love of music sometimes led to a Shetland fiddler being spirited away when walking home late at night from a dance. The fiddler might then expect to be kept entertaining the trows for a year, as they favoured long parties. A person can be **sained** or protected from trows by means of a piece of silver, a steel blade or a Bible. [O.N. *troll*: fairy]

trowe (trow) (adv) through. [L.Sc. *throu*, *throo*; O.Sc. *throuch*]

trowe-baand (trow-band) (n) a long stone extending through a wall to reinforce a building; a bond-stone. [L.Sc. *throu*: through + N. *bandstokk*; L.Sc. *band-stane*: a stone laid cross-wise through a wall]

trowe-pit (trow-pit) (n) a putting through of work (lit. 'through-put'); **trowe-pitten** energetic; deft. [L.Sc. *troo-pit*, *troo-pitten*]

trowie buckie (n) a snail shell – used by trows as boats. [N. *troll* + O.Sc. *buckie*, *bukky*: shell of a whelk or other mollusc; orig. obs. cf. L. *buccinum*]

trowie cairds (n) fern fronds, said to be used by trows for carding wool (also **ferri-cairds**). [N. *troll*: fairy + Sc. *cairds*, *cards*; Fær. *trollakambur*: troll combs]

trowie knowes (n) earth mounds under which trows have their dens or **hadds**; name commonly given to any archaelogical mounds dating from antiquity. [*trow* (N. *troll*) + Sc. *knowe*: knoll]

trow's hadd (n) a trow's den. [*trow* (N. *troll*) + L.Sc. *hald*, *hauld*: a place of stay; a dwelling; refuge]

tröni (n) a pig's snout. [O.N. *tryni*: a snout]

tröttel (trötl) (v) to talk in a low voice; mutter; grumble. [N. *tryta*: to low softly; to sulk – from *trut*: mouth; snout]

truck (truck) (v) to tread down; trample; stamp on. [N.dial. *trakka*, *trokka*]

trump 1) (n) Jew's harp (marranzano) or mouth harp, one of the oldest known musical instruments. [O.Sc. *trump*]

trump 2) (v) (of a horse) to kick; fling. [Icel. *trampa*: to tramp; kick; also (of a horse) to kick; jolt; N. *trumpa*: to push]

trumph (n) card trump; (v) to trump an opponent's card. [O.Sc. *trumph*: the chief suit in a card game (the 'ph' was retained in Scots from the original word 'triumph')]

trumsket (adj) fretful; sulky. [Fær. *trumsutur*: peevish; sulky]

trunsher (n) a large plate or platter. [E. *trencher*; O.Sc. *trincheour*, *trunschour*]

truss (n) a collection of worthless objects; trash. [N. *trus*: trash; bits of rubbish]

trusset (adj) slovenly; untidy. [N. *trussa*: a slattern]

trussie laverek (n) corn bunting (*Emberiza calandra*) (also **shurl**). [supposedly from *truss* (untidy; unkempt) but this appears doubtful, cf. Icel. *trasi*: a careless, untidy person; N. *trus*: bits of rubbish; trash; + Sc. *laverock*: a lark]

tryst (n) dilemma; trouble. [negative usage of E. *tryst*: an agreement; a mutual pledge – presumably out of limitations imposed]

tully (tolli, tulli) (n) sheath knife; large wooden-handled knife. [O.N. *talguknifr*: sheath knife]

tup (n) a ram; (v) (of a ram) to copulate with a ewe. [E. & Sc. *tup*: a ram; (v) of sheep, to copulate, cf. N. & Sw. *tupp*]

tushkar (torvsker) (n) peat-cutting tool, featuring a long, thin blade (**fedder**) set at right-angles to vertical spade, thus providing two cutting edges which work simultaneously. Tushkars are made in both right and left-handed versions, cf. Shetland reel tune *Da Left-handed Tushkar*. [O.N. *torfskeri*: a peat spade – from *torf*: turf + *skera*: to cut]

tusk (n) torsk – North Atlantic, white-fleshed fish of the cod genus having a single dorsal fin, elsewhere known as cusk, **brismak** (*Brosme brosme*). [N., Sw., D. *torsk*; O.N. *thorskr*]

tuslag (n) coltsfoot (*Tussilago farfara*), the crushed leaves of which are a remedy for coughs – hence *tuslag*. [L. *tussio*: a cough]

tuss (v) cajoling murmur; *Tuss, tuss* – used to quieten agitated animals. [N. *tos*: murmer (of talk); Fær. *tosa*: to hum; to talk]

twa (twae) (adj) two; a few. [L.Sc. *twa*]

twafaald (adj) two-fold; (of a person) doubled up. [L.Sc. *twa-fald*]

twal (twal-oors) (n) a mid-morning cup of tea (not necessarily taken at 12 o'clock). *Is du hed dee twal yit?* (Have you had your morning tea yet?); twelve; (v) *Ta twal de coo* (To milk or feed a cow at midday). [equiv. to Sc. *elevenses*: mid-morning snack; morning coffee, etc.]

twalmont (n) twelve-month; a year. [Sc.]

twartbaak (n) cross-beam between rafters. [cf. O.N. *þverr*: transverse]

twarter (adj) cross-grained. [see above; also L.Sc. *thortour*: athwart]

twartle (v) to contradict; frustrate; oppose. [E.dial. *thwartle*]

twartree (adj) any number over three, though sometimes qualified as *a peerie twartree* (a few), or *a braa twartree* (a lot); (n) a group of people. *Dey wir a braa twartree inna de hall.* [L.Sc. *twa*: two (or) *tree*]

twasper (twa-spor) (v) to travel at full speed; to gallop. [Fær. & N. *tvispora*: to run at full speed]

tweet (twit, twäit) (n) heavy work; toil. [N. *tveta*: to wrangle; dispute]; (v) to cut; split; pare; chip; whittle. [N. *tveita*: to cut; split]

tweetishee (twitasedi, twit-se-dee) (interj) fie! shame upon you! [O.N. *tvi*: fie]

twig (v) to comprehend; perceive; to tug or jerk. [Sc. *twig*, Gael. *tuig*: understand]

twilt (n) a quilt. [Sc.dial. *twill*, *twilt*]

twize (adv) twice (though often 'several'); used sarcastically – *Twize A'm heard dat!*

tyoch (adj) tough. [L.Sc. *teuch*; O.Sc. *tucht*, *tewch*]

tystie (n) black guillemot (*Cepphus grylle*). [N. *teiste*]

tyugga (tjugga) (n) young razorbill (*Alca torda*). [N. *toka*: a fool; D.dial. *tokke*: to show foolish behaviour; note: words signifying 'fool' or 'foolish behaviour' are not uncommon in bird names]

T

U

udal (adj) a term applied to land held by uninterrupted succession, without any original charter and without subjection to any feudal superiority. [O.N. *ódal*: allodial property; family homestead]

udaller (n) one who holds property by udal rights. [see above]

ufsahellek (n) one of the flat, sloping stones placed to direct rain off the top of a wall, once commonly used on thatched dwellings. [O.N. *ufs*, Sw.dial. *hofs*: eaves + *hella*: a flat rock]

uggle (v) to soil; defile. [N. *ulka*: mould; dirt]

ul (**ool**) (n) owl (also **kattyuggle**). [E. owl]

ulination (n) uproar. [of O.N. *ýla* & N. *ula*: to howl]

Ultima Thule (n) Shetland (also **Thule**). [L. *Ultima Thule*, a place beyond *Thule* and therefore unlikely to be Shetland; *Thūlē*; Gr. *Thoulē*; the Greek explorer, Pytheas, stated *'Thule is a six day's sail north of Britain, and is near the frozen sea'*; the most northerly land, variously identified as Shetland, Iceland or Greenland]

unawaars (adv) unaware. [L.Sc. *unawar*]

unbiddable (adj) intractable; unmanageable. [L.Sc. *unbiddable*]

uncan (adj) unknown; strange; odd; supernatural. [Sc. *uncanny* – in similar meanings]

unction *ung-shin* (n) auction. [E. *auction* – though supposedly originally an ironical use of *unction* (sanctimonious speech) and therefore a reference to the smooth patter of the auctioneer]

undömious (adj) immense; outlandish; incalculable; unexampled. [O.N. *dæmi*: doom; judgement]

unhaandy (**oonhaandy**) (adj) awkward; not skilful; not convenient. [Sc. *unhandy* – in similar meanings]

unhonest (adj) unseemly; dishonest. [Sc. *unhonest* – in similar meanings]

unkirsen (adj) (of food) unfit for human consumption; indecent. [L.Sc. *kirsten*: decent; proper; fitting; N.dial. *kirsten*: Christian; seemly; decent – hence *un-kirsten*]

unpossible (adj) not possible. [Sc.dial. *unpossible*]

up de latest (colloq. phrase) the most recent development; in the long run.

Up-Helly-A' (**Up-Helly-Aa**) (n) originally the cessation of the Christmas celebrations 24 days after Christmas (17th January), now the last Tuesday in January and celebrated in a fire festival with a blend of Scandinavian and Celtic elements including the burning of a 'Viking galley' (ship) presided over by a troupe of Viking **guizers** under a chieftain or **jarl**. [O.N. *uppi*: at an end + *helgr*, *helgi*: holiness, the day or time to be kept holy + *allr*: ended; finished; complete – lit. 'the whole festival season at an end']

upliftet (adj) morally or spiritually elated. [E. *uplifted*]

uploppm (**upplopen**, **upplupen**) (adj) impetuous; uncontrollable. [cf. of O.N. *hlaupa*: to leap; jump; run]

uplowsin (n) thaw (also **upslaag**, **towe**). [N. *løysing* (*snjolløysing*): a thawing; breaking up of frost]

uppadoga (adj) highly excited; uneasy in mind. [O.N. *uppi dagadr*: being out at daybreak and caught unawares – originally of trolls surprised in this way and terror-struck of impending death; subsequently by transference to persons behaving anxiously or in a state of high excitement]

upslaag (**uppslag**) (n) a thaw (also **towe**, **uplowsin**). [O.N. *slá*: to strike; to loosen; let slip]

upsteer (n) same as **steer** – a bustle; stir; commotion. *Dey wir in a rycht upsteer owre d flittin*. [O.Sc. *stere*: to stir; move]

upstropolous (adj) rowdy (also **opstropolous**). [Shet. variant on E. *obstreperous*]

upswill (**uppswol**) (n) originally a commotion in the sea near land – slight surf; now a commotion or upset of any sort. [N. *svalla*, *skvalla*: to splash; wash; Sw. *skvaia*, *svalla*: to swell; roar; *svall*: heave; swell]

uptak (n) 1) a change for the worse in weather. [Fær. *taka seg upp*: of weather – to rise to a certain state; 2) comprehension; outcome. [O.N. *taka upp*: (in sense of) to understand]

ure (n) an obsolete monetary value equiv. to an ounce of silver; the value of an area of land equiv. to one-eighth of a mark (see **merk**) and associated with feu-duty. [N., Sw., D. *öre*, from L. *aureus*: a gold coin]

V

vaar (n) heed; notice; (v) to be careful; wary; attentive. *Du'll meybe tak vaar neist time.* [O.N. *varda*: to guard; watch]

valsket (adj) weak; feeble. [cf. N., Sw., D. *valen*: benumbed with cold]

vam (vamm) (n) magical influence; hypnotic spell. [N. *vam*: misfortune; disaster; O.N. *vamm*: inflicted injury]

vanlop (vanlup) (n) heavy shower of rain; downpour. [O.N. *vatnhlaup*: a rush of water]

vaarie (n) change of direction. *See du, yun yoal's taen a vaarie.* [L.Sc. *varie* (v): to change; alter]

vaddel (vadel, vaadel) (n) a shallow place in water; a ford or tidal pool. [O.N. *vadill*: shallow place in water]

vaege (v) to wander; roam; voyage. [L.Sc. *vage*, O.N. *valka*: to drift about]

vaelensi (n) turbulent, stormy weather; a violent gale. [E. *violence (violency)*]

väir (n) a great beauty; a belle; an outstanding person or animal; (also **vire**). [Ork. & Sh. of obs. orig. cf. D.dial. *vedder*: active; lively; brisk]

vand (n) knack; ability. [O.N. *vanda*: to be particular and careful; to perform something with care]

vandet (adj) having a certain form or inclination; well shaped. [see above]

varg (verg) (n) badly performed and messy work; difficult, disagreeable work. *Hit wiz a right varg*; (v) to soil; make a mess of a job. *A'll laekly joost hae t varg wi it.* [O.N. *vergr*: soiled; dirty; Icel. *verka*: to soil oneself]

variorum (varryorm) (n) a flourish or decorative feature on furniture or china; (v) to so embellish. [L.Sc. *variorum*; of L. *variorum*: of various persons – in relation to a publication or text having additional notes of various persons *cum notis variorum*]

vass (vas) (n) identifying thread tied on a lamb to pair it with its mother; (v) to attach such a mark of identification. [the root meaning is from O.N. *vasask*: to be entangled]

vatty-kabe (vat-keb, vatikeb) (n) piece of wood fixed to the gunwale of a boat and having a notch through which a fishing line runs. [O.N. *vadr*: fishing line + *keipr*: thole]

veesik (n) folk song, esp. an ancient ballad (also **visek**). [N. *visa*: folksong; ballad; O.N. *visa*: verse; stanza]

veeve (adj) bright; clearly seen; vivid. [O.Sc. *vive*: life-like]

veevly (adv) vividly. [see above]

veggel (veggil, veggwol) (n) wooden stake or post in the byre-wall to which a cow may be tethered. [O.N. *veggr*: wall + *volr*: a round stick]

vengie (n) boisterous, noisy mob, esp. of children. [cf. O.N. *vanhagr*: trouble; injury; damage; O.N. *veina*: to wail – prob. a combination of both]

venom (n) a vicious, detestable, spiteful person or animal. [Sh. usage of E. *venom*: poison]

verdi (n) an old custom or superstition. [cf. O.N. *varðlok(k)a*: incantation]

vex (v) to grieve; to feel sorry; to be disappointed. *I wis vexed du coodna win dastreen.* [Sc. *vex* (now rarely) in this meaning]

vill (n) stroke of an oar when rowing. [probably originally *bill*: to make an eddy by pulling on an oar; N. *bull*: bubble; eddy; cf. O.N. *vorr*: a pull of the oar]

vimmer (v) to tremble; shiver; quiver. [N. *vime*: state of giddiness; Icel. *vim*: stupor]

vinster (n) bacterial stomach disease in sheep, generally brought on by rich pasture (referred to as braxy elsewhere in Scotland). [Icel. & Fær. *vinstur*, N. & Sw.dial. *vinster*: the fourth stomach of a ruminant]

virdek (virdi-) (n) a small cairn of stones or other material used as a marker; a watch-hill; common placename, e.g. Virda-water, Virdifell, Virdaskule. [O.N. *varda, vardi*: a pile of stones used as a mark on a mountain top]

vire (n) a great beauty; a belle; an outstanding person or animal; (also **väir**). [Ork. & Sh. of obs. orig. cf. D.dial. *vedder*: active; lively; brisk]

virmish (v) to be excited or worked up over something (also see **fommis**). [O.N. *fimr*: nimble; agile]

virp (v) to vomit; throw up. [O.N. *verpa*: to cast, throw]

visek (n) folk song, esp. an ancient ballad (also **veesik**). [N. *visa*: folksong; ballad; O.N. *visa*: verse; stanza]

vivda (n) unsalted mutton which has been hung in a **skeo** to dry. [probably originally *vodvakjot*: meat containing muscle; O.N. *vodvi*: muscle]

vizzie (vis, vissi) (v) to make visual; to look at; to inspect. [L.Sc. *weise*, Fr. *viser*: to look at]

voar (vor) (n) spring; seedtime. [O.N. *vār*: spring; O.N. *várvinna*: preparing of the soil in spring; also *ware, wār*: Sc. and dialect springtime]

voe (n) a narrow sea inlet, often quite long; common in placenames, e.g. Ronas Voe, Dales Voe – hence 'Vaas' which was incorrectly interpreted as 'Walls' owing to a misunderstanding when the word was taken as Scots 'waas' (walls) in late 17th century. [N. *vag*, Icel. *vogur*: bay; inlet]

vod (adj) (of houses) untenanted, abandoned, derelict. [L.Sc. *voyd, void*; O.Sc. *vode*: empty]

vord (ward) (n) high hill, esp. with cairn or watch-tower (also **wart**), now only in placenames, e.g. Saxa Vord. [O.N. *vardi*: heap of stones, as a mark; cairn; O.N. *vardhald*: watch-tower]

vyalskit (valsket) (adj) lacking in handiness or energy; slack in one's movements. [derivative of obs. Sh. *valin*: benumbed; fumbling; N. Sw. and D. *valen*: benumbed with cold]

vyld (adj) vile; loathsome. [L.Sc. *vile, vyld*]

vynd (n) a skill; talent; knack. [O.N. *vandr*: particular; *vanda*: to be particular and careful in performing something]

vyndless (vandless) (adj) lacking in care and ability; clumsy. [O.N. *vandr*: particular; *vanda*: to be particular; to perform something with care – hence *vandr*-less: careless]

W

waa (n) wall. [L.Sc. *waa*]

waa-back (n) a flat-backed paraffin lamp suitable to hang on a wall. [L.Sc.*wa-back*]

waageng (n) a lingering taste or flavour; an after-taste. [L.Sc. *wa-gang*]

waaken (wakn, wauken) (v) to awake. [O.N. *vakna*: to awake; L.Sc. *wauken*; O.Sc. *walkyn*]

waakrife (adj) unable to sleep; insomnia. [L.Sc. *waukrife*, O.Sc. *walkryfe*: wakeful]

waand (wand) (n) fishing-rod. [O.N. *vondr*: a wand; switch; L.Sc. *wand*: fishing-rod]

waar (var) (adj) aware; careful; wary; attentive. [O.N. *varda*: to guard; watch; N. *vara*: to warn; to heed; take care]

waar (n) broadleafed seaweed; kelp (*Laminaria*) which grows beyond the low-water mark in 8 to 30 metres depth of sea, as opposed to **tang** which grows in shallower water, although the words would appear to be interchangeable. [L.Sc. *wair, ware, (se-ware)*: seaweed, esp. of type used for manure]

waari (adj) covered in kelp. *A warri-baa* (a buoy covered in seaweed). [see above]

waaverin laef (n) the large-leafed plantain (*Plantago major*).

wabbit (adj) tired out; feeble. [Sc. *wabbit* (orig. *wobart*): feeble]

wadder (n) weather (chief topic of idle conversation); (v) to get to windward of. *Ta wadder de skerry*; (adj) to windward. *Shö's owre weel gyaan ta wadder.* [O.N. *vedr*; E. *weather*]

wadder-head (n) a bank of clouds, seen as portent to a change in weather. *Nort sooth is a drooth, aest wast fur a blast.* [Sc. *weather-head*]

Wadensday (n) Wednesday (also **Widensday**). [O.Sc. *Wodinsday*]

wadmel (n) thick woollen cloth once used for paying taxes. [O.N. *vadmal*: thick home-made woollen material]

wae (n) woe; (adj) sorrowful. [Sc. *wae*]

wael (wale) (n) choice; (v) to choose; select. [cf. O.N. *val*: choice; selection; O.Sc. *wale, waile*: to select]

waesome (adj) causing woe; sorrow. [Sc. *waesome*]

waev (n) swivel-catch to fasten a door. [Sw.dial. *veiv*: (revolving) wooden handle of a door]

waff (n) a faint (disagreeable) odour. [Sc. *waff*]

wairin (n) a strap of wood fixed to the ribs of a boat on which the thwarts rest. [Du., Flem. *wegering, wijgering*]

wak (n) proportion or share. *Du's got dee wak.* [E. *whack*: share]

wan (pron, adj) one (also **ean**); (v) to wane, as the tide or moon; (pt of) **win**. *He wan de race.* [Sc. *wan; ane*]

wan- (negative prefix) un-, denoting a lack, insufficiency, as in *wantrivven* = ill-thriven; *wanrestit* = unrested (see below). [O.N. *van*: un-]

wanless (wanliss, wanlos) (adj) hopeless; having no prospects. [O.N. *vánlauss*, N. *vonlaus*: disheartened; dejected]

wan-paece (n) strife; trouble. *I wiss him wanpaece for his ill-tricket capers.* [O.N. *van-*: un- + peace]

wanrest (n) restless; unease. [cf. *unrest*; O.Sc.*wanrest*]

wantrivven (adj) ill-thriven; puny; stunted. [O.Sc. *wan-thryvin*]

wanwirt (n) a thing of very little value; a trifle. [O.N. *vanvirda*: disdain; shame; L.Sc. *wanworth*: slight value]

wap (n) a blow; (v) to throw; wind around; to swing one's arms when walking. [L.Sc. *wap*]

waptree (n) the wooden rod connecting treadle to axle on a spinning wheel. [cf. N. *vapla*: to move to and fro + *tree*: any structure made of wood]; also the crank-handle for a car.

warback (warbak) (n) the larva of the warble-fly (*Hypoderma bovis*) or bot-fly (*Gasterophilus intestinalis*) which hatches from eggs laid on the legs of animals from where the larva makes its way under the skin, emerging as 'warbles' or unsightly lumps; the swelling itself. [N. *vere*: larva, in the skin of animals; E. *warble*: the small hard swelling caused by the warble fly]

wark (n) work; fuss; to-do; goings-on. [O.Sc. *wark*]

warn (n) warrant; attest. *I'll warn du's no heard de last o dis.* [E. *warrant*]

wart (n) lookout on a hilltop; the hill itself; (also **vord, ward**); used in placenames, e.g. Ward (Wart) of Laxfirth, Ward (Wart) of Scousburgh. [O.N. *vardi*: heap of stones, as a mark; cairn; O.N. *vardhald*: watch-tower]

waster (v) to go towards the west; (adj) lying towards the west; common in placenames, e.g. Wasterhoose. [L.Sc. *waster*; O.Sc. *westir*]

wastird (n) the western part of a district. [L.Sc. *wastert*: westward]

wat (v) know; an assertive declaration in phrases, e.g. *I'll wat du'll no fancy yun!*; To be sure!; I can tell you! (also **weel I wat**). [O.Sc. *wat(e)*: know; L.Sc. *wat*]

watertraa (wattertra) (n) heartburn (also **brunt rift**). [*water* + E. *throe*: a pang; pain; cf. Sc. *thraw*: throw; throw-up]

wavvel (v) to totter in an unsteady motion. *He's gyaan wavvlin aboot.* [O.N. *vafla* (v): to walk with tottering gait; L.Sc. *wavel*: to be in motion to and fro]

weeg (waeg, weig) (n) kittiwake (*Rissa tridactya*). [imitative of the bird's call 'kitty-*weeik*']

week (n) wick of a lamp; corner of the mouth. [L.Sc. *week*]

weel (adj, adv) well. *Is du weel?* (Are you well?); *Weel, weel, du keens best* (Well, well, you know best). [L.Sc. *weel*; O.Sc. *wele, weill*]

weel I wat assertive declaration – well I declare. [see **wat**]

weet (n) wet; a drink; rain, drizzle. *Hit's come a weet day*; (v) to make wet. *Ta weet de bairn's heid* – drink a toast to a new-born child. [O.Sc. *wete*; L.Sc. *weet*]

weety (adj) rainy; drizzly. [Sc.]

wedder (n) castrated male sheep. [E. *wether*]

weird fate; fortune; destiny. *Ta dree a weary weird* (To suffer a depressing fate). [L.Sc. *weird*; O.Sc. *werd*]

wengle (wenkl) (v) to meander, as a stream. [O.N. *venda*: to turn; N. *vengla*: to flutter; to fly veeringly in unsteady motion; L.Sc. *wingle*: to zig-zag]

wenglit (winglet) (adj) 1) lean, tall, ungainly person; 2) winding; twisting; given to bending. [1] cf. L.Sc. (Aberdeen) *wheeber*: lean; tall; however the etymology of this and the previous word appear to have become intermingled in regard to 2) cf. L.Sc. *wankish*: twist; interlace; entwine]

wer (worrse, wurse) (adj) worse. *Shö wiz far wer/worrse/wurse as him at sailin*. [L.Sc. *war*, *wars*; M.E. *wurse*; O.E. *wyrsa*; O.N. *verre*]

wha (pron) who. [L.Sc. *wha*]

whaal (hwal) (n) whale. [O.N. *hvalr*; L.Sc. *whaal*]

whaanious (adj) extremely large; huge. [orig. obs.]

whaap (whaup) (n) curlew (*Numenius arquata*). [L.Sc. *whaup*, poss. imit. of the bird's cry and cogn. with *whelp*: a puppy]

whaar (kwaar, whaur) (adv) where. [O.N. *hvar*: where; whither]

whaarm (hwarm) (n) rim of the eyelid. [O.N. *hvarmr*: the eye-lid]

whaasay (whaarsay, whaarsaymeko) (conj) as if to say; (n) a pretence. [L.Sc. *wha say*, also *whaarsay*]

whaase (pron) whose. *Whaase dug is yun?* [M.E., O.Sc. *quas*; *quhais*]

whaasel (whaasle, hwasel) (n) asthmatic wheezing; (v) to wheeze. [O.N. *hvæsa*: to hiss; whistle]

whalp (hwalp) (n) a whelp; puppy. [O.N. *hvelpr*, L.Sc. *whalp*: a whelp]

whan (adv) when. *Whan's dee midder comin ta stay?* [Sc.]

wharve (hwarf, hwerf) (v) to turn over or rake together mown hay. [O.N. *hverfa*: to turn; N. *kverva*: to turn hay; also *kvervla*: to spread hay]

whatten (whattna, whatn) (adj) (interrog) what kind of. *Whatten an onkerry is dis?* [L.Sc. *whatten*, *whatna*; O.Sc. *quhaten*]

wheef (hwiff, kwiff) (n) a swipe; a blow; a box on the ears; a whiff; agility; power. *Der a göd wheef in him*; (v) to puff; to inhale, as on a pipe or cigarette. [L.Sc. *wheefle*: a puff; a blow; also cf. Sc. *whiff*: to aim at, and fail to hit, a ball; N. *kufsa*: to bustle; run about]

wheefer (n) a large object (also *eever*). [cf. O.N. *ærinn*, *yfrinn*: excessive; abundant; very large; also S.dial. *övra*: to increase in vigour and growth]

wheeflication (n) excuse. [cf. L.Sc. *qualificate*: conditional; under certain limitations]

wheelbaands (n) thin intestines of sheep, once dried and used as driving-belts on spinning-wheels, also referred to as **wheel-guts**. [O.Sc. *quheill-band*]

wheesht (interj) hush! Be quiet. [Sc.dial. *whisht*, *wheesht*]

whenk (hwink) (n) sudden sideways movement or glance. [N. *kvima*, *kvimsa*, Sw.dial. *hvimsa*: to fidget; bustle about; Icel. *hvima*: to move quickly and unsteadily; to look round slyly]

whet (quet) (v) quit; stop; (also **white** in pr t). [L.Sc. *white*: quit]

whid (hwid) (n) a quick, darting motion; a whim. [O.N. *hvida*: a fit; attack; a squall of wind; O.Sc. *quhyd*: a squall]

whilk (n) the sound of swallowing; a gulp; (v) to gulp; (also **clunk, kwilk**). [Sw.dial. *kulka, kolka, kålka*, D. *kulke*, Fær. *kulka*: to gulp; to drink in high draughts]

whillie (n) the smallest of fishing boats; a skiff – usually 2-seater. [cf. N. *whelli*: underbark; skin (of potato); O.N. *hvelja*: whaleskin; E. *wherrie*]

whin (conj) when. [Sc. *whan*, *whin*]

whirk (whark, hwark, kwerk, kwirk) (n) the instep; corresponding part of a boot or shoe; (also see **yarken**). [O.N. *kverk*: the angle below the chin; the throat; also the sole of the foot; Icel. *kverk*: an angle; the innermost edge of a curve]

whiss (whissen) (v) to question; to quiz; cross-examine. [E. *quiz*: interrogate]

white kaitrins (n) grass-of-parnassus (*Parnassia palustris*).

whitrit (whitterit, whitrat) (n) stoat (*Mustela erminea*). [L.Sc. *whitrat*: (white-throat) O.Sc. *quhytred*]

whummel (hwuml, hwumel) (v) to capsize; overturn. [O.N. *hvelva*, N. *kvelva*: to turn a hollow object bottom up; Sc. *quhemle*]

wi (prep) by; with; of. [L.Sc. *wi'*, O.N. *vid*: with]

wid (n) wood. [O.N. *vidr*]

widdie (n) in phrase: *Ta play de widdie wi it* – bring to grief; the laying waste of a plan – *De wadder played de widdie wi wir trip sooth*. [L.Sc. *widdie*: willow canes or other flexible wood that can be twisted into rope; iron chains; the gallows rope – *cheat the widdie* (escape hanging)]

Widensday (n) Wednesday (also **Wadensday**). [O.Sc. *Wodinsday*]

widdergaets (waddergaets) (adv) counter-clockwise; contrary to the sun's course; (also see **sungaets**). [Sc. *withershins*, O.Sc. *widder*, O.E. *wither*: against; contrary + O.Sc. *gate*: way]

widderin (n) canine distemper. [presumably so named for its withering effect]

widderwis (adj) contrariwise; awkward; perverse; (see **widdergaets**). [O.E. *wither*: against; contrary + *wise*: ways]

widge (v) to fidget; shift uneasily. [of same root as **wig** (see below)]

wig (hwig) (v) to wriggle; shake; wag; move to and fro. *He wis wiggin on his feet*. [N. *kvika*: to wriggle; be restless; Icel. *hvika*, Sw.dial. *hveka*: to wriggle; waver]

wig-at-de-waa (n) a hanging pendulum clock. [Sc. *wag-at-the-wa*]

wilkie (wolki) (n) razorbill (*Alca torda*). [O.N. *alka*: the auk; Icel. & Fær. *álka*]

will (v) to become lost; go astray; (pt) **wilt**; (pp) **wilt**. [O.N. *villr*; Sc. *will*, *wull* (adj & adv): at a loss; astray]

willna (v) will not. [Sh. variant on Sc. *winna*: will not]

willsom (willisome) (adj) misleading; that which leads one astray. [O.N. *villusamr*; L.Sc. *wilsome*]

W

win (v) to go; to obtain; to earn; (pt) **wan**; (pp) **wun**. ('*Send help ta da needy whaarever dey be, Bit I canna win, sae You needna send me.*' – *Bül My Sheep*, Rhoda Bulter.)

winderfil (adj) causing admiration. *Shö's winderfil for her age*. [E. *wonderful*: admirable]

windlin (n) wisp; bundle, esp. of straw. [L.Sc. but also cf. O.N. *vindli*: a wisp; N. *vindel*: twisted tuft; N. *vondul*: a bundle of hay or straw]

windspeil (windspell) (n) a windmill; wind turbine. [cf. O.N. *spjel*: to thrust out arms and legs; der. N. *spjelka*: to make awkward movements with the arms]

winglit (adj) see **wenglet**

winnish (v) to waste away; pine; become emaciated. [L.Sc. *wainish*, form of E. *vanish*]

wint (adj) to wish; desire; be accustomed or inclined to. *He wis aye wint t geng d sam wye*. [extension of E. *want*: to wish; desire]

wip (v) to bind; whip round with string; coil; entangle, ravel; (also **wup**, **wupple**). [N. *vipla*: to entwine; wind; plait]

wir (adj) our. *Wir Laureen* – said of a family member; also we are (we're). *Wir aye blyde ta see dee* (We're always glad to see you); and occasionally – were. *Wir dy bairns playin wi wir dug?* (Were your children playing with our dog?) [Sc. *wir*; *wur*; *wer*]

wird (n) word. [Sc.]

wir eens (n) one's immediate family. *Wir eens göd t Aberdeen at de helli*; also **der eens** their family members and **dy eens** your family members. [Sc.]

wires (waers) (n) knitting needles, made of steel and pointed at both ends. When knitting Fair Isle, Shetlanders use three such needles to create a circular, seamless garment (elsewhere knitters commonly use four needles). [Sc. *wire*: a knitting needle; O.Sc. *weir*]

wirhoos(e) (wiroos) (n) our house (also **wirs**). [Sc.]

wirlie (wirli, worli) (n) gap in a fence or wall through which a stream flows. Common croft name where such a conjunction occurs. [O.N. *árhlid*]

wirry (v) to worry; (of an animal) to harrass or attack; (of an object) to choke. *Du'll wirry on yun bacon*. [L.Sc. *worry, wirry*]

wirrieation (n) an altercation between dogs; a fight. [see above]

wirs (wirse) (poss adj) ours; (n) our house (see **wirhoos**). [Sc.]

wirsells (pron) ourselves. [Sc.]

wirset (worsit) (n) knitting yarn made from wool (also **yorn**); (adj) made of wool – *a wirset joopie*. [E. *worsted*: a type of knitted yarn originally spun in Worstead, Norfolk, consisting of two strands of wool lightly twisted together – the traditional method of spinning Shetland wool]

wirsom (wirsam) (n) discharge from a sore; also *wirsam-midder* – the core of a boil. [L.Sc. *wursom*, O.E. *worsm*: pus; Fær. *vágsmódir*, Sw.dial. *varmor*: core of a boil]

wirt (n) worth. *Hit's no wirt de budder* (It's not worth the bother). [E. *worth*]

wish (v) to wash; (pt) **wösh**; (pp) **wishen**. [Sh. form of E. *wash*]

wiss (v) to wish. [Sc. variant on E.*wish*]

wit (n) sense; intelligence. *Hae wit*; (v) to know. *I wit dat*; **witted** *He witted shö wisna dere* (he had it to be/it was his opinion that she wasn't there). [N. *vett*: to know]

witchie klokk (n) a large beetle (see also **hointiclock**, **hundiclock**). [O.S. *clok*: a beetle; S.dial. *klocka*: a beetle]

witteens (witted) (n) information; (v) to insist; express. [N. *vitende*: knowledge; L.Sc. *witter*]

witter (n) barb on a hook; a tangled mass. *It gied in a witter*; (v) to be caught, as on a hook; to buckle; to tangle. [Mid.Du. *wederhake*: barb]

wiz (pron) us. *You Tell Wiz!* former Radio Shetland programme inviting listeners' complaints; (v) (pl of) was. *Da bairns wiz playing ida burn*; (also **wir**).

wizzen (n) food passage in the throat; oesophagus; gullet. [L.Sc. *wizzen*, variation on E. *gizzard*]

woollie-horse (n) an adjustable wooden frame, also referred to as a **jumper-board**, on which to stretch or shape a finished knitted jumper or cardigan to correct size; also used to reconstitute an old garment which may have shrunk, or to prevent shrinkage; (see **jimp**; also **dress**). (Produced in a number of patented designs the woollie-horse appears to be a Shetland innovation although the concept of dressing knitted garments in this manner is now universally acknowledged as desirable for certain yarn types.)

wösh (v) (pt of) wash; (pp) **wöshen**. [E. *wash*]

wrasle (wrastle) (v) to struggle; to strive; wrestle. [L.Sc. *warsle*]

wrat (v) (pt of) write (also **wret**). [Sh. form of E. *wrote*]

wrest (v) to sprain; wrench a muscle or joint. [N. *reista*: to twist; L.Sc. *wrest, wreist*: a sprain]

wrestin-treed (n) black wool tied with special knots round a sprain and accompanied by incantations to effect a cure. [N. *reista*: to twist; L.Sc. *wresting-thread, wrestin-string*]

wret (v) (pt of) write (also **wrat**). [see **wrat**]

wrowt (wrocht, wrouht) *w-rocht* (n) (pt of work) worked. *He wrocht on de rodds*; (also **rowt, rocht**). [E. *wrought*]

wupple (wupl, wuppel, wup) (v) to become entangled about the legs; to walk in an unsteady manner. *He göd wupplin alang de röd*; (also see **wip**). [L.Sc. *wipple*: to wind; twist]

wye (wey) (n) way. [L.Sc. *wey*: way]

wylk (n) periwinkle (*Littorina littorea*); whelk; (also see **buckie**). [L.Sc. *wulk*: whelk]

W

Y

ya (adv) yes; affirmative – with a tendency to iterate – *Ya, ya*; (also **yae**). [N., D., Sw., Fær. *ja*]

yaag (v) to fault-find; nag. [Fær. *jagga*: grumble; find fault; nag]

yaager (yagger) (n) small trader; pedlar. [Du. (*haring*) *jager*: a Dutch herring-fleet tender which brought stores and equipment from Holland to the fleet (16th cent.) and took back the catch. Enterprising Shetlanders clandestinely sold fish and other produce to the Dutch *yaggers* at higher prices than they otherwise got under their obligations to the laird]

yaarm (v) to whimper; bleat, as a sheep; (also **nyaarm**). [O.N. *jarma*: to bleat; Fær. *mjarra*: to whimper; mew; bleat]

yackle (yackel) (n) a molar tooth. [N.dial. *jakle*, O.N. *jaxl*: a molar]

yae (adv) yes; affirmative – with a tendency to iterate. *Yae, yae! Weel, weel!* (jokingly) yes, certainly! (also **ya**). (O.N. *já, já! vel, vel!*]

yalder (jalder) (n) loud, continuous barking; (v) to make a loud, raucous noise, esp. of a dog barking when in pursuit. [O.N. *hjaldr*: din; clangour; chatter; talk; N.dial. *hjal*: a scream; yell]

yalk (n) a yelp; bark; (v) to yelp; bark, as a dog. [imit. of the sound – E. *yelp*]

yallicrack (n) an uproar; commotion; a noisy quarrel. [N. *jala*: to shout; yell; cry; L.Sc. *yaul*: to yell + L.Sc. *crack*: animated chatter; gossip; talk]

yallows (n) jaundice in sheep. [cf. E. *yellow* (jaundiced)]

yallowsis (n) an illness in grazing animals caused by eating large quantities of St John's Wort (*Hypericum perforatum*). [so named for the yellow flower of the plant and not related to symptoms]

yammalds (n) twins. [O.N. *jafnaldri, jafnaldra*: of equal age]

yamse (adj) greedy; eager for; enthusiastic. [N. *jafsa*: to snap at something with the mouth, but assimilated with N. *jamsa*: to chew; munch]

yap (v) chatter incessantly – imit. of a yapping dog.

yarfast (jardfast, yerfast) (n) straw rope for securing a hay-stack; (v) to 'earthfasten'; tie down anything in danger of being blown away. [O.N. *jarda*: to earth; bury + O.N. *festa*: to fasten]

yarg (jarg) (n) incessantly complaining or wrangling; (v) to complain vociferously; to carp. [Sw.dial. *jarga*: to chew something tough; to grumble; raise objections]

yark (jark) (n) a grab; tug; a gulp of drink; a large bite; a large person. *For siccan a yark o a boy*; (v) to push; jerk; grab; tug; to snap with the mouth; (also see **wherk**). [E.dial. *yerk*: jerk; tug]

yarken (jarkin) (n) the instep; space between thumb and forefinger; side-stitch of a shoe. [O.N. *jarki*: outside edge of the sole of the foot; Icel., Fær. *jarki*: edge of the sole of the foot]

yarken ellishon (n) a shoemaker's awl (also **ellishon**). [O.N. *jarki*: outside edge of the sole of the foot + O.N. *alr*: awl + L.Sc. *shoon*: shoes]

yarn winds (n) adjustable device to hold a hank of yarn while it is being wound into a ball. [D. *garnrulle*: yarn reel; N. *garnvinde*; Fær. *garnvindari*: yarn reel; wool winder; Icel. *garnvinda*: swift; E. *swift*]

yarta (jarta) (n) properly, the heart, now a term of endearment. *Child of my heart*; *peerie yarta*. [O.N. *hjarta*: the heart]

yasp (jasp) (adj) active; eager; lively. [N. *jabba*: to run; trip lightly]

yatlen (yetlin) (n) cast-iron kettle or griddle; tallow candles formed by repeated dipping of wick in melted tallow; (adj) of cast metal; strong; thoroughbred, esp. of blood; rich red, as newly shed blood; [L.Sc. *yetlin*: article made of cast-iron; deriv. of *yat*: to pour; gush, as *yatlin bluid*]

yatt (v) to pour in a large quantity. [see **yark (jark)**: a large draught]

yatter (jatter) (v) to jabber; chatter; carp on about something. [D. *jadre, hjadre*: to jabber; tattle; Sw.dial. *jatträ*: to babble; lisp]

yield (adj) barren (of land and unproductive animals); not giving milk; (v) to stop milking a pregnant cow prior to calving. [L.Sc. *yeld, eild*, O.Sc. *yheld*, O.N. *geldr*: dry of milk]; Origin of island name Yell, due to the extensive area of unproductive land.

yikka (jiker) (v) to snarl, as a dog. [cf. Sw.dial. *järga*: to fret; grumble; to raise objections]

yird (jard) (v) to bury in earth. [O.N. *jarda*: to earth; bury]

yirn (v) to curdle – the effect of adding rennet and heat to milk. [O.Sc. *yirne*: to curdle]

yirnin (n) rennet. [O.E. *rinnen*, E. *earning*: rennet]

yirnin girse (n) common butterwort (*Pinguicula vulgaris*) used as a substitute for rennet (also see **ekkelgirse**). [*yirnin* (see above) + *girse*, O.Sc. *girse*, E. *grass*]

yittel (n) a gland, esp. of the neck; swollen gland. [N.dial. *eitel*; Icel. Fær. *eitill*]

yoag (joag) (n) horse mussel (*Modiolus modiolus*). [N. *odskjel, ovskjel*]

yoal (n) a six-oared boat, of lighter and more rakish build than a **sixern**, having two masts and a jib sail and capable of being rowed by three men with two oars apiece; popular in competitive racing at regattas. [L.Sc. *yole*; O.Sc. *joall*; E. *yawl*; O.N. *jolle*; Sw. *jolle*]

yock (n) a grab; (v) to grab; grasp firmly; set upon. *Shö made a yock at him as he gied by*. [L.Sc. *yoke*: neck-harness, but in sense of to collar; grab; O.Sc. *yock*]

yooder (joder, yudder) (n) udder. [O.N. *júgr*: udder]

yorn (Yell) (n) knitting yarn (also **wirset**).

yowe (n) a ewe; female sheep. [Sc. *yowe*; O.Sc. *yhow*]

yöl (n) yule(tide); the festive season; Christmas; the yule dram. [O.N. *jōl*; E. *yule, yuletide*]

yölgirse (n) meadowsweet (*Filipendula ulmaria*). [cf. O.N. *jóll*; N. *jol*: wild angelica]

yuck (n) an itch; an urge; (v) to itch. [Sc. *yuke, yuck, youk*: to itch, cf. M.Du. *jeuken*]

Y

yucky (adj) itchy. [Sc. *yuky*, *yucky*: itchy]

yuggle (jugl, jugla) (n) an owl (also **ul, kattyuggle**). [O.N. *ugla*: owl]

yuglet (joglitt) (adj) colour description applied to sheep which have white circles round the eyes and darker bodies, or converse. [Fær. *eyglittur*; O.N. *auga*: eye + *litr*: coloured]

yulter (yolter, julter) (n) edible sea-urchin or shell thereof (*Echinus esculentus*); (also **scaddiman's heid**). [Icel., Fær., N. *igulker*]

yun (pron) that; the thing you know of (interchangeable with **dat, datn**). *Yun coo is gotten a host* (That cow has got a cough). [Sc. and Sc.dial. *yon*]

yundru (adj) at a distance; over there. [E. *yonder*]

Z

Zetland (n) Shetland; former official nomenclature – ZCC (Zetland County Council), now SIC (Shetland Islands Council).

Tabu (taboo) words used at sea by the deep-sea or 'haaf' fishermen

THE practice of using tabu words at sea arose out of superstitions that go back into antiquity and are related to placating pagan sea gods – amongst other things. Strictly speaking these words were not 'tabu' in themselves but rather were the words used to avoid the tabu of 'land' words when at sea. Not surprisingly, ministers of religion and all things pertaining to them came in for special attention. It can be seen that almost all of these words are of Norn origin, giving rise to the observation that the demise of the language throughout Shetland is closely related to the cessation of haaf fishing, an activity undertaken by a majority of menfolk up until the mid- to late 19th century. Indeed, of over 420 words listed here, only 25 are not of Norn extraction. It is as if freed from the shackles of the land with all its restrictions and subservience to the Scots crown, the fishermen were at liberty to speak the language of their hearts. It is very probable the last place Norn words were being strung together with any semblance of fluency was at the deep-sea fishing in an open boat over 150 years ago. Having said that, it is equally likely that the words carried some deeper significance the meaning of which is lost in the mists of time.

Most of the words are nouns and many relate to animals or objects that have been left behind on land but cannot be called by their 'land' names. Other words have to do with activities associated with fishing and the fish themselves. These words in particular (over 160) give the strongest indication that the whole business of fishing was surrounded with a belief that the sea was a hostile environment in which forces beyond the control of the fishermen must always be treated with special deference – this belief even extending to the collection of bait on shore when a fisherman might give the indirect answer *sjusamillabakka* (between the shore and the ebb) when asked where he had been.

It will be seen there are several different words for some animals, especially the pig, mouse, horse and cat. This is partly to do with the sense that the speaker wishes to convey, for instance a mouse may be called **grokoll** (*the grey-headed one*) or **fotlin** (*the light-footed one*) or it may indicate a regional difference – Unst fishermen did not necessarily use the same words as Foula fishermen. What they had in common was the belief that one must not use 'land' words as it was unlucky to do so. If a mistake was made one might need to 'touch cold iron' to avert disaster.

With the demise of haaf fishing went much that was colourful and curious about Shetland's past, although there seems to have been a desire to keep at least some of the quaint words alive, leading to 21st century Shetlanders using words that were once the exclusive domain of deep-sea fishermen. Examples include **dratsi**, *the otter* and **russi**, *a horse*. In other words it may be said the tabus have finally been broken – or have they?

The following words are sourced exclusively from Jakob Jakobsen's *An Etymological Dictionary of the Norn Language in Shetland*. They do not necessarily represent all that is known on the subject. There are a number of other words associated exclusively with the deep-sea fishing – words related to fishing grounds, landmarks and the industry of fishing generally. These were not tabu words as such and would have been used as readily on land as at sea and therefore are not included here.

Note that there is no letter 'C' in the alphabetic list which is in keeping with the dominant Norn content – there being no 'C' in the Norse alphabet of the time.

English nouns represented by multiple tabu words in Norn: (see following Norn list for etymology)

basket (fishing-basket) bjesnek; skalv

boat (ship) basek; far; farlek; sjar

boot (sea-boot) ler; lør; stafalir; stenglin; stivalir

buoy brill; kolla; pilen; pinnek; pinni; ponni; pulgin; roller

cat drinj; firfoden; foder; fodin; fudin; jarmek; jarmer; kisek; kisert; klurer; mjawi; njarm; njau; njauer; rami; sidi; skavin; skavansi; snistel; snister; spjaler; vender; venga; vengla; voler; winsi; wissek, wissert, yarmer

clergyman beni-mon; hoiden; loder; predikanter; prestengolva; sjuski; søski; uppstander

cod galti; knabi; knavi; sjukkola

cow brølek; burek; dronjer; halin; nut; snult

dog beni; benibiter; bjenek; raeki; sjuski; søski

fish fisk; fusk

fire (and associated words) aber; agl; birtek; brenna; brenner; burt; eld; emek; fona; furin; hildin; ilder

fishing (hook, line and sinker) arvi; brus; damp; gred; griper; hadin; kavi; molek; nokki; pikki; redskab; sandkorn; snør; wolhard

hen (cock) flokner; hjonsa; hunek; jappi; jonsa; klur; kokrin; kriel; skrofer; skrogin; skrovin; tunskerri; yappie

halibut baldin; drengi; glaffi; keita; lager; leger; pigvar; plousi

horse (mare) gjonger; heslin; hobiter; hokken; horda; niggi; pertek; russa; russi; sjalti; skjud; skjut; snegger

hut (booth, fishermen's booth) habagoitlek; hoid; hoslek

ling hulefer; hwidi; longa-fish; mamsa; skudra

mackerel fogri; rolli

mouse bisper; bohonnin; fitlek; fitlin; fitnik; fittek; foitlin; fotek; fotlin; ifetlek; grokoll; murin; rinner; skerdin; skirrek; skjorrin; sma'-fit; vokonnin

otter birren; borren; bruni; dafi; dratsi; drillaskøvi; fibi; fibbi; halin; lotage; tik

pig (swine) birsi; dronger; galti; gronter; grontjel; grundswirl; harki; hjosi; moddin; moddvit; pobi-rontli; pottisidna

sea (waves and the fishing grounds) brimtod; dekk; festo; flör; hollost; landbrim; ljog; log; mar; millabakka; sjusamillabakka; veda

sheep (ram) grømek; jarmek; jarmer; klovin; radien; rodin; skobback; skobbek; skupi; skupek

wind daggastø; gro; gula; odestø; stora-broken; stø

woman (wife) fru; halihwiffer; hemelt; hospra; hosper; hosten; kuna; moia; nigda

Norn to English tabu words (with etymology)

A

aber (v) sharpen up; liven. *Aber op de birtek* (get the fire blazing by poking it); (also **agl**). [Sw.dial. *abra, appra*: set to work energetically]

aftag (Fetlar) (n) mitten; sea mitten. [orig. obs.]

agglovan (aglavin) (n) fire tongs. [N. *agge, ange*: notch; tooth; fork of a cleft tool + O.N. *klovi*: forked implement]

agl (agel, aggel) (v) to get to blaze. *Agel up de birtek*; (also **aber**). On a long sea journey an **eld** or fire-kettle was carried in which there were live coals to be used for cooking purposes. [N. *alka*: to irritate]

anklovan (n) tongs (see **agglovan**).

anti (n) oil-lamp. [Fær. *ana*: to shine or burn brightly]

apateg (Yell) (n) mitten; sea mitten. [orig. obs.]

arm (n) tail-end; end. [O.N. *arm*: extremity; extreme edge]

arvi (n) end; broken end of fishing line. [see above]

B

baldi used in reference to ling – *baldi her*: close its eyes (when protruding from its head). [see below]

baldin (n) the halibut. [O.N. *baldinn*: powerful; headstrong; Lapp. *baldes*]

basek (n) ship. [prob. deriv. of *basel* – N., Icel., Sw. *basa*: to splash, etc.]

beni (benibiter) (n) bone-biter (dog). [Lapp. *baena*, Finn. *peni*: dog]

beni mon (n) clergyman (see **bønus**). [N. *boena-madr*: man of prayer]

berel (n) a basket; creel. [O.N. *berill*: vat to contain liquid]

bigg (biggin) (n) barley (partly preserved as a tabu term but also still used in placenames today, e.g. Buggerslit, Papa Stour.) [O.N. *bygg*]

birren (borren) (n) the otter. [N. *borre*: proud, harsh fellow; *byrren* (adj): angry; fierce (of animals)]

birs (birsi) (n) pig; swine; (lit. 'the bristling one'). [L.Sc. *birs*: bristle; *birsy*: bristling]

birtek (n) fire (also **brenna**). [O.N. *birta, birti*: clearness; light; shining]

bisper (n) mouse (also **bohonnin, fitlek, fitlin, fitrik, fittek, faitlin**). [N. *bispur*: tramp; knave]

bjenek (n) a dog (also see **beni, benibiter**). [Sw. Lapp. *piædnak*: a dog]

bjesnek (n) fishing basket. [N. *bidne*: a vessel (cup, pail)]

bjorg (n) house, esp. a manse. [O.N. *borg*: a fortified place; castle]

blink (n) a flash; a gleam. *I see a blink* – I catch a gleam (of a fish below the surface of the water). [D. *glippe* (v): to gleam; flash]

blobelti (n) peat; prob. *blue-belti* (very hard peat). [Icel. *böllti*: iron or leaden ball]

bloda (n) (dirty) bilge water. [N. *bloti*: dampness; liquid]

bohonnin (n) a mouse, ironical application of *búhundr* (watch dog).

bova (n) a bed; box-bed. [Icel. *pauf*. Change of 'p' to 'b' is not unusual in Shet. Norn (Jakobsen)]

brenna (brenner) (n) fire; blazing fire in a hearth; (also **birtek**). [O.N. *brenna*: burning fire]

bri (v) sharpen. *Bri de skøni* (Sharpen the knife). [O.N. *bryna*: to sharpen]

brill (n) buoy made of hide; fishing buoy. [Fær. *prilla*: an animal skin]

brimtod (adj) sound of breaking surf. [N. *brimtot*]

brolli (brui) (n) brother – used in jocular address. [Sw.dial. *brui*: trolls; witchcraft]

bruni (n) the otter – the brown one.

brus (n) a sinker; the lead on the end of a hand line. [cf. Icel. *brúsi*: a jar]

brø (v) to tar. *Brø de far* (Tar the boat). [O.N. *bræda*: to tar]

brølek (n) a cow (lit. 'the lowing one') (also **burek**). [O.N. *baula*: a cow – from (v) *baula*: to bellow]

bunki (n) reel on gunwale over which fishing line is hauled. [N. *bunke*: roller in a loom]

burek (n) a cow. [(see above); N. *bura*: to bellow]

burt (n) fire. [see **birtek**]

bø (n) a churn. [Icel. *byoa*: a vessel; tub; Fær. *byoi*: a milk pail]

bønhus (n) church. [O.N. *bænhús*: house of prayer]

D

dafi (n) otter (also see **dratsi**). [from N. *dava*: to saunter – deriv. O.N. *dof*: loin; the hind part of animals]

dag (n) mitten. [orig. obs. see **afatag**]

daggastø (n) wind with rain. [O.N. *dogg*: dew; moisture + *stø*: wind]

daikel (n) a compass. [corruption of E. *dial*]

damp (n) end of fishing line. [D. & N. *tamp*: a piece of rope]

danser (n) a species of small shark; a hoe or dogfish. [D. *danser*, prop. *den dansende*: the dancing one]

dekk (n) the sea-bottom. [O.N. *dokk*; N. *dokk*, *dekk*: hollow; depression]

dertek (n) sea boot. [cf. Icel. *dart* (v): heavy gait; *darka*: to walk heavily]

djadd (v) in exp. to *djadd de glonter* – to snuff the wick in an oil-train lamp. [L.Sc. *dad*: a sudden and violent stroke]

djub (djup) the sea. [O.N. *djúp*: depth; depths of the sea]

doma (adj) sensation; impression – applied to taste or smell. *Der nae doma on de fish* (having neither taste nor smell, the fish will not bite). [O.N. *dámr*: taste]

drager (n) one of the runners over which a boat is dragged. [O.N. *hlunnr*]

dratsi (n) an otter (lit. 'one who walks heavily and slowly') (also **dafi**). [O.N. *dratta*: to move with a heavy, slow gait; cf. Icel. *dratthali*: the fox]

draw (n) halyard. [O.N. *drag*]

drengi (n) halibut (also **keita**). [O.N. *drengr*: unmarried man]

drillaskøvi the otter (lit. 'the one that drags its tail'). [see **dratsi**]

drinj (n) the cat (lit. 'the slow, idle one'). [Sw.dial. *dryna*: to be slow, sluggish; to idle; loiter]

drolti (n) a codfish (formerly in Norn, a clumsy fellow). [N. *drulta*: to move heavily, with a rolling gait]

dronjer (n) a cow; sometimes a pig. [N., Icel., Fær. *drynja*: to low softly]

drøg (adj) substantial; abundant; large. To *sni de nibord owre drøg* (cut the bait too big). [O.N. *drjúgr*]

duk (n) a sail; boat's sail. [O.N. *dúkr*: cloth; a length of woven material; Du. *doek*: linen cloth]

E

eld (n) fire. [O.N. *eldr*: fire]

emek (n) fire. [O.N. *eimr*: steam; in poetry also fire]

F

fang (v) to tie an overhand knot in a damaged section of handline. [O.N. *fanga*: to grip; capture]

far (n) a boat. [O.N. *far*: a conveyance; a vessel; N. *fjørefar*: a four-oared boat]

farlek (n) a boat. [see above]

fedek (fiddek, fiedek) (n) bucket; pail. [O.N. *fat*: a vat; *fata*: a pail for fetching water]

feger (feg) (n) a periphrasis for the sun. [O.N. *fagr*: fair; beautiful]

fell (v) to scald or half-boil. *Fell de flodreks* (half-boil the limpets). [O.N. *vella*: bring to the boil]

festa (n) a hook over the fire on which a pot could be hung. [O.N. *festr*: a rope; cord; chain]

festo (n) the sea-bottom; fishing bank. [O.N. *vost*: fishing ground; fishing bank]

fibi (fibbi) (n) an otter (lit. 'the soft-haired one'). [derive. of *fib*: downy; soft hairs; O.N. *fifa*: cotton grass]

firfoder (n) cat (lit. 'the four-footed one'). [O.N. *fjórir*, N. *fire*: four]

fisk (n) fish. [O.N. *fiskr*]

fitlek (fitlin, fitrik, fitsek) (n) a mouse. [see **fotlek**]

fittek (n) mouse; cat. [see **fudin**]

fjal (v) to hide; disappear. [O.N. *fela*, Fær. *fjala*: to hide]

fjedin (n) a whale. [O.N. *feitr*: fat; *feitingr*: animal covered with blubber]

fjora (n) limpets found on the foreshore and used for bait. [O.N. *fjara*: ebb-tide; foreshore]

flada (n) the flat one – flatfish. [O.N. *flatr*: flat]

fladrek (n) limpet. [N. *fladra*: small splinter; Fær. *flidr*: limpet]

flokner (n) a fowl; hen. [O.N. *flognir*: a poetical name for a raven, from *fljúga*: to fly]

flör (n) sea-bottom; a shoal or bank in the sea. [cf. O.N. *golf*: floor]

fodek (see **fedek**)

fodin (foder) a cat. [see **fudin**]

foger (see **feger**)

fogri (n) a mackerel. [deriv. of O.N. *fagr*: fair]

foitlin (fotlin, fotlek) (n) a mouse. [N. *foetlingr*: a small foot; light foot]

foleks (n) folk; people; men. [O.N. *fólk*: people]

fona (n) fire. [O.N. *funi*: flame]

forso (n) half-boiled, chewed limpets spat out on the surface of the sea to lure fish (also **fross**). [N. *frøsa*: to snort; splutter; gush]

fremd (n) 1) head, esp. of fish used as bait; 2) a high, steep point of land. [O.N. *fremd*: headland]

fru (n) a woman; wife. [O.N. *frú*: mistress of the house; a lady; Ger. *frau*]

fudin (n) a cat. [*fótingr*: lightfooted; O.N. *fótr*: a foot]

furin (n) fire. [O.N. *fúrr*: fire]

fusk (n) fish. [O.N. *fiskr*]

G

galti (n) a hog. [O.N. *galti*, *galtr*]

gap-stick (n) cylindrical wooden tool for removing hook that has been swallowed by a fish. [O.N. *kafli*: cylinder; stick]

genger (adj) of the sun at sunrise. *De sjiner is upon his gengers* (the sun is rising). [D. *ganger*: a saddle-horse]

gi'e (v) to fail; to go to pieces. [L.Sc. *gie*: to give; N. *giva seg*: to fail; give up]

gjonger a horse. [O.N. *gangari*: a steed; saddle-horse]

glab (n) an opening; a space – used in association with finding fishing grounds by watching landmarks. *He (the hill) maks i de glab* (the hill appears in the opening (dale, gap, cleft)). [N. *glap*: a hole; interstice]

glan (glani, glannel, glankett) (n) a whetstone. [Icel. *glan*: the brightness of smoothed and polished objects]

glid (glida, glidde) (n) the sun. [O.N. *glit*: splendour; shine; glitter]

glaffi (n) nickname for halibut. [Sw.dial. *gluffi*: a glutton; N. *glufsa*: to gobble]

globeren (n) the moon. [Icel. *glápa*: to stare; glare]

glom (n) the moon; also (rarely) a lamp. [O.N. *glámr*: a dull gleam of light]

glub (n) 1) a gap; ravine. 2) appetite. *Der nae glub on de fusk* (the fish are not biting). [N. *glup*: a gap; ravine; *glop*: a glutton]

glunta (n) the moon. [Sw.dial. *glona*, *gluna*, *glana*, D.dial. *glyne*, N. *glana*: to stare; gaze; N. *glane*: a luminous spot on the horizon]

glurek (n) an eye. [O.N. *glyrna*: an eye (cat's eye)]

gola (n) wind; blast. [O.N. *gola*, *gula*: a squall of wind; blast]

golin (n) hoe or dogfish. [N. *gaale*: a fool]

golti (golte) (n) a cod. [O.N. *galti*, *galtr*: a hog]

gred (n) a fishing long-line. [N. *greida*: gear]

griper (n) fishing hook; tongs. [E. *grip*]

gritten (n) rumbling thunder; a thunderclap. [N. *gnulta*, *grylta*: to roll; boom, as thunder]

gro (n) wind; a gentle breeze. [O.N. *grádi*: a gentle breeze ruffling the surface of the water]

grokoll (n) a mouse (lit. 'the grey-headed one'). [O.N. *grár*: grey + *kollr*: the head]

gronter (grontjel) (n) swine; pig; (lit. 'the one who grunts'). [N. *grumta*, *grymta*: to grunt]

grundswirl: (n) swine; pig; (lit. 'he that roots in the ground'). [O.N. *grund*: ground + Icel. *svarfla*: to rummage about; to fling here and there]

grød (v) to become turbid; to become or be indistinct. [N. *gruta*: to become dim (cloudy)]

grømek (n) a ram. [O.N. *grimr*: poetic name for a ram]

grødek (n) a pot. [O.N. *gryta*: a pot]

grøta (n) [see above]

gula (n) wind. [O.N. *gula*: wind; a squall of wind]

gunska (adv) very well; quite well. [D. *ganske*]

H

habagoitlek (n) booth; fisherman's hut. [E. *habitat*: dwelling + O.N. *kot*: hut]

hader (n) fish hook (lit. 'a holder'). [O.N. *hald*: a hold; grip]

hader (n) a tiny, poor fish. [N. *hatra*: constantly to persecute; try to exterminate]

hald (halt) (v) to hold. *Had dy hands and tak a blag* (Stop work and take a rest). [O.N. *halda*: to hold]

halihwiffer (n) woman; wife; a disparaging term – *the one who does her work badly*. [N. *kufsa*, *kufta*: to bustle; run about]

halin a cow; otter; (lit. 'the long-tailed one'). [O.N. *hali*: the tail]

haltagonga (v) stop your gait! stop your speed! [O.N. *halda*: to hold back; stop + O.N. *ganga*: going; walking]

handi (n) a small shark; hoe. [O.N. *hann*: he]

harki (n) swine. [Fær. *herkja*: to eat greedily]

hekla (n) the ray (fish). [O.N. *hekla*: a cloak]

hema (hemelt) (n) wife. [L.Sc. *hamald*: that which belongs to the home or house]

heslin (n) horse. [O.N. *hestr*: a horse]

hildin (n) fire. [O.N. *eldr*: fire]

hjonsa (n) a hen. [O.N. *hœna*: a hen]

hjosi (n) swine; a young pig. [cf. **harki**]

hobiter (n) the horse (lit. 'the one that grazes'). [O.N. *bita*: to bite; to graze]

hoid (n) a hut; fisherman's booth. [Sw. *hydda*: a hut]

hoidin (n) clergyman – he who waves his arms (from the pulpit). [N. *hytta*: to wave the hand; to threaten]

hokken (n) the horse. [Du. *hakkeneie*: a small horse]

hollost (n) deep-sea fishing grounds. [O.N. *áll*: a gutter; a furrow; a deep depression; also *vost*: fishing-ground]

honger (n) a kettle; pot; (lit. 'the hanging one'); in exp. *väir de honger* – turn the pot (to facilitate even cooking of the contents). [O.N. *hanga*: to hang]

honnek (n) a boat's foghorn; horn for holding snuff. [O.N. *horn*]

horda (n) a mare. [poss. N. *hordel*: an animal that consumes much]

horin (horek) (n) a seal (lit. 'the hairy one'). [Icel. *hárhamur*: hairy skin; N. *haarham*: the outer hairy skin]

hospra (hasper, hostan) (n) wife. [O.N. *húsfrøjya*: mistress of the home; wife]

hudek (n) a gaff. [N. *hytt*: a pike; a small gaff]

hulefer (n) a very big ling. [O.N. *úlfr*: a wolf]

hun (n) a gaff. [O.N. *húnn*: a cube-shaped piece of wood]

hunek (n) a hen. [O.N. *hœna*: a hen]

hutrikin (n) a gaff. [N. *hytt*: partly a point; spike; top; tip; partly in special sense a small gaff for taking up fish]

hwadi (n) a gaff. [O.N. *hwati*: a sword]

hwida (n) ling – the white one.

høslek (n) a hut; straw-thatched house. [Ger. *häuslein*: a small house]

høli (høleli) (in exp. *geng høleli* – pull slowly. [O.N. *hægliga*: quietly; gently]

I

ifarek (n) shoe. [Fær. *inferd*: the mouth of a shoe]

ifetlek (n) a mouse; a small, lightfoot (lit. 'the extremely lightfooted one'). [O.N. *idgnógr*: abundant; plenty; Icel. as an independent word *perpetual motion*]

ifudien (n) a cat. [see above]

ilder (n) fire. [O.N. *eldr*]

J

jappi (n) a hen (lit. 'a cheeping, jabbering creature'). [N. *jappa*: to jabber; talk with tiresome repetition]

jarmek (n) sheep; cat; precentor (leader of singing in church). [O.N. *jarma*: to bleat]

jarmer (n) sheep; cat; precentor (leader of singing in church). [O.N. *jarma*: to bleat]

jemelt (n) a woman. [see **hema**]

jonsa (n) a hen. [see **hjonsa**]

jorin (n) a seal. [see **horin**]

K

kabbi (n) a cod. [N. *kabbe*: stump; lump; stick; cylinder – word often used in Shetland as names for fish]

kavi (n) sinker on a fishing line; something diving down. [O.N. *kaf*: depths of the ocean]

keger (n) stomach of ling or cod; inflated stomach. [Fær. *kikur*: (inflated) stomach of a whale; N. *kik*: sheepskin taken off in one piece and inflated for a buoy]

keita (n) halibut. [N. *kveita*]

kerro (n) spinning wheel. [N. *kirra*: to tremble; quiver; Sw. *kirra*: to swing]

ketthuntlin (n) a cat. [O.N. *ketta*: female cat]

kipperwari (n) tongs. [O.N. *kippa*: to snatch; pull]

kirks (n) scissors. [O.N. *kyrkja*: to pinch]

kisek (kisert) cat – partly as a pet name. [Icel. *kisa*, Sw.dial. & N. *kiss*: cat]

klepp (n) a gaff. [O.N. *kleppr*: a staff, supplied with an iron hook, by which large fish are hauled into a boat]

kliksi (n) eagle. [O.N. *klaka*: to cry, used in ref. to the eagle]

klingr (klinger) to turn around; *klingr dee!* – an exclamation addressed to any large fish when hooked. [O.N. *kringla*: a circle; ring; disc]

klir (kliri) (n) a cock. [O.N. *klidr*: bird's cry]

klister (n) butter. [D. *klister*: paste]

kliven (n) cleft implement; tongs. [O.N. *klofi*: a cleft; Fær. *klovi*: tongs]

kloster (n) chapel; church. [O.N. *klaustr*: a convent; monastery]

klovi (n) cleft tool; tongs. [see **kliven**]

klovin (kløvin) (n) a sheep; a cloven-hoofed animal. [O.N. *klauf*: hoof]

klurer (n) a cat (a scratcher). [O.N. *klóra*: to scratch]

klut (n) a sail; a boat's sail. [O.N. *klútr*: a clout; rag]

knabi (n) a cod. [O.N. *knapi*: a man; fellow]

knavi (n) cod. [see above; also E. *knave*]

knubbi (n) potato; prop. a log, club. [Sw. *knubbe*: a short gnarled stick]

kogi (n) a seal (lit. 'the peeping one'). [O.N. *kaga*: to peep]

kogi (n) the land; high ridges seen from the sea; (lit. 'that which peeps out'). [see above]

kokkasødi (adj) applied to various sea-birds and associated with their call – an auk; cormorant; long-tailed duck; Manx shearwater, etc. (The cry of a sea-bird was taken as omen of bad weather.) [onomatopœic]

kokkel (n) a compass; prop. a lamp. [N. *kokle*]

kokrin (n) a hen – the cackling one. [N. *kokra*: to emit monotonous sounds; to cackle]

koll (n) head, esp. head of a fish. [O.N. *kollr*]

kolla (n) a buoy made from sheepskin, prop. something clipped and round. [N., Fær. & Icel. *kolla*: a wooden vessel without handles; O.N. *kolla*: a polled animal]

kom (v) in phrase *kom til itsel* – of a fishing line at breaking point. [O.N. *koma*: to happen]

korka (korkin) (n) oaten bread. [O.N. *korki*: oats]

krekin (n) a whale. [N. *krake*: a large marine animal]

kriel (n) a cock. [Icel. *kría*: a sea-swallow; N. *kria*: to shout; rejoice]

krug (n) a thole-pin in a boat. [O.N. *krókr*: hook; loop]

krug (v) to sail a vessel. [O.N. *rista krok*: of a ship on the sea; to cut a curve]

kuna (n) woman; wife. [O.N. *kuna*]

kupa (n) boat's scoop. [N. *kupa*; Icel. *kúpa*: a round vessel; a bowl]

kwern (n) a mill. [O.N. *kvern*: a quern; hand-mill]

L

lager (n) halibut (also **leger**). [N. *lega*; Fær. *legukalvi*: a large, full grown halibut]

lagstøt (v) to turn; *lagstøt de skalv* (turn the basket round). [O.N. *støyta*: to turn upside down]

landbrim (n) surf; break of waves on the shore. [O.N. *brim*: surf]

laverni life; living; used in the sense of 1) crop; harvest; 2) mirth; noise; 3) a crowd; flock. [O.N. *liferni*: life, conduct of life; N. *liverne*: mode of life, esp. gay life]

leger (n) halibut. [see **lager**]

legviser (n) a compass; *soind de legviser* (look at the compass). [O.N. *visa*: to show; to direct]

ler (lør) a boot; sea-boot. [Du. *laars*: boot; also cf. O.N. *ledr*: leather]

ligger (v) to lie; lies (untruths). [O.N. *liggja*]

lju (adj) mood; humour; sound; in exp. *Dir nae lju on de fish* – the fish will not bite. [O.N. *hljod*: sound]

loband (n) grommet. [O.N. *loda*: to cling fast; to stick]

loder (n) a clergyman (lit. 'the talking one who preaches'). [O.N. *láta*: to talk; emit a sound]

log (ljog) (n) the sea; ocean. [O.N. *løgr*: any liquid; water; sea; ocean]

log (v) to wash; bathe. *I logged my lookers* (I washed my eyes). [O.N. *lauga*: to wash; bathe]

lomm (v) to grow light, in exp. *See du, shö lomms op* (See you, she (the fish) is appearing below the surface of the water). [O.N. *ljóma*: to gleam; shine]

londi (n) the puffin. [O.N. *lundi*]

longafish (n) the ling. [O.N. *langa*]

lotage (n) the otter. [N. *lutra*, Icel. *lötra*: to walk slowly and leisurely]

lør (n) a sea-boot (see **ler**).

M

mamsa (n) a ling. [N. & Fær. *mamma*: mother]

mana (n) land, esp. the mainland, as opposed to the sea. [O.N. *magn*: the main part of a thing]

mar (n) the sea; fishing grounds. [O.N. *marr*: the sea]

milla(bakka) (n) between the sea and the coast (see **sjusamillabakka**). [O.N. *millim*: between]

mjawi (n) a cat – the mewing one. [N. *mjaua*; D. *mjaue*]

moddin (modder, moddvit) (n) swine, prop. 'he that roots up earth'. [N. *modda*: to root]

moia (n) woman. [N. *moja*: a stout, vigorous and somewhat coarsely built woman]

molek (n) a certain length (40-50 fathoms) of fishing long-line. [O.N. *maale*: a coiled fishing line of about 20 fathoms]

mondi (n) a feeling, suggestion, sensation applied to the nibble of a fish at a baited hook. *I felt de mondi o him*. [O.N. *munr*: mood; mind]

mud (muud) (n) mood; temper. [assoc. with above, O.N. *modr*: (violent) emotion]

muls (v) to preach. [O.N. *mæla*: to speak]

munger-hoose (n) a church. [O.N. *munka-hús*: a monastery]

murin (n) a mouse. [N. *mura*: to walk quietly; to potter]

mød (n) mood; temper; humour; (see **mondi, mud**).

N

nebrod (n) bait; fish cut into pieces; bait-box containing fish suitable for bait in deep-sea fishing. [Icel. *nidurburdur*: the act of lowering bait in the sea; the actual bait]

neggi (n) the horse. [O.N. *gneggja*: to neigh]

nigda (n) wife; prop. 'the grumbling one'. [O.N. *snegda*: a quarrelsome woman]

njarm (njau, njauer) (n) a cat (lit. 'the mewing one'). [Fær. *mjarra*: to whimper; mew; bleat]

nokki (n) a hook; fish-hook. [Icel. *hnokki*: a small iron hook on a spindle; N. *nokke*]

nut (n) a cow. [O.N. *naut*: a head of cattle]

O

oddi (n) a point; tongue of land. [O.N. *oddr*: a point]

ondi (adj) small. [O.N. *ogn*: a husk]

ondestø (n) mist or drizzling rain accompanied by a light breeze. [O.N. *anda*: to breathe; N. *anda*: to puff + *stø*: wind]

ongastø (n) a contrary wind; wind from the opposite quarter. [Icel. *andstædur vindur*: contrary wind]

P

pertek (n) a mare. [D.dial. *perd*: a mare; Fær. *pert*: a horse]

pigvar (n) halibut. [D. *pighvarre*; Sw. *piggvar*: turbot]

pikki (n) a gaff. [O.N. *pikka*: a pickaxe]

pilen (n) a buoy, more prob. the upright point on a buoy. [O.N. *píla*: a point; an arrow]

pinni (pinnek) (n) fishing buoy. [see above]

pirrena (pirraina) (n) a girl. [N. *pir*: young, delicate creature + poss. O.N. *hæna*: a hen]

plousi (n) halibut. [orig. uncertain, cf. Ger. *pladise*, E. *plaice*, N. *flaassa*: something wide and shallow]

plumper (n) the cusk (torsk – fish), prop. 'a clumsy fellow'. [N. *pump, pumpa*: a short, stout, clumsy fellow]

pobi (n) hill; anything prominent or projecting. [N. *pappe*: a conical round hill; a pap]

pobi-rontli (n) a pig; prop. 'the fat, round grunter'. [N. *pappe* (see above) + *grontli*, N. *grumsta*: to grunt]

polta (pulter) (n) the cusk (torsk – fish). [Icel. *pölti, pöltr*: a small globe; convex object]

ponni (n) fishing buoy. [see *pinni*]

pottisidna (n) pig; swine. [O.N. *svin*: swine]

predikanter (n) clergyman. [O.N. *predika*: to preach; Fær. *praeikumadur*: preacher]

prestengolva (n) clergyman (lit. 'the one in the cassock'). [O.N. *predika*: to preach + *kulf*: a cowled cloak]

pulgin (n) a buoy. [D. *puld*: round top; head]

pulter (n) the cusk. [see **polta**]

R

radien (n) a sheep. [cf. N. *rate*: a wretched sheep; *a vaarsrak of a sheep*]

rakki (n) a dog. [O.N. *rakki*]

ramek (n) an oar. [Fr. *rame*]

rami (n) cat (lit. 'that which has claws or paws'). [N. & Sw.dial. *ram, ramm*: a paw; claw]

redskab (n) fishing tackle; a fishing line. [O.N. *rudskapr*: implement]

rem (n) boat's oar. [Fr. *rame*: oar]

rikabaand (n) grommet; loop to hold an oar on a boat's gunwale. [O.N. *hrikka*: to creak – the sound made by friction in such a loop when the oar is in use]

rimbel (n) rounded top or elevation. [N. *rymbydl*: placename assoc. with rounded hill]

ringalodi (n) iron rings and hook by which a pot hangs over the fire; the kettle itself. [O.N. *hringr*: a ring + *hadda*: a pot hoop]

rinner (n) a mouse (lit. 'the one that runs'). [O.N. *renna*: to run]

ro (n) a sailyard. [O.N. *rá*]

rodin (n) a sheep, esp. one in an emaciated state. [Icel. *hrota*: wretched, lean ewe]

rolki (n) a young coalfish (piltek); a jocular term with the root meaning of bundle; bundle-shaped. [N. *rulka*]

roller (rölli) (n) fishing buoy made of hide. [N. *rolv*: a bundle; *rulle*: a roll]

rolli (rölk) (n) a mackerel. [N. *rolv*: a bundle; a round, stout fellow]

rottan (n) a rat. [O.N. *rotta*: rat]

rungklows (n) tongs. [O.N. *rong*: the rib of a boat + *klovi*: a cloven tool; pincers]

russa (russen) (n) a mare. [O.N. *hryssa*]

russi (n) a horse. [O.N. *hross*]

rølli (n) a fishing buoy made of hide. [see *roller*]

S

sandkorn (n) stone sinker on a fishing line. [cf. O.N. *korn*: a grain, thus a small stone]

segel (n) a sail, esp. a promontory which when seen from the sea, resembles a sail. [O.N. *segl*: a sail]

sel (v) to break. *Wir stong is selt*. [N. *seila*: to incline; to lean]

semek (n) sewing needle. [N. *søyma*]

sidi (n) a cat – a whimperer. [cf. N. *syta*: a whiner; (v) *syta*: to moan; whine; complain]

sjalti (n) a small horse. [O.N. *hjalti*, *hjaltr*: a man from Shetland (Hjaltland)]

sjar (n) boat; fishing boat; a small whetstone. [cf. L.Sc. & E.dial. *shard*, *sherd*: a fragment – thus an old, unseaworthy boat]

sjiner (n) the sun (lit. 'the shining one'). [O.N. *skina*: to shine]

sjukkolo (n) cod. [Fær. *kúla*: 'thick-head']

sjusamillabakka: (n) between the sea and the shore. (If a man had been gathering bait at low tide and was asked where he'd been, he would be unwilling to give a straightforward answer as it may spoil his luck, thus he'd evasively say 'sjusamillabakka' – between the sea and the shore.) [O.N. *sjór*: the sea + *milla* (millim): between + *bakki*: river bank; shore]

sjuski (n) a dog; clergyman. [N. *ljursken*: thievish; Fær. *ljóvskur*: thievish, also knavish; malicious]

skalv (n) a basket made of rope for holding coiled fishing lines. [O.N. *skjalf*: trellis work]

skavin (skavnasi) (n) cat (lit. 'he that scrapes'). [O.N. *skafa*: to scrape; smooth]

skarnsi (n) cat (lit. 'nose-scraper'). [see above]

skäil (*skile*) (n) a boat's sail. [O.N. *skyli*: protection, shelter]

ske (skega) (n) a sail. [Fær. *skeki*: a clout; rag]

skeni (skoni) (n) a knife. [L.Sc. *skean*, Gael. *sgian*: a knife]

skerdin (n) a mouse. [cf. N. *skjerra*: a shy animal]

skirrek (n) a mouse. [see above]

skjort (stjort) (n) a tail; the tail of a large fish. [O.N. *stertr*: a tail]

skjorrin (n) a mouse; a rat (Whalsay). [N. *skjerra*: a shy animal]

skjud (skjut) (n) a horse. [O.N. *skjótr*: a horse for conveyance]

skobback (skobbek, skupi, skupek) (n) a sheep. [L.Ger., Du. *schaap*, poss. deriv. O.N. *skopa*: to run]

skøn (skøni) (n) a knife. [see **skeni**]

skøvek (n) a foot; a large clumsy foot. [N. *skjæpa* to stagger along]

skrofer (n) a hen (lit. 'the scraper'). [Icel. *skráfa*: creak; scrape; rustle]

skrogin: (n) hen. [see above]

skudra: (n) a ling. [N. *kjøda*, trout]

skupi (skupek) (n) a sheep. [L.Ger., Du. *schaap*]

sma'-fit (n) a mouse (small foot). [see **foitlin**; L.Sc. *sma'*: small]

smellek (smeller, smoiller) a gun (lit. 'one that smacks, cracks'). [O.N. *smella*: to smack; crack]

smi (n) a smithy; a blacksmith. [O.N. *smidja*: a smithy]

smjongni (n) an eel. [O.N. *smøygjen*: supple; slippery]

smoiler (n) a gun. [see **smellek**]

snapp (n) a knob; round top; originally used in Fetlar tabu language to describe south point of Funzie Ness (now so named Snap). [O.N. *knappr*: a knob; round top]

snäit (n) the cusk. [O.N. *snád*, *snædi*: a meal]

sne (snei) (v) to cut; cut up bait. [O.N. *sneida*: to cut]

snegger (snigger, sneggen, sniggin) (n) a horse (lit. 'the one who neighs'). [O.N. *hneggja*: to neigh; whinny]

snistel (snister) (n) a cat (lit. 'the sniffing one'). [Sw.dial. *snustär*: to sniff; scent]

snold (snoldi) (n) an ugly face. *Der an ill snold upo de fish* (the fish will not bite). [O.N. *snáldr*: snout; Fær. *snáldur*: ugly face]

snult (n) a cow (lit. 'the pushing, butting one'). [N. *knolta*: to push; butt slightly]

snør (n) a handline used in fishing. [O.N. *snæri*: a string; a line; a fishing line]

soin (soind) (v) to see. *Does du soind de ponni?* (do you see the buoy?); look at. [O.N. *sjónd*: sight]

soinnek (soindelek) (n) the eyes. [see above]

spjaler (n) cat; (occas. dog); (*the sprawler or player*). [Fær. *spæla*, Icel. *spila*: to play]

spongi (n) eel. [O.N. *smøygjen*: supple; slippery]

spord (n) tail. [O.N. *spordr*]

stafalir (stivalir) (n) a boot. [O.N. *styfill*]

stakka-milja-bakka (see **sjusamillabakka**)

steng (n) mast of a boat. [O.N. *stong*: a pole]

stenglin (n) thigh boot; fisherman's high, waterproof boot. [N. *stanga*, *stinga*: to walk stiffly and jerkily]

stiven (n) stocking. [N. *stuva*: sock]

stjort (n) the tail of a large fish. [O.N. *stortr*: a tail]

stong (n) (see **steng**)

stora-broken (n) (of a boat) shattered by the wind; driven by wind onto the shore and dashed against rocks. [O.N. *stædi*: wind (see **stø**)]

stu (see **stø**)

sulin (n) the sun. [O.N. *sólin*]

swett (n) to splash; sprinkle; to bale a boat. [N. *skvetta*: to splash; sprinkle; throw away liquid]

swettek (**switek**, **swattyek**) (n) a boat's baling scoop. [see above]

swimmek (n) a saw. [N. *svim*: smart; quick; convenient; easy to handle]

sølfeng (n) butter. [O.N. *sufl*: some fat to eat with bread]

sør (n) south; in the south; towards south. [O.N. *sudr*]

søni (**sjøni**) (n) a horse. [ety. uncertain]

søski (see **sjuski**)

T

tik (n) otter. [O.N. *tik*: a bitch]

tobi (**tobilingi**) (n) cormorant. [N. *taap*, *taape*: a fool; Fær. *tapulingur*: a fool; simpleton]

tread (**trid**) (n) thread. [O.N. *prádr*]

tree (n) wooden materials. [O.N. *tré*: wood; mast]

triv (v) to catch hold; recited in a verse by Fetlar fishermen *triv i*, catch hold. [O.N. *prifa*: to grip; grasp]

tunskerri (n) a cock. [O.N. *keri*: male bird]

U

uppstander (n) clergyman (lit. 'he who stands up during the service').

uriin (n) a seal – the hairy one. [Icel. *hárhamur*: hairy skin; N. *haarham*: the outer hairy skin]

uru commotion in the sea; strong current. [O.N. *úró*: unrest]

usoindali (adj) that which is unlucky to see or meet on the way down to the shore for fishing – esp. a cat or a woman. *De cat is a usoindali animal*. [O.N. *úsýniligr*: unsightly; repulsive + *sjond*: to see]

utili (adj) untimely; unlucky, as in *utili to meet*; (see above). [N. & D. *utidig*: untimely; an importune time]

V

vabb (n) water. [N. *vabba*: to go splashing in the wet]

väir (v) in exp. *väir de honger* – turn the pot over the fire (to move contents from one side to the other when boiling). [D. *vir*, *virne*: whirl; twirl]

veda (n) water; wet. *Swit de veda ut o de var* (bale the water out of the boat). [O.N. *vaeta*: wet; moisture]

vender (v) to turn in a certain direction; *Vender de var* (turn the boat contrary to the sun); also of the turn of the tide. [O.N. *vendr*: to turn round]

vender (n) cat (lit. 'the wanderer') (also **vengla**). [O.N. *vandre*: wander]

venga (n) cat (lit. 'the mewer or wailer'). [O.N. *veina*: to wail]

versbrolli (n) brother-in-law. [O.N. *ver*: law + *brolli*: (little, dear) brother]

versmoia (n) sister-in-law. [O.N. *ver*: law + *moia*: woman]

vissek (n) piece of wood nailed to boat's gunwale over which line is hauled. [cf. N. *vise*: overlapping edge on side of vessel]

viväind (v) to turn around. [O.N. *venda*: to turn]

vissek (**wissert**) (n) a cat. [N. *vinsa*: to bustle; to toss; *vins*: a giddy person]

vokonnin (n) mouse (a corruption of **bonhonnin**).

voler (n) a cat (lit. 'the mewer'). [O.N. *vála*: to wail]

W

widdk (n) a piece of peat. [cf. O.N. *vidr*: wood, as in fuel]

winsi (n) cat. [N. *vinsa*: to bustle]

wirm (v) to break; *Wirm dee fast* (break your fast; have breakfast). [O.N. *hverfa*: to turn around]

wolhard (n) sea bottom, esp. fishing grounds. [O.N. *allhardr*: very hard]

worin (n) a seal (lit. 'the hairy one; the hair-fish'). [N. *haarham*: the outer hairy skin]

Y

yappie (n) a hen. [N. *japla*: to jabber]

yarmer (n) a cat. [see **jarmer**]

yungie (**yungers**) (n) a horse, esp. a foal. [O.N. *ungr*: young]

Ø

ød (adj) large and of good quality. [O.N. *itr*: excellent; considerable]

Addenda

1. Some word groups which may be helpful to crossword writers and students –

all tied up

baak; bö-rep; bucht; caddel; eel-towe; faize; fast; gointek; greemik; hank; horn-towes; humlibaand; kiarr; kishie-baand; link; lowrie-towe; raep; rep; sheet; simmonds; snaar; snöd; tedder; toam; tows; tömikins; tyal; wip; wrestin-treed; yarfast; note: **string** = a strong sea current.

boats and boating

aandoo; aff; baand; boo; bore; börep; canny; cloot; cuddy; cuggle; boat's draa; dycal; eela; eft; eft-taft; far; fast; fastibaand; fendy; fitlinn; fleet; flit-boat; foreroom; foretaft; forrard; fourareen; gabbord; geng; haaf; haddibaand; hank; hassens; hinnyspot; horn; huggistaff; hunnik; kabe; kannie; keeldracht; laag; lay; linn; looderhorn; mid-taft; nile; nile-hol; noost; owse-room; owskerri; ranksman; reebins; room; röv; scöp; seafeardy; sem; shoard; shoo; shölibrod; sixern; skaer; skaer-taft; skat rooth; skott; sool; stammerin; taft; tilfer; tows; vatty-kabe; wairin; whillie; yoal.

come wind, come weather

aester; bat; be-aest; be-nort; be-sooth; be-wast; bittersie; bittersie; blatter; blen; daachen; dill; distress; dirl; ettersome; flan; gabs; galder; guff; goosel; gulder; laar; loor; mell-moorie; mirkabool; moorie-caavie; norderly; pampero; pirr; ree; regenwistie; sair; slud; snitter; soch; sook; stoor; swap; vaarie; waster.

coming to blows

beetle; boofel; bult; dad; dang; dart; ding; doose; dunt; hat; hitten; laaber; ledder; lunder; pexins; shappet; skelp; strick; swap; wheef; note: **hit** = (pron) it.

rain, rain, go away

a weet; blashy; boo o wadder; dag; doontöm; drush; grop; Lammas-speet; plump; raag; shug; skub; slester; slud; slurd; slushy; smush; speet; töm; tömald; vaanloop; weety – all are words to describe different sorts of rain; note: **rain** = (v) to glare.

sheepish words

aalie-lamb; almark; anyister; biggiflay; blaegit; blisset; buggie; bül; byelsit; byoags; caa; caain-time; caddel; caddie-lamb; cast; catmoagit; crook; crö; crugset; dill-bells; drave; gimmer; greenbowe; gulmoget; half-oot-afore; half-oot-ahint; haslock; hems; hentilagets; kransit; kwarkabus; lavilugget; lungie; mooed; moorit; nyaarm; paes-wisp; piece; pirl; reddins; rit; roo; setnin; sheep's gaet; sheephaddin; sholmark; sholmet; songie; stoo; sturdy; tag-set; tup; vaas; vinster; wedder; wheelbands; yaarm; yowe; yuglet.

2. English-Shetland word list (readers are advised to check dialect list for context, variations and detailed meanings of individual words. Also see 'Nature Study' addendum for all flora and fauna words.)

A

able fierdy
abnormal tooth bittel
above abön
abundance footh
ache nyaag
acquainted acquant
across owre-by
additionally firbye
adorn divvish
adze eetch
afraid faird
aft (of boat) eft
after efter
aftertaste waageng
against alang
agitation tird, tirse
ailment brash
ailment (contagious) feerie
ajar ajee
alert aaber
all aa
allow lat
almost maistlins
alms aamos
alone alane, lane
also benon
always aye
amber laamer
angry birsie, ill-bistet, tirn
ankle cöt
ankle sock cöttikin
annoy irg
annoyed gaggit, ill-plaesed
antics atfirts
anxiety amp
anxious kibby
anything ocht
appease cöllie
apron brat, peenie
are ir
argue traep
armful skurtfoo
armpit oxter
arrested taen up
arse erse
artful sloomit
as if sammas
ash ess
ask ax, spör
askew skavel, skyefset
astound bombaze
astride stridey-legs

asunder asundry, sindry
ate öt
attest warn
attractive boannie
auction roup, unction
aurora mirrie dancers
autumn hairst
aware awaar
awful hellsest
awkward oonhaandy
awl (shoemaker's) ellishon

B

baby's napkin grethy-cloot
backbone riggie
backwards backlins
backwash (sea) affrug
bad luck ill-sunse
bad tempered crabbit
bag pockie
bale (as a boat) owse
ball baa
ball (of wool) clew
barbed wire toarny-waer
bark (v) yalder
barley bigg, bere
barrel hoop gird
barrel stave scowe
barter troke
bask bee
basket cuddie, kishie
bathe, wash beek
beak neb
beat lunder, scud, beetle
bed böl, scratcher (sl)
bedridden bedral
been (v) bön
beetle clock, hundiclock
before afore
beg tig
behind ahint
belch rift
belittle nochtify
belle vire
bellow (v) bröl, gölbröl
bemused stumsed
beneath anaeth, anunder
besides firby, forby
bespoken feft
between atween
bewitched mösed, santed
bilge owse-room
birthplace (childhood or spiritual home) bonhoga
bird fool
bit grain
bitch bick
bite shill
bitter (cold) aari, atteri
bitter (taste) ramse
black swart
blaze aze
bleat nyaarm, yaarm
blemish blae, blett
bless sain, bliss
blister blibe

blizzard caavie, moorie
block (of wood) stab
blood-blister stenloopen
blood relations blöd-freends, sibb
blotch scam
blow (as wind) blaa
blur mirr
boat, ship far
bogeyman boky
boil (v) ramp, skruttle
boisterous oonmoderate, owre-steer, uploppin, vengie
bone ben
boot böt
booty proil
boredom langer
boring teddisome
bosom bosie, skurt
boss tapster
both baid
bother fash
bottom (sea bed) boddam
bought bowt, coft
bound (v) spang
boundary hagmark
bow (of boat) boo
boyfriend laad
brace paal
braces strops
bradawl broag
brains harns
brand new spleet new
brat oolet
brazen browdened
bread breid (Yell)
break brack
breathless bursin, gaa-bursin
breeze laar
brew (of tea) browst
bridge brig
bristles birse
brittle froch
broke brook
bronchitis brooncaidies
broody clockin
broody hen clocks-midder
brother bridder
brothers briedder
brought broucht, brocht, browt
brown broon, moorit
bruise blue-melt
bubble (n) blibe
bubble (v) rutl
bucket pell
build bigg
bulky whaanious
bullock strick
bundle (of clothes) cloo-bing
buoy bowe
burden fracht
burned brunt, colcoomed
burned to ashes roo scadded
burst spret, spring
bustle (v) tird
butt (as a ram) bult
buttermilk kirn-mylk
buttermilk (thin) gyola, druttel

C

cabbage kail
cabbage stem kastik, runt
cackle claag
cake hufsi, khoik, tjoik (Whalsay)
call cry, kall
calm platt
capable fierdy
caper moy-foy
capsize hwimble, whummel
caraway seeds carvy-seeds
carcase crang, ro
card caird
caress kyoder
cartilage bröski
castrate lib
cattle baess, kye
cattle-fodder baess-maet
cautiously tentily, peerie wyes
cease lin
celebration foy
chafe nidd
chaff caff, anns
chair shair
chamber-pot grethy-pot, shanty
chance shance
change shange
chase scunge, shaste
chatter, gossip bledder, clash, nyitter
cheat swick
cheekbone sheekbenn
cheep pleep
cheerful canty, croose
cheerless dreich
chest (lg) girnal, kist
chew showe
chickenpox nirls
child bairn, ting
childhood bairndom
chimney shimley
chimney-head craaheid
chin shin
choice wael
choke shock
chop shap
church kirk
churn kirn
clamour raldi
claw claa, cloor
claws (esp. of cat) crammicks
clay pipe cutty
clear ripe
clearing (of clouds) tinnin
cleft geo
cliff face bank(s)
clockwise sungaets
close cropped snoiltit
closed steekit
cloth cloot, swabb
clothe dink
clothes claes
clothes-line raep
clove clowe
clumsy bulderit, clushit, gaevalos, haandless, kefsi, vyndless

clutch (of eggs) ort
coagulate sturken
coal (burning) taand
coarse rushie
coat (as of paint) cootch
coax tize
cobweb moose-wup
coffin kist
co-habit bidey-in
coir kiarr
cold caald
cold (of stormy weather) bitterness
cold (very) caald-rife
cold wind snitter
colic booel-cramp
collapse faa by, rummel
colossal sygonical (N.Yell)
colt staig
comb kame, redder
comely sonsie
common (n) outrun, scattald
commotion kollyshang, lundilog, steer, splore, upsteer
compass (boat's) dycal
compete kyemp
complain girn, graim, krom, nyirg
congeal lapper
confuse mer
contrary camshious
cool cöl
copulate (of animals) brind, tread
corn stack skroo
corpse corp, leek, krang
cotton thread pirm treed
cough host
counted kyaandit
counter-clockwise widdergaets
cow coo
cowardly skreebie
cowshed byre
crawl arl, oag
creak snyirk
cream raem
crease lirk
creature craetir
crept kroppm
cripple (n) lemminder
cripple (v) mirackle
croak kurrip
crockery laem
crooked skave, krolkit
cross (adj) tirn
cross-grained twarter
crouch crug, hoorkle
crown croon
cruel haethenous
crunch crump
crush brootch
crutch heck
cry greet, sprech
cupboard press
curdled run
currant curn
cut klip, nyiggle, snee
cut (with sickle) risk
cut close snibb

D

dale daal, quam
dance (n) rant
dance (v) link
dark mirk
dawdle drittle
dawn dimriv, greek
daughter dochter, dowter
deafen daev
dealings curry-raag
decay mooter
decorate penk
decorated variorumed
deep-sea fishing haaf
defecate (sl) cockie
defile uggle
demean below
diminish dwine
dense (as fog) steekit
dent benkle
derelict vod
despondent dumpised
destroy sink
detain apper
devil soaroo
diarrhoea robbi-rutl, skitter
difficult varg
dig dell, hock
diligence leid
dip (in water) dibe, dook
direction ert
drizzle raag, röd
dirty aggled, eltit, pickit
disagreeable ill-vaandit
disappointment bluntie, dooncome, sitter
disgrace tash
disgust stugg
dishevelled tooskit
dishonest unhonest
disperse skail
distract mar
distressed pitten-aboot
disturbance cuttanoy, onkerry
ditch stank
divulge lat on
dog hund
doleful doely
doll dukkie
domineering gowsterit
dough levin
downfall firsmo
downhearted dimsket
downpour tömald, vanlop
doze dov, neeb, sob
drab demaloorie
drain golgriv, runnick
dram toot
draw draa
drawback begunk
dread dreid (Yell)
dredge draig, garl
dregs brucks
dress riggament
drip dreep, raep
drive out skunge

drizzle grop, raag, röd, shug, skub, slurd, smush
drove (v) drave
drown smore
drowsy neebin owre
drudgery daddery
drunk foo, paloovious
drying wind sook
drystone enclosure crub
duck deuk
dull demaloorie
dung muck
durable oot-tack
dusk dim, hömin
dust coom, stoor, steuch, styooch
dwelling – or group of biggin(s), bister
dyke daek, gord

E

eager aaber, kibby
ear lug
earth aert, möld
east aest
easterly aesterly
economy raad
eerie oorie
eggshell skurm
either edder
elbow elbuck
emaciated meesery
embellish busk
embers emmers
empty (adj) töm
endure akkadör, dree
enervated machtless, moyenless
enormous eever, whaanious, wheefer
enough anyoch
entangle buckle
entertainment funs, jorum
entice luck
epilepsy nedfallsot
equal morrow
equitable (of weather) dörkable
everyone aabody
everything aathing
ewe yowe
excessive overly
excrement cockies, drit, sharn
excuse wheeflication
exhausted daddit, debaetless, depooperit, disjasket,
    forfochen, hurless, maegered, mankit, moyenless,
    pooskered, pyaagit, ootmaagit
expect lippen
extinguish (as fire) coll-slock, slokk
extreme odious, terrible
eye ee
eyebrow ee-wharm
eyelash ee-breer
eyelid whaarm
eyes een

F

fact fack
fade dwine
faint blöv, faa asoond, fent

105

fairly braaly
faith feth
fall faa
false faase
family blöd-freends, wir eens
fart frad, prut
fasten key, sneck, snib, tedder (of animals)
fat spikk
fate weird
father faider
fathom faddom
feast foy
feather fedder, pen
fed-up ganselled
feeble lemskit, little wirt, pör, valsket, wabbit
fellow billie, sheeld
fester bell
fever feerie
few twartree
fidget fidge, widge
fight fecht
find fin
firmament lift
fishing fly flee
fishing rod waand
fist nev
flake, sliver fliss
flame lowe
flap (as a loose sail) blatter
flash blink, flaacht
flatten flatsh, swirten
flatter fyaarm
flirt flenk
floor flör
flounce whenk
flounder (v) bummel
foam froad, saatbrack
fog stumba
folk (colloq) bairns
folksong veesik
fondle köli
food maet
fool gomeril, spjetak
foot fit
footpath gaet
footstep fit stramp
footwear feet
force gaase
forehead broo
foreshore rocks craigs
forgive forgie
forgot firyat
foul guggle
found fan, fun
foundation stone boo-stane
four fower
four-oared-boat fourareen
fragment skoilt, skroil
fray faize, treff
freckle fairntickle
fretful raamished, trumsket
friable bruckly
friendly cosh
frighten fleg, gluff
frolicsome glafterit
from fae, frae

frost (severe) bonfrost
froth gub
frothing barmin
frown snurl
fruit pudding curn pudding
full foo
fumble trivvel
fun maddrim
furrow furr
fuss fam
fussy pernickety

G

gable gaevil
gaff huggistaff, klipp
gale pampero, vaelensi
gall gaa
gallop twasper
gander genner
gape gaan
garbage truck essikert
garment plaag
garter gertan
gasp fetch, pew, pyaa
gate grind
gather gadder, hent
gave gae, gaed
gaze gaan
generous frugal
gentry jantry
gift aamos, gyurd, hansel
gift (conditional) kyoab
give gie
gizzard gözren
glad blyde
glare rain
glazed glerlit
glimmer gloor
glimpse glisk
glint glink
glove gliv
gnaw knaw, shaav
go geng, win
goose gös
gosling gaeslin
gossip gaep, news
got gotten
grain puckle
grand braa
grandfather daa
grasp mitten, yock
grass girse
grass clumps chug
grease creesh, gree
great greht, grit
greedy yamse
gridiron braand-iron
grief döl
grimace sham
gristle bröski
groceries errands
ground grund
grumble dronj, girn, njarg
grunt groint

106

guizer grulik, skekler
gullet wizzen
gulp glaep, kwilk, whilk
gum goom
gurgle cruttle
gust (of wind) gooster, swapp

H

had hed
hailstone haily-puckle
hair-lip kirk-mark
half-witted glaiket
halter greemik
ham joint skenkhoch
handful nevfoo
handkerchief sneet-cloot
handle (n) heft
handline dorro
hang hing
happen skae
hardened harned
hardship tralldom
harp (v) irp
harness bend
harassed doggit, trachled
harsh harsk
harvest hairst, hird
haste roose, scad
hateful condwined
haunch hench
haunches hookers
have hae
hawk (as clearing throat) kreks
haycock cole
hayrick dess
haze ask, shask
head pow
headland bard, knab, mool, mull, ness
headlong headleens
headsquare nyepkin
headstrong ram-stam
healthy owre-weel
heap bing, coose, roog
heartburn brunt rift, hertscad, watertraa
hearth hert-stane
heat haet
heed ant, anse, leet, seem
heifer quaig
held höld
hermaphrodite songie
heyday tamto
hiccups hicksi
hide hoid, hiddle
high-jinks karrant
high-spirited filska, filsket, liftit
hill byurg, houll
hillock heogue, knowe
hinder happer
hip hench
hip bone nyuggelben
hit baff, dadd, lunder, strikk
hoard poase
hoarfrost shaela
hoarse hairse

hocks (cattle) affcuttins
hoe howe
hoist hunkse, hyst
hold hadd
hollow boss, toom
home hame
hoof cliv
hoofprint clivmett
hook, peg cleek, crook
hooves – sound of clivgeng
hopeless wanless
hospitable inbös
hot-water bottle laem-pig
hound (n) hund
hour oor
house hoose
hover laav
how foo
however hooenever
howl yowl
hubbub kabbi-labbi, hooro
huddle crug
huge whaanious
hullabaloo klurmose
hum noodel, nön
hump (on back) cröl
humour (mood) cant
hunger fantation
hungry fantin
hunt hunse
hurry scad, skrit
hush! wheesht
uly hurda
husk (n) sid
husk (v) kwiss
hut (esp. fisherman's bothy) böd

I

idiot, stupid person dereeshion, föl
immense undömious
immigrant (to Shetland) incomer, soothmoother
impetuous uploppm
impress deer
in ita
incite igg
inclined wint
indigo dye blue-litt
industrious eident
infectious disease smit
infertile jaa
infirm creeksit
information witteens
infuse mask
ingle-nook shimley-neuk
injure masheeve, mirackle
injury faat
inlet voe
insects boags
inside inna
insomnia waakrife
inspect vizzie
instep (of shoe) whink
intercept kep
into intil, itil

intoxicated mortal, stimin
intractable inbiggit, unbiddable
invite bid
iota eetimation
iron yatlen
irritable crabbit, ill-naitered, starty
islet holm
isolated backaboot
it hit
itself hitsel

J

jam jeely
jaundice gulsa
jaunt reenkie
jaws shocks
jerk hwenk, nyig
jersey gansey
jew's harp trump
jollification glant
jump jimp, loup
jumped jamp

K

kidney neer
kin sib, freend
kindling kendlin
kinsman freend
kiss smoorikin
kitten kettlin
knack kan, vand, vynd
knitting makkin
knitting needles maakin waers
knitting (work in progress) sock
knob hivvet
knot (v) drang
know ken
known kent

L

labour trachle, varg
lacerate sklent
ladder trap
lame gammy
lamp kolli
lane closs, strodie
large muckle, stour, whaanious
last hidmost, lest
last night dastreen
laugh gaff, laach
lazy döless, sweerie, longsome
laziness sweetra
learning laer
leather (thick, as sole of shoe) bain
leave laeve
ledge skelf
length lent
leprous spilt
lie lee
light licht

light gust (of wind) bat
light snow feevil
limp hirple, lemse
limpet lempit
linoleum oil-cloth
litter (as straw in a barn) bizzie
litter (of puppies, etc.) laachter
little grain, litel, peerie, skaar
load lod
loan len
loathsome vyld
lobe lapple
loft laft
lonely lanerly
long lang
loose slagget
loosen lowse
lot footh, hantle, immense, lok
loud noise dunder
louse gunnie
lower a sail duss
lowermost nedmost
lovable currie
lull, abate (of wind) daachen
lurid glowerit

M

maggot maed
make mak
makeshift riggamifixin
malicious ill-vicket
mallet maal
mantelpiece brace
mare russa
mark mett
marrow-bone merky-bane
mash shap
master mester
match mak
matchless morless
meander wengle
meat – beef, mutton flesh
medicine pheesic
merriment gleers
mess murg, scutter, slutter
middle hert-holl
midwife howdie
might micht
milk mylk
mimic scoarn
minute quantity sint, skaar
mirage hedimoo
mire gag, poosie
miserly naaber, nearbegyaan
mishap misanter
misshapen croppened, skevelled
mislaid tint
misleading willsom
mist ask, barber, shask
mite moot
mix mell
moan monn, nyoag, oob
moderate (of weather) dörkable
moderation hag

modicum mention
moist soolp
molar yackle
moment start
Monday Monenday
money penga
month munt
mood key, lay
mood – esp. bad mood cob on
moon mön
mope ool
morsel lip, mooth, peel
morose trumsket
moth moch
mother mam, midder, moder
mottled eeskit, marlet
mouldy blue-finsket, blue-niled, föti, nildet
mound toog
mouse moose
mouth gab, gob, mool
mouthful sheeksfoo
mucus snurt
mud glaar
muddy puddle dub, purt
mumps branks
murmur imper
muscle pain creeks
mushroom paddock-stöl
must man
muster (as sheep or cattle) caa
mutter tröttel
muzzle mool-baand

N

nag bamp, nyarg, pirg, sharg, yaag
nappy grethy-cloot, hippen
near in aboot
neck craig
needy ill-aff
neighbour neebour
neighbourhood neebrid
neither nedder
nephew oy
nestling, young bird burd
nevertheless still an on
next neest, neist
nickname töname
night nicht
nightmare mara
nimble fjask, nyiff
nimble (esp. of old people) feespin
nipple paap, prummek
no na, nae
noisy footsteps clooter
noisy speech gabbleation
none nane
nonsense brølek dreet, hellery
nook cro, nyook
north nort
northern nordern
northerly be-nort
nose neb
notice seem
nourishment dreach

now eenoo, noo
nudge nug
numb doven

O

oafish gufset
oar aer
oats aets, coarn, havr
oatmeal aetmell
oatmeal scone brönnie, kröl
obedient biddable
obey anse, ant
obstinacy stoit
obstinate onstaandin, siccar, traan
occasional anterin
odds and ends bölliments, scran
off aff
offer applös
off-putting aff-bidden
oil lamp kolli
oilskin sken joop, smooky
old aald, owld
once eence
one ean, ee, wan
only bit, ony
opposite fornest
other idder, tidder
otherworldly fey
ought ocht
our wir
ourselves wirsells
outcome efterklaps, uptak
outcry cabbi-labbi
out-of-doors furt
over by, owre
over-excited owre-end
overturn cummel, heeld, kepsweevil
oxen owsen

P

pack saddle (wooden) klibber
paddle japple, plootch
pail daffik, pell
pain (in muscles or joints) benwark
palm (of hand) löf
pane peen
pant pech, stunk
paper bag pockie
parboil leep
parhelion gaa
particle mott, nirt
party foy
passageway transe
pat clap
patch clamp
path gaet, bröd
path (along cliff top) banks gait
pause salist
peat paet
peat (coarse, mossy) bluster, skyumpik
pebble riddlie
pedlar packie, yaager
peek peeg

peel flae
peep teet
peer (v) coag, glinder, keek, skile, stime
peevish freksit, frumset, ramist
pencil calafine
penis pillie, pintle
people fok
perceive twig
perceptive gleg
person bein, craetir, eemage
perverse traan, widderwis
pet lamb caddie
phosphorescence (on sea) mareel
pig grice
pile bing, roo, roog
pillow booster
pimple boolik, plook
pin preen
pinafore peenie
pinch kläip
pine (v) dwine, winnish
pipe stroint
plant (v) set
platter trunsher
plead prig
plough ploo
ploy reenk
plunder roan
pocket knife jocktaleg
poison pooshin
poke proag, ripe
pony röl
post stab, stoop
potato taatie
potato masher shappin-tree
potter (v) dingle, footer, ooril, plooter
pound beetle, pund
pout sleb
poverty pörta
power föshin
powerless crachtless, foshinless gaevalos, machtless
prank prettikin
prattle bledder, gabble, sheeks
predict spo
preen prink
premonition feyness, foregeng
presentable onlookin
press feeze, pram
pretence makadö, pit-on
prim pernyim, perskeet
proceed warily caa canny
prostrate gröflins
proud prood
provisions errands
provoke irg, pirvok
pucker snipper
puff guff, pech, wheef
pummel boofel
punishment pexins
puny wantrivven
puppy whalp
purr grinnd, nurr
purse (v) knep, nyep
push putt, shiv
pushed, hit dang
put pat, pit

Q

quantity (mass) boady, dose, footh
quarrel argie-bargie, cangle, rammi, tölli
quench slock
quiet quide, wheesht
quilt twilt
quiver mirl, vimmer
quiz whiss

R

rabbit hole kyunnen hadd
ragged pellet, trefset
rags rinty-pells, taavrins
ram (n) tup
ransack raase
rascal smatshet
rasp risp
rather redder
rattle rinks
ravine gyill
reach reck, rex, raex
ready clair
rebound stot
recover better
rejects (n) oot-waelins
relatives blöd-freends, sib
relish keetchin
reluctant ellis, laith
remainder brucks
remnants akker, ormals
remorseless haagless
repeat tell
replete stuggit
reprobate reebald
render speechless clumpse
resemble tak efter
reside bide
resin roset
resonate runk
retch byock
revelry bachus
revive kukker, kyukker
riddle guddick
ridge rissie
right richt
rinse rensh, synd
ripple geel
rivet (v) clink
roam stravaig
robustness book
rock baa, craig
rocky hill byurg
roe raans
rogue trooker
roll rowe, rowl
roof röf
root(s) röt, taas, taeger, tavrins
rough coorse, ruckli
row (a boat) aandoo
rowdy opstropolous
rowdy dispute collyshang
rowdy mob catticloo
rubbish bruck,hellery

rumble rummel
rummage reesel, rumse
rump humpigumpi
rumple tooder
run rin, sprit
rush (v) bang, breenge

S

sack sekk
saga stoal
salivate slaver
salt saat
satisfactory owre göd
saturate sab
Saturday Setterday
saunter daander. drittle
saw saa
scarecrow gluff, taatie-boky
scarf gravit
school scöl, skule
scold flite
scone bannock
scoop (for baling a boat) owskerri
scratch cloor, cram, scart, skam, skrovvel, skruffel
scorch scooder
scowl skoolm
screech skröl
scrub scoor
scuff skröfl
scythe sye
sea-foam löragub
seagull maa
sea-mist (esp. v. cold) barber
sea-spray brennastyooch
sea urchin julter, scaddiman's head
seaward fram
seaweed tang, waar, tari
seaworthy fendy, sea-feirdy
seesaw hedderkindunk
senile doitin
sensitive feelin-herted
separate sinder
seven seevin
several twartree
sew shew
shabby slushit
shafts trams
shake batter, shak, shiggle, titter
shall sal
shall not sanna
shallow shaald
shapeless slagget
share wak
sharp blow knoilt
shawl hap
she shö
sheaf shaef
sheath-knife tully
sheaves shaeves, stooks
sheep-fold crö
sheepskin bag buggie
sheet ice glerl
shell scurm
shelter lee, skyug

shimmer risen, vimmer
shine sheen
shirt sark
shiver pipper, nitter, stirn
shoo! (interj) cösh, keest
short tempered tirse
short sock fitty
should sood
shoulder jokhel, shooder
shoulder-blade hyocklebane
shout gouster, rout
shove shiv
shovel shivvel, shöl
show shaa, shew
shower (of rain) speet
showoff (n) cramper
shrewd canny
shrill laugh skirl
shrink kling
shrug hunkle
shuffle sköfs, smuks
shut steek
shy, timid blate
sibling sutshkin
sickened scunnered
sickle hyook
sickly neebit, öliklörum, skyoamit
sideways sidlins
sieve syer
sigh seich
sight sicht
simpleton gock, snöl
simmer soose
since syne
sinew sinnen
singlet joopie, spenser
sinister osmil
sinker (as on fishing line) cappie
sit down dip
skiff whillie
skill cast, vynd
skim scoom, skeet
skimpy crimp
skirt (n) cott
skull harnpan, skult
sky lift
slake slokk
slander miscaa
slate sclate
sleepless waakrife
slice skelp
slide slidder
slim smaa
slink smoot
slipper patan, smuck
slobber slepse
slovenly slefset, trusset
slovenly person sloo
slow-witted stookie
sluggish döless, dulskit
slurp soitl
sly sleekit
smack pay
small minkie, mootie, peerie, sma
small holding croft
small person oorick**

small quantity coarn, skaar
smart prunk
smear clert, clime, kline
smell fyunk, guff, vaam
smirk smeeg
smithereens ötna, shalmillens
smoke reek
smoke-cured reestit
smooth slicht
smother smoor
snail's shell trowie buckie
snappish snippet
sniff snyösk
snigger sneester
snippet paek
snort snush
snout (pig's) tröni
snow (n) snaa
snow (v) sneeb
snow storm (severe) blinndin moorie
snub forsmo
so-so noo an sae
soaking drookin
soft fozie, saft
softly peerie wyes
solder sowder
somersault headicraa
song sang
soot (coating a utensil) ime
sort mallivoag
sorrowful wae
sound soond
sour cassen, kassen, shilpet, soor,
south sood, sud
spank skelp
spanner runch
spark spunk
speak spaek
speck millin
speechless stumsed
spiced mince sassermaet
spinal cord möni
spine riggie
spit teoff
splay spjaal
splint spyolk
splinter(s) skelf, skelderin
spongy fozie
spoon spön, spune
spotted spricklet
spout (of kettle, etc.) stroop
sprain wrest
spray (v) sproan
spring (n) spoot, voar
sprint sprit
sprout (as seed) breer, sproot
spurt frush, speer
squall flan, gandigooster, scudder
squeak peester
squeal (as a pig) reein
squeeze birze, nyivvel
squelch julk
squint gly, skave, skew-wheef
squirt scoot
stagger swaander

stallion russie
stammer mant
star starn
starve fant
steamy ölg
steep slope clave
steer (n) stot
stiff hansper, spaegie
stile stiggy
sting swee
stomach hert, muggie, puggie
stone sten
stone cairn virdek
stood stöd
stool stöl
stoop (v) djuk
stop quet, whet
stove lid blinnder
strange uncan
stranger fremd
straw gloy, strae, stylk, taek
straw basket böddie, kishie
straw bed flatshie
straw mat flakki
streaked reebie
streamlet burn, stripe
strength maugerment, pooer, stimna
stretch stent
stiffen stivven
strife wan-paece
strike (as a heavy blow) beetle, soge
strong, robust bördly
struggle bassel, pengle, wrasle
strut stritt
stubborn traawirt
stumble snapper, stengle, stoiter
succumb neeve
such sic
suffocate scoomfish, smore
sulk dort, toint
sultry ön
superb clinkin
supply plenish
surf laebrack
suspect doot, jalouse
swallow, gulp clunk, swally
swamp poosie, sukkamire
swarm mird, screed, scry
sweetheart hinny
swim soom, sweem
swipe wheef
swivel swill
swoon swarf

T

tainted cassen, soor
taken taen, tön
tangle reffel, witter
tangled mass clewball
tap (v) klapp, pick
taste (v) preeve
tatter rintypell
taught laerned, teached, towt

tea tae
teapot stroopie
tear (v) raive, rive
teardrop taer
tear-stained begrutten
teat prummek
tedious teddisome
telltale clipe
tenant (small holding) crofter
tenure tack
tepid loo
testicles nackers, pongs
tether tedder
that dat
thatch taek
thaw towe, uplowsin
the de
their der
them dem
then dan
they dey
thick steekit, swaara
thick mist dag, stumba
thick smoke fyunk
thief tief
thigh hoch, tee
thirst trist
thirsty shokkin, tristy
this dis
thought towt
thowel-pin kabe
thrash laaber, ledder, pey, tresh
thrashing beetling
three-legged stool creepie
threshold göt, treshel-tree
thrifty hain
thrive stivvle
throat craig, trot
throb tift
through trowe
throw baal, tro, wap
thud boof, dunt
thunder tjordin
thumb toom
Thursday Försday
tickle kittle
tidal current roost
tide rip snaar
tidy redd, rig, snug
tilt coup
timber support dwang
tinkle rinkel
titbit tabnab
to ta, tae, til
toe tae
toil tweet
told telt
tone deaf timmer
tongs tengs
tooth tanyik
top heicht
top-heavy tap-swaar
torch (battery type) blinkie
torment hatter
totter wavvel
touchy himst, pirrie, sary

tough tyoch
tousled tooderie, tooskit
towel tooel
toy laalie
trade, barter cose
tramp (v) stramp
trample truck
trash truss
tremble pirm
trick plunky
trickery jookerie-packerie, manyugilti
trickle dreeple
trifle bee-bo, fismal, wanwirt
triviality bee-bo
trouble tryst
trousers breeks
trowel trooen
trudge platch, studge, troag
trudge heavily buks
trundle hurl
truth trath
Tuesday Tiesday
tuft tiv, toosk
tumble raab
tune spring, tön
turf, sod fael, poan
turf wall faelly-daek
turmoil stramash, styooch
turnip neep
turn-up (on garment) flipe
twice twize
twilight dim, hömin
twinkle glans, plink
twins yammalds
twist kenk, snöd, traa
two twa, twae
two-fold twafaald

U

ugly ill-faared, ill-laek
unacclimatised oonbemmed
unaware oonawaars
unconscious asoond
under anunder
underclothes inside claes
undernourished ill-trivven
undress afkled
unease wanrest
unexpected oonlippened
unknown uncan
unless aless
unlucky ill-luckit, oonteelie
unruly obstropolous, owre-geen, pultrous
unruly hair feetiks
unserved oonsaired
unsteady fitless
untidy kyufset, tremsket
unwell, ailing badly
upon apo
uproar cabbie-labbi, hubbelskyu, ulination, yallicrack
urine greth, pish
us wiz
use ös
usual öswal

V

vacillate swidder
valance paand
valley daal
valley mist dallamist
vertebrae tivlik
very aafil, horrid
vest simmit
vibrate dirr, mirr
vie kemp
vigour pooster
vivid veeve
vomit virp

W

walk geng, traivel
walk noisily clump
wall waa
wander bulwaaver, stravaig, vaege
wary vaar
wash synd
washer röv
watch-tower vord
wave (n) dy, lae
way gaet, wye
weak, feeble depooperit, föshinless
wean spend
weather wadder
weather (inclement or stormy) coorse
Wednesday Wadensday, Widensday
week ook
weekend helly
weep gowl, ool
well weel
westerly wasterly
westward wastird
wet weet
wether (sheep) wedder
wheeze whaasel
when whan, whin
where hwar, kwar, whaar
whey (sour) blaand
whim whid
whimper nyurl
whine plöt
whinge girn
whirl birl, tirl
whirlwind sweevel
whirr birr
whisky (sl) screecham
whisper hark
whistle pjöfl
who wha
whole hale, hale-an-hadden
whose whaase
wind (as very light breeze) blen, laar
windbreak, shelter (n) böl
windpipe hass, trapple
wipe dicht
wish wiss
wisp lisk
witch heksi
with wi

within athin
within hearing cry-rek
without ithoot
wobble cuggle
wood wid
wooden bucket (sm) daffik
wooden toggle snyivverie
wooden vessel cog
wood shavings spells
wool oo
wool (from dead sheep) beni-plukkins
woollen ooen
woollen cap toorie kep
woolly ooie
work trift, wark
worked rowt, wrowt
worry wirry
worse warse, wer
worth wirt
wrench runch
wring trist
wrinkled ruckly
write scrit, skrieve
wrong rang
wrote wrat, wret

Y

yarn crack
yarn (woollen) wirset
yawn gant
yearling ewe gimmer
yearn grein
yelp yalk
yes aye, ya, yae
you dee, du
your dy
yours dine

Z

zenith croon ida lift

3. Nature Study (English/Shetland)

ANIMALS & INSECTS

ant mooratoog
beetle clock, hundiclock, witchie klokk
butterfly kail flea
cat fooden
cattle kye
cow coo
dog hund
duck deuk
ewe anyister, yowe
flea flech
goose gös
gosling goeslin
hen with chickens clocks-midder
horse russie
horse (young) staig
insects boags
kitten kettlin
maggot maed
mouse (field or wood) hill moose
mouse (house) moose
otter draatsi
ox, oxen stot, owsen
pig gaat, grice
pilot whale (long-finned) caain whaal
porpoise neesik
puppy whalp
rabbit kyunnen
ram tup
seal (common) tang fish
seal (grey) sylkie (selkie), haaf fish
sow soo
stoat whitrit, (whitrat)
whale whaal
woodlouse sclater

BIRDS

Arctic tern tirrick
Arctic skua alan, scooty alan, shooie (sjui)
cormorant scarf, muckle skarf, hiplin
cormorant (immature) brongie
corn bunting docken sparrow, shurl (sjorl), trussie laverick
curlew whaap, stock-whaap
dunlin ebb sleeper, plivver's page
duck (eider) dunter
duck (long-tailed) caloo
fulmar maalie
gannet solan
golden plover (lapwing, dotterel, ringed plover) plivver
great skua skooie
greylag goose grey gös
guillemot longie
guillemot (black) tystie
gull (black-headed) hoodie maa
gull (common) pikka maa
gull (glaucous) (in juvenile plumage) burgie, Iceland skorie
gull (great black-backed) baagie, swaabie
gull (herring) maa
gull (juvenile) skorie
gull (lesser black-backed) peerie swaabie, saed fool
great cormorant loren
great northern diver emmer gös
great skua bonxie
heron hegrie
hooded crow craa
kittiwake weeg
lapwing tieves nacket
little auk rotchie
mallard stock-dyook
manx shearwater kokkasodi, leerie
meadow pipit teetik, hill sparrow
merlin peerie haak (hawk), smirl
owl kattyuggle, ul, yuggle
oyster catcher shaalder
peregrine stock haak, (hawk)
pigeon doo
puffin norie, tammie norie
raven corbie
razorbill sea craa, wilkie
razorbill (young) tyugga
red-breasted merganser herald deuk
red-throated diver loom, rain gös
redshank ebb cock
ringed plover saandiloo
rock dove blue doo
rock pipit hill-sparrow, banks-sparrow, teetik
sanderling ebb fool
seagull maa
shag scarf
skylark laeverek
snipe horse-gock, snippit
snow bunting snaaie fool
starling stari, stirlin
storm petrel alamootie
terns (collective) pikkatari
twite lintie
wheatear shakk, stenkle, stinkle, sten-shakker
whimbrel peerie whaap, tang-whaap
white-tailed eagle erne
wren robbie cuddie, sistie moose

FISH & SHELLFISH

angler or monkfish masgoom, marool
barnacle rooder
basking shark brigdi, hobrigdi
blue shark hobrand
butterfish brunklet, swarfish
clam (edible) cuffey
coalfish (1st year) sillek
coalfish (2-4 years) piltek
cod kabbi, tusk, torsk, sjukkola
common whelk bucky
common whelk (empty egg cases of) marshun
conger eel sleeky
cowrie shell grottie-buckie
crab (esp. brown crab) partan
cuttlefish skeetek
dogfish (lesser spotted) blinnd hoe
dogfish (piked) hoe
fan mussel sooter
flounder fluke
gunard crooner
haddock (small) pinger

halibut, turbot baldin, keita
herring (immature female) smatchie
horse mussel yoag
ling (young) olick
lion's-mane or giant jellyfish sara-slob
mackerel fogri
mussel (small) craa peel
periwinkle wylk
pollack lör, lyrie, lythe
razor shell spoot, skeptin
saithe saed
salmon laks
sandeel geddek, saandy eel
sand-gaper shellfish or blunt gaper smisslen
sand hopper sea flech
scallop harpey
sea scorpion plucker
sea-urchin julter, scaadiman's heid
spotted blenny swarfish
spurdog blue hoe
stickleback banstickle
torsk (young) brismak
torsk tusk
trout troot(s)
wolf-fish stenbiter

INSECTS

blue-bottle or maggot fly matlo
bumble bee drummie-bee
common or house-fly bee
devil's coach horse beetle eterskap
earwig forkietail, skordi (skurdi)
horse-fly clegsie, klek(si)
woodlouse sclater

WILDFLOWERS

alpine lady's mantle milsprinda
autumn gentian dead man's mittens
bearded lichen auld man idda daek
bird's foot trefoil katticloo
bog asphodel skeetitrumps
bogbean gulsagirse
coltsfoot tuslag
common butterwort ekkelsgirse, yirnin girse
common chickweed arvi
crowsfoot craatae

daisy kokkaloori
dandelion bitter-aks
dog rose (wild briar) klonger
fern (bracken) fairy's caird, trowie's caird
grass of parnassus white kaitrins
heather ling
hemp nettle (day nettle) daa nettle
hogweed kecksie
lousewort sookie
marsh marigold blugga
marsh ragwort gowan
meadowsweet yölgirse
meadow buttercup craafit
mugwort bulwaand
primrose mayflooer
purple orchid curl-dodie
red clover smora, red
scurvy grass banks girse, sailor's hope
sea campion buggiflooer
sea mayweed muckle kokkaloori
sorrel soorik
thrift (sea pink) banks flooers
yarrow sholgirse
yellow iris seggi-flooer
yellow rattle dog's pennies
white clover smora, white
wild angelica limmerick
wild radish runshick
wild thyme taegirse

4. Days of the week
(de ook)

Monenday
Tiesday
Wadensday
Försday
Friday
Setterday
Sunday

5. Numbers

ean (wan)	**six (sax)**	**eleeven**
twa (twae)	**seevin**	**twal**
tree	**eight**	**twinty**
fower	**nine**	**hunder**
five	**ten**	**thoosan**

6. Some colloquial expressions:

a piece a wark – a difficult or complicated thing, even a startling piece of news may invoke this reaction. *De plane hed ta laand in Inverness on de wye ta Glasgow. Hit's a piece a wark.*

a piece fae – a long distance from. *Dey bide a piece fae de rodd.*

a tongue at can clip cloot – said of a sharp-tongued person.

aald age doesna come itsel – said when a physical ailment or lack of ability accompanies the onset of age.

aathin turns up bit whit's brunt or stown – everything turns up except that which is burned or stolen.

aert-kent laek de moorit yowe o Hascosay – as well known as the brown sheep of Hascosay; universally known (which is more than can be said for the legendary Hascosay ewe, the story of which appears to have been forgotten).

A'm joost gyaan tae stand on de flör – said when one visits another's house and wishes to indicate an intention to remain only a short while and therefore will not take a seat.

apo de day/night – during the day/night.

apo de links o his neck – under threat of hanging.

as fur dat – said in response to a remark which has come as no surprise.

at de lang an de lent – eventually; after some time. *He turned up at de lang an de lent.*

atween de bed and de fire – said of someone who is in poor health.

back an fore – now and again; now and then.

be me feth! – I assert (lit. 'by my faith'). *Be me feth he'll no be plaesed.*

bocht med – commercially manufactured goods as opposed to home made.

boys a Bressa! – said on hearing something surprising or wonderful. *I wan de lottery dastreen. Boys a Bressa!*

brook up a hostin – start coughing.

da brucks a da helly – the last of the weekend.

dat sam – quite so.

dere's a loss – it doesn't matter; ironic response to news that something of little worth is not about to be forthcoming.

dere's wis and dere's hit – (lit. 'there is us and there is it') a more or less senseless phrase used to close a conversation.

dir a want aboot him/her – he/she is lacking in IQ.

dis'll no buy a cott (peenie) fur de bairn – said to interrupt or end a time-wasting, long-winded conversation.

dry as a hummlibaand, bit dey wir nae end tae de lest at wiz atil him – said of an old man who seemed to be wearing well.

dunna du craa sae croose – don't be too boastful, you may be courting disaster.

dunna say clowe – don't say a word.

du sall hear aboot it – you will be told off.

du's no fey yit! – (ironic) you still have your wits about you!

every man tae his own kist lid – everyone to his own opinion.

fit fur (for) tyin – in a rage. *Peerie Tammie brook de window an his midder wiz joost fit fur tyin.*

foo's du livin? – how are you?

God be aboot me – said in surprise at hearing something amazing or outrageous. *Shö's gyaan ta Aberdeen ta buy a pair a shoes. God be aboot me, ir dae nae cheaper wye as dat?*

gyaan at de hadd – moving with the aid of a support, e.g. a child learning to walk, an inebriated person, or someone walking on icy ground in the face of a gale.

gub, snar, snap! – used to describe a sharp-tongued person (see meanings under individual words).

hae ye bön awaar? – have you seen? *Hae ye bön awaar a Lowrie?*

heads tae traas – heads to toes, as children sometimes sleeping several to a bed.

he's bön him a day o im – it's been a remarkable day, perhaps of weather, or one in which a great deal of work has been done and the speaker is exhausted.

he/she needs it aa – a 'politically incorrect' expression used to describe someone who is slow or backward. [E. *not the full shilling*]

he's him a laad o him (he's him a laad o it) – he is a bit of a character, bad fellow, gets up to things that are usually naughty or negative.

he's nae day – said of bad weather.

hit'll aye be somewye – it will all turn out right in the end.

hit's aa needed – sarcastic remark in response to perceived outrageous, ridiculous or extravagant behaviour. *De cooncil is spent £50,000 pittin an underpass in fur deuks ta geng trow. Hit's aa needed.* Also used as a throwaway comment in conversation where a disinterested listener seeks to trivialise what has been said.

hit widna be winderful – it will not be a surprise. *Hit widna be winderful if it rained afore night.*

horreed fine/splendid – a seemingly contradictory way of expressing approbation.

if A'm/wir spared – if God let's me/us live. *A'll see dee de moarn, if A'm spared.*

I hear dee – response made to a surprising or shocking remark, with the emphasis on 'hear'.

I keen A'm carin – despite lit. meaning 'I know I'm caring', it means the opposite 'I don't care'.

I ken every lith o his rigg – I know him thoroughly.

ir you doin away no sae bad? – are you well and in good spirits?

is du gyaan oot dis year? – are you going to the Up-Helly-A' festival this year?

laek a drookled skoorie – said of someone who is soaked (like a drenched seagull).

laek a gös glyin at thunder – like a goose squinting sideways at thunder; a sideways glance.

lemm (laem) laalie – literally a china toy but used in the sense of something useless; used to describe a woman who shows little prospect of being a good wife. *Steer du clear o her fur shö's joost a lemm laalie.*

livin an life tinkin – said in response to an enquiry about one's health. *Foo is du? A'm livin an life tinkin.* (I am alive and thinking to stay alive.)

loobit tae an loobit helsin – 'lukewarm tea and lukewarm welcome'.

loss me end – suffocate; breathe one's last. *I gaffed till I towt I wid loss me end.*

mad aerly/late – very early/late.

mak a lang airm – an invitation to guests to help themselves at the table.

mak fur (for) de hoose – go home. *He's comin on a moorie so du better mak fur de hoose.*

neebin ower de fire – said in response to an enquiry after someone's health. *Foo's dee midder? Shö's joost neebin ower de fire.* (She is not too well and nodding by the fireside.) It can also be said in jest of someone who is perfectly well.

never win oot a de bit – no end to one's work.

no fur a day an a dim – not for a long while. *A'm no heard fae wir fok fur a day an a dim.*

noo an sae – *so*, so; faint praise.

paekin awa – (lit. 'pecking away'), as in plodding on.

poosie aet dee – may you fall in a bog and be swallowed up (said in frustration to an argumentative or troublesome person).

rattle a hellery – said of something below standard quality. *Yon aald car du selt me is joost a rattle a hellery.*

seeven lang an seeven short – a long period of time. *I waited seeven lang an seeven short but shö never turned up.*

shö/he nearly gaed by hersel – she/he nearly died laughing (or of shock or embarrassment).

shö's/he's got a rycht cob on da day – she/he is in a bad mood.

shö's/he's weel at hersel/himsel – she's/he's a hefty/fat person.

shö's her a leddy o it – the feminine version of above.

sookin anunder snaa – said of a fine day when the ground dries quickly, often the forerunner to snowy weather.

still an on – nevertheless; regardless. *Yun's a fancy hat shö haes. Still an on hit's no fur wearin tae de kirk.*

up de latest – the most recent development; in the long run.

won/wan de lent – reached an intented destination. *He lost his pocket money afore he wan de lent a Lerwick.*

whit's no made fur de penny? – sometimes said when shown some new gadget or device.

Binominal checklist

Flowers – plants

auld man idda daek bearded lichen (*Cladonia portentosa*).

aertbark tormentil (*Potentilla erecta*).

arvi chickweed (*Stellaria media*).

banks-flooers thrift, sea pinks (*Armeria maritima*).

banks-girse scurvy grass (*Cochlearia officinalis*).

bark root (*Potentilla erecta*).

bitter-aks dandelion (*Taraxacum officinale*).

blugga marsh marigold (*Caltha palustris*).

buggiflooer (bogiflooer) sea campion (*Silene vulgaris. subsp. maritima*).

bulwaand mugwort (*Artemesia vulgaris*).

burra (bora) heath rush (*Juncus squarrosus*).

craatae meadow buttercup (*Ranunculus acris*).

curl(ie)-dodie early-purple orchid (*Orchis mascula*).

daa nettle hemp nettle (*Galeopsis tetrahit or G. versicolor*).

dead man's mittens autumn gentian (*Gentiana amarella*).

dilse seaweed, the common dulse (*Palmaria palmata*).

docken dock (*Rumex –*).

dog's pennies yellow rattle (*Rhinanthus minor*).

droo sea lace or dead man's rope (*Chorda filum*).

ekkelgirse common butterwort (*Pinguicula vulgaris*).

eksis girse dandelion (*Taraxacum officinale*).

fairy's caird fern, bracken (*Pteridum aquilinum*).

gaa-girse stonewort (*Chara vulgaris*).

gowan marsh ragwort (*Senecio aquaticus*).

grice ingan vernal squill (*Scilla verna*).

gulsa-girse marsh trefoil or bogbean (*Menyanthes trifoliata*).

hinnywar dabberlocks – edible seaweed (*Alaria esculenta*).

Johnsmas flooer (Johnsmas-girse) ribwort plantain (*Plantago lanceolata*).

kaitrins, white grass-of-parnassus (*Parnassia palustris*).

kattikloo common bird's-foot-trefoil (*Lotus corniculatus*).

kecksie (keksi) hogweed (*Heracleum sphondylium*) or wild angelica (*Angelica sylvestris*).

kokkaloorie (kokkeloori) common daisy (*Bellis perennis*).

limmerik (limrek) bog asphodel (*Narthecium ossifragum*).

ling heather (*Calluna vulgaris*).

lucky-lines (lukki-lines) long (up to 8 metres) sea lace or dead man's rope (*Chorda filum*).

lucky minnie's oo bog cotton or cotton grass (*Eriophorum augustifolium*).

marlek (marlok, marl) eel grass (*Zostera marina*).

mayflooer (meyflooer) primrose (*Primula vulgaris*).

meldie (meldi) corn spurrey (*Spergula arvensis*).

milsprinda (melspindra, millspindra) alpine lady's mantle (*Alchemilla alpina*).

moorek silverweed (*Potentilla anserina*) also vernal squill (*Scilla verna*).

muckle kokkeloori sea mayweed (*Matricaria maritima*).

okrabung (ekrabung) tuberous oatgrass (*Arrhenatherum bulbosum*).

quigga (kwigga) couch grass (*Elymus repens*).

raggie-willie ragged robin (*Lychnis flos-cuculi*).

runshick (runshie) wild radish (*Raphanus raphanistrum*) or charlock (*Sinapis arvensis*).

sailor's hope scurvy grass (*Cochlearia officinalis*).

seggie-flooer (seg, sig, siggie) yellow iris (*Iris pseudacorus*).

shickenwirt chickweed (*Stellaria media*).

sholgirse (sholgry grise) yarrow (*Achillea milliefolium*).

skeetitrumps wild angelica (*Angelica sylvestris*).

smora clover (*Trifolium pretense*).

sookies lousewort (*pedicularis sylvatica*).

soorik (surek) sorrel (*Rumex acetosa*).

taegirse (tæger?) wild (creeping) thyme (*Thymus praecox*).

tuslag coltsfoot (*Tussilago farfara*).

yirnin girse common butterwort (*Pinguicula vulgaris*).

yölgirse meadowsweet (*Filipendula ulmaria*).

Birds

alamootie (alamuti) storm petrel (*Hydrobates pelagicus*).

alan (aalin) arctic skua (*Stercorarius parasiticus*).

baagie (bagi, baki) great black-backed gull (*Larus marinus*).

banks-sparrow (-sporrow) rock pipit (*Anthus spinoletta*).

blue doo rock dove (*Columba livia*).

bonxie (bunksi, bonksi) great skua (*Megalestris catarrhactes*).

brongie (brongiskarf) immature cormorant (*Phalacrocorax carbo*).

burgie glaucous gull (*Larus hyperboreus*) in juvenile plumage.

caloo (kallu) long tailed duck (*Clangula hyemalis*).

corbie raven (*Corvus corax*).

craa hooded crow (*Corvus corone cornix*).

dirri du (doo) storm petrel (*Hydrobates pelagicus*).

docken sparrow corn bunting (*Emberiza calandra*).

dunter eider duck (*Somateria mollissima*).

ebb cock redshank (*Tringa tetanus*).

ebb fool sanderling (*Calidris alba*).

ebb-sleeper dunlin (*Calidris alpina*).

emmer gös great northern diver (*Gavia immer*).

erne white-tailed eagle (*Haliaeetus albicilla*).

grey gös greylag goose (*Anser anser*).

hegrie (hegri) heron (*Ardea cinerea*).

herald (herald deuk) red-breasted merganser (*Mergus serrator*).

hill-sparrow (-sporrow) meadow pipit (*Anthus pratensis*).

hiplin cormorant (*Phalacrocorus carbo*).

hoodie maa black-headed gull (*Larus ridibundus*).

horse-gock the snipe (*Gallinago gallinago*).

Iceland skorie glaucous gull (*Larus hyperboreus*) in juvenile plumage.

kattyuggle (kattyuggla, kattool) owl – various species (*Strigidae*).

kokkasødi manx shearwater (*Puffinus puffinus*).

laeverek skylark (*Alauda arvensis*).

leerie (liri) manx shearwater (*Puffinus puffinus*).

lintie twite (*Acanthis flavirostris*).

longie (longvie) guillemot (*Uria aalge*).

loom red-throated diver (*Gavia stellata*).

loren (lorin, lorn) great cormorant (*Phalacrocorax carbo*).

maa gull, esp. herring gull (*Larus argentatus*).

maallie fulmar (*Fulmarus glacialis*).

muckle skarf cormorant (*Phalacrocorax carbo*).

norie (nöri) puffin (also **tammie-norie**) (*Fratercula arctica*).

peerie haak (hawk) merlin (*Falco columbarius*).

peerie swaabie lesser black-backed gull (*Larus fuscus*).

peerie-whaap whimbrel (*Numenius phaeopus*).

pikka maa common gull (*Larus canus*).

pikkatari (collective) terns (*Sterninae*).

plivver golden plover (*Pluvialis apricarius*).

plivver's page dunlin (*Calidris alpina*).

rain-gös red-throated diver (*Gavia stellata*).

robbie cuddie wren (*Troglodytes troglodytes* subs. *Zetlandicus*).

rippek kittiwake (*Rissa tridactyla*).

rotchie little auk (*Plautus alle*).

saandiloo (sandilu) ringed plover (*Charadrius hiaticula*).

saed fool lesser black-backed gull (*Larus fuscus*).

scooty-alan (skuti-alen, scootie aalin) Arctic skua (*Stercorarius parasiticus*).

sea craa razorbill (*Alca torda*).

shakk wheatear (*Oenanthe oenanthe*).

shalder (sjalder) oyster catcher (*Haematopus ostralegus*).

shooie (sjui) Arctic skua (*Stercorarius parasiticus*).

shurl (sjorl) corn bunting (*Emberiza calandra*).

sistie moose wren (*Troglodytes troglodytes* subs. *Zetlandicus*) (the mouse's relative).

skarf (scarf) shag (*Phalacrocorax aristotelis*).

skooie great skua (*Stercorarius skua*).

skorie young gull (*Laridae*).

smirl merlin (*Falco columbarius*).

sna fool (snaw-ful) snow bunting (*Plectrohenax nivalis*).

snippik (snippek) a snipe (*Capella gallinago*).

solan (solon gös) gannet (*Sula bassana*).

spooie (spui) curlew (*Numenius arquata*).

stari (stirlin) a starling (*Sturnus vulgaris*).

stenkle wheatear (*Oenanthe oenanthe*).

sten pikker turnstone (*Arenaria interpres*).

sten-shakker (stenskik) wheatear (*Oenanthe oenanthe*).

stock-dyook (-deuk) mallard (*Anas platyrhynchos*).

stock haak (hawk) peregrine (*Falco peregrinus*).

stock-whaap curlew (*Nermenius arquata*).

swaabie (swabek, swartback) great black-backed gull (*Larus marinus*).

swartback great black-backed gull (*Larus marinus*).

tang-sparrow water pipit, rock pipit (*Anthus spinoletta*).

tang-whaap whimbrel (*Numenius phaeopus*).

teetik (titek) meadow pipit (*Anthus pratensis*).

tieves nacket lapwing (*Vanellus vanellus*).

tirrick Arctic tern or common tern (*Sterninae*).

trussie laverek corn bunting (*Emberiza calandra*).

tystie black guillemot (*Cepphus grylle*).

tyugga (tjugga) young razorbill (*Alca torda*).

weeg (weig) kittiwake (*Rissa tridactyla*).

whaap (whaup) curlew (*Numenius arquata*).

wilkie (wolki) razorbill (*Alca torda*).

Fish, shellfish

baldin (baldung) halibut (*Hippoglossus hippoglossus*); turbot (*Scophthalmus maximus*).

banstickle stickleback (*Gasterosteus aculeatus*).

blinnd hoe (ho) lesser spotted dogfish (*Scyliorhinus canicula*).

blue hoe (ho) spurdog (*Squalus acanthias*).

brigdi (bregdi) basking shark (*Cetorhinus maximus*).

brismak young torsk (*Brosme brosme*).

brunklet butterfish (*Pholis gunnellus*).

bucky (buckie) common whelk (*Buccinum undatum*).

craa peel small mussel (*Mytilus edulis*).

crooner grey gurnard (*Eutrigla gunardus*).

cuffey quahog – edible clam (*Arctica islandica*).

fluke flounder (*Platichthys flesus*).

fogrie (fogri) mackerel (*Scomber scombrus*).

geddek (giddek) lesser sandeel (*Ammodytes tobianus*); greater sandeel (*Hyperoplus lanceolatus*).

grottie-buckie type of cowrie shell (*Trivia monacha*).

harpey scallop of *Pectenidae* family.

hobrand (hobrin) blue shark (*Prionace glauca*).

hobrigdi basking shark (*Cetorhinus maximus*).

hoe (ho) piked dogfish (*Squalus acanthias*) or spurdog.

julter (yulter) edible sea-urchin (*Echinus esculentus*).

keita halibut (*Hippoglossus hippoglossus*).

laks a salmon (*Salmo salar*).

lör (lythe, lyrie) pollack (*Pollachius pollachius*).

marool (marul) angler or monkfish (*Lophius piscatorius*).

marshum cluster of empty egg cases of common whelk (*Buccinum undatum*).

masgoom (marsgum) angler or monkfish (*Lophius piscatorius*).

olick (ollek) ling (*Molva molva*).

partan crab; common edible crab (*Cancer pagurus*).

piltek coalfish (2-4 years) (*Pollachius virens*).

plucker (plukker) sea scorpion (*Myoxocephalus scorpius*).

rooder barnacle (*Cirripedia*).

saandy eel lesser sandeel (*Ammodytes tobianus*); greater sandeel (*Hyperoplus lanceolatus*).

saed saithe – commonly coley or coalfish (*Gadus virens*).

scaddiman's heid, (Lerwick) **scabbiman's heid** the sea-urchin or the shell thereof (*Echinus esculentus*).

sara-slob lion's-mane or giant jellyfish (*Cyanea capillata*).

sea-flech the sand hopper (*Talitrus saltator*).

sillek (sillock) coalfish (1-2 yr) (*Pollachius virens*).

skeetik (skitek) cuttlefish (*Sepia officinalis*).

skeptin razor shell (*Solenidae*).

sleeky conger eel (*Conger conger*).

slöb jellyfish (*Aurelia aurita*).

smisslen (smirslin) sand gaper shellfish or blunt gaper (*Mya truncata*).

sooter fan mussel (*Pinna fragilis*).

spoot razor shell (*Solenidae*).

stenbiter Atlantic wolf-fish – also known as Atlantic catfish (*Anarhichas lupus*).

swarfish butterfish (*Pholis gunnellus*).

troot(s) trout (*Salmonidae*)

tusk North Atlantic, white-fleshed fish of the cod genus having a single dorsal fin; elsewhere known as cusk, brismak, torsk (*Brosme brosme*).

wylk periwinkle (*Littorina littorea*).

yoag (joag) horse mussel (*Modiolus modiolus*).

Animals

caain whaal long-finned pilot whale (*Globicephala melas*).

draatsi (dratsi) (sea) otter (*Lurtra lutra*).

haaf fish grey seal (*Halichoerus grypus*).

herrin hog minke whale (*Balaenoptera acutorostrata*).

hill moose field or wood mouse (*Apodemus sylvaticus*).

kyunnin rabbit (*Oryctolagus cuniculus*).

moose house mouse (*Mus musculus*).

neesik (nisik) harbour porpoise (*Phocaena phocaena*).

sylkie (selkie) grey seal (*Halichoerus grypus*) or common seal (*Phoca vitulina*).

tang fish common seal (*Phoca vitulina*).

whitrit (whitrat) stoat (*Mustela erminea*).

Insects

bee common or house-fly (*Musca domestica*).

clegsie klek(si) horse-fly (*Tabanidae*).

drummie-bee bumble bee (*Bombus*).

eterskap devil's coach horse beetle (*Staphylinus olens*).

forkietail earwig (*Forficula auricularia*).

kail flea (kale-) large white (butterfly) (*Pieris brassicae*).

matlo blue-bottle or 'maggot fly' (*Calliphora vomitoria*).

mooratoog (muratug, möratu) ant (*Formicidae*).

sclater woodlouse (*Oniscus asellus*).

skordi (skurdi) earwig (*Forficula auricularia*).

thoosan taes centipede. [Sc. lit. 'thousand toes' and consequently a gross exaggeration as the most common centipede in Britain is the brown centipede (*Lithobuis forficatus*) with 15 pairs of legs. Of other species the garden centipede (*Geophilus*) has the most with 40-80 pairs of relatively short legs – no taes]

warback (warbak) larva of the warble-fly (*Hypoderma bovis*) or botfly (*Gasterophilus intestinalis*).

Bibliography

Barnes, Michael P. *The Norn Language of Orkney and Shetland* (The Shetland Times Ltd. 1998)

Bulter, Rhoda *Shaela – Shetland Poems* (Thuleprint, Shetland, 1976)

Cluness, A. T. *The Shetland Book* (The Shetland Times Ltd. 1967)

Edmondston, Thomas. *An Etymological Glossary of the Shetland and Orkney Dialect.* 1866, (Sh., Ork.)

Graham, John J. *The Shetland Dictionary* (The Shetland Times Ltd 1979, 2000)

Guy, Christine M. *Songs and Sights of Shetland* (Shetland Arts Trust. 1995)

Jakobsen, J. *An Etymological Dictionary of the Norn Language in Shetland* (London & Copenhagen, 1928-32)

Malcolm, D. *Shetland's Wild Flowers* (The Shetland Times Ltd. 2003)

Nicolson, James R. *Shetland* (David & Charles, Newton Abbott, 1972)

Ramsay, Dean. *Reminiscences of Scottish Life and Character* (T. N. Foulis, Lond. & Edin., 1912)

Robertson, T. A. *Mair Laeves Fae Vagaland* (The Shetland Times Ltd. 1965)

Robertson, T. A. & **Graham**, John J. *Grammar and Usage of the Shetland Dialect* (The Shetland Times Ltd. 1991)

Robertson, Thomas. *Personal Dictionary and Notes* (Shetland Archives)

Saxby, Jessie M. E. *Shetland Traditional Lore* (Edinburgh, 1932)

Shetland Isles Ordnance Survey Maps (1:25,000) nos. 466 – 470 (O.S. Southampton, U.K. 2003)

Stout, Margaret B. *Cookery for Northern Wives* (T & J Manson, Lerwick, 1925)

Tulloch, Lawrence. *The Foy and other folk tales* (The Shetland Times Ltd. 2006)

The Chambers Dictionary (Chambers Harrap Publishers Ltd. Edinburgh, 2006)

The Oxford English Dictionary (20 vol.) (Clarendon Press, Oxford, 1989)

The Shorter Oxford English Dictionary (2 vol.) (Oxford University Press, 1973)

Online:
Dictionary of the Scots Language (DSL)
Dictionary of Old Scots Tongue (DOST)
Dictionary.com
Shetland Dictionary.com
Shetlandic in a Context of Linguistic and Cultural Identity (John M. Tait)